prairie university

prairie

A History of the University of Nebraska

university

Robert E. Knoll

Published by
the University
of Nebraska
Press and the
Alumni Association of the University of Nebraska–Lincoln: Lincoln & London

Library of Congress
Cataloging in Publication Data
Knoll, Robert E.
Prairie university: a history of
the University
of Nebraska / Robert E. Knoll
p.   cm.
Includes bibliographical refer-
ences and index.
ISBN 0-8032-2717-5 (cl: alk. paper)
1. University
of Nebraska – Lincoln – History. I. University of Nebraska – Lincoln. Alumni Association. II. Title. LD3668.K66 1995 378.782′293—dc20 94-36729 CIP

© 1995 by the University of Nebraska Press.
All rights reserved
Manufactured in the United States of America
The paper in this book meets the minimum re-
quirements of American National Standard for
Information Sciences – Permanence of Paper for
Printed Library Materials, ANSI Z39.48-1984.

Frontispiece: Lincoln, 1871, looking northwest
from the capitol. The massive building in the
upper left is University Hall. (UNL Photo Lab)

The text type is Monotype Octavia, designed
by Will Carter and David Kindersley, & set by
Keystone. Book design by Richard Eckersley

Corporate bodies are like persons, long vaguely swayed by early impressions they may have forgotten. Even when changes come over the spirit of their dream, a sense of the mission to which they were first dedicated lingers about them, and may revive . . . . — George Santayana, *Character and Opinion in the United States* (1920)

Contents

xi Contents

Illustrations

Preface

This book is an essay in the history of a western university. Agreeing with Emerson that any institution is the lengthened shadow of one person, I have attempted to identify the people who have left their marks on the University of Nebraska. Decade by decade, leaders of the University have reflected national and international ideas and modified them to the circumstances of the prairie state. Chancellors, some wise and some less wise, have had influences; but so have regents and professors, legislators and students, citizens and passers through.

In this rather personal account I have tried to identify central issues, record responses to them, and indicate resolutions reached. I have striven to make it readable, and brevity is the soul of wit. It is not a record of fiscal battles, for financial concerns only reflect wider, basic philosophical assumptions. This book reports the doings of men and women on a western stage of the national educational drama, spotlighting leading performers in important, changing scenes. My central attention has been given to the Lincoln campuses, both because they were the defining segments of the University in its first century and because other campuses present unique problems.

Though initially I had no central thesis, I found patterns rising from the materials I have examined. It might be useful to spell these out here, for they are only implied in the narration. In the first generation of its history, the chancellors, the professors, and the public at large were concerned to define the public nature of a public university. By 1890 the University of Nebraska, like American public universities everywhere, was no longer nonsectarian and had become secular. Never ceasing to be an agency committed to encouraging moral responsibility, it drew away from religious doctrine. A tension between religious authority and

academic authority remained for the next century, but dogma ceased to be a defining issue by the end of the first quarter century.

In the second quarter century, from about 1890 until about 1920, the University became a collection of professional colleges assembled around a core of common learning. Here doctors, lawyers, merchants, and chiefs were educated and accredited. The nineteenth-century justification for higher education as a place where Christian gentlemen were prepared for public service gave way to the idea of a university as a place where men and women were prepared for professional responsibility. Most of the colleges – agriculture, engineering, medicine, law, business, pharmacy, dentistry – were established as divisions of the University by 1920.

In the third quarter of the University's history, from about 1920 until about 1945, the University actively participated in what one historian has identified as "the culture of aspiration." The University had always been a means of upward mobility, a way to raise one's status; but now with increasing numbers coming to the University, it became an accrediting agency socially as well as professionally. The people one knew, the clubs one joined, the fraternities one was invited into, were seen to be as important now as the courses one took or the training one received. This concern for "contacts" was not new, of course, but these decades saw the growing importance of extracurricular life. This was the generation of raccoon coats and football stadiums.

In its fourth quarter century, after World War II, the University aspired to become a research institution. Federal money was the pump primer. Though the University had been committed to research almost from its earliest days, it now saw research as the distinguishing characteristic of a major institution of higher learning. Aspiration sometimes outreached performance in these years, but the research ideal of the comprehensive university became established.

The last quarter century of the University's history has seen yet another change. Now the University has become increasingly an experiment station, not just for agriculture (it has been that at least since the Hatch Act of 1887), but for medicine, engineering, business, and various social activities. University research and development is now increasingly justified by its relationship to the state's economic growth. The University remains an accrediting agency for the professions, a channel of upward mobility for the ambitious, and a laboratory of pure research for the curious; but the supporting public is now invited to see it as a place where applied research may help bring prosperity to the region.

Nobody asked me to write this book, but many have encouraged me. I have been associated with the University of Nebraska since 1940, when I came to it as a freshman, and I have been on its faculty since 1950. I have thus personally lived through more than a third of its total existence. All my family – my wife, my children (except one), my brother and sister – have earned degrees here. My parents graduated with bachelor's degrees in 1910. Because I knew Louise Pound (class of 1892) and other members of her generation rather well, I have had firsthand reports of life at the University from its very start. In these pages I have tried not to put total trust in such reports and have sought to check my memory with reference to official and unofficial records. These records, located in Love Library, are full and partially indexed. I have consulted campus newspapers and publications. Every detail in these pages rests on documentary evidence. The conclusions are of course my own. Where possible I have talked at length with persons who participated in University life, and several sections of this essay have been read with critical eye by persons involved in what I have described. These readers have kept me from errors. Much of what is reported here cannot be checked by living witnesses, for this is more than contemporary history.

If this book is opinionated, its judgments are not hasty; and if important persons and events have been only sketched, I hope the sketches are not idiosyncratic. As I have said on other occasions, I would rather be conventional than wrong. This book is addressed to any reader who would like to know what it was like to found, develop, and live within an institution of higher learning that was far from major population and power centers, an institution that yet participated in the cultural movements of the times. If you had the hours, I could tell you much more than I have put down here.

prairie university

1. Founding a Land-Grant University

The Morrill Act of 1862

The history of the University of Nebraska begins with the passage of the Morrill Act in 1862. With this law, the U.S. Congress provided endowment lands for public universities and influenced the direction not only of American education but of American society generally. Education became the channel of upward mobility in the United States, and the democratic ideal of equal opportunity was made more possible. The State of Nebraska accepted federal lands in 1869, became part of this land-grant system, and embraced the Morrill definition of education. It was entirely consistent with the mood of the times, for pioneer Nebraskans saw the West as the hope of new men unburdened by a past.

The land-grant university has often been cited as America's greatest contribution to higher education, and it certainly pioneered important innovations. It elevated the "useful" arts, sciences, and professions to academic respectability, worthy of study alongside the classical disciplines of ancient languages and pure mathematics. The Morrill Act assumed that higher education should be available to all qualified persons at low cost, throughout a full lifetime. The university was thus seen as a functioning part of a total society, not as an addendum or an ornament, and not the prerogative of the few or the solace of the leisured. Not all the implications of the Morrill Act were immediately recognized by the new universities like the University of Nebraska, but the central assumption implicit from the start was that the University was both a responsibility of its citizens and a service available to them all.

The Morrill Act of 1862 was designed "to promote the liberal and practical education of the industrial classes in the several pursuits and professions of life."[1] (Later, in 1887, the Hatch Act would provide for establishing experiment stations at land-grant colleges, thus defining the public university as an agent of growth through research as well as a transmitter of received knowledge, and so placing it at the cutting edge of a new society.) Congressman Justin S. Morrill, who sponsored the bill which endowed "industrial universities" with western lands, was a remarkable man, a Vermont merchant turned statesman who served in Congress longer than any other man in the nineteenth century. By 1860 agricultural-industrial colleges had been tentatively established in Michigan, Iowa, Maryland, Pennsylvania, and elsewhere, but Justin Morrill and others of his generation did not want to settle the land with trade schools. They opposed class legislation for farmers and mechanics, for they wanted "the teaching of science [not vocationalism] to be the leading idea"; by *science* they meant all departments of systematized knowledge.[2] Like Thomas Jefferson they wanted to illuminate as far as practicable the minds of the people at large through a "general diffusion of knowledge."[3] Morrill's land-grant university was a lineal descendant of the Jeffersonian ideal, and the grandparent of the state universities was the University of Virginia, not Harvard.

The Morrill Act had in effect questioned assumptions about the purposes of higher education. Traditionally colleges had seen it as their responsibility to educate Christian gentlemen for public service. Their fundamental commitment was to the development of moral character. Noah Porter, the conservative president of Yale, spoke for many when he said upon his inauguration in 1871, "A noble character becomes light and inspiration, when dignified by eminent intellectual power and attainments,"[4] but the new "liberal and practical education" doubted the validity of the pious assumption that the university was fundamentally devoted to ethical uplift. The Morrill Act seemed to assume that a college had practical responsibilities, and it had in effect taken higher education out of the exclusive control of the churches. Education became secular. But just what *secular* meant in this context was not at all clear, nor was it clear how *secular* differed from *nonsectarian* or *interdenominational*.

Andrew D. White and Ezra Cornell confronted this problem head on in founding Cornell University (opened 1868) and so did Daniel Coit Gilman when he served as president (1872–75) of the new University of California in Berkeley (opened 1869) and then as founding president of Johns Hopkins University in Baltimore (1875–1901). White agreed with Gilman: a university was "a group of agencies organized to advance the arts and sciences of every sort, and train men as scholars for all the intellectual callings of life."[5] They, like Charles W. Eliot at Harvard (president 1869–1909), freed their institutions from traditional orthodoxies. Like the whole society, universities, including the frontier University of Nebraska, were caught up on a seismic conflict of faith. The old religious certainties were being called into question by the spirit that produced Darwin, and literal readings of the Holy Scriptures were questioned by the Higher Criticism of biblical texts. Conservatives opposed "broad-gauge" Christians — that is, fundamentalists stood against those who wanted to reconcile new facts and old convictions. All were of course professing Christians. Who and what would form higher education?

A State University for Nebraska

In the 1850s Nebraska, still only a territory, had not been immune to the educational ideas then abroad. Acting Governor T. A. Cuming, a college man himself, in 1855 had urged the Nebraska territorial legislature to establish a university here, and within the next decade more than two dozen charters were issued for "Nebraska University" at various proposed locations — Fontanelle, Omaha City, Saratoga, Wyoming, Nebraska City. The earliest historian of education in Nebraska observed that the University of Nebraska "seems to have been on wheels (as were so many

of the towns)."[6] Proposals were so frequent that the legislature had blank charters printed to hand out to enterprising developers, who thought that a newly platted town might attract more settlers if they made provision for higher education within its precincts. None of these "universities" took root, however, and most of the platted towns remained on paper. In 1867 Mount Vernon Seminary was established on the Missouri bluffs just west of Brownville; it survives as Peru State College and is thus the oldest institution of higher education in Nebraska.

A genuine state university did not exist until 1869, when the first state legislature met in Omaha. In haste the legislature unanimously approved a charter on 15 February 1869 in order to claim the federal lands provided under the Morrill Act. The act of 1867 which had located the capitol in Lincoln also located the University there and provided that "the State University and State Agricultural College shall be united as one educational institution."[7] It also placed the penitentiary and the insane asylum in the new "Capitol City," an artificial municipality supported by public institutions and, as such, subject to envious criticism for the next century. The 1869 charter is important not only because it was an enabling document but because it attempted to specify the role and purpose of the new university. This was to be the state's only comprehensive university, and the new industrial arts and the traditional arts were to be studied together. Unlike Iowa and Kansas, where the state university and the land-grant college were separate, Nebraska, like Wisconsin and Minnesota, was to be served by a single institution where all branches of learning could be mutually supportive.

The impetus for chartering the University was the federal offer of free land. Nebraska could claim 30,000 acres for each of its congressional representatives, to a total of 90,000 acres. Upon becoming a state in 1867 it had received under the enabling act of 1864 46,080 additional acres for the support of a university. The total endowment for the University was thus 136,080 acres. When the legislature adopted the charter, it assumed that the federal endowment would support the University with little additional cost, but it did in fact assess a property tax of one mill per dollar (cut to one-fourth mill in 1871) for the University. The legislators could hardly realize that the land would yield little return for many years. The Homestead Act of 1862 and the generous railroad grants of the 1860s and 1870s depressed the value of public lands appreciably, and the whole nation suffered from a general agricultural depression through the last third of the century. The promise of financial support for public universities was thus chimeric, but it encouraged the founding of colleges across the country nonetheless. From the start they were in straitened financial circumstances, but Nebraska fared somewhat better than other states in the sale of its public lands. The sums received by all states from Morrill land averaged $1.65 an acre, but in Nebraska the sale of educational lands had brought the state an average of $8.37 per acre by the time it was halted in 1897.[8] Some people thought the school lands should have been retained as a permanent endowment.

The original charter deserves close examination, for it broadened the provisions of the Morrill Act. It specifies that the object of the University of Nebraska "shall be to afford to the inhabitants of the state the means of acquiring a thorough knowledge of the various branches of literature, science, and the arts." This institution was for the "inhabitants": not the citizens or the youth, but persons of all ages and conditions. It was to reach out to all the people. It made explicit provision for the admission of women. Section 18 of the original charter reads, "No person shall, because of age, sex, color, or nationality, be deprived of the privileges of this institution. Provisions shall be made for the education of females apart from male students in separate apartments or buildings; *Provided*, That persons of different sexes of the same proficiency of study may attend the regular college lectures together." In the subsequent years some persons have questioned whether the charter assumed "separate but equal" facilities for women, but in fact the issue never arose. Women were enrolled along with men from the beginning.

The burden of learning rested on the student, for the University offered "the means of learning"; it did not presume "to educate." It offered "thorough knowledge," that is, more than elementary fundamentals provided in common schools. And the charter called for the "various

branches of literature, science, and the arts," not just the industrial branches so much talked of in the previous decades. This then was not to be a trade school. The charter made no provision for religious instruction but did not deny the fundamental importance of religion: the University was a nonecclesiastical institution of a kind new in the country because the idea of secularity had not yet been clearly defined. The University of Nebraska was thus a nondenominational, coeducational institution, comprehensive and public, devoted to the study of fundamental principles and to their general application.[9]

Its seal, designed by Allen R. Benton, the first chancellor, has an open book in its center, not a plow or a microscope or a cross, surrounded by words in Latin: *Literis dedicata et omnibus artibus* – "Dedicated to letters and all the arts." Symbols of science, art, engineering, agriculture, law, and patriotism surround these words. This university was to be a place of learning devoted to public service, building on the classical past for an undiscovered future.

Augustus F. Harvey (1830–1900), who wrote the bill establishing the University and saw it through the legislature, was typical of his time and this place. He had come to Nebraska City with his brother, Henry, in 1856 and this colorful and gifted pair held various offices in the territory. Henry was superintendent of public instruction for some years, and handsome Augustus – " 'Gus' for short, otherwise 'Ajax' " – served as city engineer in Nebraska City. In the 1860s the brothers had a newspaper. Another publisher of the time, Dr. Frederick Renner, said of them later that they were "usually hard workers, and managed to get a fair patronage during the summer and fall of 1866; but they had the failing that they could not stand prosperity. When the month was up and collections satisfactory, the happy event had to be celebrated to the neglect of all, even the pressing work." Dr. Renner continues: "Both brothers, aside from this 'wee failing,' were as good natured and as high-minded gentlemen as ever came to Nebraska from Washington, D.C."[10] Augustus was employed as surveyor for the committee authorized to select the site of the new capitol city, which they did in July of 1867, and he and his family invested heavily in lots there.[11] In proposing the establishment of the University in the legislative session of

1869, he may have hoped to feather his own nest by becoming its chief administrative officer. Like many frontiersmen in early Nebraska, the Harveys saw the new country as opportunity, not responsibility. Like most of their contemporaries, they operated less from a Puritan ideal of service than from the pragmatic aspiration of getting ahead.[12]

Augustus Harvey was clearly a gifted man. In writing the University bill, he drew on the charter of the University of Michigan at Ann Arbor, not the land-grant college at East Lansing. The University of Michigan was the most firmly established of the state universities. Its 1837 charter was based on an earlier document, prepared by U.S. Circuit Judge Augustus Woodward, who in May 1814 had conferred with Thomas Jefferson as he was planning the University of Virginia. "The effect of this institution [the University of Virginia] on the future fame, fortune and prosperity of our country, can as yet be seen but at a distance," Jefferson wrote, but "our sister States . . . will bring hither their genius to be kindled at our fire."[13] The University of Michigan can be said to have kindled its fire from Jefferson's university and so, in time, did the University of Nebraska. The tradition of the public, secular university, open to all qualified applicants, thus came to Nebraska from high antecedents. "Let our Countrymen know," Jefferson had written (1786) in the full flush of Enlightenment optimism, "that the people alone can protect us against these evils [of ignorance and tyranny], and that the tax which will be paid for this purpose is not more than the thousandth part of what will be paid to kings, priests and nobles who will rise up among us if we leave the people in ignorance."[14]

﴾ Building a University

The government of the University of Nebraska was placed in the hands of a board of twelve regents: nine from the judicial districts, initially appointed by the governor but subsequently to be appointed by the legislature, and three ex officio members, the governor, the superintendent of public instruction (yet to be named), and the chancellor (after the 1877 revision of the state constitution, the number was reduced to six and they were directly elected). The state university was clearly part of state government and answerable to the people. The first board met on 3 June 1869 to organize itself and plan for a University building and again in September to lay the cornerstone, but did not think it necessary to meet a third time until December 1870. The University was thus without direction during the first year and a half of its existence. Even Augustus Harvey seems not to have recognized the range of responsibilities of the university whose charter he had written, and perhaps this frontier state had little fundamental interest in higher education, its attention being addressed, rather, to breaking the sod, building roads, and setting up towns on the prairies. When the board met for the fourth time, in January 1871, the contracted building was practically completed and the members declared themselves entirely satisfied.

Lincoln, the site of the new University, had been established as a result of sectional rivalries. Legislators from south of the Platte in the 1867 session were determined that Omaha, the largest settlement in the state and north of the Platte, not remain the capital. Unable, however, to agree on another site, they designated the governor, the secretary of state, and the auditor as a commission to locate a new seat of government within a specified area south of the Platte and west of Omaha. The name originally designated, Capitol City, was changed to Lincoln by a north Platte legislator in an effort to draw south Platte Democratic votes away from the measure, "but sectional loyalty overrode political considerations, and South Platte Democrats promptly approved the new name."[15]

Though the commission described the area as "gently undulating," with "rich timber and water power available within short distances," the prairie was in fact nearly featureless, with scarcely a tree.[16] Obsessed with the potential value of the saline deposits in the northern half of Lancaster County, they located the new city in a salt basin where the town of Lancaster had a population of fewer than thirty people. The saline deposit never proved up and the new city drew farther and farther away from it to the south and east. People complained for years that Lincoln water was saline and undrinkable, and at the June 1871 meeting of the Board of Regents, a University committee was instructed to build one or two cisterns at the University building to collect fresh water.[17]

"The commissioners who located and laid out the capital city and set aside four blocks for the University campus, must have selected the location of these four blocks [10th to 12th, R to T streets] when blindfolded," a partisan of the University was to write fifty years later. "No good angel whispered to them of seats of learning set upon the hills. The gentle slopes of the Antelope valley were ignored, and a site bordering on Salt Creek valley and inevitably in the path of railroads, then imminent, was chosen."[18] The railroad arrived in 1870. Campus landscaping, poor at best, rarely survived the hot winds of Nebraska summers, though from the first the Board of Regents set aside money ($500 in September 1871) "for laying out and beautifying of the grounds." It was reported that the campus differed little in appearance from the prairie about it for a number of years. Citizens tethered their family cows on it; children picked violets and buffalo beans there. Almost immediately it was recognized that insufficient land had been set aside for the University. Roscoe Pound said generations later that his father, Judge Stephen B. Pound, had suggested to the commissioners that four square blocks was hardly room enough for a university; but the commissioners ignored the protest, and so for the next century the University had to buy back land which ought to have been part of the initial settlement.[19]

The first building was to be pretentious, but like the new state capitol, it was poorly constructed. The capitol, built in 1868 and budgeted at $40,000, had cost $75,000 and was so badly made that it had to be replaced within a dozen years. The University building was to be paid for by the sale of lots in Lincoln and not to cost more than $100,000. The regents were eager to get the University in operation in order to secure the appropriated Morrill lands; and when a Mr. R. D. Silver arrived in Lincoln in June 1869 promising to set up a plant for the manufacture of bricks – 12,000 a day, he said – he was awarded a contract for $128,480, well beyond the specified $100,000. Controversy followed, of course, but construction proceeded. A brass band was imported from Omaha for the

cornerstone-laying festivities on September 23, and a "grand banquet" was given in the evening. H. W. Caldwell recorded that "the banquet – thanks to the good people of Lincoln – was enjoyed by fully a thousand people, dancing being indulged in from 10:00 until 4:00 o'clock."[20] The band and banquet cost "the good people of Lincoln" nearly $2,000.

The building, in the "Franco-Italian" style and more imposing by far than the capitol half a mile to the south, rose on the plains as a monument to both the hopes and the politics of its day. It stood where Ferguson Hall now stands, at Eleventh and S Streets, and it must have looked to many students as it looked to Alvin Johnson coming to the University from the farm: "The building before me seemed huge and majestic. It had four strata of windows, some of them lighted, under a mansard roof. The building was topped with a square tower."[21] Another student born and reared in a sod house remembered that "the old red brick main building was as beautiful as the Parthenon, and O Street, though built of wood and sun-dried bricks, could not have been surpassed in attractiveness by the marble palaces of Rome." The Lincoln newspaper defended the excessive expenditure on the edifice, asserting that so fine a building would not soon have to be "pulled down and built over again."[22]

From the start the University building was unsatisfactory. The locally manufactured bricks turned out to be soft, the roof leaked, and the furnace did not heat the rooms, let alone the corridors. "Early generations of students remember the ugly and insatiable stoves that made winter use of the old chapel possible, but never comfortable," one of the early students recalled. Huge ash heaps, where townschildren loved to play, accumulated west of the north wing of the building.[23] The construction had been largely unsupervised, and within a few weeks after the regents approved it on 18 January 1871, critics found the structure dangerous. When three professional architects examined it in June, they declared it "safe for the present and probably for years to come," but rumors persisted. On 18 March 1873, after consultation with another set of architects, new foundations were ordered under the north wing because there soft brown sandstone, not the specified limestone, had been set almost without mortar and the supporting walls were crumbling. Robert D. Silver, the builder, seemed to feel no responsibility for the inadequacy of the building. In April 1873 he even offered to undertake repairs at a cost of $7,410. By June 1873 the Board of Regents determined what everybody had known all along: extensive graft had been involved from the start. Governor David Butler had been impeached in 1871 and removed from office because of his "incredible laxity in the handling of the state's financial affairs," including the construction of the University building.[24] Neither Butler nor Silver seems to have been disgraced. These were free-wheeling times and the distinction between public trust and public opportunity was not sharp.

The building, now called University Hall, continued to give trouble. In 1877 yet another group of architects, this time all from Nebraska, were consulted. On the strength of their report, on 6 July 1877 the board decided to pull it down and erect another on its site at a cost of $60,000, $40,000 of which was to come from Lincoln. Some Lincoln citizens feared that should the building be razed, the University would be moved, perhaps to Nebraska City, more likely to Omaha, and so they hired consultants from Iowa and Chicago, who declared the building easily repairable. In August 1877 a new foundation was ordered at a cost of $6,012 and the roof was repaired at the further cost of $1,625. These sums were paid by the city, and despite repeated billings, the city was never reimbursed by the state. After 1877 no further attempts were made to remove the University from Lincoln, but more money had to be spent on the building – a new slate roof, for example, was put on in 1883 – using up funds that might have gone for educational purposes.

This building, whose cost suggested that it was built for the ages, hardly survived fifty years. Old "U Hall" had a place of sentimental importance to many graduates of the University; and if it had been soundly constructed, much of the early hostility to the University might have been turned away. As it was, the building was the center around which storms rose and broke.

❧ Chancellor A. R. Benton and the Faculty

At its January 1871 meeting, only its fourth, the Board of Regents not only accepted University Hall but appointed the first chancellor. Henry Tappan, the former head of the University of Michigan and the man who established it as the nation's leading state university, was optimistically nominated for the post, but Allen R. Benton was elected on a second ballot. Benton, an ordained minister in the Christian Church, knew his name had been put forward by the Reverend D. R. Dungan, regent from Pawnee City and also a minister in the Christian Church, but he "took no steps to secure the position," according to a colleague, Samuel Aughey, in a Charter Day address of 1881. He was therefore "taken by surprise when, in the beginning of 1871, he was notified of his election."[25] Early in February he came to meet the regents in Lincoln. He had impressive credentials: a student of the ancient languages, he had been president of Northwestern Christian University (now Butler University) in Indiana from 1861 until 1867, and upon going to Mount Union College in Ohio had become president there too. He was about to return to the presidency of Northwestern Christian when the Nebraska offer came, but his visit to Lincoln was so mutually favorable that he rejected Indiana and took up his duties in Nebraska in June 1871.

A contemporary account of the February meeting gives something of Benton's character and explains why he was so favorably received: "Meeting the regents at the appointed time, he frankly told them he regarded his election as a great compliment, but that he gave them perfect liberty to rescind their action in his case, or to choose another for the position." After all, he had a presidency waiting in Indiana. "He also gave advice as to salaries, especially that of the chancellor, which he considered, under the circumstances of a new state like Nebraska, altogether too high." He had been offered $5,000 but accepted $4,000. "He wished them to retrieve any false step which they had taken in the election of chancellor. In other words, he was ready to sacrifice his own interests for those of the university, if, in the opinion of any of the regents, the two interests were in conflict."[26] In 1873 he offered to return $500 if the board would appoint an assistant to the professor of science, who was overworked. The size of the proposed salaries, like the cost of the University building, suggests that the board, supported by the legislature, had high aspirations for their university – or that they knew nothing of the nature of universities.

Critics and friends of the University were alike pleased by Benton's generous spirit. One of his first students, George E. Howard, said of him fifty years later: "Chancellor Benton had just the qualities of heart and mind, the breadth of humanism, needed in the transition stage. While he was an enlightened and faithful representative of orthodox Christianity, he was able firmly to grasp the new ideal of public education as the safeguard of society. He was tolerant in his daily walk and conversation. He was a refined gentleman; a scholar accomplished in the humanities of his day. Furthermore, he was a good teacher; for he was both chancellor and professor of 'intellectual and moral science,' besides finding time on the side to teach classes in Latin, Greek and history."[27]

In accepting his appointment, Benton and the Board of Regents agreed that the University was to open in September 1871; nothing could be gained by delay and politically much could be lost. They had to decide what a state university was to be. The Board of Regents tried to resolve or at least dodge basic theological, dogmatic issues by making the University ecumenical; the expression then was *pansectarian*. Early they let it be known that it was "the purpose of the Board, to have the different Christian denominations represented in the various chairs,"[28] and they solicited nominations to the faculty from the various churches. In a generation before graduate schools and in a country vastly underpopulated, where but to the churches could the board have gone for faculty, time being short? The clergy was then "the learned profession" and those rare graduates who hoped for academic careers often had church affiliations. The board's appeal to the churches was expedient. Had there been time, young men and women from the more populous East might have welcomed invitations to the West. Nebraska professors were to be paid $2,000 a year, a sum equal to the pay of assistant professors at Harvard; Benton's $4,000 was equal to the salary of a full professor at Harvard. In addition, for some enterprising people, the West represented an opportunity to remake a world, a chance to leave a mark on virgin land. Benton's letters to his father communicate some of the excitement that he, and many other people in those days, felt. They also indicate that he hoped to make some money as real estate values rose, but so did everybody else.

By April the regents had assembled a faculty. All but one, G. E. Church, who was to be principal of the preparatory school at $1,500, were active in their churches. They named an ordained Methodist minister to the chair of ancient languages: S. H. Manley; an ordained Episcopalian to the chair of English literature: O. C. Dake; an ordained Lutheran to the chair of natural sciences: C. H. Kuhns, who refused but nominated Samuel Aughey, another Lutheran minister; and an elder in the Presbyterian Church to the chair of mathematics: H. E. Hitchcock. At least four, perhaps five, of the regents were themselves clergymen, and Augustus Harvey's replacement as secretary of the board, Henry T. Davis, was also a minister. "This virtual stamping of the principal state school as protegé and ward of the church was doubtless due in part to the still surviving belief or concession that the inculcation of religion was the most important part of even public education," one contemporary historian noted.[29] There was of course much talk of a "Godless" state university, and in their appointments the board attempted to forestall criticism.

The professors, decent and honorable men, were none of them much above mediocre, Roscoe Pound said later. George Howard of the class of 1876 and subsequently a celebrated scholar said, "Not one was of transcendant ability. Most of them were persons of strong character and high ideals. The dominant conservatism of the group was a real safeguard in undertaking the then bold experiment of determining the methods, planning the curriculum, and starting the traditions of a secular, a public, University for a pioneer society."[30] They often taught subjects outside their specialties just as public school teachers in later generations were expected to fill in where they had not been trained. O. C. Dake, "professor of rhetoric and English lit," taught French as well as English philology; H. E.

Hitchcock taught astronomy and German as well as mathematics; but Samuel Aughey was the real polymath: as professor of "chemistry and natural sciences," he taught botany, zoology, geology, chemistry, and occasionally German and even Greek. When he was absent, his classes were "taken" by other teachers. One must conclude that higher education initially was not very high.

Chancellor Benton addressed himself to the relationship of the state University to religion in his inaugural address, 6 September 1871. "It is worthy of note, that the most devout of our educated men are most likely to be interested in education; and by some general law of affinity, are attracted to this kind of labor," he said. Historically the church had supported higher education for its own purposes, but society now looked to its institutions of higher learning to help with growth and change. Acting Governor W. H. James, president of the Board of Regents, proclaimed in his opening remarks that in America "the avenues of greatness are alike open to all, so the doors of this institution are thrown wide open to all. This is as it should be. Science, scholarship, letters, are of no sect. They are of all sects, because they are of humanity itself. To insist upon sectarian education is to insist upon binding the infant mind with an iron cord. No restrained or imprisoned infant grows into the perfect Apollo." He then referred to an inscription at the new Cornell University: "Above all nations is humanity." He continued, "let it be carved in imperishable gold upon [our] gates: 'Above all sects, is truth.' "[31] From its beginning, the new University of Nebraska was participating in the broadening intellectual currents of the nation.

❧ The Curriculum

Chancellor Benton arrived in Lincoln, then a village of some 2,000 persons, in May 1871 and assumed his responsibilities on the first of June. Though his teaching staff had been appointed by the Board of Regents, it was his task to establish a curriculum and to prepare the University building, already under attack as unsafe and unfit for occupancy. Since the state did not have a system of secondary schools from which students would naturally

move to the University, Benton and the Board of Regents established a two-year "Latin School" for preparatory students as well as a four-year curriculum for collegiate students. The course of study was rigorously classical. In the first year of the Latin School, what we would now call the eleventh grade, students were to study Latin and mathematics, with a nod at English grammar, history, geography, and physiology; in the twelfth grade they had more Latin and mathematics but could now choose between Greek and German. They all studied a bit of ancient history and all had some "rhetorical exercises, embracing composition and elocution."

The collegiate course was no less rigorously prescribed and classical. With only brief instruction in classical history and English philology, the students were to study Latin, Greek, and mathematics through four years. In their last two years some modern languages — French and German — and some science — geology, physical science — varied the diet a bit, and seniors were to study philosophy and political economy. This "Classical Course" could be varied in the "Scientific Course" by substituting zoology and physical science for some of the classical languages, but, according to the catalog, "the students of this course will recite, as far as their studies coincide[,] with those in the Classical Department — using the same text books." Provision was made for irregular students in the "Selected Course": "Special students will be admitted to the classical or scientific course, select[ing] from the general course such studies as they may prefer, with the advice and under the direction of the Faculty."[32]

This enforced and extended study of the classics was standard in the colleges of mid-nineteenth-century America, however inappropriate to frontier Nebraska it might now seem. Defenders of the curriculum argued that the ancient languages and mathematics disciplined the character and developed clear thinking. Further, they inculcated a sense of moral responsibility. President Noah Porter of Yale said at his inauguration in 1871: "To hold the student to minute fidelity in little things is an enforcement of one of the most significant maxims of the Gospel."[33] President James McCosh of Princeton was no less rigorous in defending the classical curriculum as the main channel of educational disciplines.[34] It was assumed that knowledge was virtue (it was Francis Bacon who observed that knowledge was power). With professors as models of probity who could influence students, build character, and promote good order in society, Benton's classical curriculum was squarely in the conservative tradition.

Benton and the Board of Regents were fully aware that this curriculum was not in harmony with the terms of the Morrill Act, which called for study of the "useful" arts. But in 1871 no model for the new land-grant industrial university had yet been devised, and agricultural and industrial colleges were encountering violent opposition wherever they were tried. In Nebraska no "professor of agriculture" was appointed by the board during the months before the opening of the University, but in December 1871 Samuel R. Thompson of Rock Bluffs, Cass County, was named to that post. He was instructed to spend the winter among agricultural schools in the East in order to see what they were doing. The question confronting him and the board was both practical and theoretical. Was the University to establish a model farm for the edification of agriculturists or was it to be a place of practical instruction? The ideal of research had not yet been formulated.

The subsequent reports of experiences with industrial education elsewhere were disheartening. In December 1873 the board was told: "At the late National Educational Convention, held at Elmira, N.Y., which was attended by about 1000 delegates from all parts of the country, it was stated that only three out of the graduating class of the Massachusetts Agricultural College at Amherst, will turn their attention to farming, and this is said to be the best institution of the kind in the country." Since, in the Seventies, Nebraska was still underpopulated, many people thought a department of agriculture would only seduce people from the land, not improve the rural economy. "Dr. McCosh of Princeton, in his address to the Convention on Upper Schools, maintained that the Agricultural Colleges are not accomplishing any great good," the board was told, "and that they are not entitled to any great endowment. The general opinion among educators present at the convention was that these institutions, in their special work of educating farmers was lamentably disproportion-

ate to their cost."[35] In Nebraska the problems were postponed. An agricultural college was not organized until the fourth year of the University, when fifteen young men enrolled in an agricultural course, and in that year, on 24 June 1874, the board purchased the Moses Culver farm of 320 acres some three miles northeast of Lincoln, on what is now Holdrege Street, for $55 an acre. It was more than a decade before full support was given to an agricultural-industrial college as more than a trade school.

Students and Campus Life

When the University opened its doors, nobody could know how many students would appear, and the board and the chancellor were gratified that 130 matriculated, more than they had anticipated. Of that number, 110 were in the preparatory school; five, including one woman, were collegiate freshmen; two were sophomores; and one was a junior. Twelve, including six women, were irregular students. The one junior, J. Stuart Dales, was to have a life-long connection with the University. (He had come to Nebraska with the Bentons because of his attachment to their daughter, Grace, whom he subsequently married, and, after taking one of the first two degrees awarded, he became secretary of the Board of Regents, a post he held for the next fifty-seven years.) All these first students were enrolled in the College of Literature, Science and the Arts, for this was the only organized college. Six colleges had been specified in the University charter, but their time had not come.

Chancellor Benton and the board should not have been surprised at the size of the student body or its composition. Other state universities had begun with similar numbers of unprepared students. The University of California had opened with twenty-seven students in 1868; the first graduating class at the University of Minnesota, founded in 1851, numbered just two young men, and the University of Wisconsin had graduated its first class in 1854 with two men. In 1865, 290 of its 331 students were in preparatory or special work. The University of Missouri had forty-six students in the year it took advantage of the Morrill Act endowment. When Kansas University began in 1866 with a faculty of three, not a single student was prepared for college work. The Illinois Industrial University began in 1867 with an enrollment of fifty, very few prepared for college work.[36] By comparison, the collegiate and Latin School enrollments in Lincoln were quite respectable.

In 1871 the method of instruction at the University of Nebraska and elsewhere was mainly recitation. College training consisted principally in reshaping others' thoughts in the student's language, in parroting fact and opinion uncritically. Teachers were little more than proctors, hearing lessons out of standard textbooks, and students were expected to be in classrooms many hours a day. No research was required of students and they were not asked to use the library, the professor of English remembered later.[37] The library was in fact small. In five years it grew to about 2,500 volumes but was open only a few hours every week. Laboratory work was unheard of. The high spirits of the pioneer students found fulfillment outside the classroom. Literary societies played an active part in the education of both Latin School and college students. The Palladian Society was the first of these. Founded in the fall of 1871 shortly after the University opened, it was intended "to help build up and perfect the moral and intellectual capacities and in like manner the social qualities" of the students. At first it was restricted to male membership, but after the founding of the Adelphian in 1873, women were admitted and regularly became officers. For the next twenty-five years the Palladian Society and its rivals, first the Adelphian and then the University Union and later still the Delian, were the center of social and intellectual life in the University community. They met weekly and had rooms in University Hall. Louise Pound, of the class of 1892, described their activities: "The programs of the literary societies consisted of varied features. Staple were the 'essay,' the 'oration,' the 'recitation,' with such musical numbers as were available interspersed, and the program closed normally with a 'debate.' Social sessions followed, sometimes varied by the serving of 'light refreshments,' such as doughnuts, apples, popcorn, or more rarely, ice cream; and there were promenades through the long corridors."[38]

The faculty, including the chancellor, and townspeople often attended the Saturday night debates and participated in the discussions that grew from them. The debates were on such questions as "The pulpit affords a wider field for eloquence than the bar," "Chinese immigration is beneficial," and "War advances civilization." Woman suffrage was a subject of lively interest from the first years of the University. Students remembered these spirited meetings all their lives, and the student newspaper repeatedly spoke of the practice young men and women received there in public speaking and open discussion. Commonly the editors contrasted the controversy of the literary societies with the stultifying discipline of the classical courses.

The furnace did not heat University Hall, and by June 1873 twenty-five or thirty stoves had to be placed in the classrooms to make them usable. "Early generations of students remember the ugly and insatiable stoves that made winter use of the old chapel possible, but never comfortable," one student recalled. "With its wealth of bleak walls, its stained and perilous ceiling, a more uninspiring room cannot well be imagined, but pioneer spirit was not so easily daunted."[39] A steam-heat plant was not installed until 1885. Here was Emerson's "plain living and high thinking."

❧ Benton's Departure

In his early years Benton and his family were pleased with what they found in Nebraska. "This is to me the best country I have ever lived in," he wrote his father on 11 April 1873. "I should not be surprised if we remained here as long as we live," he wrote a few weeks later. But within a year he was considering a return to Northwestern Christian University. He got on well with his Board of Regents and felt himself to be warmly accepted wherever he went, he said, and he thought that he was establishing the University soundly. But though secure in his post, he was, willy-nilly, in the center of storms. He wrote to his father on 12 March 1875: "One half of our Board have just been elected by the legislature, and it would not surprise me if we have some difficulty between the two parties [fundamentalist Christians and more liberal 'broad-gaugers'].

The half just elected are all Free Religionists or Broad-gauge men. A little ring was formed in the legislature and they elected themselves." Trouble did not come quite as quickly as he had feared, and on 30 June 1875 he wrote, "Our Board here have just met and everything passed off well. The Broad-gaugers are so much in the minority practically that they can do nothing. They desire, I know, my place of influence and compensation, but I expect to hold it until I voluntarily resign it. I suit the majority and who cares for the rest." But within a month Benton decided to return to Indianapolis, where his old college had realized enough money to pay him a salary commensurate with what he received at Nebraska. "I shall have been here for five years, have got the University nicely underway. Enjoy the highest respect of people here, and this makes a good condition of things to leave," he wrote his father on 31 August 1875.[40]

When the time came, however, the Bentons left with reluctance: "Our work here is going forward pleasantly and smoothly, and it will be something of a trial to leave it," he wrote on 22 January 1876. He had reason to feel that he had the respect of Nebraskans. At his final commencement exercises in 1876, two students, unannounced, acting for the community, presented him with a "handsome silver pitcher and a pair of elegant gold-lined goblets," and one of them spoke of the affection the students felt for the chancellor. Too overcome to respond, Benton could only pronounce the benediction.[41] *The Hesperian Student* reported later (1 May 1882), "Ex-Chancellor Benton has been tendered a professorship in the University. . . . Few men were ever admired and respected by the students as was Mr. Benton when Chancellor here." The Bentons did not sever their connections with Nebraska. They left their daughter Grace, now married to J. Stuart Dales, in Lincoln; and their daughter Mattie later married W. E. Stewart, who became a Nebraska judge. Benton's grandson Benton Dales was a professor of chemistry at the University from 1903 until 1917, and the first chancellor himself returned to Lincoln in his old age, to die in 1914.

Chancellor Benton did not leave Nebraska only because of the controversies. The fact was, the state was undergoing severe financial difficulties in the Seventies. With a monetary panic in the East in 1873, the price of farmers' crops dropped disastrously; sometimes farmers could not even sell their wheat and corn. Grasshoppers were a serious menace through 1876, and the drought of the middle Seventies was terrifying. It can be no wonder that enrollment at the University failed to keep up with the population growth of the state, falling to one hundred in 1874, and that pioneer enthusiasm was tempered. Fortunately for both the University and the state, the later Seventies saw considerable recovery, but by then Chancellor Benton was in Indianapolis.

The achievement of the first years was that the University survived. It had no built-in constituency, no religious, economic, social, or intellectual support group such as ancient European and earlier American universities had had. It had not grown organically — it was not established to satisfy recognized needs. Rather, it was set up by fiat, federal fiat at that, and it was "emphatically the seeker and not the sought," an early professor wrote.[42] This circumstance was not unique to Nebraska. All land-grant institutions in greater or lesser degree had to prove themselves to an indifferent public.

2. Defining a University: 1876–1891

❧ The Eighties

In 1876 Edmund B. Fairfield, a religious and educational conservative, found himself chancellor of a university which, like other universities of the time, was developing differently from anything he had known. In the next decade the prescribed classical curriculum was modified and students were offered electives. Increasingly the professors saw themselves as scholars, not proctors. The University became more than an academy.

The University changed physically, too. After some controversy, the first expensive telephone was installed in 1882; it cost $4.50 a month. In the spring of 1884 the first typewriter was purchased for $115; typewriters had been in use at the capitol since 1879. (By 1890 a "Type-Writer Built for a Student" was advertised for $15.) In 1885 the chancellor's and steward's rooms — the steward was the business manager — were fitted out as offices complete with wash basins. In 1886 the chancellor was provided with a fountain pen, at a cost of $2.50; L. E. Waterman had produced the first such pen two years earlier. "Water closets" were put into the basement of University Hall in 1887. In this decade J. Stuart Dales, the secretary-steward, gave larger and larger portions of his time to the University until in 1889 he had a salary of $1,800 a year. In 1889 the acting chancellor was authorized to employ a clerk at a salary not to exceed $960; the salary of John Green, the janitor-engineer, was $1,020. Professors were paid $2,000 in the Eighties; the chancellor got $4,000; and the new dean of the Industrial College, Charles E. Bessey, was hired in 1884 at $2,500, a salary that caused some professorial envy.

❧ Frontier University

The Eighties began in controversy. Chancellor Benton's replacement, Edmund B. Fairfield, was caught between uncompromising fundamentalists, who feared with some justice that they might break if they bent, and modernists, who had to respond to charges of atheism. Edmund Burke Fairfield (b. 1821) had once been president of Hillsdale College in Michigan (1849–70), where he had been active in Michigan politics, and had more recently (1875) become president of a normal school in Pennsylvania. Like Benton, Fairfield, a Congregationist, was an ordained minister. Less personable and more given to politics than Benton, he seemed unable to grasp the distinction between a secular and a nonsectarian education; and he resisted modifying the classical curriculum of mathematics and languages. The dogmatic concerns of the times can be gathered from a circular widely distributed in a regents' election in 1879. Addressed "To the Voters of the State, Regardless of Politics," it read: "Our children's welfare should be nearer, and dearer, to us than party ties. Their education, moral and intellectual, is our highest duty. The question is, shall it be entrusted to infidel, or broad guage [sic] hands?" The sheet endorsed A. J. Sawyer, who was "in favor of a high standard of morals, and believe[d] that the bible affords such a standard."[1] The names of ministers in Presbyterian, Christian, Congregational, Methodist, and Baptist churches were affixed to the document, but these ministers quickly denied that they had had anything to do with the flier. This name-calling, they said, was beneath their dignity. Sawyer was defeated, and never again has a member of the clergy been elected to the Board of Regents.

Newly appointed faculty in the Eighties were similarly

divorced from official religious affiliation. Students (and parents) who wanted instruction guided by theological concepts could go to Doane College, founded by Congregationalists in 1872; Creighton University, a Jesuit college founded in 1878; Hastings College, a Presbyterian school founded in 1882; or Nebraska Wesleyan University, a Methodist college opened in 1887 after several false starts. The state university moved away from its "pansectarian" disposition into something like modern secularism.

This secularism was identified with the new "scientific spirit," and in an 1881 Charter Day address, Samuel Aughey, the best-known member of the faculty at the time, defined it. Clarifying the differences between the older religious institutions and the new public university, he said "the time had come when an advance should be made on traditional methods of education" and "a University was needed – a University 'by the people and for the people' – an institution which should be expressive of the intellectual life, not of the past or present, but of all time. To accomplish this, an institution was needed where pre-eminently the scientific spirit should obtain. . . . The scientific spirit pre-eminently makes its inductions from facts – facts in nature, in consciousness, in language, in the life of the people, and the development of an epoch." The scientific spirit searches for descriptive truth and does not rely exclusively on received, prescriptive truth: "[It] is the spirit that is revolutionizing our times."[2]

Samuel Aughey – the name was pronounced OW-e – was predominantly a man of the New West, an enthusiast whose excitement about the new world sometimes clouded his judgment. His eagerness to help shape a new society attracted men and women to him, and he was for nearly a decade a leading booster of it. Born in 1831 and raised on a Pennsylvania farm, he went to college and theological seminary at twenty. An ordained Lutheran pastor, he subsequently held a church near Philadelphia, but he lectured throughout the surrounding counties on scientific subjects as well as politics. Controversial and restless, he made various explorations to the West in 1860 under the auspices of the Smithsonian Institution, and it was said, probably erroneously, that he was the first white man to explore the Niobrara River and the first geologist to visit the badlands

of the Dakotas. In 1864 the Reverend Aughey brought his family to Dakota City, Nebraska, as a home missionary, but in 1867 he resigned his pastorate "through failing health" to devote himself almost exclusively to scientific work. He made geological, mineralogical, botanical, and conchological collections in Dakota, Nebraska, and Wyoming, and after 1869 he worked as a civil engineer (he had briefly practiced surveying in Pennsylvania when young). In 1871 he was appointed professor of chemistry and natural science at the University, where he taught a full range of subjects, upon occasion even hearing recitations in German and Greek for the ailing professor of languages.

Nothing seemed too much for him. At the University, Aughey conceived it his responsibility not only to teach but to answer the scientific questions put to him by the citizens of the state. Those who thought they had discovered deposits of coal sent him samples for analysis, temperance groups who wanted alcoholic beverages checked came to him, and farmers with sick beasts brought the contents of beastly stomachs for examination. For more than ten years at the University he worked indefatigably. *The Hesperian Student* reported on 1 December 1882 that "the professor of Natural Science [was] usually in his room from early in the morning until after eleven at night" when he was in Lincoln. He was much less faithful in teaching his classes, and the student paper also reported, on 16 January 1882: "Professor Aughey is still in Washington and his classes have been distributed around to anyone kind enough to take them." The confining and regular work of the University was not congenial to this restless temperament, and when in November 1883 some rumors arose about "forged endorsements" on a paper that he had issued, he resigned his professorship and would not return even when charges were dismissed. Claiming failing health again, he went off to become geologist for the Wyoming Territory. His health seems to have recovered, for he continued a strenuous life of exploration. He died in 1912 at age eighty-one.

In his day Aughey was important in Nebraska, for it was he who promoted the doctrine that "rainfall follows the plow." His speeches and publications boosting the trans-Missouri West as suited for agriculture were reprinted by the railroads to encourage settlement in the

Great American Desert. His explanation for this increase in rainfall is ingenious. As the land is broken, he said, the absorbative power of the soil is increased and the land becomes "like a huge sponge. The soil gives this absorbed moisture slowly back to the atmosphere by evaporation. Thus year by year as cultivation of the soil is extended, more of the rain that falls is retained to be given off by evaporation, or to produce springs."[3]

In Aughey a "sanguine, bilious temperament" was combined with diligence. If none of his studies measure up to modern standards of accuracy, they at least began a systematic examination of the country. Roscoe Pound, who took a doctorate in botany at the University of Nebraska in 1897, later called him a "charlatan": "He assumed he knew things he didn't know and didn't know enough to know he didn't know them."[4] But Lawrence Bruner, the son of an early regent who became an internationally celebrated entomologist, credited Aughey with arousing his scientific interest in insects; and Charles E. Bessey, his successor as professor of botany, said of him at his death: "Let us honor him for his scientific spirit which he maintained here in the day when science was small and weak, and which he carried to the end of his long life."[5]

"The Trio of Sampsons"

Aughey did not attempt to reform the University. Perhaps he was not so much interested in education as he was in opening the West. Four men a generation younger than he took upon themselves the task of educational reform and became thorns in Chancellor Fairfield's side. The four were rather like Aughey: they had come west because they saw opportunity to shape a new world with advantage to themselves. "They were all men of uncommon aggressiveness and ability," Albert Watkins, an irascible but meticulous early historian of the state, wrote a few years later. "Having decided that the chancellor ought to go, they set about with systematic energy to attain their end." Three of the Young Turks had, like Aughey, joined the University from other institutions. Theirs was "a spectacular campaign resulting in the annihilation of the forces on both sides. The trio of Sampsons who thus deliberately dragged

down the Philistine temple upon their own heads, afterward won distinction in other walks of life."[6]

George Church, the oldest of the Sampsons, "constitutes really the disturbing element," the *Hastings Nebraskan* said in February 1882. "He has such a positive personality, such peculiar views, and such ambition, that it is probably impossible to put any Chancellor in the University, with whom he will agree, or work in harmony." Perhaps he wanted to be chancellor himself; some people thought so. Born in 1843 and educated at Antioch College in Ohio and the University of Michigan, he became the head of the University Latin School when it was founded in 1871. Far from erudite, he was a brilliant teacher who inspired his students to play over their heads. A "devout Unitarian," according to the *Omaha Republican*, and thus outside the pale of Christian orthodoxy, he nonetheless in 1875 became professor of Latin in the University and was awarded a leave on part pay to study in Europe. A freethinker before studying in Berlin with Ernst Curtius and Theodor Mommsen, celebrated ancient historians, in 1877–78 he got a new vision. Discontent with proctoring, he wanted to inaugurate "scientific" investigations of scholarly topics; lectures, not recitations; and discussions rather than paraphrases of received texts. He scandalized the Methodist and Presbyterian ministers by drinking in public with his adult students and by encouraging them to go hunting on the Sabbath.[7] In later years he became a judge in California.

George Church was not alone in questioning the curriculum, the teaching methods, and the faculty's responsibilities for their students' morals. He found a sympathetic colleague in young Harrington Emerson. Emerson was more brilliant than Church and even more colorful: he was said to know nineteen languages. Born to a Presbyterian minister in 1853, he was educated at the Royal Bavarian Polytechnik institute in Munich and in Italian and Greek universities. Chancellor Fairfield appointed him tutor of modern languages at $1,500 a year in 1876 at age twenty-three, and when he came to Nebraska, he borrowed money from his father so he and his brother could invest in land and a flour mill at Milford. The business venture was not a success, so he devoted his considerable energies to the University.

Becoming secretary of the faculty and overcoming Fairfield's objections, Emerson insisted that thorough academic records be maintained in a card file. Within the University, he complained to his father, there was "no system laid down for state instruction and every professor thinks for himself." Like Church, Emerson believed that teaching was more than drill and that classwork was more than recitation. Much of what passed for University teaching could be done by tutors at less than half his salary: "Let us do work worth $2000 and raise our standard." Like Church, he was impatient with the restrictions on his private life. "The Chancellor of the University sometimes makes me wish I was a farmer, poor, but entirely free," he wrote his father. "For the University's sake, I must wear a padlock on my mouth and a chain on my feet."[8]

One can detect elements of Emerson's future career in his response to the West in the Seventies. It was Emerson who later invented the term "efficiency engineering" to describe a kind of management, and it was he who first sold American industry on the importance of standard accounting methods. He insisted on the virtues of line and staff organization. Between 1882 and 1896 he was what we would call today a management consultant to banks and railroads in the West, and then in 1896 he examined industrial plants and mines in the United States, Mexico, and Canada for a British syndicate. From 1896 to 1898 he established some of the first long-distance mail routes in Alaska and down the Yukon, and investigated marine cable routes through Alaska to Asia. Controversial throughout his life – he died in 1931 – Emerson reorganized the world for greater efficiency and profit, beginning with the University of Nebraska.[9]

The third young critic of Chancellor Fairfield and the conservative University regents was George Woodberry. In later years he became professor of comparative literature at Columbia, editor of Shelley, and biographer of Edgar Allan Poe. A more unlikely member of the frontier it would be hard to imagine. Hired in 1877 at $1,500 upon his graduation from Harvard, where he had been a favorite of Charles Eliot Norton, historian and founder of *The Nation*; James Russell Lowell; and President Charles William Eliot, George Edward Woodberry had been recommended by Henry Wadsworth Longfellow. He was twenty-three years old. He had been brought to an appreciation of the Mediterranean culture of Homer, Dante, and the Old Masters by Norton, and when he wrote to Norton of the bare solitude, the cultural poverty, the raw town – Lincoln – and the undeveloped landscape of Nebraska, he feared that he would become as barbarous as his surroundings. He was a spokesman for what Santayana identified as "the genteel tradition." Shortly he associated with Church, Emerson, and a few laymen in town; and when he resigned his post at the end of the year to become an editor on *The Nation*, Fairfield was not displeased.

And yet in 1880 he returned to Lincoln, his reappointment arranged by Church, Emerson, and "a few strong friends . . . mostly politicians."[10] To Woodberry the West was not the Land of Opportunity as it was to Harrington Emerson, nor a conquerable world as it was to Church, but he responded to it in his genteel way, too. Years later, recalling an extended trip through the unmarked country, he spoke of an exaltation he found there. He "plucked a natural trust for the future, a reasonable belief in Providence, and a humble readiness to accept the partial ills of life." Here a man "establishes a direct relation to God, which is also a reality of experience, as vital in the cry for aid as in the offering of thanks."[11]

When Oscar Wilde visited Lincoln in the spring of 1882, Woodberry spent many hours with him, fascinated by his religion of beauty as well as by his conversation. The two young men were of an age, just under thirty. Woodberry wrote to Norton, "He is better than his theories." Wilde lectured under the auspices of the Presbyterian church. The Presbyterians had been among the severest critics of Woodberry's casual disregard for social proprieties, and Woodberry told Wilde, "The nearest I have come to going to church for a long while was in attending your lecture." Wilde replied, "Oh, Mr. W., that is the most bitter thing that has been said to me."[12]

Woodberry had the same troubles with Chancellor Fairfield and the conservative regents that Church and Emerson had. Coming from Harvard, where President Eliot had inaugurated a nearly complete elective system, he found the narrow offerings at the University of Nebraska antiquated. Woodberry and his young colleagues were eager to participate in the momentous changes of their time. They demanded that students elect their own course of study, that professors teach their subjects with scientific impartiality, that both students and professors engage in independent investigations. Professors were intellectual guides, not moral preceptors, they believed.

By 1882 the University was in an uproar. The newspapers of the state had much to say about the controversies, and when the Board of Regents met in January 1882 with only four regents present, they decided by a vote of three to one to "dispense with the services" of Church, Woodberry, and Emerson as of 30 June.

The report explained their actions: "A lack of harmony, an 'irrepressible conflict' in the Faculty, a matter well understood throughout the State," led the board to their dismissal.[13] A storm followed, the newspapers filled with charges and countercharges, the language often extravagant and the charges extreme. The editor of the *Omaha Bee* wrote on 1 February, "The state university is supposed to be the highest development of our public school system not of our Sunday schools," and *The Watchman* of Omaha on 4 February called the chancellor "a slimy religious fanatic." When the board met at their annual meeting in June, they decided to dispense with the services of Fairfield as of 30 September. For all his intransigence, Fairfield was abused. He had simply stood by his fundamentalist principles and found himself out of step with the times.

George Howard as Survivor

George Howard, the fourth of the rebellious young men, was the only one to survive the purge of 1882. He had come to Nebraska in a covered wagon with his cousins in 1868, and after studying at Peru State College, then called Montclair College, he took his B.A. degree at the University of Nebraska in 1876 at the age of twenty-seven. Thereupon he went to Germany and France for two years. During his absence he wrote fully to the campus newspaper reporting on European universities, and when he returned he became first a teacher of English and history and then,

from 1879 until 1891, professor of history. History was a new subject in the curriculum. Samuel Eliot Morison reports that "as late as 1884, President Eliot [of Harvard] could declare without contradiction 'The great majority of American colleges . . . have no teacher of history whatever.' "[14]

Always eager to break new ground, Howard imported the new European "scientific" history to Nebraska. The new historians were concerned, above all else, with discovering the origins of those institutions which had hitherto been conceived of as fundamentally static. Such a method challenged the absolute stability of orthodoxy. A splendid lecturer, he quickly became the most popular teacher on the campus, drawing more students than any other teacher. Lecturing itself was a new thing. Accustomed to reciting from textbook summaries, the students delighted in hearing a scholar gather information from various sources in order to draw independent conclusions. Howard required them to write "library papers," that is, reports of original investigations on set topics. Within a few years he established the University's first seminar, in which a group of students and a professor researched a subject together. At his insistence the library was open to students longer periods of time; earlier it had been a faculty bailiwick, open only to professors, who had their own keys. Howard became librarian, insisting that books be available to all and that the holdings be expanded.

Though not physically large, Howard was formidable. With piercing eyes and a straightforward manner, he brooked no nonsense. Some thought him a bit humorless. He relished competition as well as novelty, making demands on himself and those around him. Why of the Young Turks was he alone not dismissed in 1882? Perhaps he was secure as a local defender of the University, a graduate who had returned to his alma mater. Apparently he did not challenge conventional social conduct – did not drink beer in public – and though he saw the University as a secular institution, he did not deny that it had a responsibility for moral instruction. In an essay, "The State University in America," which he published in *The Atlantic Monthly* in 1891, he said, "Comparative science is more likely to foster honesty and truthfulness than a regimen of conduct, and the laboratory is the best academic police system ever invented."[15] He saw the University essentially as a service to society. He wrote in 1889, "The state must concern herself with the economics of government and with the pathology of the social organism." He continued, "Hereafter only men carefully trained in the schools can safely be placed at the head of state departments."[16]

Howard was an advanced thinker, favoring an elective curriculum, freedom of inquiry, research into all areas of experience, and equal opportunity for men and women alike; and he was in substantial agreement with Church, Emerson, and Woodberry. He can be said to be one of the two intellectual founders of the University of Nebraska; Charles E. Bessey was the other. The Young Turks had lost their battle in that they had now to prepare for new careers, but they won their war and the University was changed permanently by their action. The elective system which they had championed was established and the study of ancient languages and pure mathematics never again dominated the curriculum. The secular as opposed to non-sectarian nature of the University was determined, and religious issues never again became central in discussions of University purposes. Fairfield left Lincoln, and from the summer of 1882 until January 1884, Henry E. Hitchcock served as acting chancellor. Hitchcock, a rather colorless man, had often sympathized with the Young Turks, but he taught a celebrated Sunday school class at the Presbyterian church and was beyond criticism.

J. Irving Manatt and the Faculty

During the summer of 1882 Lucius A. Sherman, who had just taken his Ph.D. in English philology at Yale, was appointed to the chair vacated by George Woodberry. In November he wrote to his friend J. Irving Manatt: The University "has a fair start, but is far behind what it should be, owing to a chronic row between the late chancellor and three of the younger professors. These latter, if indeed not the former official, prostituted the university to their strife, and did very little work for the students. Their successors are of a different stamp, and are willing to do

their best for the university. A good dispositioned, long-suffering chancellor seems alone to be wanting." Sherman defined the place of the chancellor: "You know the idea of a Chancellor that prevails here: some one to kick at, who shall be responsible for everything, though powerless to shape a policy, or inaugurate change." Sherman was personally very happy: "I cannot conceal my enjoyment of the work here, – would not if I should try. So pardon the obtrusive raptures of my honeymoon. There are drawbacks, of course: but less than I expected to find."[17] After a considerable delay, upon recommendation of the faculty the regents offered the chancellorship to Sherman's Yale colleague. J. Irving Manatt accepted in January 1884. He apparently had Sherman's assurance that the faculty was eager to cooperate with him, and the evidence is clear that they were.

The University in the 1880s was ready to progress. It was fortunate to have Charles H. Gere, publisher of the *Lincoln Journal*, as member and president of its Board of Regents from 1882 to 1892. Through his influence the University expanded physically and academically. Three new buildings were added: a chemistry laboratory in 1885 (later Pharmacy Hall); Grant Memorial Hall, an armory-gymnasium; and Nebraska Hall, home initially for the Industrial College, in 1887–88. Like University Hall, these were not closely supervised in their construction and were accepted finally without meeting the architects' specifications. The defects in Nebraska Hall were especially egregious, and though the building was remodeled in 1908, it remained troublesome for the next three generations.

Gere was also instrumental in upgrading the quality of the faculty. He supported George Howard as new professor in history. In 1882, Grover E. Barber replaced George Church as professor of Latin, L. A. Sherman replaced Woodberry as professor of English, and Hudson Nicholson took the chair of natural science formerly held by Aughey. All were men of energy and ability, a considerable improvement over the staff that Chancellor Benton had had to work with.

The new chancellor, like his friend L. A. Sherman, had a Ph.D. from Yale, but before that he had taken a doctorate at Leipzig in Germany. He was a man of settled opinions, and when he arrived in Nebraska on 1 January 1884 from

Marietta College in Ohio, where he had been a professor of Greek, he resolved to "overhaul the faculty by removing a bit of dead timber." Within three or four years he did indeed preside over the appointment of a number of persons of distinction. Charles E. Bessey, the botanist, was the most important appointment of his years. Lewis E. Hicks, who had studied with the renowned scientist Louis Agassiz, became professor of geology; A. H. Edgren, a profound student of Sanskrit and modern languages, taught comparative philology and later joined the Nobel Commission in Sweden; D. B. Brace, who took his Ph.D. in Berlin under the brilliant physicist H.L.F. von Helmholtz, made fundamental investigations into the nature of light; Rachel Lloyd, the second woman on the faculty, came to the University with a Ph.D. from the University of Zurich and studied sugar beets for the benefit of Nebraska agriculture; F. S. Billings made investigations into hog cholera that changed swine culture.

The "dead timber" which Chancellor Manatt identified included Ellen Smith, the first woman appointed to the University faculty. The regents had wanted a woman on staff from the beginning, and Chancellor Fairfield had brought Miss Smith from Hillsdale College, where, working her way through college, she had impressed him with a "passionate earnestness and a staunch nobility."[18] In 1877, at age thirty-nine, she became a tutor in the Latin School, where Roscoe Pound remembered that she placed more emphasis on learning the rules of grammar than on reading or translating.[19] Later principal of the Latin School, she was known as "Ma" Smith behind her back, and she inspired respect to the point of fear "even by those whom she rebuked for their shortcomings."[20] She told hulking farm boys when they needed baths and instructed girls in ladylike behavior. When her records showed that students were dilatory or failing, she called them to her office, remonstrating and cajoling.

In 1886 Ellen Smith was made "Registrar and Custodian of the Library," relieving Howard for research and teaching. Something of a curmudgeon, she was hardly the person to make library facilities easily available, but she tried to bring order out of the chaos of the collection of some 7,000 volumes. Her system of classification was am-

ateurish at best, for it was hardly more than an accessions list. In 1889 almost singlehanded she moved the library from its single second-floor room in University Hall to two large first-floor rooms, but the quarters remained unsatisfactory. In 1891 she was replaced by Professor George McMillan, more of Manatt's dead timber, who had grown so deaf that he could no longer hear his classes in Greek, but he was no improvement. "Ma" Smith continued her petty tyrannies from the registrar's office. Successive chancellors wanted to retire her, but no system of pensions existed. They wanted to retire the superannuated McMillan and the aging Henry Hitchcock also, but state law forbade paying salaries, even retirement stipends, without returning labor. Manatt and his successor could only wait out the years, more or less impatiently.

With her thin hair pulled tightly into a bun, Ellen Smith became a campus character, and in 1894 the editorial board of the quarter-centennial yearbook decided to dedicate their volume to "Ellen Smith – Registrar." They feared to ask her permission, frightened of her celebrated fury, but they got an unexpected response. " 'O, the dear children!' she exclaimed," an editor reported to the board. "Eyes whose steely darts had transfixed freshmen lowered in a strange mist, then she said, 'Tell them I love them all. I am proud of the honor.' "[21]

True to his conservative principles, Chancellor Manatt was concerned with the moral character of the faculty and even traveled to New York to interview H. H. Wing, a recent graduate of Cornell University, and his parents to determine if he was well bred. He was apparently sufficiently genteel, for in 1885 Wing was appointed professor of agriculture. Manatt inquired into the religious commitments of the faculty generally and at one time commented on Rachel Lloyd's church attendance. An Omaha newspaper reported that he called her "an infidel," but this he denied. He told the Board of Regents "that he has understood, and continues to suppose, that Mrs. Lloyd is a communicant of the Episcopal ch[urch] – though this is only an inference from the fact that, prominent and influential among the testimonials on which she was appointed here, was one from the Bishop of Kentucky in which (if the Chancellor's recollection is not at fault) she is spoken of as an excellent Christian lady."[22]

Manatt did not fully understand the nature of the new public university or the limits of his authority. When he failed to renew Mrs. Lloyd's contract, reporting that he "had causes not for public debate," the faculty voted unanimously (with one abstention) to reinstate her. He fell into controversy with the faculty over the appointment of D. B. Brace also. When Brace was about to leave Nebraska for another job, the chancellor did not protest sufficiently and the faculty unanimously recommended to the regents that Brace be retained, that the chair of physics and chemistry be divided, and that $5,000 be set aside to equip a physics laboratory. Charles E. Bessey, dean of the Industrial College, pressed the board to expand the sciences and related industrial activities, both theoretical and practical. By June 1888 the weekly faculty meetings had turned into an administrative council where both appointments and allocations of funds were decided, and Bessey's recommendations about industrial education were passed directly to the Board of Regents, over the chancellor's head.

By summer 1888 the chancellor and the faculty had reached an impasse, and at their July meeting the board, urged on by the student body, which included Roscoe Pound, an eighteen-year-old senior; the Alumni Association; and the faculty, dismissed Manatt in a stormy session. In September they appointed Bessey as acting chancellor and Lewis E. Hicks, professor of geology, as temporary head of the Industrial College and the agricultural experiment station. Within weeks Bessey made appointments and policy decisions which had been hanging fire for a year; Manatt seems to have been paralyzed by his own satiric temperament and the hostility of the faculty. The mood of the time can be gauged by a story in the campus newspaper, The Hesperian, for 1 October 1888: "We understand that Professor Hunt [secretary of the faculty] met the ex-chanc. on the street one day, and after passing, turned around and called out, 'Say, Chancellor, what are you doing now?' " The Hesperian remained vindictive through the whole next year.

Manatt was out of his element in the democratic frontier community of which the University was a part. As chancellor, he had no model, either in the eastern universities like Yale, themselves searching for a reconciliation of

the orthodox and the new, or in the German universities like Leipzig, where so many of the rising scholars developed research methods. In his four years as chancellor, Manatt worked with the state's high schools for a closer articulation of the curriculum, but without fully comprehending that a grounding in the traditional classical studies was not enough for the new world, and his arrogance and sarcasm alienated many with whom he had to work. Stubborn and uncollegial, he could not, in the view of his faculty, "harmonize a faculty of divergent ideals and contrary theories on the new education."[23] The editor of The Hesperian wrote 1 October 1888 of Manatt and his administration: "The cardinal difference between the administration of the present and that of the past is that the students now receive such usage as gentlefolk may expect and claim. Here there is certainly no necessity for ironclad discipline; and to us there is nothing more obnoxious than ostentation and parade of authority." The young editor goes on: "It is not easy to imagine how our recent trouble could have been adjusted more satisfactorily. Unsought by the university, discord came and increased, until it became unbearable." Happily those times were past: "A unique and pleasing feature of the whole affair has been the [present] perfect harmony between professors and students." Clearly Bessey, popular teacher-scholar, had established a new atmosphere.

For the second time in a decade a chancellor had been dismissed because he could not work with his colleagues. Why was this? In some fundamental respects the failure of the two chancellors was quite dissimilar. Fairfield failed because he took an untenable intellectual position on curriculum; by 1880 the classics and pure mathematics could not be the sole road to scholarship. Manatt failed because he was constitutionally disinclined to compromise. A martinet, he usurped authority not his, and men and women of the New West were not prepared to accept arbitrary assertion of power.

Irving Manatt and Charles Bessey made a striking contrast. Bessey, with only a very spotty elementary and secondary education, entered Michigan Agricultural College in 1866 and graduated brilliantly in 1869. Thereupon he went to teach botany and horticulture at Iowa State College of Agriculture in Ames. In time he became its acting president. Both Michigan and Iowa State were pioneers of the new popular college defined by the Morrill Act of 1862. Bessey studied on two occasions at Harvard with the great Asa Gray, who exerted a lasting influence on his scholarly habits of mind by modifying his strong practical inclinations. He urged theoretical considerations. Nevertheless, Bessey's ideas of higher education were formed in East Lansing and Ames; he remained a practical man of the West with a strong sense of public responsibility. He was a pragmatic descendant of eighteenth-century rationalism.

Manatt, on the other hand, came out of a tradition of ecclesiastical authoritarianism descending from the seventeenth century. A splendid student of the classics, like President Noah Porter of Yale he resisted the revolutionary movements then stirring in higher education. Manatt and Porter looked backward, out of step with the new egalitarian times, and thought that education was more the transmission of received culture than the assemblage of new data in the service of a new world. Subsequently Manatt had a distinguished scholarly career, serving as U.S. consul at Athens (1889–93) and then as professor of Greek history and literature at Brown University, where he remained until his death in 1915.

❧ Charles E. Bessey

Charles E. Bessey remained acting chancellor from 1888 until he found a successor in 1891, James H. Canfield. He refused to accept the chancellorship permanently because his overriding interest lay in plant research and teaching, and in his first report to the Board of Regents in 1885 he defined his position. This report attracted the attention of the editor of *Science*, then as now an influential journal, who quoted it on page 1 of his 20 February 1885 issue. Bessey asked for "two classes of experiments designated as 'popular' and 'scientific'; the first designate to reach immediate results, and the second to establish general principles." The first, "popular" investigations are constantly being made by private enterprise, he said, whereas the second are appropriate to experiment stations and colleges which have special apparatus and staff. Bessey distin-

guished between pure and applied research, as the modern jargon has it; and for all his concerns for local problems and practical results, he gave primary place to fundamental research. He saw a university as a kind of research center where scientific experiments searched out fundamental principles underlying natural experience.

Bessey had long been an advocate of experimentation as a benefit to agriculture, and when in the early Eighties the United States Department of Agriculture considered setting up research centers, he was consulted. His definition of purpose was quoted verbatim in the bill that was adopted, after some delay, on 2 March 1887 as the Hatch Act.[24] This act established research centers, called experiment stations, in connection with Morrill Act land-grant colleges. It provided an annual appropriation of $15,000 to each state with which to conduct research. On 31 March 1887, the Nebraska legislature moved to take advantage of the federal offer, and the Nebraska Agricultural Experiment Station was created. Though $15,000 was no great sum even in 1887, when the total University biennial appropriation for 1887–89 was $166,200, it was enough to entice the legislature into committing Nebraska to a long-term program.

Even before the federal government had acted, Bessey and the Industrial College had begun publishing results of research. Urged by Bessey, the Board of Regents as early as June 1886 had provided for the establishment of an experiment station for the investigation of the diseases of domestic animals; and short bulletins dealing with problems of plants, animals, and soils had appeared before 1887. The station's first official publication, issued in 1887, was by Lewis E. Hicks, professor of geology, and dealt, significantly enough, with irrigation in Nebraska. A variety of others followed shortly.[25]

Farming groups could not always see the advantage to themselves of agricultural research or indeed of education in agriculture. They saw the young men going to college from the farm, never to return; and the research seemed unnecessary where so much rich land lay undeveloped. They were defensive in dealings with theoretical professors, trusting their own practical experience almost exclusively. The 1888 legislature clearly put "the farm" on the defensive when an independent committee of agriculturists investigated charges of incompetence and waste there. How the Moses Culver land out on Holdrege Street could be used to best advantage was slow in being decided. In his report to the regents, Hicks of the Industrial College pressed for a professional scholar in the chair of agriculture, not a "so-called practical professor who affected to teach all subjects to boys who understood the practical aspects better than himself." He was referring to Harvey Culbertson, the University's first graduate in agriculture, who had been superintendent of the farm and an instructor of agriculture, from 1876 until relieved by the board in 1884. "Professor C. E. Bessey [who came to the University in 1884] has not only commanded greater respect from the practical horticulturalists of Nebraska than the so-called practical man ever could, but he has, at the same time given the University admirable service as a scientific botanist," Hicks said.[26]

Ever since Chancellor Benton and the regents had bought the Moses Culver farm in 1874, the University had been trying to define its function. The Hatch Act and Bessey determined that to be fully useful, education was to be oriented to research. Now officially and fundamentally the University, not just the Industrial College and the agricultural division, was a research center, devoted to the discovery and dissemination of new knowledge, not just to the transmission of received lore. Not a trade school, it was an institution of higher learning. Bessey's shadow fell across the next century.

❧ The New Faculty

The faculty at the University agreed that research was a necessary part of their responsibilities. On 18 November 1887, they spelled out exactly the requirements for their various ranks and, in doing so, defined themselves. They saw themselves as a self-governing, scholarly community; and at the 18 June 1888 meeting of the board, the regents agreed that for promotion to full professorship, candidates must give evidence of "literary or scientific activity" over and beyond "ability and experience as teachers" and "degrees and honors." Associate professors, on the other hand, need not yet give such evidence of literary or scientific activity. In short, professors were active scholars. They were to be appointed by a committee of their peers working with the chancellor.[27]

But the University professors did not define themselves as research scholars exclusively or even primarily. They did not separate teaching and research: that separation was not to come for some sixty years. Bessey himself had early made a mark with a textbook, undertaken at Asa Gray's suggestion, *Botany for High Schools and College* (1880). Immediately gaining recognition, this volume has since been judged to be "the single most important book published in American botany."[28] It was seminal because it insisted that students examine natural data before arriving at philosophical generalizations. Bessey, like his colleagues, was concerned with guiding students to the analysis of direct experience. While acting chancellor, Bessey was also president of the Nebraska State Teachers Association.

Bessey had occasion to define the relationship of science to education in an address delivered in Buffalo, New York, when in 1896 he was president of the National Education Association. He said that though there had been a conflict between the advocates of science and those of the old "culture-studies," this conflict was false. The usefulness of science is not its presumed money-getting value. Bessey said, "Let us hear less in the school of the practical value of science. Let us emphasize its vastly greater importance in the making of men [and women]." He continued, "The proper pursuit of science should develop a judicial state of mind toward all problems."[29] Bessey did not claim that science had an exclusive hold on the development of a judicious state of mind. In his report to the regents for 1889, he wrote that "this working one's way through a subject has become a marked feature of the University, and is by no means confined to its scientific side either. It is the dominant idea in the University."[30]

In 1887 the faculty asked the regents to allocate money for the publication of University Studies, a series of research monographs rather analogous to the experiment station bulletins. Such a series, the professors said, would bring fame to the institution; Johns Hopkins University was eminent in part because of its faculty publication. Five hundred dollars was provided at the June 1887 meeting of the Board of Regents, and in April 1889 Bessey reported that several studies had appeared, attracting international attention. Of his faculty of eleven professors, six had published in the series. In addition, George E. Howard had a five-hundred-page book on the nature of local governments in publication at the Johns Hopkins University Press, and Howard Caldwell, also of the history department, had a commission to write a monograph on Nebraska for a government series dealing with education in the various states. Bessey reported that these professors all taught very heavy loads. The professor of English taught twenty-one hours a week on eight subjects; the professors of modern languages taught seventeen hours and put in many more hours of tutorial instruction. Bessey wondered how the faculty had the time to get all their work done.

Hudson Nicholson, professor of chemistry, combined his research with local needs. *The Hesperian* reported 16 December 1889 that when he was in Germany he had "noted the similarity of soil between that of northern Germany, given up to sugar beet culture, and that of western Nebraska. He thought that beet culture might be made profitable in this state. Some experiments had been made by Germans at Grand Island. Within a year the Wellfleet company of English capitalists had started works in Lincoln county. Now capital wishes to know how much sugar the Nebraska beet will yield, and where beets can be profitably raised. These questions the chemical department of the University has undertaken to answer." Seeds were distributed to farms, sample beets collected, and Nicholson and others traveled throughtout western Nebraska assembling samples of soils. Thirty counties became involved, and beets grown on the University farm were analyzed by Rachel Lloyd and a graduate student assistant to Nicholson. These analyses indicated where beet growing might prove most profitable. The immediate advantage to the state of scientific research at the University was obvious.

The humanities — literature, languages, history, philosophy — felt neglected, as is clear in the departmental requests to the Board of Regents for funds in April 1889.

L. A. Sherman in English and Grover E. Barber in Latin were self-consciously modest in their requests, acknowledging the needs in science as great; but they and George Howard of history pressed for greater library facilities. By 1890 the University library had grown to about 11,000 volumes. The arts were similarly marginal, even though the newly formed Nebraska Art Association (then called the Hayden Art Club) had had a successful showing of the painting "The Wise and Foolish Virgins" in its initial exhibition in 1888. Indeed, people had come from all over the state and paid a handsome fee, fifty cents, to look at that large allegorical picture.[31] Bessey said that musical instruction was available in nearly every town in Nebraska (he did not speak of its quality), and he thought it necessary at the University if for no other reason than to help in chapel services! He and the board did not seem to find the arts central to the University experience.

❧ Student Life

By 1890 the University was stronger than it had ever been before. The *Hesperian* said 15 December 1888 that "among the students, general opinion seems to be that the term just at a close has been the most prosperous that the University has seen in years. In every way progress is apparent. . . ." Activity in the literary societies was vigorous, for there, the newspaper noted, "students are beginning to learn that the work afforded by the literary societies is worth more to them than any other study in the University curriculum [because] . . . the ability to appear well before an audience is not inherent" but can be learned through training. The students were high-spirited: "The first match game of football ever played at the U. of N. took place Saturday November 23 between the elevens of the Senior and the Sophomore classes," *The Hesperian* reported on 2 December 1889, the seniors finally winning "owing partly to an error by the Sophs." For some time the students had been agitating for intercollegiate football, asserting that competitive sports would increase school spirit. The paper announced with some delight that "the foot ball committee have accepted the challenge of the University of South Dakota to play us a game of foot ball here, at any time after next Saturday." The "Western Interstate Foot-Ball Association," comprising the states of Missouri, Kansas, Nebraska, and Iowa, was organized 28 December 1891, according to the 1892 yearbook, *The Sombrero*; and in 1894 the Nebraska team was the first to be recognized as the champion of the Missouri Valley colleges.[32] Big Red had begun.

Student enrollment continued to rise, slowly. In 1887, 157 were enrolled in college; in 1888 it was 173; and in 1889 the number was up to 191. The Latin School enrollment was steady at about 130. The number of graduate students increased from none in 1887 to eleven in 1888 and twenty-six in 1890. The total enrollment in 1887 was 381, but in 1890 it exceeded 500. In the Nineties the University was to see a startling growth, but the Eighties prepared the way. The University had come to the end of its beginning by 1890.

To commemorate the University of Nebraska's first quarter century, Willa Cather, managing editor of *The Hesperian*, solicited comments from alumni and faculty in 1894. She published their essays in the "Quarter-Centennial Number," dated 15 February 1894. What these persons chose to remember both defines the state of the University and marks its progress. Amos Warner, a brilliant member of the class of 1885 who, unhappily, died prematurely, wrote of how he and the business manager of the student newspaper had "batched" (as they said) on the second floor of a ramshackle frame building on O Street. "Our one room was so small that the bed lounge on which we slept had to be folded up and the bedding piled on top of it every morning before we could sit down to breakfast. Our kitchen table was also our dining room table, and also our study table. This insured our washing the dishes promptly so as to get the table to put our books and papers on." Such "tenement house problems did not interest me as much then as they have since." Public baths were available down the street for a small fee, in a barber shop. In the early Eighties, H. C. Peterson recalled, "Lincoln was either a Venice of mud or a Sahara of dust. There was not an inch of pavement, sewer, street railway, or electric wire in the town." East of Thirteenth Street there was not a brick

building, and the courthouse yard was a cornfield, the capitol grounds a dark, deserted meadow of timothy.

In the Eighties an infant medical college was organized by local physicians holding classes and laboratories wherever space could be located, and one small room in University Hall was used as a "skeleton closet." Acquiring bodies with which "the boys" could study anatomy was something of a problem and became a local scandal. One morning the residents of Lincoln awoke to see "CASH FOR STIFFS" painted in eleven-foot letters across the roof of University Hall. "Who the artist was is a mystery to this day," Peterson reported in Cather's "Quarter-Centennial Number."

To later generations the amount of energy expended over the formation of fraternities in conflict with the literary societies seems astonishing. For some years the editors of *The Hesperian* fulminated against the Greek-letter societies which challenged the Palladian, the Union, and other literary groups. The history of the conflict is reported at length in Cather's quarter-centennial issue, where it was taken with great seriousness. Will Owen Jones, by 1894 editor of the *Lincoln Journal* and benefactor of Willa Cather, could conclude his essay, "The Barbarian Revolt," by saying: "In my opinion there are few things more worthy of approving mention during this quarter centennial celebration than the barbarian revolt of 1884." In that year the literary societies excluded all members of the fraternities from their membership, thus dividing the student body decisively.

The issue was not trivial. To the pioneer students as to the pioneer society generally, the West represented a new start, an opportunity for growth without privilege. The egalitarian ideal was precious. The fraternities were groups of persons committed to one another through secret oaths and ceremonies. They set up what the "barbarians" saw as barriers to equal opportunity. In place of an open society where every man and woman stood on his or her own merit, competing on equal terms for whatever prizes lay before them, the Greek-letter societies established a closed society in which a selected few promised one another advantages of friendship, opportunity, and as-

local, ruined, serviceable

sistance. Where the literary societies were developed in the early decades to teach all who wanted to know how to speak in public, how to organize their thoughts, and how to conduct meetings, the fraternal organizations sought to give advantage by place rather than by accomplishment. By 1894 all this seemed to some, including Willa Cather, an argument now settled, and settled not in favor of the simplicities of the pioneer ideal. *The Hesperian* no longer carried editorials against the fraternities. Indeed, in assuming the editorship in the fall of 1893, Cather announced that it was not to be a continuing controversy in her pages. She herself was not a member of either a literary society or a fraternity.

⁊ॐ *The Nature of the University*

Late in life Allen Benton told Henry H. Wilson, one of the students who had been attracted to the University by the chancellor when he was on a speech-making tour about the state, that the two things in his career as chancellor that gave him most satisfaction were the establishment of the college farm and the designing of the seal of the University, the latter of which he accomplished while on a long railway journey in the East. The seal summarized Benton's view that a university was essentially a place of learning applied to the various human needs.[33] The establishment of the University farm dramatized one view of higher education. The existence of the farm demonstrated that this university was called to applied as much as to basic scholarship. Charles E. Bessey, who arrived in 1884 and served as acting chancellor from 1888 until 1891, and Martin Massengale, who became chancellor nearly one hundred years later, in 1981, were two of a kind. Both agriculturists, Bessey in horticulture and Massengale in agronomy, they conceived of the University as responding to the issues of this time and this region. Bessey by the weight of his character and the clarity of his mind permanently marked the University, and because of him the University of Nebraska seemed more like Michigan State University, a land-grant college committed to public service, than it was like the University of Michigan, a place of comprehensive scholarly research. In the first years, given the state's indifference if not hostility to higher education, perhaps Bessey's insistence on the local, the immediate, the serviceable, was the only means by which the University could have survived.

3. "A Golden Era": 1891–1900

Dean Bessey, who reluctantly served as acting chancellor after the firing of Manatt in 1888, was a superb scholar and an inspiring teacher but had no interest in administration, and the University had in effect no leadership until Canfield came in 1891.

1891

When James Hulme Canfield arrived in Lincoln in the summer of 1891, he found a city of some 35,000 people claiming to be twice that large. Though it was just passing from rawest frontier into civic order, this was no barbaric place. Some of the firstcomers, college-bred, brought their Greek grammars with them, and others brought money, expecting to make it grow in the country. High expectancy was in the air, for the world lay all before them, and, they thought, Providence was their guide — Providence aided by energy, high ambition, and an eye to the main chance. If trees were scarce, the newcomers planted more; if the mud was deep, they planned pavement. Bliss was it to be alive, and to be young was very heaven.

Like the city, the University perhaps exaggerated its merit in the early Nineties, but within the decade it took its place as one of the Big Four of state universities, along with Michigan, Wisconsin, and California. Under Chancellor Canfield, the University of Nebraska became a mecca for young men and women who left their mark on their time. Willa Cather remembered the Nineties: "In those days there were many serious young men among the students who had come up to the University from the farms and the little towns scattered over the thinly settled state. Some of those boys came straight from the cornfields with only a summer's wages in their pockets, hung

on through the four years, shabby and underfed, and completed the course by really heroic self-sacrifice. There was an atmosphere of endeavour, of expectancy and bright hopefulness about the young college that had lifted its head from the prairie only a few years before."[1] Canfield's precocious daughter, the novelist Dorothy Canfield Fisher, reflected the temper of the time and her father's attitude: "Above all it was new. It was crude because it was new. And because it was new, both town and University had the iridescent glamor of life beginning, for which almost anything is possible because little has yet been tried. The very air over the campus was glittering bright with what might be."[2]

Chancellor Canfield

"Chancellor Canfield by happy fortune came to the University just when the special problems of the time required such special talents as were his," W. F. Dann, professor of Greek, wrote a generation later. "There was particular need of buoyant optimism and glowing prophecy."[3] James Canfield was in fact one of the young men who had gone west with the youthful vigor of a hopeful time. He was a little larger than life, and he left a permanent imprint on the University of Nebraska. He was the first of the great chancellors the University was to know in the next century.

After graduating brilliantly from Williams College, Williamstown, Massachusetts, in 1868 at age twenty-one, Canfield left his native soil for the farthest West, at least the West that his thirty-four dollars would take him to. He began working in Iowa on the railroad and soon became a division superintendent. Despite his delight in those years, he went to St. Joseph, Michigan, in 1872 to study and practice law; but by the time he was thirty, he concluded that teaching was his true profession. Through President John Bascom at the University of Kansas, another Williams alumnus, he went even farther west to become professor of history and allied subjects there. No scholar, he was a wonderful platform speaker with a full voice and great craft in telling stories. Enormously popular on and off campus though controversial because of his support of free trade in a protectionist region, he became president of the National Education Association in 1890 and a national figure. In 1891, at the age of forty-four and the height of his energy and aspiration, he became chancellor of the University of Nebraska, nominated to that post by Acting Chancellor Bessey.

Canfield assumed his duties in July. "He was very simple and direct in his methods and hated display and formality," Bessey later reported. "In the morning [of July 1], he walked in[to the chancellor's office] and holding up his hand began reciting the oath of office, . . . and then being the duly qualified chancellor, he went to work."[4] Immediate results were obvious everywhere. The University was "pregnant with great things," according to the University's first historian, who was there, but "system was lacking. Ideas were present, but organization was wanting."[5] This Canfield provided "so enthusiastically that when the students returned from the summer vacation, they hardly recognized the University," according to the yearbook, *The Sombrero*.[6] The campus newspaper, *The Hesperian*, reported on 6 October 1891, "The hedge and the row of cottonwoods on the north and east sides [of the campus] have been cut down, also the hedge on the south. The gas pipe fence has been taken down, and the earth around the campus has been removed to make room for the stone walks and iron fence, now being constructed."

Students and the people of the state were charmed immediately. The professors resisted a bit, but within a year or two even Canfield's severest campus critic told him that he "could do more in the state and with the state in one evening than anyone else ever could in a month."[7] During his first year in office he traveled some 10,000 miles around the state, talking to everybody. In subsequent years he traveled only 8,000 miles a year addressing any group that

would have him. The University, he said, belonged to the citizens and its doors were open to all: Canfield was an egalitarian, a western democrat, an idealist. The University, he said repeatedly, was only grades thirteen, fourteen, fifteen, and sixteen in public education and developed "no superior class, only superior individuals." Children of farmers and professional people, of widows and bank presidents, all should have opportunity for as complete an education as they were capable of utilizing. Nebraska and the Great Plains suffered severely from depression and drought in Canfield's years, but these difficult times he took only as opportunity. "If you cannot earn," he told his audiences, "you can at least learn." He told journalists, "I may not know Nebraska from alpha to omega, but I know it from Arapahoe to Omaha." People came through mud and weather to hear his fervent message.[8]

Canfield did not attempt to explain the University only orally; he wrote for the press and encouraged faculty and staff to do so also. He asked the professors to accept speaking engagements through a kind of speakers' bureau; and he invited every organization, from the horticulture society to teachers' associations, to make use of campus buildings. He early proposed a campus "convention hall," but the depression kept that from materializing. Visitors to the campus were greeted cordially – earlier they had been shunned or neglected – and tours for them were arranged. Indeed, sometimes classes and legitimate academic activities were postponed to provide for visitors and their meetings. Women had always been provided for in the University and had been active on campus from earliest days, and they were welcomed now. Canfield himself offered a course entitled "The Status of Women in America," and the *Omaha World-Herald* reported in 1892, "Co-education is a feature which insists on intruding itself constantly upon the attention of the visitor."[9] When Canfield arrived in 1891, the enrollment stood at some 500 students; within four years it had climbed to some 1,500, and by 1900 it was at 2,000. By 1897 the University was fourteenth in size among the 300 American universities and colleges. Ninety percent of its students were Nebraskans. The citizens were embracing their University.

❧ The Students and Campus Life

On campus Canfield was popular and available. It was said that he knew every student by name. "Our chancellor may wear an imposing hat, but he never talks through it," Willa Cather wrote in *The Hesperian*, 15 November 1893. Walking to University Hall at seven in the morning from his home on S Street, he remained until dark. He saw himself as a surrogate *pater familias*. When one student, a freshman from Grand Island, was injured in a football match at Doane College, he typed out a letter to the father on his Remington typewriter:

| | University of Nebraska |
| *Chancellor's Office* | Lincoln, Nebr. *11/15/91* |

Dear Mr. Nusz:

I have just thought best to send you a telegram to the effect that the newspaper reports about your son's injury are not true. I feared that some of this talk might reach your ears and make you uneasy.

He played with the University eleven in the football game at Crete yesterday. Just at the close of the game he got a heavy fall, striking on the left side of his head. It knocked him senseless for a few moments. He was well cared for, however, and rallied enough to come back with the boys [to Lincoln]. They took him to his room here, where he was soon in a heavy sleep. They came to me at once about him, as I have instructed them to do always if anything happens to the boys; and I went to his room at about ten o'clock. I did not like to have him pass the night without the attention of a physician, so called one; who said he thought there was nothing very serious, though Chauncey's memory had not come back to him. That is, he could not recall the game nor how he got hurt. This morning I had him brought [to my home] by the carriage to prevent the danger of taking cold, and put him to bed in a quiet room, where he has been all day in care of my wife and son. He has slept much, has taken food with relish, his memory is coming back, he is in no pain, has no marks of violence, has no fever, and the Doctor says will doubtless be all right again in the morning. I shall give him a good hot bath before he goes to sleep for the night, and shall keep him with us til he is as good as new.

Do not worry about him. I will keep you posted if he does not.
Very hastily but

> *Very Cordially Yours*
> *James H. Canfield [signed]*
> *Chancellor*[10]

Within a week or ten days the Nusz boy returned to classes, but he postponed further football.

From its beginning football was an enthusiasm. Before the first intercollegiate game the students agitated for competitive sports, thinking that they would increase school spirit. In 1890 a University football team defeated the Omaha YMCA, and in the spring of 1891 it defeated Doane College – but in the fall Doane beat them. The first real achievement, however, was the defeat of Illinois in Lincoln in 1892, the star of the game being a ruggedly handsome black tackle and fullback from York County and Lincoln, George A. Flippin. In 1892 the University of Missouri forfeited a game rather than play against a black athlete, but Flippin's teammates insisted that he remain on the team. Very popular, Flippin was not only an athlete but a campus leader and became president of the Palladian literary society. He subsequently took his M.D. degree at the University of Illinois Medical School in Chicago (1900) and in 1907 returned to Stromsburg, Nebraska, to help his father, Dr. C. A. Flippin, establish the first hospital in that area.

The president of the Board of Regents, C. H. Morrill, commented on Canfield's attitude toward football. At first both men had been much opposed to it because it was "so brutal." "Very soon after this [conversation about football] the University team played in Omaha and won the game. A great number of University students and almost half the people in Lincoln were at the depot to welcome the boys on their return; the University band was playing, bells were ringing, whistles blowing, and the rejoicing was general, especially in University circles. The Chancellor was at the depot – he could not resist taking part in the occasion – and when the column was formed, he proudly marched at the head through the streets. This act of the Chancellor's won the everlasting friendship of the boys; they worshipped him and ever afterwards willingly made what they considered a sacrifice when he requested them to do so."[11] Canfield's initial instincts may have been right; within ten years the tail threatened to wag the dog. By 1901 the athletic department was paying the football coach more for three months' work than professors were paid annually.

Canfield was universally respected. Louise Pound said in 1909 that he was "possibly the best-loved man ever connected with the government of the University." She remembered that "enthusiastic applause greeted his every appearance among us." Samuel Avery, himself chancellor after 1910, remembered that Canfield posted typewritten notices on a central bulletin board over his signature. "It was customary to step over about 10 o'clock in the morning to read the bulletin board and one would hear the word exchanged: 'Well, I wonder what Jimmie's got for us this morning?'"[12]

Canfield had a remarkable group of students to work with. They included a future chancellor of the University, Samuel Avery; a future distinguished governor, George Sheldon; a future president of the Modern Language Association, Louise Pound; a future president of the American Historical Society, William Westerman; a future president of Purdue University, Edward Elliott; a future eminent Chicago physician, Charles A. Elliott; a founder of plant ecology, Frederic Clements; a future Pulitzer Prize–winning editor of the *Omaha World-Herald*, Harvey Newbranch; young Dorothy Canfield, the chancellor's daughter, who became a distinguished woman of letters; and Willa Cather. The student body contained others like Olivia Pound and Jessie Towne who marked communities but did not become widely famous. One wonders on what meat these people fed.

Roscoe Pound was perhaps the most brilliant person in all this brilliant community. Young Pound, later dean of the Harvard Law School, had been a fixture on the University campus since he was ten years old. His mother, recognizing early that Roscoe and his two sisters, Louise and Olivia, were unusually gifted, had tutored them at home. Judge Stephen Pound, their father, taught them Greek, and at age ten Roscoe was enrolled in University German, where he led his class. For the next years he was a faithful

attendant on the cadet battalion, interesting himself in military tactics, even plotting movements with his wooden soldiers at home. The undergraduates found the bespectacled young man attractive, for, though bright to the point of genius, he was full of high spirits. He took his B.A. degree in 1888 at age eighteen, majoring in botany. Professor Bessey was thought by Judge and Mrs. Pound to be the strongest man on the faculty and therefore a fit teacher for their precocious son.

Though Roscoe was full of pranks, he enthusiastically studied plants as directed. When Bessey became acting chancellor in 1888, Pound assumed responsibilities for the Botanical Seminar, a more or less formal gathering of half a dozen of Bessey's students. It was called, with undergraduate gaiety, the Sem. Bot. The laboratory in the new chemistry building (finished in 1886) was its usual meeting place. This group read serious scientific papers to each other; twenty-one were read between October 1888 and April 1889. They also made life miserable for the "lits," students of letters, challenging the rest of the school with their cry "Show me a Lit." On one occasion they renamed the faculty with spurious and sarcastic Latin tags invented by Roscoe. The seminar's motto, *Canis Pie* (dog pie, or mincemeat pie) was undoubtedly invented by Pound and resulted in pie as the standard treat after their Thursday evening meetings.[13]

When Pound went off to the Harvard Law School (1889–90), supported with money saved from his three jobs, the Sem. Bot. languished, but upon his return the young lawyer revitalized it, combining high spirits and serious study. Pound practiced law in Lincoln from 1890 on and quickly became so prominent in his profession that he was named in 1896 by the state Supreme Court to a bar examinations board. As first secretary of the Nebraska State Bar Association he managed all association affairs. In the evenings and on weekends and holidays, Roscoe continued his study of botany and engaged in serious research with Frederic Clements. The two entered their laboratory by windows, since doors were officially locked after closing hours. Through their quantification of plant geography, building on foundations laid by Bessey, the two young men by 1896 had undertaken *The Phytogeography of Nebraska*, a study of the relationship of plants to environment, which earned them their Ph.D. degrees, Pound in 1897, Clements in 1898. The contiuum that Darwin had discovered for biology, Pound and Clements applied to ecology, a recent historian has said, and in doing so they won permanent places for themselves in the history of American science.[14] It can be argued that the modern study of ecology began in Bessey's laboratory and was developed by Bessey's students. But after 1898 or so, Pound gave his full attention to the law, yielding what was to have been a brilliant career in botany.

Frederic Clements was not quite so colorful as Pound, but, unlike Pound, he remained a botanist. The original Sem. Bot. in 1886 had been made up of undergraduates, but after 1889 all the members were graduate students. In 1892 the Sem. Bot. accepted new undergraduates who, upon examination, were given the status of *novitii*; one detects the playful hand of multilingual Pound. Frederic E. Clements was the first of these. He was only eighteen in 1892 (Pound was all of twenty-two), the son of an English photographer living in Lincoln. Unlike Pound, he played football in high school and college and served as a cadet officer under Lt. John J. Pershing. He tramped the fields collecting specimens, frequently dressed in military-style clothing — jodhpurs, laced field boots, campaign hat — with a youthful insouciance that matched Pound's. Clements's doctorate in plant ecology was held up one year because of a language requirement, but in 1898 when he got the degree — he was not yet twenty-four years old — he married Edith Schwartz, a teaching assistant in German. Thereafter she became a student of ecology and took a Ph.D. in botany in 1904, and he learned languages, eventually even Polish. On their honeymoon in Colorado the pair took up forest ecology, the beginning of a lifetime scholarly collaboration. Within ten years after receiving his Ph.D., Clements had an international reputation, accomplishing his monumental work in ecology in spite of diabetes. This illness forced him to a rigorous regimen of work and diet and contributed to a remote and chilly manner in later years; but in the Nineties, Clements, Pound, and the other members of the Sem. Bot. had a lighthearted enthusiasm that attracted some of the best and the brightest University students to their scientific circle.

❧ The Faculty

Charles Bessey set the pace, but he was not the only remarkable faculty member. By 1892 the faculty consisted of some forty teachers, counting graduate assistants, instructors in the Latin School, and adjunct professors in music and art. Their teaching load was heavy, averaging something like twenty hours a week in class; but of this forty, sixteen had doctor's degrees (this was a full generation before the Ph.D. became a requirement for college teachers); ten had studied in European universities, primarily German; and seven had spent a year or longer at Johns Hopkins, the new research university founded in 1876. There were nine adjunct professors of law in a newly established law school, all practicing attorneys.

Several individuals were poised for fame. Lawrence Bruner, who took his baccalaureate degree in 1880, was already established in entomology. The son of a member of the University's first Board of Regents, and a professor at the University after 1888, he had earned a reputation for brilliance through his work on insect pests. When locusts invaded Argentina, Bruner was sent to South America in 1897 as a special investigator; he had been field agent in entomology for the United States Department of Agriculture since 1879. DeWitt Brace was another with a growing reputation. Educated in Germany, he had been on the staff since 1887. By 1897 he was doing research on the nature of light at the forefront of physics. Einstein is said to have drawn on his pioneering study. Hudson Nicholson and Rachel Lloyd of the chemistry department had helped found Nebraska's sugar beet industry, and by the middle of the decade annual Sugar Institutes were held on the campus for farmers and developers. Frank Billings had investigated hog cholera in 1886 and continued his researches into other animal diseases until he left the University in 1893 because of his vitriolic temper and extreme contentiousness.

These University scientists were committed to pure research but they were equally concerned with its practical applications. A school of agriculture for persons not otherwise registered in the University was established in 1896; employing "the laboratory method of instruction," it attracted increasing numbers to twelve-week courses. Ever since Chancellor Benton's day, the University had attempted to give farmers the benefit of its technical knowledge, and Farmers' Institutes, both on campus and off, had grown appreciably under Bessey's urging. Through this work Canfield's fame was matched across the state by Bessey, Bruner, and Billings.

In 1891 George E. Howard, the most popular teacher on the campus, or at least the one who attracted the most students, left Nebraska to become a member of the founding cadre of Leland Stanford Jr. University in Palo Alto, California. Howard's monograph on the local constitutional history of the United States, published by Johns Hopkins University Press in 1889, had attracted considerable scholarly praise. His colleague, Howard W. Caldwell, remained in Lincoln, but he had neither the fire nor the intellect of his mentor. In 1892 Fred Fling joined the history department. He had enough fire for two people and in his long career at the University of Nebraska built a considerable reputation as a historian of the French Revolution. He was also to play an important part in the University community, as we shall see in due course.

❧ L. A. Sherman

The University's two most prominent teachers of the humanities in the Nineties, Lucius A. Sherman in English and August Hjalmar Edgren in modern languages and Sanskrit, were both infected by the scientific virus and attempted to turn their literary studies into scientific inquiries. They tried to apply to letters the methods which were producing such brilliant results in the investigation of the physical world. The results were uneven at best. The humanities, that rich vessel containing the ideals and the aspirations of humankind, were seen by them frequently as a collection of artifacts to be examined for their sources, analogues, influences, and historical parallels. Insofar as science is a search for source, philology in its search for verbal, grammatic, and syntactic etymology was scientific; but insofar as philology is an examination of aesthetic and ethical values, language studies cannot be scientific. This distinction between the descriptive and the

prescriptive was not clear in these first decades of flaming scientific success; perhaps the distinction is not clear to social-science relativists to this day.

Lucius A. Sherman came to the University of Nebraska in 1882 from Yale, where he had taken his Ph.D. in 1875. There he had studied with William Dwight Whitney, the great philologist and lexicographer. A little man, rather waspish and ambitious, Sherman was head of English, dean of his college, and, finally, dean of the Graduate School. Born in 1847, he retired in 1929 at age eighty-two. His most important book, *Analytics of Literature* (1893), attempted to put literary criticism on a scientific basis. "Twenty years ago," he wrote in that book, "the college study of Physics and Chemistry consisted of recitation in assigned pages from a text-book, just as in Greek Grammar and Metaphysics," but as this "dogmatic" mode of teaching gave way to newer experimental modes, so the recitation of received opinion needed to give way in the study of literature. Just as students were now engaged in firsthand experience with physical properties, so students of literature must be involved with literary properties. Literary students should not be mere reporters of their masters' opinions any more than student scientists. Sherman sought to identify the *elements* (his emphasis) which compose excellence and beauty in literary works, assuming that just as *elements* could be identified in chemistry, so they could be identified in literature. The student, in a personal laboratory, his study, by numbering and diagraming words and sentences, would come in time "to discern and interpret every manner of excellence and beauty for himself" with something approaching scientific accuracy.[15]

Sherman's schemes were not universally admired; indeed, from the first, some of his students, Willa Cather and Louise Pound among them, said his scientific certainty amounted to little more than word counting. Louise Pound thought his book was silly, and Willa Cather thought it arid pedantry. Cather had been a campus character from her first day in Lincoln, coming as she did for a year in the University Latin School before enrolling as a freshman in 1891. She first planned a scientific course, but within months her essays were published in local papers and her direction was set. She cut quite a figure with her

1. University Hall, at the north end of Eleventh Street in 1873, when the population of Lincoln was about 8,000. (UNL Photo Lab)

2. Allen R. Benton (1822–1914), first chancellor of the University (1871–76). Though an orthodox Christian, "he was able firmly to grasp the new ideal of public education as the safeguard of society." (UNL Archives)

3. The agricultural campus, three
miles northeast of the city campus, in
1875. This half-section of land had a
small stone house, seen here in the center, for a caretaker, and a larger frame
building appropriate for a dormitory.
These grounds replaced a "model
farm" near the site of the present state
fairgrounds and became an "experimental farm." (UNL Photo Lab)

4. The cadets at the rear of University Hall, 1877. The Morrill Act of 1862 prescribed that military tactics be included in the curriculum of land-grant universities. "Students are generally provided with dark colored pants, so that the only extra expense will be for coat, cap, and gloves, and this ought not to exceed from $6.00 to $12.00, depending upon the quality of cloth chosen by the student," the University's *Sixth Annual Register and Catalogue* of 1877 asserted. Note the well in the left rear: its water was brackish. (UNL Archives)

5. Literary society room in University Hall in the 1870s. Will Owen Jones, later editor of the *Lincoln Journal*, wrote that "social distractions in the early part of my experience were found mostly in the Friday meetings of the literary societies," and, he went on, "the young people of the little city were bubbling over with social gaiety all the time. . . . The sons and daughters of the pioneers, some of them fresh from the sod houses on the homesteads, were catching their first glimpse of the glories of the ancient and the modern world. It was an enchanting and inspiring time." (UNL Photo Lab)

6. Samuel Aughey (1831–1912) was professor of natural sciences at the University from 1871 until 1884, when he retired, angry that he was accused of passing off borrowed scientific information as his own. He was a great proselytizer of the theory that "rain follows the plow"; perhaps he invented the theory. (UNL Photo Lab)

7. Medical college students in front of University Hall, 1885. Opened in 1883 with eighteen students, fourteen in daily attendance, the college promised an M.D. degree in three years. The graduating class of 1886 numbered six women and nineteen men. The college was discontinued in 1887 because of public and professional hostility. (UNL Photo Lab)

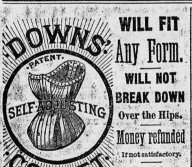

8. A portion of the front page of the *Nebraska State Journal* for 10 June 1885. Notice the announcement of the bath house. When plumbing was installed in Grant Memorial Hall, there was considerable controversy over the proposal that the baths be opened to students not enrolled in gym classes. (UNL Archives)

9. Steel engravings of Lincoln were published in *Harper's Weekly*, 10 August 1889. This picture views Lincoln northwest from the capitol; the campus is to the right of the center, in the distance. (UNL Photo Lab)

10. "Qualitative laboratory" in the new (1885) chemistry building. Here Rachel Lloyd, professor of analytic chemistry, and H. H. Nicholson, experiment station chemist, analyzed the sugar content of Nebraska beets to discover their commercial viability. (*Sombrero '92*, UNL Archives)

11. James H. Canfield (1847–1909) was the first great chancellor of the University of Nebraska (1891–95). In an 1893 letter he said, "The western atmosphere is crisp. Its breezes blow freely. It ministers to life in the largest sense of the word. It demands activity, earnestness, unselfishness and plenty of red blood rather than 'blue.' Here a young man's future is safe; safe in recognition, and what is far more to the purpose, safe in usefulness." The photograph is from the *Sombrero '92*, which was dedicated to him. (UNL Archives)

12. Greek recitation room in University Hall, ornamented with plaster casts of classical statuary and a framed print of Virgil reading the *Aeneid* to the court of Augustus. (UNL Photo Lab)

13. Chancellor Canfield at home with his daughter, Dorothy, and son, James. Notice the plush draperies, oriental rugs, classical casts, and Old Master prints on the walls: European culture was imported to the prairie frontier. (UNL Archives)

14. The football squad as pictured in the *Sombrero '92*. The second man from the right, front row, is Chauncey Nusz, the player who received Chancellor Canfield's solicitous attention after being injured in a game. Second from left, second row, is George A. Flippin. In 1892 the University of Missouri forfeited a game rather than play a team that included a black man, and Omaha's Paxton Hotel threatened to refuse him service until his teammates, "bent on seeing that the civil rights bill is enforced . . . manfully stood up for their fellow student." (UNL Archives)

15. The campus, looking north from Eleventh and R streets in 1894. The fence, erected in 1892, remained in place until 1922, when it was moved to surround Wyuka Cemetery. The walks were still wooden, though wider than earlier. (UNL Archives)

16. Louise Pound (1872–1958) took a degree in English philology in 1892. A champion in tennis and golf, she was an enthusiastic bicyclist, even when the roads were hardly more than tracks. She wrote, "Campus life, though somewhat Spartan, was stimulating, [with a] serene expectation of a world which was to grow consciously better and better." (Nebraska State Historical Society)

17. Willa Cather, about 1895. The boulder behind her was brought to the campus by the class of 1892 because Professor Aughey had discovered on it what he took to be pre-Columbian petroglyphs. It is now on display in front of Morrill Hall. The pine tree is still living, in the sculpture garden west of Sheldon Memorial Art Gallery. (Nebraska State Historical Society)

18, 19. Grant Memorial Hall was an armory, gymnasium, sports arena, auditorium, dance pavilion, and music hall. Soldiers Memorial Hall was added onto it in 1899. These views, looking east into the light, show the women with Indian clubs, a staple in gymnastics of the day, and the men in a variety of exercises including fencing, which was taught to both men and women by Lt. John J. Pershing. (*Sombrero '92*, UNL Archives)

20. Ellen Smith (1838–1903) came to the University in 1877. Something of a curmudgeon, she became registrar in 1884 and in 1886 she was put in charge of the library. Over her door, students said, the motto ought to be posted: "All hope abandon, ye who enter here." (UNL Photo Lab)

21. Lt. John J. Pershing (1860–1948) had commanding presence even as a young professor of military science and tactics from 1891 until 1895. As a teacher of elementary math he was un- feeling in his military discipline, but he never forgot his students, and he called them by their names when they met many years later. (Nebraska State Historical Society)

22. Erwin H. Barbour (1856–1947) is seen here on a horse, leading an 1894 geological expedition to the state's Pine Ridge and Badlands region. Beginning in 1891, he and his staff made extensive fossil collections for the state museum now in Morrill Hall. (Conservation and Survey Division)

23. The Sem. Bot. — Seminarium Botanicum — was a group of enthusiasts who gathered around Professor Bessey to read research papers and promote scholarship. In this 1896 photograph are, in the back row, Roscoe Pound, later dean of the Harvard Law School (far left); Albert F. Woods, later president of the University of Maryland (second from left); and F. E. Clements (fourth from left), founder of plant ecology. H. B. Ward, first dean of the University College of Medicine and later the "father of American parasitology," sits in the middle. Seated at the far right, beside the bearded Bessey, is Lawrence Bruner, world-famous entomologist. Bessey's son, E. R. Bessey, himself a noted botanist, sits on the floor in the foreground. (UNL Archives)

24. Willard Kimball (1854–1939) at his desk in the School of Music, which he founded. Brought to the University in 1894 by Chancellor Canfield, he built a two-story brick building for the School of Music at Eleventh and R streets, just off the campus. In 1899 he added a third floor. The handsome pictures and furnishings of the office contrast strikingly with the prairie frame house seen through the window. (UNL Photo Lab)

25. The old library, now Architectural Hall, in about 1903. The bicycles laid against the fence in front of University Hall, which is off to the right and not shown in this view, imply a growing prosperity – and improved roads. (UNL Archives)

boyish haircut, her independent ways, and her outspoken opinions. Many students did not like her, for she lacked the "kindness, sociability, and wit" that earned girls like Minnie De Pue popularity. But even as an undergraduate she achieved more than a local reputation with her theater reviews in the *Lincoln Journal*. Professor Sherman admitted her as a freshman to upper-division study of Shakespeare, but in later years she did not apply her gifts to classroom exercises, and her open contempt for the "Sherman method" kept her from getting a teaching assistantship in the Department of English in 1896.

Louise Pound was more circumspect, but to the end of her long life she found Sherman's *Analytics* an object of high amusement. Louise was only just less gifted than her brother Roscoe, and had, like him, been educated at home before entering the Latin School at age fourteen. She had her baccalaureate degree by the time she was twenty (1892), but she also had a diploma in "harmony, piano, and sight reading" and any number of trophies for her excellence in competitive sports as well, her spirit sharpened by Roscoe's brilliance. Like him, she was exceedingly jolly, loving jokes, pranks, and parties; and like him, she had enormous reserves of energy. Many of her college contemporaries thought her "cold-hearted," perhaps because they were not well acquainted with her, or perhaps because of her competitive spirit. She competed with Roscoe. She could read as fast as he, but she could not remember everything as he did. She could, however, beat him in sports, for there he could only umpire and lead the cheers, his eyes being weak from childhood measles. A beautiful, rather slight girl with lots of red hair and brown eyes, she had an intensity that matched Cather's.

❧ A. H. Edgren

August Hjalmar Edgren was a match for Roscoe Pound in sheer brainpower and energy. It was probably Sherman's influence that brought him to Nebraska; both had been students of Whitney's at Yale, where Edgren had taken his Ph.D. in 1874 after only two years of study. His distinguished career as a philologist – ultimately he called himself a "linguistic scientist" – was really his second or third career. Born in Sweden in 1840, he enlisted in the U.S. Army of the Potomac upon graduating from the Swedish Royal Military Academy in 1860; the American Civil War, he said, "was primarily a battle between light and darkness."[16] He returned to his native Sweden in 1863, having been commissioned as a first lieutenant for bravery in action. His military career began to pall when in 1867–68 he studied in France and Germany, and so in 1870 he returned to the United States to take a baccalaureate degree in physical sciences at Cornell, in one year. He only found philology when he went to Yale for the Ph.D. There he became Whitney's favorite student. In a single year he became proficient in half a dozen arcane languages, including Sanskrit. In 1877 he published an English-German dictionary with his mentor and various studies of Sanskrit, a subject in which Whitney was a world expert. He translated the classical writers of India into both Swedish and English, and his favorite English poets, Tennyson and Longfellow, into Swedish. He was a prodigious worker. At one time he slept only every other night in order to have sufficient time for study.

He came to the University of Nebraska in 1885, from the University of Lund, for he thought Sweden offered little chance of academic or financial advancement and the open spirit of the West attracted him. The new and untried appealed to him, so in the summer of 1889 he spent six weeks in Mexico with a student friend. "[T]hey had experiences which would furnish anecdotes and pleasant memories for many years to come," *The Hesperian* reported on 1 October 1889. But though he had remarkable success in America, both in building his department and in lecturing in summer Chautauquas in New York, he took a position at the newly opened University of Gothenburg in 1891 with a sharp decrease in salary. His Danish wife had been homesick in Nebraska. Perhaps he was too. In two years he became the University of Gothenburg's first *Rector Magnificus*; but in 1893 he returned to the University of Nebraska. "My love for Sweden has never abated," he said,[17] but the chance to build in the West called him back.

Edgren's second stay in Nebraska was not as rewarding personally as he had hoped. He found himself yearning for Sweden and Gothenburg, he lost money on his American investments, and he became thoroughly disgusted with the manner in which business was conducted in the West. But his scholarship continued. He published monographs on Sanskrit, German, and Romance languages; studies in comparative philology written in Swedish, German, French, and Latin; and he edited dictionaries of German, French, and Italian. He wrote German, French, Spanish, Italian, and Sanskrit grammars and edited school texts. He published two volumes of his own poems and several volumes of translations. With his military haircut and bearing, his personal discipline surprised no one.

Edgren helped shape the nature of the University of Nebraska. Eagerly participating in the graduate program in the Eighties with George Howard, Charles Bessey, and Lucius Sherman, he revived it in 1893, and in 1896 became graduate dean in the first organized graduate college west of the Mississippi. He set up entrance and residential requirements, detailed programs for degrees, and defined standards. Seventeen professors at the University were qualified to offer graduate degrees, he thought. By 1898 he could claim that "only three state Universities and about twelve other institutions have a larger graduate attendance" than the University of Nebraska.[18] The two largest departments were English, with some fifty graduate students, and history, with thirty-eight; botany, with fewer students, continued to be the premier research department, but the first Ph.D. degree, awarded to H. N. Allen in 1896, was in physics; the second was awarded to Roscoe Pound in plant ecology in 1897.

Edgren's final return to Sweden in 1901 was understandable; he was invited to be one of the five directors of the Nobel Institute of the Swedish Academy, only then being established. He died two years later of a heart attack and was buried on the same day as his older daughter, who had been grievously ill. His other two children remained in America. His son Arthur took an engineering degree from the University of Nebraska in 1907 and lived out his life in Lincoln.

❧ Lt. John J. Pershing

Canfield provided strong leadership for this glorious company. When he arrived in Lincoln, he found Lt. John J. Pershing newly appointed commandant of cadets. Pershing, age thirty-one, had wanted this appointment since at least 1888 and had received it through the political machinations of his brother James. James, like the Pershing parents, lived in Lincoln. An 1886 graduate of West Point, John Pershing had found little intellectual stimulation in the frontier posts where he had been stationed. Canfield came to "regard Pershing in a way as 'one of his students,'" Dorothy Canfield Fisher remembered later, "and gave him a great deal of good advice about the way to manage his life, which I think the rather stiff West Pointer needed." At Canfield's suggestion, Pershing studied law while in Lincoln and took a degree. He "knew that a full-blooded young man of that age . . . really wouldn't have enough to do to keep him out of mischief" just with training the cadet battalion. The chancellor's daughter remembered that the lieutenant "had a reputation for – well, it wouldn't be called drinking nowadays when everybody does it, but of not being the most sober member of society."[19] In addition to drilling his undergraduates and studying law, Pershing also taught geometry in the Latin School, rather badly. Altogether a disciplinarian, he never introduced his young charges to the pleasures of logical proof.

Pershing had command in his bearing and authority in his manner, authority enough to quiet crowds. But he also got enormous affection from his cadets, who never forgot him, or he them. Many years afterward he could still recall their names and dispositions. On 28 August 1899 he wrote to the president of the Board of Regents suggesting that note be made on campus of those students who had served in the Spanish-American War. He proposed that "a memorial tablet or tablets be placed upon the walls of the chapel"; and to start the subscription for this memorial, he placed $50 at the disposal of the regents, a considerable sum in 1899 for an army officer.[20] Such a tablet was in fact struck and fixed on the west facade of Grant Memorial Hall, the University armory, where it remained until the building was razed in 1958. It was then moved to the Military and Naval Science Building. Pershing later said that every army officer ought to have an association with a university as he had had; it provided a broadening influence.

Mary Jones & L.i.b

When he died in 1948 he provided in his will that $1,500 go for the purchase of a gold medal for annual presentation to the best student soldier in the University of Nebraska ROTC.[21] Canfield and Pershing were a happy match.

❧ Mary L. Jones and the Library

In 1892 Canfield brought Mary L. Jones to the University as "acting librarian." (His commitment to libraries is illustrated by the fact that he served as librarian at Columbia University from 1899 until his death in 1909.) When he arrived at the University, all members of the faculty carried keys to the library, which was opened to students only a few hours a day. The keys were a privilege that the faculty was reluctant to relinquish, and when the new chancellor brought up the matter at a faculty meeting, spelling out the reasons the keys ought to be turned in, the faculty resisted. Thereupon Canfield announced that the lock on the library door had already been changed.

On her arrival, Mary L. Jones, class of 1885, had just completed two years of training at the Albany School of Library Economy, where she studied with Melvil Dewey, the author of the celebrated Dewey decimal classification for cataloging (1876). She immediately undertook to establish the University library, which had grown to 12,000 volumes, on a rational basis, but found that "no records of any value, no catalogues, or anything that goes to make up the machinery of a modern library existed."[22] She was thus obliged immediately to make an author, title, and subject card catalog (the revolutionary card catalog had been introduced at the Harvard library in 1861). This took several years. Very shortly the chancellor placed in her hands all purchasing, including periodicals, and through her association with book dealers she developed an efficient system for acquisitions, to the delight of the chancellor — and the faculty also, once they got used to yielding to her authority. Newspapers reported that Miss Jones, as she was always addressed, and her assistants were "conducting one of the best regulated university libraries to be found anywhere" and that "Miss Jones has achieved the feat of being popular alike among the learned and the unlearned."[23]

Mary Jones did not confine herself to the library or even to the University but traveled extensively about the state talking to various clubs and organizations. Hired at $150 a month, she was soon given a raise to $160 and then $170, but even so her salary was appreciably under the $2,000 that professors received, because she was paid for eight months only. She was called "assistant librarian" though there was no "librarian" except herself. Canfield wanted to give her a full voice and a vote in the Faculty Senate, with a commensurate title of adjunct professor of bibliography. Like that of the other women on the faculty and women elsewhere at the time, however, her advancement was resisted. As the years passed and she continued to meet such discrimination, Mary L. Jones became increasingly belligerent, but during her Nebraska years she was not yet militant.

The new library building consumed a good deal of Canfield's attention. When the legislature in 1891 appropriated less money for it than the regents and the chancellor thought necessary, they decided "to take the funds already in hand, lay the foundation for the entire building, and complete the wing as far as that could be done,"[24] hoping to receive additional funds in subsequent appropriations. They found, though, that it was impossible to get more money in 1893, however diligently Canfield and the president of the Board of Regents lobbied. Nebraska in the Nineties suffered from drought and depression. The library could not, thus, be completed, and the building contracts had to be carefully renegotiated. Canfield reported to the regents on 1 August 1893, "It is no small matter to break a contract in two, settle up all accounts, and get out without loss and without a law suit."[25] When classes began in September 1893, the half-finished building was surrounded by mounds of earth and forests of weeds. The campus newspaper reported that the Populist legislators, in refusing the money to complete the building, "have builded themselves a monument more lasting than brass in the unfinished library building, which stands on campus like some Old World ruin or a last surviving relic of the Chicago fire." The editor continued: This "is still a lasting memorial of the consummate meanness and sublime pig-headedness of the last legislature of the great People's Party."[26] In the spring of 1895 the new legislature appropriated necessary funds and the library was finally completed.

Planning had begun before Canfield arrived and during its construction he assumed active supervision. He was determined that this new building be so sound that it not need the constant repair that old U Hall and the newer but even less satisfactory Nebraska Hall of 1888 required. In his diary he wrote, "It seems almost impossible to cure the radical defects of 'public work,' " but he nonetheless insisted on finding "a suitable person as inspector of all labor and materials as to quality."[27] His concern paid off, and unlike the other early buildings on the campus, this one needed no extensive overhauling for nearly a century and remains structurally sound to this day. Later Willa Cather gave an account of the building: "It was constructed of red brick, after an English model. The architect had had a good idea, and he very nearly succeeded in making a good thing, something like the old Smithsonian building in Washington. But after it was begun, the State Legislature had defeated him by grinding down the contractor to cheap execution, and had spoiled everything, outside and in. [University officials,] both young men then, had wasted weeks of time with the contractors, and had finally gone before the Legislative committee in person to plead for the integrity of that building."[28] The old library is now Architecture Hall.

❧ Music from the University

The musical life in town was notably rich. When Carrie Belle Raymond came to Lincoln in 1886, she very soon became organist at the First Congregational Church, and within two years had organized a May Festival which became an annual event. It consisted of a series of concerts and recitals, first at her church and later at the Lansing Theater. Following her lead, other churches developed splendid choirs and together they presented such oratorios as Handel's *Elijah*, Haydn's *Seasons*, and Gounod's *Messe Solenelle*, as well as semireligious contemporary works now sunk into oblivion. In 1900 alumni of the University, through a committee headed by Professor Law-

rence Fossler, collected several thousand dollars to buy the pipe organ from the Omaha Trans-Mississippi Exposition. It was installed in Grant Memorial Hall. Mrs. Raymond, who had become director of music at the University in 1894 upon Canfield's invitation, presented regular organ recitals there, sometimes supplemented with instrumental and choral groups. Though she was primarily an organist and choral director, she was adept at arranging music for whatever instruments were available. If the programs seem rather miscellaneous to later generations, the quality was apparently high. Mrs. Raymond was indefatigable. In her earliest years, though she had prepared the choruses and instrumental groups, she invited a man to conduct in public; but after 1891 she directed orchestra and chorus herself. The local people were delighted, thinking this the first time a woman was general conductor. Her annual Christmas presentation of *The Messiah* was continued annually for some fifty years even after her death.

Besides developing vocal and instrumental groups, Mrs. Raymond also brought orchestras of national repute to Nebraska. At various times she got the businesses of the town to underwrite not only the May Festival, whose budget came to several hundred dollars, but performances of the symphony orchestras of Minneapolis, New York, and Chicago, whose budgets were larger. A small, attractive woman, married into the prominent Raymond family, she established her own identity quite independent of them. In 1924 the Lincoln Kiwanis Club presented her with their Distinguished Service Award for her major contributions to the life of the city and state, and the carillon tower at the First Plymouth Congregational Church was dedicated to her memory after she died in 1927.

The University School of Music enriched the musical life of the community. Conceived as a self-supporting institution in 1892, it had an uneasy quasi-official relationship with the University. Willard Kimball, the director, had found money to put up a building without tax support, and he hired teachers who received University appointments but got no University pay: an anomalous arrangement. Canfield was proud all his life of helping to found this school. The students took standard courses within the University but paid extra fees for instruction in music. Although they received University degrees, the Board of Regents refused to assume financial responsibility for the school. When Kimball's contract expired in 1903, he wanted his school to become a regular part of the parent institution, with himself as dean, but the board refused to accept it. The School of Music thus remained a proprietary adjunct to the University long after other proprietary colleges had been absorbed.[29]

❧ Chancellor Canfield Resigns

Rather suddenly, in 1895, James Canfield announced his resignation. He had accepted the presidency of Ohio State University, a smaller and less prestigious institution far to the east. It was not clear why he should have left Nebraska. Perhaps his wife, Flavia, enamored of the fine arts and cultivated society, wanted to escape the rawness of the West. In Lincoln she involved herself in the art department and women's clubs so thoroughly as to cause some resentment. She and her husband were ill-matched, he full of democratic gregariousness and she all sensitivity and willfulness. Only a few months before his resignation Canfield had written in *The Hesperian* of 19 December 1893, "The western atmosphere is crisp. Its breezes blow freely. It ministers to life in the largest sense of the word," and many years later his two children wrote of his Nebraska experience: "We had no impression of failure, for that great wind of material disappointment served but to fill the educational sails which our father spread wide over the University. The catastrophe, the sudden crash of both agriculture and industry, the wasting away of the foundations of economic life, were felt by Chancellor Canfield not as the tragic end of hopes for higher education in Nebraska, but as the soundest possible evidence of the need for higher education."[30] It is sad to report that his egalitarian energy did not suit Ohio as it had Nebraska and that his subsequent career was disappointing. His Nebraska chancellorship was the climax of his life.

James Canfield's record as chancellor is unsurpassed in the whole history of the University of Nebraska. He left the University three times as large as he had found it. In his four years it grew from 530 to 1,550 students, almost all of them coming from within Nebraska; and he set it on its permanent course. "To him more than to any other one man, perhaps more than to all other men, was due the bringing of the people and the university into touch and sympathy. The university was not known by many and was appreciated by fewer when he came. When he left it was the pride of the State as a whole," Howard Caldwell, professor of history in Canfield's tenure wrote.[31] Canfield could say with justification in his farewell remarks, "The University of Nebraska stands easily today [5 June 1895] in the 'big four' of State Universities."[32] *The Hesperian* had claimed on 1 February 1895: "Ours is the third State University in the country. . . ." The usually hostile Omaha press referred to Lincoln as "the Ann Arbor of the West," with only a slight irony.[33]

Canfield developed laboratories, the museum, and the library, and acknowledged the particular nature of a land-grant college, building on service aspects that Bessey and others had initiated. He put the agricultural experiment station on a professional basis, over the initial but impermanent protests of its staff; and, like his predecessors but with greater vigor, he encouraged agricultural and industrial short courses on and off campus. Twenty-five years later, persons could recall that "the achievements of Chancellor Canfield's comparatively brief administration stand out in clear and shining relief, and it is only sober truth to say that he, more than any other man, ushered in the golden era of the University's prosperity and greatness."[34]

Canfield's resignation was met with disbelief and distress by everybody, especially the students. Across the state the newspapers expressed regret. At a dinner given in his honor a couple years later, Willa Cather, speaking for "the Old Guard – the class of '95," said: "When we first came to the University from the towns and villages and country places everything looked big to us. The University was big. The seniors were the big boys and big girls. The professors were big – awesome and mighty – to be spoken of in low tones and whispers. And the Chancellor – that was a conception of greatness beyond our comprehension. Since those days our pictures have changed somewhat as was to be expected. Some of the lights we found did not shine so brightly to other eyes. Some of the big boys and girls gradually grew less in stature as we came nearer to them – and the professors – well we finally grew to be able to speak in audible tones of them. But the Chancellor – he looked big not only to us – to the faculty and to the state but we found that he appeared even larger to people in other states." Cather concludes: "While we are ever modest and ever reverent of the claims of other Chancellors, we think of Chancellor Canfield as a French Bishop did of that great berry the Strawberry. 'Doubtless' he said, 'God Almighty could have made a better berry than the strawberry – but doubtless God Almighty never did.' "[35]

George E. MacLean and a New Administration

When Canfield announced his resignation, the Board of Regents promptly elected George E. MacLean to take his place, recommended as he was by Canfield. "With the year 1895–96 came the change of administration," *The Sombrero* of 1898 reported. "Among the reforms of this year, the one of greatest moment was the discontinuance of the preparatory course [the Latin School] and the organition of the Graduate School. This raising of the standard of work in the University was simply putting into practice what we had long been qualified to do. The School of Mechanic Arts was established. The Library Building was opened, affording some relief to University Hall. *The Nebraska Literary Magazine* made its appearance, and *The University Monitor* commenced and ended its existence within this year. A system of fellowships and scholarships was established, and a chapter of Phi Beta Kappa organized."[36] The year 1895 also saw the establishment of the School of Agriculture and a summer school primarily for teachers. The Nebraska chapter of Sigma Xi, the science honorary, was founded two years later.

George MacLean never attained Canfield's popularity. A handsome man, born and educated in New England with a divinity degree from Yale and a doctorate from Leipzig, he pronounced *culture* without the *r*. MacLean was formal where Canfield was sociable, he was an elitist where Canfield was egalitarian, and he was an intellectual where Canfield was intelligent. Louise Pound wrote of him later that he was "polished in manner and somewhat given

to the language of Old World compliment. A few thought him over-effusive at the cost of sincerity."[37] From the beginning MacLean rubbed students the wrong way. *The Hesperian* reported on 4 October 1895, "We are sorry that Chancellor MacLean was moved to tears when he saw the barren and generally impoverished condition of our laboratories, – sorry, not so much for ourselves as for other universities. For we are informed on good authority that our chemical laboratory, so far as equipments are concerned, is second to but one in the United States; that our botanical laboratory is, in the same respect, the peer of any in the west, and that our psychological laboratory in its present quarters is fully up to the very best standards."

A scholar, MacLean analyzed the educational scene with off-putting prescience. In his inaugural address he asserted that professors were essentially scholars whose function it was to stimulate research. Undergraduate colleges should prepare students for higher education, that is, for research. He said that the professions of law and medicine, then frequently taught in proprietary schools outside universities, needed the support of university scholarship. Following the lead of the German universities, Harvard, and Johns Hopkins, he was on target, as the next decades showed. But this did not please the frontier Nebraskans. Alvin Johnson, founder of the New School for Social Research, wrote later that Nebraskans thought the University's mission was "to bring the light of education and culture to the prairie," and that local responsibility took precedence over a commitment to general learning.[38] MacLean was out of place in a frontier university.

Restlessness on Campus

The Hesperian constantly compared the University's achievements with those of neighboring universities and colleges "in the East." In defensive pride they reported victories and defeats on sports fields, taking unsportsmanlike delight in overcoming teams from Doane College and the University of Kansas. Debate and oratory contests were similarly celebrated. Crowds of people attended competitive events, and when attendance fell off, the student body was scolded for a lack of school spirit. It is as though the students and their elders of the Nineties were concerned with winning, no matter what the contest. This was a world of assertiveness, of individual initiative, of ambition; a world where some were tempted to take whatever advantage they could. Students in University Hall complained that their personal belongings were not safe in the cloakrooms and that "swiped" books turned up in second-hand stores. Football was subject to criticism for corruption, including professionalism.

Campus politics was intense. In 1894 Adam McMullen, a campus politician and fraternity man, sought to represent the University in an oratorical contest in Indianapolis with an oration which he had bought, not written. In April, Willa Cather, editor of *The Hesperian*, wrote, "We adore you Adam, because you belong to the great brotherhood of man, but we can't stand your manners," and in a mass meeting on May 21 the student body voted 349 to 150 to censure him. They refused to allow him to represent their university. Campus politicking persisted, nonetheless, and *The Hesperian* reported on 1 February 1896 that "the frats got the offices [on campus] and did what they pleased with them. It was the spoils system in practical operation." It may be worth noting that Adam McMullen became governor of Nebraska for one term in 1924.

Another student uprising occurred when a popular teacher, Harry K. Wolfe, revealed that the manipulation of rules extended to the faculty. Since departmental budgets were based on student credit hours, every department tried to report as large a number as possible. Sometimes departmental figures were falsified, "cooked," as the slang had it. Harry K. Wolfe, a native Nebraskan from the class of 1880, returned to the University's Department of Philosophy in 1889 after taking his Ph.D. in Germany in 1886. At Leipzig he had studied with Wilhelm Wundt, who was among the founders of the new subject of experimental psychology. Indeed, Wolfe was one of the first two Americans to earn a Ph.D. in this discipline. At home he set up the first undergraduate psychology laboratory in the nation, perhaps in the world, and taught his students the rudiments of scientific psychology – the measurement of

human responses, the testing of human reflexes, and the like.

A young and energetic man, outspoken, impolitic, and son of a prominent Populist, he quickly became one of the most successful teachers on the campus. He demanded support for his laboratory and sometimes got it, but at the cost of favor with Chancellor MacLean and the regents. When he found that a colleague was falsifying records to his department's advantage, he reported it to MacLean. Though the records were subsequently corrected, Wolfe was accused of meddling, and the next year the chancellor dismissed him from the University. (Rules of academic tenure had not yet been formulated.) The chancellor's recommendation was sustained by the Board of Regents.[39]

Hearing that Wolfe had been fired, the campus erupted. At a mass meeting the next day, 27 April 1897, the chancellor's name was hissed and petitions were circulated asking that the regents reconsider their action. Of course they stood their ground, but the controversy continued, exacerbated by Wolfe's continued presence in the state. He refused offers from other universities and became superintendent of public schools in South Omaha and later principal of Lincoln High. A marvelous teacher, he was finally, in 1906, reinstated at the University, where he inspired a notable number of psychologists.

MacLean was insistently impolitic. When he arrived in Nebraska, he found a library newly organized on the latest professional principles by a professional librarian. He promptly told Mary L. Jones that as soon as he could find a male, he would replace her. Though he got the Board of Regents to name her adjunct professor of bibliography and acting librarian, he was known to be searching for a man before she resigned to go to the University of Illinois in 1897. In the fall he brought John D. Epes to the campus. Epes had no professional training, and by spring the students were in rebellion against his high-handed treatment of them. They marched around the campus and into his office, disturbing classes and general peace. MacLean replaced him with James I. Wyer, who, like his brother Malcolm, became a national figure in library science. MacLean was much better in theory than in practice. In his report to the regents on 27 April 1897 he wrote, "Doubtless the severest task laid upon the Regents and the final test of administration is to be found in the performance of the duty to suggest removals or wisely to select appointees."[40]

When George MacLean was invited to become the president of the University of Iowa in June 1899, he accepted promptly, though at the time the University of Iowa was less prestigious than the University of Nebraska. When he left Lincoln, few regretted his departure; and though he stayed at the University of Iowa until removed in January 1911, his administration there was also stormy. The next chancellor at Nebraska, E. Benjamin Andrews, was adroit, personable, and courageous, a man of great integrity.

4. From College to University: 1900–1908

❧ The New Century

When E. Benjamin Andrews came to the University of Nebraska in 1900, a future there seemed possible. Canfield had left the University in 1895 three times as large as it had been when he arrived, and its faculty was equally enlarged. He had taught the people of the state to think of this as *the* university, their university; and for the next eight decades (at least) this loyalty persisted. Chancellor George MacLean had attempted to build on this enthusiasm, but his cool manner put Nebraskans off, and his foresight went unacknowledged. When he resigned in 1899, Dean Bessey of the Industrial College once again reluctantly became acting chancellor and continued to represent the University to the state. He served only until Elisha Benjamin Andrews could take office.

If Canfield persuaded the state of the importance of the University to its citizens, E. Benjamin Andrews gave it form, a form that persisted through the next century. It continued to grow, from 1,500 students in 1895 to 2,200 in 1900 to 4,000 in 1910; and the new chancellor organized it. Until 1900, schools and colleges had appeared as circumstances demanded, but the total suffered from both administrative and ideological confusion. What should an institution of higher learning be in a western state? What was its fundamental nature? How were its parts related to the whole and the whole to Nebraska?

The questions were not unique. Everywhere institutions of higher learning were defining their responsibilities in the last decades of the nineteenth century. Charles W. Eliot unified Harvard's semiautonomous schools into a university when he became its president in 1869. Daniel Coit Gilman refounded the University of California at Berkeley between 1872 and 1875; and in 1887 Yale, assuming the title of university, officially centralized its graduate and professional schools. Everywhere universities began to perceive of themselves as collections of professional colleges, not simply academies for the enlightenment of the young.

In 1900 the Nebraska state university was not yet a collection of colleges, but it had possibilities. The 1899 *Sombrero* reported that a bill "providing adequate revenues for the increased demands of the growing institution passed both houses of the legislature with scarcely any opposition and was signed by the Governor on the morning of the Thirtieth Anniversary of the University." "The Golden Age of Nebraska" was approaching its meridian.[1]

❧ Chancellor Andrews

When Benjamin Andrews became chancellor of the University of Nebraska in 1900, he was already well known both locally and nationally. After serving as president of Denison University in Granville, Ohio, from 1875 until 1879 and studying in Germany, in 1884 he was granted an LL.D. *in honore* by the University of Nebraska, Chancellor Manatt being a friend of his. In the spring of 1889 Bessey approached him as a possible candidate for the chancellorship at Nebraska (Bessey was trying to escape the post), but Andrews wrote that he could not entertain the flattering invitation. He did not tell Bessey that he was at that very time considering the presidency of Brown University, his alma mater. He was a spectacular success there from 1889 until 1898. In a generation of great college presidents, Alexander Meiklejohn, himself president of Amherst College and a commanding figure in the history of American education, said in 1917 after Andrews's death, "My impression is that no one in the last half-century has so captivated, so dominated an American College community as he did."[2] Andrews had visions of making Brown a graduate institution like the University of Chicago. At Denison he had earned the admiration of both William Rainey Harper, the University of Chicago's founding president, and John D. Rockefeller, its benefactor, but for all his persuasiveness, he could not collect the enormous funds such an enterprise required.

At Nebraska, Andrews hoped to build a national university, but, like Canfield, he never forgot his responsibilities to the local undergraduates. Indeed, he took a paternal interest in them, even providing for the penurious out of his own pocket. With great affection the students called him "Bennie" behind his back, rather as they had called Canfield "Jimmie." They loved him. Never very strong, he insisted once, when taken ill in Chicago, on returning home to Lincoln. There his train was met by 400 students in an impromptu demonstration of "fond attachment and reverence." Taking the horses from their shafts, they quietly drew his carriage through the streets to his home on R Street. Too weak to address them from his porch, he recognized their affection and whispered to his companion, "I really don't deserve it."[3] Andrews rarely appeared at University convocations that he did not receive an ovation.

Elisha Benjamin Andrews took the prophet Elisha as worthy of emulation. He thought that "duty meant not meditation . . . but life – earthly life too – actively, practically lived."[4] A man of great courage, he survived calamities over the years that would have destroyed an ordinary person. When young, he injured his left leg so severely that he had to be tutored at home for two years and only returned to classes on crutches. When the Civil War began, he enlisted at seventeen, still handicapped. Commissioned in 1863, he was wounded in 1864 at the awful siege of Petersburg and lost his left eye. Most of his subsequent pictures present his right profile.

Andrews's moral courage was as great as his physical courage. He came to Nebraska after an intellectual storm at Brown that exhibited it. Exhausted, he took a sabbatical in Europe in 1896, and in a private letter expressed some sympathy for free silver. Bimetallism was then a highly controversial topic, an anathema to conservatives. When his private letter was published, without his permission or knowledge, the Corporation of Brown University, fearing loss of financial support for their increasingly expensive institution, asked him to withhold public statements on this subject. Andrews promptly resigned his presidency, writing that the absence of "reasonable liberty of utterance" made the most ample endowment of little worth.[5] The faculty, the alumni, and the students supported him vigorously; and shortly a "memorial" signed by President Daniel Coit Gilman, now of Johns Hopkins University, President Charles William Eliot of Harvard, and other prominent persons in and out of academia protested the action of the corporation. By September the corporation reconsidered and Andrews withdrew his resignation. In October he was invited to lecture in Nebraska.

Andrews remained at Brown for one more year, celebrated but uneasy; and in 1898 he moved to Chicago to become superintendent of the troubled public schools there, a post to which President Harper had nominated him. As at Brown, he was marvelously successful, for he freed the schools from external political control, but in 1900 he left Chicago to become chancellor of the University of Nebraska. His greathearted spirit quickly won over all parties there, E. L. Hinman, professor of philosophy wrote. "It was recognized at once that the new leadership was clear in purpose, resolute in decision, academic in its standards, and influential in its popular appeal – a strong administration."[6] Another of his faculty colleagues said that Andrews "had the heart of a boy, which was the secret of his great hold on the students."[7] He had an infectious good humor, and his chapel talks were forthright and exuberant. When he found himself in error, he frankly and courageously acknowledged it, and in 1903 he publicly said about his support of free silver: "I have to admit that it was an astounding mistake, and that I was in great and inexcusable error."[8]

Andrews earned loyalty from his staff. In the spring of 1902 he was invited for a third time to head the University of Wisconsin, already famous for its academic excellence and its defense of free inquiry, with a salary of $10,000, twice what he received in Lincoln. A convocation was quickly called in Grant Memorial Hall, where a capacity crowd of students and faculty urged him to remain in Nebraska. Some of his most distinguished colleagues – Charles E. Bessey, Fred M. Fling, Howard W. Caldwell, Laurence Fossler, Henry B. Ward, Ellery Davis – testified to their admiration for him, and the *Daily Nebraskan*, the campus paper succeeding *The Hesperian*, reported on 28 May, "A number of the professors offered to contribute a part of their salaries to help make up the difference in salary received and the salary offered." Very shortly thereafter Andrews announced that he would stay at Nebraska "for a number of years," and on 21 July 1902 he wrote to the Board of Regents, "Gentlemen: While deeply sensible of your kindness in recently advancing my salary and believing that this new figure is not greater than a Chancellor of this University ought to earn and receive, I am unwilling, so long as the University is compelled to the rigid economy it now exercises, to accept for my services any higher renumeration than I have hitherto had, and therefore beg permission to continue for the present to be paid at the old rate."[9]

Andrews had the support of his Board of Regents as well as the students and faculty. Charles H. Morrill, the most prominent regent, served ten years as president of the board. An active Republican and political conservative, he had initially voted against Andrews's appointment but very quickly became his sturdy supporter. Like Charles Gere, president of the board a decade earlier, Morrill helped move the University from provincial to national prominence and recognized in Andrews "a practical visionary." Morrill had made a fortune in banking, land management, and town development, and for a decade had given his energies and money toward developing the University. He organized annual geological expeditions into the state from the University and sustained them with generous gifts. He regarded E. H. Barbour, the state geologist and professor of geology, as a kind of genius. Perhaps Barbour was. He found remarkable paleontological specimens, especially great fossil beasts, which he and his staff mounted in the state museum, to the delight of generations of schoolchildren, their teachers, and parents. Full-length

portraits of Barbour and Morrill hang in Morrill Hall, the museum named in his honor. Both are clearly vigorous, intelligent men, who, like Andrews, intend to leave the world richer for their having been in it.

Andrews's private life was not fortunate. Not especially well married, he saw one of his two sons die in infancy and the other, said to be brilliant, become an alcoholic. By September 1904 the latter had to be confined to the Hospital for the Insane in Lincoln, this in a generation when alcoholism was regarded with moral obloquy, and Andrews had to disown his son's debts in the public press. "Once, at Lincoln, a group of unthinking students, knowing that Andrews was within earshot behind a closed door, tried to gain some amusement at his expense by singing: 'O, where is my wandering boy to-night?' As they sang, the door opened and Andrews emerged, his face drained of color. Then in a broken voice he said, 'I hope, young men, the day will never come when any of you will know what agony may be back of those words.' Terribly ashamed the students silently went away."[10]

❧ The Undergraduate Competitive Spirit

Andrews seemed to understand the undergraduate taste for competition. Collegiate football was being played with gathering popularity in his years, but controversy continued about the brutality of the game. Bills to outlaw football were introduced in the state legislature in 1897 and in 1898; by 1900, however, the general enthusiasm seemed uncontrollable. Bleachers and grandstands were constructed on the athletic field at Tenth and T streets, and by 1901 the team was identified as the Cornhuskers, the name invented by Charlie (Cy) Sherman, a local sportswriter. The school colors of scarlet and cream, prominent at sporting events, had been selected after much argument in 1893. Three thousand fans accompanied their team to Minnesota at three dollars each in 1901, and in the next three seasons Walter Cowles "Bummy" Booth coached a winning streak of twenty-four games. A story in the 24 October 1903 *Lincoln Journal* said, "Nebraska occupies a unique position in western football. Too strong to find fearful competitors, the Cornhuskers can almost weep with Alexander the Great because they have no more teams to conquer."[11] Reports of brutality, graft, and professionalism dulled the victories, however, and in 1905 "Bummy" resigned. In 1907 the football team won its first conference title and serious speculation about a football stadium began.

Andrews sought to direct the passion for competition into academic channels. In 1901 he brought Miller M. Fogg to Nebraska to set up the "Nebraska system" of training in argumentation and debate. Andrews had known young Fogg at Brown, where Fogg had taken a master's degree in 1895; he took a second at Harvard in 1901. In Nebraska he quickly established debate as an important undergraduate activity. A historian of "the student writer" at the University has noted that "the student who wanted to be 'where the action was' in the 1870s would have been an active member of one of the literary societies [as George Howard was]; in the 1880s, he would have entered one of the oratorical contests [as Louise Pound did]; in the 1890s, he would have been an editor for one of the student publications [as Willa Cather was]; and in the 1900s, he would have been a member of the University intercollegiate debate team."[12] Debating became part of the regular curriculum, with the classes in argumentation attracting some of the best student minds. The intercollegiate debate program was supervised by a debating board of faculty and students. Everybody was involved in debate.

The "Nebraska system" was a four-year course of study and its teams won all their contests. After one of these debates, Chancellor Frank Strong of the University of Kansas remarked: "I feel as if I had been going through a cyclone on an express train." Victorious returning teams were met at the railway station by cheering students, faculty, and Chancellor Andrews. All could see that "these intellectual contests involve, equally with athletics, the pride and honor of their alma mater," *The Sombrero* of 1906 observed.[13] The enthusiasm was "almost wholly due to the high order of ability and tireless energy which [Fogg] brought to the work," *The Sombrero* of 1903 had said,[14] and Fogg became a hero, like a football coach. This debating mania was contagious. In 1908 Fogg organized the Nebraska High School Debating League, and for the next fif-

teen years the enthusiasm for debate spread to small towns across the state, earning debaters the fame ordinarily reserved for athletes. When Fogg died suddenly in 1926, he was widely and deservedly mourned.

❧ School Spirit

The chancellor was eager to develop a sense of camaraderie at the University. Greek-letter societies, which competed among themselves as well as with the literary societies, seemed to divide the campus into self-serving groups; and in convocations Andrews complained of cliques. The prominence of Theta Nu Epsilon, TNE, was taken as evidence of the lack of community, for TNE, the sub rosa drinking fraternity, challenged all authority. It saw itself as a law unto itself and strove to monopolize campus offices and University affairs. In 1905 the Board of Regents mandated an interfraternity council "to correct, discipline, and impose punishment" as necessary to bring order to the campus.

In part as a reaction to TNE, the Innocents Society, modeled on senior societies on eastern campuses, was organized in 1903 "to advance University interests at every possible point," the *Daily Nebraskan* reported on 25 April. Initially proposed by Roscoe Pound, it was sponsored by G. E. Condra, professor of geology and director of the state geological survey. Condra was a public-spirited young man who developed a following both on and off campus. His memory for names was his pride. On more than one occasion he astonished groups by calling every person in a large banquet hall by name. He liked advising student groups and proposed that each year thirteen men from the senior class be selected as Innocents, on evidence of leadership, character, and service, and that distinguished alumni also be invited to join. This was a self-perpetuating society. The insignia was Mephistopheles in profile, surmounting crossed tridents. Its color was red, in reaction to TNE, whose membership was secret and whose red emblem was a skull and crossbones. On state occasions the Innocents appeared in red pseudo-monastic robes. Their ritual of initiation was built around the seven deadly sins and seven matching virtues, and the young men took papal names. Apparently Condra was interested in papal history and ritual, rather surprisingly in strongly Protestant Nebraska. Only in 1934 was this papist-moralistic ritual revised, by Hartley Burr Alexander, professor of philosophy. Meetings were held initially in the belfry of old University Hall and later in the organization's own rooms in University Hall. When the Student Union was constructed in 1938, a "secret" room was provided there, with private keys for members of the Innocents Society.

In 1905 a women's group corresponding to the Innocents Society was organized, to which thirteen women were invited annually. Called Black Masque, it was, like the Innocents Society, "to provide a means by which class and University spirit can be called for and used to accomplish desired ends," the *Daily Nebraskan* said on 4 April. In 1921 this local organization was affiliated with the national Mortar Board organization. Beginning in 1916, new members of both societies were identified on Ivy Day, a spring festival held after 1901 on the first weekend of May. As Ivy Day flourished as a full holiday, it became honors day for student leaders. In 1912 the first May Queen was crowned, and in 1923 Kosmet Klub, an undergraduate theatrical organization, sponsored the first Interfraternity Sing. In 1927 the Associated Women Students began an Intersorority Sing. All these campus activities attracted considerable attention, and for years Ivy Day was front-page news across the state.

Living accommodations for students concerned Andrews. In those years most students lived in private homes or in boarding houses; and though a dozen fraternities and nine sororities were organized on campus, only a few had yet established living quarters. In 1906 a privately-owned and -operated women's dormitory was opened on the corner of Twelfth and Q streets, with "the hearty endorsement of the faculty of the State University," its advertisements read. Rooms cost from five to twenty-four dollars a month, and meals were available at three dollars a week. Hayes Hall, as it was called, was closely chaperoned. Mrs. W. E. Barkley, whose multimillion-dollar estate was to build and endow the Barkley Memorial Center for Speech and Hearing Disorders seventy years later, was named acting dean of women in 1905. She saw herself as guardian of decorum

and felt it incumbent upon her to give the girls instruction in table manners and social conduct. Perhaps instruction in the social graces was necessary for persons coming to college from a rough country, but she became the object of considerable student laughter. No provisions were made for housing male students, some of whom "batched" around town. Not infrequently parents from outstate Nebraska moved to Lincoln so their children could attend the University while living at home.

Alvin Johnson, who had been a student in the Nineties, returned to the University from Columbia University in 1906. He said, "The student body had changed with the swelling prosperity of the state. There was no longer in evidence the kind of student I had known, particularly one who had walked from Loup City, a hundred and fifty miles, with a broken ankle, to save a few dollars on railway fare." Perhaps Johnson was idealizing his undergraduate years. But now, he said, "the dean of women was growing haggard and gray, breaking up parties on campus benches where the young men's wooing was getting too *handgreiflich*, as the Germans say – too 'handgrabbish.' "[15]

Andrews looked outside the University for means to construct a student activities center. In 1903 he persuaded his old friend John D. Rockefeller to offer the University $66,666.66 if citizens would match it with $33,333.33 for a "social and religious building." This was the first time the Rockefellers had made such an offer to a state university. In anticipation, Andrews quietly and personally bought the southeast corner of Twelfth and R streets, off campus, before rumors drove up lot prices. He formed a town-gown solicitation committee, and by the end of the year half the needed sum was raised.

But the building became controversial. William Jennings Bryan announced, "Rockefeller's money smells too much of oil to allow him to put a building on our campus," and newspaper editors quoted Ida M. Tarbell and other muckrakers, asserting that a "receiver of a gift becomes partisan of the giver." The *Omaha World-Herald* campaigned against it, asking, "Shall a memorial to John D. Rockefeller be erected upon the campus of the Nebraska State University?" The editors of the campus newspaper replied to the Omaha paper on 5 February 1904: "The

World-Herald has much to say about Nebraska selling her honor. The World-Herald never had any honor. If it ever had, it would have sold out long ago if the price had been offered." Other critics raised questions about the religious purposes to which the building was to be put, fearful that separation of church and state was here violated. But by June 1904 the required $33,333.33 was raised (at one point Andrews had pledged his personal, meager fortune to underwrite the project), and in December 1904 the regents authorized construction.[16] Those fearful of sectarian restrictions on the building need not have worried. Within a year the second floor was remodeled for social functions — that is, for dancing — and plays and "frivolous entertainments" were regularly presented in its theater.

Andrews was successful in getting state money for classroom buildings and laboratories. In 1904 he got nearly $60,000 for a city campus physics laboratory and more than $50,000 for an agriculture hall at the farm. Altogether the state built five new buildings on the ag campus and four on the city campus during his tenure. The administration building caused grief because Thomas R. Kimball, its splendid architect from Omaha, had grossly underestimated its construction cost; even when terra cotta was substituted for stone, it came to nearly $40,000. Kimball's rather elaborate structure with its R Street porte-cochère and banded pillars was a focal point of the campus until it was unfortunately torn down in the 1950s.

The University as "Haven of Dissent"

The pattern of the modern university was set in these years. Early in the University of Nebraska's existence, free inquiry was threatened by religion: religious authority challenged academic authority. After about 1890 the independence of the University was threatened by economic interests. Moneyed groups sought to define the limits of inquiry. Andrews had had firsthand experience with this threat at Brown, and he made Nebraska one of the strongholds of free inquiry. In these years "a few academic establishments, notably Nebraska, Wisconsin, and Cornell, developed into recognized havens for dissent," Laurence R. Veysey concludes in his history of the American university.[17] The University of Nebraska had long harbored dissenting opinion, often supported by George Howard, the popular professor of history, but in 1891 Howard had left Nebraska to found the Department of History at the new Stanford University, one of President David Starr Jordan's first faculty appointments.

At Stanford, Howard was joined in 1893 by Edward A. Ross, a fire-eating young liberal who had convictions about social injustice. He was to become a founder of modern sociology. In the 1896 election Ross worked for the Democrats and against McKinley, and Mrs. Stanford, the Maecenas of the university, conferred with Jordan about silencing him. Jordan resisted but suggested to Ross that he find another job elsewhere. In 1900 when Ross opposed Asian immigration — Chinese laborers had helped build the railroads from which the Stanford money had come — and did not firmly oppose municipal ownership of public utilities, Mrs. Stanford again approached Jordan. Reluctantly and hesitantly obeying Mrs. Stanford's dictum, Jordan fired Ross on 12 November 1900. The next morning in his classroom Howard defended Ross's right to dissenting opinions and denounced Jordan's action and Mrs. Stanford's part in it. By December 14 Mrs. Stanford was demanding an apology from Howard, which he refused to make, and on 12 January 1901 he resigned from the university. He was past fifty years old, without immediate prospects for another job. Six other professors followed suit and the whole matter of academic freedom became a national issue. Out of the ensuing and similar controversies the American Association of University Professors was founded fifteen years later by John Dewey, A. O. Lovejoy, and other academic giants.

Andrews, hearing of the Stanford firing, on 12 December 1900 offered Ross a lectureship in sociology beginning in the second semester at a salary of $2,000 a year, the going rate. Ross gladly accepted and found Nebraska to his liking: "The air there has a winey effect, pleases the lungs as sparkling Burgundy pleases the palate," he wrote later. "Many a day I found that just to respire was intoxicating."[18] In due course Howard also came to Nebraska. After teaching briefly at Cornell, Wisconsin, and Chicago, he returned in 1902 upon Andrews's invitation and remained for the rest of his distinguished life, retiring only at age seventy-five.

Another splendid young "radical" who joined the staff in Andrews's administration was Alvin Johnson, crusading editor of *The New Republic* in the next decade and founder of the New School for Social Research in the decades after that. A farm boy who had come to the pioneer University in Canfield's day and was admitted under special dispensation by the chancellor over "Ma" Smith's objections, he became one of A. H. Edgren's prize students in languages. By 1906 he had established a reputation at Columbia University as a freethinking young economist. Over the objections of its authoritarian president, Nicolas Murray Butler, Johnson returned to Nebraska, place of his homesick dreams. There he became the second man in a department headed by W. G. Langworthy Taylor, a brilliant if neurotic student of William James's. Taylor disciplined his unsteady constitution only by sheer will power, with the result that his lectures were sometimes momentarily incoherent and his social conduct erratic. He kept a couple of fierce Kentucky horses which he rode every afternoon to exercise his rebellious spirit.

Alvin Johnson, a liberal in an already conservative state, found the students in newly prosperous Nebraska uninterested in economic theory, public finance, and labor management. The "idyllic faculty society" which he had remembered from undergraduate days now seemed rife with internecine warfare and restrained by puritanical rules. Even Andrews, whom Johnson thought huge mentally and morally, could not impose a necessary sense of community. Johnson himself was too much the determined maverick, the pioneer free spirit, to be satisfied anywhere but in a world of his own making, and after two years he moved to Texas; he did not stay there either.[19]

Andrews not only hired independent thinkers for his University; he also addressed social issues. In 1902 he invited Booker T. Washington to be commencement speaker. Controversy resulted, but the storm was brief. The *Daily Nebraskan* reported on 11 February 1902 that "not more than five persons in the class have serious feelings [i.e., misgivings] about the action." In 1906 Andrews recalled Harry K. Wolfe to service, knowing that he had been fired

without cause by an earlier administration. Within a year he made him head of a department. Like Howard and Ross, Wolfe was to leave a mark on his profession.

In the first decade of the new century, Nebraska was without doubt settling into patterns of etiquette and orthodoxy, but the University under Benjamin Andrews harbored varieties of opinion and encouraged arguments which looked sometimes like quarreling, at other times like debate. In this small world, personalities became involved. E. A. Ross was convinced that his discussions with Roscoe Pound influenced Pound's fundamental attitudes toward the law; Louise Pound said that Hartley Burr Alexander's views of culture influenced her approach to folklore; and Charles Bessey's confidence in the scientific spirit shaped a whole generation of men and women, in and out of his laboratory. Andrews was not afraid of controversy. Apparently he was not afraid of anything.

The Pattern of the Modern University

The organization of the twentieth-century University of Nebraska was set in Andrews's administration. Ellen Smith, then registrar, was a last remnant of the early informal years, and when in February 1902 she half-offered her resignation, discontent with her meager salary, the Board of Regents (and the chancellor) quickly accepted it. Her office became a bureau of registration and records with a new, vigorous staff; and the chancellor's office expanded to include a secretary for publicity and administration. Before "Aunt Ellen" Smith could "go back east," where it was rumored she had some small property, she became seriously ill and in February 1903 she died of cancer. The University held two funeral services, perhaps half in guilt: her ruggedness added to her charm, it was said. The women's activity building, a Queen Anne–style mansion on the corner of Fourteenth and R streets, was subsequently named in her honor, not without irony: in the 1892 *Sombrero* the editors had suggested that over her door ought to be affixed this sign: "All hope abandon, ye who enter here."

The chancellor brought order to administration, and the faculty was similarly organized. By 1903 the ranks of instructor; adjunct, assistant, and associate professor; and professor were established. In April 1904 the bylaws of the Board of Regents, that is, the operating constitution of the University, were revised and distributed to faculty and staff. This document thenceforth regularized hiring, resigning, duties, and responsibilities and ran to only seven typewritten pages. On 23 October 1906 the board named twenty "head professors" for the various departments. This administrative structure was necessary because of the University's increasing complexity. In 1900 there were 56 persons of professorial rank, but in 1908 there were 390.[20] According to a Carnegie Foundation Report of 1907, from 1896 to 1906 state support for the University of Nebraska had grown fivefold; the only comparable western state university was the University of Illinois, whose support had grown sixfold. California's support in these years had only doubled.[21] In 1909 the University of Nebraska became the eighteenth institution invited to join the Association of American Universities, a select group of research universities formed by Harvard, California, Chicago, and Johns Hopkins. By 1910 it was the twelfth largest university in the nation and one of the six largest state universities.

The curriculum for both high school and University was set in this decade. In 1898 a standard course of college preparatory studies was recommended to the high schools by the University inspector of high schools, J. W. Crabtree, who became president of Peru State Normal School and later the indefatigable secretary of the National Education Association. This standard course consisted of four years of Latin, four years of English, three years of mathematics, three years of science, and additional years of German and history, the texts recommended by professors at the University in the various subject-matter fields. Students deficient in high school courses could enroll in Teachers College High School before fully matriculating at the University. Across the state many high schools and communities protested what they saw as University dictation, but the curriculum with minor modifications was pretty well set for at least a generation.

On campus the Board of Regents in April 1905 spelled out the basic curriculum of the College of Literature, Science and the Arts. In addition to one hour of physical education or military science, every student would take courses in fundamental areas of learning: English and the classics; modern languages, possibly including Swedish and Czech; history; philosophy or economics; mathematics; physical science; and biology. Beyond these requirements each student was to have electives in about half the remaining undergraduate courses, but no student was to take more than forty hours, one-third of the total course load, in a single department. Thus an essential core was established for secondary and university education. The content of courses and their quality necessarily varied from school to school and from decade to decade, but this curriculum was consistent with the definition of education across the country. In the first thirty years of its existence, the University curriculum had been sternly classical, requiring students to be disciplined, as it was thought, through the study of classical languages and mathematics; the central method of instruction was recitation from an established text. This had now changed, and the change was officially stated. Students were now encouraged to experience various areas of learning, and they were taught by lectures and in laboratories as well as by recitation. Some more or less independent library work was common. The other undergraduate colleges offered variations on this basic pattern specified by the College of Literature, Science and the Arts.

❧ The University and Its Colleges

Daniel Coit Gilman, one-time president of the University of California and founding president of Johns Hopkins University, said in 1902 that "the complete university includes four faculties – the liberal arts or philosophy, law, medicine, and theology."[22] A public, land-grant university was much more comprehensive. Chancellor Andrews's University excluded theology for political reasons; but in addition to the liberal arts, law, and medicine, it needed to provide for engineering and agriculture as well as the emerging professions of pharmacy, dentistry, and business. The relationship of teacher training and graduate studies both to the total University and to the professional

Ag campus

colleges needed to be defined. Although William James in his celebrated essay "The Ph.D. Octopus" warned in 1903 against replacing the scholar-philosopher with the professional expert, it was the issue of professionalism with which Benjamin Andrews was engaged.[23] In these decades universities everywhere became the standard educating and accrediting agencies for the professions.

The Industrial College and the College of Agriculture. The original charter of the University of Nebraska called for a college of agriculture; but in 1877 it was incorporated into a general Industrial College, whose purposes were not at all clear. Neither agriculture nor engineering was yet regarded as a learned profession. When Charles Bessey became dean of the Industrial College in 1884, he was determined that it not be a subcollegiate trade school as some proposed; and when the Hatch Act of 1887 provided money for establishing an agricultural experiment station, Bessey wrote to the Board of Regents, "It was not the intention that it should be a school of low grade, but a *College*."[24]

The issue was political. In 1884 after investigating the University farm the Nebraska Board of Agriculture had recommended that it offer short courses in practical agriculture and the mechanic arts. This board said that the farm and agricultural education ought to be separated from the University. Bessey and Chancellor Manatt resisted vigorously, and the retention of the agricultural-industrial college within the University was a near thing. When the separatists were finally defeated, college activities could be conducted at research levels; and by 1900 various farmer institutes, short courses in agriculture, and extension activities began to demonstrate the utility of scientific research. Farmers' doubts about the value of University standards began to disappear.

When Benjamin Andrews became chancellor in 1900, he was appointed director of the agricultural experiment station almost pro forma: his predecessor had served as director during his years in office. But within a few months Andrews divested himself of this responsibility, and in July 1901 Edgar A. Burnett, professor of animal science, became associate dean for agriculture, Bessey remaining

dean of the Industrial College. Burnett moved from Nebraska Hall, home of Bessey's Industrial College, to University Hall to dramatize his independence. As early as December 1899 Bessey had proposed that a new campus for agriculture be built "on the farm," and during the next decade this was accomplished. Agricultural students continued to take basic subjects in the College of Literature, Science and the Arts, but in 1903 Burnett and his faculty assumed authority over their total curriculum, discipline, and degrees. In 1904 Agricultural Hall was built at the farm and the agriculture campus was laid out, in all probability upon the advice of Thomas R. Kimball, who was working with Andrews at the time. In 1908 the legislature gave the College of Agriculture autonomy. Dean Burnett thereupon moved his office to the farm, and agriculture was on its own with the hearty endorsement of Dean Bessey and the chancellor.

The considerable achievements of research in the experiment station here and those across the country have not always been recognized in nonagricultural circles. Dealing with practical problems, station scientists discovered new principles that were important far beyond immediate utility. They did basic research in the new fields of biochemistry, genetics, plant physiology, bacteriology, and plant ecology. They worked on the cutting edge. Often farm boys with midwestern degrees, like T. A. Kieselbach, not Ivy Leaguers with German doctorates, changed the face not only of American agriculture but of agriculture around the world; and they established theoretical principles of general scientific value.[25]

The College of Engineering. The engineering divisions of the Industrial College were becoming increasingly important by 1900. Electrical shows illuminated campus buildings as early as 1896, and increasing numbers of students enrolled in the three branches of engineering in which courses were offered: mechanical, civil, and electrical. In addition, the Industrial College offered technological short courses for those not aspiring to degrees. Its School of Mechanic Arts was a kind of trade school.

The new professional engineers agitated for specialized degrees, not simply the bachelor of science available to all students; and when their "long standing grievance" was brought to Andrews's attention in the spring of 1902, he promptly agreed to rectify this oversight. It took some time. On 17 January 1905 the *Daily Nebraskan* observed that engineering was flourishing all over the country — "Provisions must be made here as in Michigan for increase and expansion" — and in 1908 Dean Bessey claimed that some 600 students were enrolled in the engineering departments. Only in 1909 was an independent College of Engineering finally established, by an act of the legislature.

The first dean of engineering was Charles R. Richards. He had been on the campus since 1892, first as a teacher of manual training, then as professor of mechanical engineering. Since 1896 he had directed the School of Mechanic Arts, and though this subdegree technological program did not attract as many students as had been anticipated, Richards showed himself an able administrator. He was made associate dean for engineering when Burnett became associate dean for agriculture, and in 1909 both men were named deans of their respective colleges and the old Industrial College was abolished. (Bessey became "dean of deans" head professor of botany.) Richards had a teaching staff of fifteen professors with numerous assistants, and he designed and supervised the splendid new mechanical engineering laboratories building himself, giving particular attention to lighting, direct radiation heating, and mechanical ventilation. It cost $115,000. Many years later, after he had become president of Lehigh University in Bethlehem, Pennsylvania, the building was renamed for him.

The development of the College of Engineering was strengthened by the presence of distinguished scholars on the faculty, DeWitt Brace of physics being one of the most notable. Educated at the Massachusetts Institute of Technology and Johns Hopkins University before taking his Ph.D. at the University of Berlin, he set up a full physics laboratory when he arrived in Lincoln in 1887 at age twenty-eight, and offered a variety of new courses. Invited in the next decade to join the faculties of Purdue, Texas, and Princeton at twice his Nebraska salary, he elected to remain in Nebraska. Ellery Davis, dean of the College of Literature, Science and the Arts, suggested that he stayed

because he felt momentum here, and indeed by 1900 Nebraska was in fourth place among physics departments in size of laboratory budget, exceeded only by Harvard, Cornell, and MIT. In these years he met and married a young librarian, Elizabeth Russell Wing, whose family operated a small fruit and vegetable farm on the edge of town and had come to Lincoln so that she, her sister, and her brothers could attend the University.[26]

Brace inspired his colleagues in research and gathered students around him. He assisted with electrical engineering, sharing laboratory space and research apparatus with a young associate professor named Robert Owens, known as Bobby. The Department of Electrical Engineering was born in the physics department with Brace acting as father, mother, and midwife, the historian of the physics department has written.[27] By 1897 he was investigating the double refraction of light due to ether drift and publishing papers that attracted international attention. In those days there were no supply houses, so he constructed his string-and-sealing-wax apparatus himself, helped only by the University carpenter, one self-taught technician, and an "expert mechanician" who was a deaf mute. Elected vice president of the American Physical Society, he became vice president of the American Association for the Advancement of Science as well in 1902. When he died suddenly and prematurely in 1905 of septicemia resulting from an infected tooth, tributes to him came from all over the world. With Brace gone, the physics department settled into becoming a service department, an adjunct to engineering and agriculture, and was not deeply involved in independent investigations. The new physics building was named for Brace at the request of colleagues and students. Significantly, it became Brace Laboratory, not Brace Hall, as though to emphasize Brace's commitment to research.

The College of Law. The College of Law had a beginning outside the University. In 1888 a number of young men reading law in the offices around town gathered together for systematic study in a makeshift Central College of Law. Roscoe Pound was among them, encouraged by his father, Judge Stephen Pound. In 1891 the Lancaster Bar Association, in which Judge Pound was active, persuaded the University regents to take over this proprietary college. Instruction was by rather disorganized and desultory lectures. In 1893 Judge M. B. Reese, former chief judge of the Nebraska state supreme court, became dean of the University's new law college and for ten years he set up a regular series of textbook courses, staffed largely by practicing attorneys, in a two-year program. By 1900 law schools across the country were instituting three-year curriculums and Chancellor Andrews was eager that his University be as professional as they. Reese was reluctant to change, insisting that enrollment in his two-year course would so increase in competition with three-year schools that the college would be a source of revenue. Andrews disdained profit-making colleges; and when Judge Reese finally resigned in 1903, he called on young Roscoe Pound to take his place. To comfort old Judge Reese, the law students had a smoker in his honor, and the class of 1904 gave him a gold-headed cane. He replied by saying that his ten years as dean were the happiest of his life.

In appointing Pound, Andrews was in effect refounding the college. Pound had been for some years active in the local bar association. Indeed, he dominated it as he had dominated the botany seminar earlier. Fired to an interest in the law after his single year (1888–89) at Harvard, as dean he saw to the raising of entrance requirements, the reorganization of the curriculum into a three-year course, and the introduction of the case system of instruction. He set up practice courts as laboratories and strengthened the library. When two years later he and his college did not get the funding he thought imperative, he imperiously resigned, but the legal profession and the law students protested so vigorously that he was reelected dean on his own terms. Pound's account of "Legal Instruction at Nebraska," published in *The Sombrero* of 1905, concludes with some doggerel (from Pound's pen, no doubt) which ninety years later seems strikingly prescient:

BACK TO THE FARM, MEN
It's all off now.
Back to the shovel,
Back to the plow.
Before judge and court
You'll stand no show,

Woman's time is here,
Man had better go.
As co-eds increase
Three fold each year,
Law will soon become
A woman's sphere.[28]

In and out of University circles, Roscoe Pound was universally respected, his genius acknowledged. In 1906 he delivered a crusading lecture in St. Paul, Minnesota, which was to the legal profession what the Flexner Report of 1910 was to the medical profession: "the spark that kindled the white flame of progress."[29] To this day a bronze plaque marks the place in the Minnesota capitol where it was delivered. In 1907 Pound accepted a professorship at Northwestern University. As soon as the news of his imminent departure was out, University classes were dismissed, the college band led a grand march through the campus, and students and professors made speeches extolling his virtues. But the decision was made, and he left. When Andrews had to resign the chancellorship in 1908 because of ill health, it was offered to Pound; the break was complete, however, and Pound moved on to Harvard. His sisters, Louise and Olivia, remained in Lincoln. His successor in Nebraska was a Harvard man, recruited by him. The College of Law had become professional.

Medical Education. In frontier days medical education was sketchy at best, and though the public was concerned to protect itself from quacks and horse doctors, it had no agreement concerning methods of training or of licensing physicians. Traditionally an aspiring doctor studied as an apprentice with a preceptor, first reading with the doctor, presumably to get information, and then riding with the doctor to get experience. He might hear a few medical lectures in a medical school, but he had limited laboratory instruction and little experience with anatomical dissection.

As early as 1869 the Omaha Medical College was organized by local physicians, but for a decade it had no students, buildings, hospital, or dispensary. In 1875 the state legislature discussed the feasibility of establishing a medical college as part of the University in Lincoln, but nothing came of it because of limited funds and limited hospital facilities for clinical training. Finally in 1880 the "Nebraska School of Medicine, Preparatory" opened as a private institution in Omaha, and in the next year, building on the preparatory year, the Omaha Medical College was reorganized and instruction began. A three-year graded course was planned, but attendance was required in only two courses of lectures, each of twenty weeks' duration.[30] Like similar institutions of the time, it was able to offer the student "the sum of medical knowledge," W. F. Milroy, M.D., professor of clinical medicine, said, but a generation later, in 1908, "only the resources of a great university were adequate to cover it."[31] In the 1880s a frame structure was put up adjacent to St. Joseph's Hospital, where at least initially the hospital staff would not permit clinical instruction because of an ancient professional feud.[32] Fourteen students enrolled in the first class, each paying tuition of thirty dollars; among them was W.H.C. Stephenson, the first black physician in Omaha.[33] In 1893 the frame building was replaced by a four-story brick structure, and by 1896 the three-year curriculum was extended to four years and basic sciences and clinical training had been introduced. Designed as a proprietary institution, the Omaha school was theoretically self-supporting, but the whole venture was financially insecure and academically weak.

The legislature had established a second medical school in Lincoln in 1883 as the University of Nebraska Medical College. It occupied a couple of rooms in University Hall and used an amphitheater built in part of the large room given to the museum. A later medical yearbook reports that "the dissecting room was in another part of the city and was in constant danger of the police looking for mysterious things. The preserving vat for subjects was in an unknown basement reached by an alley entrance, and all material was secured in some mysterious manner and handled in the same way."[34] Dissecting "material" was difficult to come by; "how it was obtained deponent saith not."[35] Local papers printed sensational stories about medical students raiding cemeteries. In 1887 the University Medical College was terminated, in part because of costs but more because of public apprehensions.

Early on, physicians recognized that affiliation with a university was desirable for medical education, and in

1892, under the leadership of Henry B. Ward, a professor of zoology, they encouraged the University to establish a two-year premedical curriculum. In 1902 the University accepted primary responsibility for medical education in the state and invited the Omaha Medical College to join it. Ward was its first dean and a four-year course leading to the M.D. degree was set up. It required two years of basic science study in Lincoln and two more years of clinical training in Omaha. In 1905, at Ward's behest, the medical college extended its program to six years, with an academic B.S. degree preceding the medical degree. Admission standards were appreciably raised, and in 1908 Ward persuaded the faculty and regents to require that two full years of general college education be added to courses in basic medical science. By 1908 Nebraska was one of the select medical colleges ranked Class A by the American Association of Medical Colleges, and in that year Ward was unanimously elected president of the American Association of Medical Colleges. In 1909 the University catalog reported that the Royal College of Physicians and Surgeons in London had added the University of Nebraska to its very short list of American institutions whose graduates could be admitted to its final examination on the same basis as graduates of the best English schools.

In 1909 Omaha doctors and others in Omaha persuaded the legislature to appropriate $20,000 toward a new Omaha campus, at Forty-second and Dewey streets, then far removed from the center of the city, on a site selected by Dean Ward. The official history of the College of Medicine reports that "several of the prominent faculty members bought up adjacent properties to be sure that the college would have adequate space for its future growth," but this would also ensure that the college could not later be moved to Lincoln.[36] Many of the reforms that Abraham Flexner recommended in the celebrated report on medical education in the United States and Canada that he made for the Carnegie Foundation in 1910 were anticipated in the University Medical College; and when he visited Nebraska in preparing that report, he "warmly praised the individual teaching in laboratory and clinic" which he found there. He said its like "could not be found elsewhere west of the Allegheny mountains." "He was confident," the

Teaching & R

Daily Nebraskan reported on 28 April 1909, "that Nebraska had all in all the best school in the West." In 1912 the American Medical Association classified the Nebraska College of Medicine as the only superior institution in the region; the Association of American Medical Colleges likewise granted it superior status.[37]

Credit for the achievement of these high standards, this "quick leap from an era of proprietary medical schools to a university school of medical sciences[,] must go to Ward for his forcefulness and foresight," the official history of the medical college reports.[38] His pictures show him to be blue-eyed and square-jawed, a man not easily intimidated. He was very well educated, with years spent in German universities and a Ph.D. from Harvard. But, unhappily, he was rejected as dean of the College of Medicine in 1910, in part because he was not an M.D., in part because he was not from Omaha, in part because of the personal ambitions of Omaha professors, primarily Irving S. Cutter and Charles W. M. Poynter, both of whom became deans in due course. Ward went to the University of Illinois, where, influential both locally and nationally, he became known as the father of American parasitology. Illinois's gain was Nebraska's decided loss.

The relationship of the College of Dentistry to the University was uneven. A dental department had been added to the Omaha Medical College before it became a part of the University, but, entirely unsuccessful, it was not part of the 1902 union. A proprietary dental college founded in Lincoln in 1899 sought to join a university, first Cotner University, a new and aspiring religious institution in a Lincoln suburb, and then in 1903 the state university. But the state was unwilling to assume additional financial responsibility, and the Lincoln Dental College did not become part of the University until 1918, when the federal government requested that the University take it on as a war measure. Only in April 1919 did the legislature fully accept it. In Chancellor Andrews's day, dentistry remained financially independent, but the Lincoln Dental College enrolled its students in University courses in basic science under contract as a "patron college."

The College of Pharmacy also had its start in Andrews's decade when Rufus A. Lyman proposed that the University assume responsibility for it. The Pure Food and Drug Act of 1906 set the national standard for drugs; but a proprietary school of pharmacy had appeared in Omaha, and, said Lyman, it and other such pseudoeducational institutions filled the drugstores with incompetent dispensers of nostrums and habit-forming concoctions. To protect the public, pharmacists should be trained and licensed by the state. The faculty resisted adding another college to a university already extended, but in April 1907 the Board of Regents, encouraged by Andrews, established a school of pharmacy as a unit within the medical college under the direction of Lyman. Lyman was very astute politically, and he loved power. In 1915 this school became an independent college. Lyman remained its dean for thirty years, and then stayed on as dean emeritus for another eleven years. His college remained small and expensive. Eventually it was reincorporated into the College of Medicine and moved to Omaha, where a controversial $3.4 million building was put up for it in 1976.

Teachers College. Teachers College was a special case. Did teachers require extended, specialized professional training like lawyers, physicians, pharmacists, and engineers, or was theirs an art so closely related to subject matter as to be inseparable from it? Early in the history of the University, students asked for instruction in pedagogy, often then called didactics, and such courses were occasionally offered. Harry K. Wolfe, professor of philosophy, in 1893 was the first to teach them; and because of his interest in experimental psychology, he, like Brace in physics and Bessey in horticulture, was on the cutting edge of his profession. Through his influence a department of pedagogy was set up in 1895, and G.W.A. Luckey, nominated by Wolfe, was brought here to become its first professor. A student of the eminent psychologist and educator G. Stanley Hall, Luckey received his Ph.D. from Columbia University in 1901, and under him courses in the philosophy of pedagogy burgeoned. Instruction in teaching methods continued to be offered in academic departments, where pure research was not yet seen as superior to teaching nor was preparation of school texts yet seen as less worthy than the writing of specialized monographs. Indeed, Chancellor Andrews himself wrote (1894) a multi-

WJB opposes pension fund 1909. Now till 1958

volume history of the United States addressed to general readers which remains readable to this day. He also offered an enormously popular course in practical ethics which was far from technical.

When Wolfe was invited back to his alma mater in 1906 from Lincoln High School, where he had been principal, the chancellor and regents began studying the feasibility of making the Department of Education, as the Department of Pedagogy was now called, into a college. In 1908 the regents established the Teachers College, with a model high school in the basement of The Temple. This new college was initially divided into five departments and required its graduates to take fifteen hours of pedagogical courses. It was empowered to award a teacher's certificate, but certification requirements had to be approved by the College of Literature, Science and the Arts, now called the College of Arts and Sciences. This limitation displeased the Teachers College staff. It remained a collegiate school within the older college until 1922. Until 1908 certificates had been issued rather arbitrarily not only by state colleges and normal schools but by county and city school superintendents. With this new Teachers College the University hoped to make the quality of public instruction more uniform and rigorous.

There was friction between the subject-matter professors and the professors of pedagogy from the start. Wolfe was a colorful and influential teacher, and he produced an astonishing number of national leaders in the next generation,[39] but Luckey did not enjoy the respect that came to Wolfe. He was thought by some to lack the cultivation that students and colleagues expected of an educated man. From his early days, subject-matter professors were supercilious about him and the tone he set. Professors of history, mathematics, the sciences, and English were convinced that he and the "educators" made professional claims that they could not sustain and that they inflated concern for teaching methods with ridiculous jargon.

❧ The End of the Andrews Administration

By the time Chancellor Benjamin Andrews resigned as of January 1909 because of ill health, the essential structure of the University was either established or promised. The College of Business Administration remained unorganized, but Andrews anticipated it. "It is a great pity that our poverty forbids the University of Nebraska from instituting such a [commercial] department at once," he was quoted as saying in the *Daily Nebraskan* on 26 March 1903, and in 1913 the School of Commerce was in fact established, with J. E. LeRossignol as its director. It became the College of Business Administration in 1919. No new college was then formed for more than fifty years.

The gravest disappointment of the Andrews years was the local defeat of a pension plan for professors offered by the Carnegie Foundation for the Advancement of Teaching. In 1905 Andrew Carnegie had endowed his foundation with $10 million for a pension fund, and in 1908 he added $5 million more so that public as well as private institutions might participate in it. These were enormous sums, comparable to Harvard's total endowment at the time. In 1909 the University of Nebraska asked the legislature to approve its participation. At first the legislature seemed favorably disposed.[40] Then, in February, William Jennings Bryan attacked it, branding it "the most insidious poison that has ever entered the body politic," for through it the professorate would become lackeys of organized wealth. After heated debate the measure was narrowly defeated.

In those early years few persons lived into advanced age, so the problem of penury among aged professors was not general, but each year the question of retirement became sharper. When the magnificent Bessey died in harness in 1916 at age seventy, his friends felt it necessary to set up a memorial fund to support his widow, much to her embarrassment. Others – Barber, Bruner, Caldwell, Howard – were hardly better off when they reached old age. It may be significant that after the proposed Carnegie pension plan was defeated because Bryan and the Populists "did not want to see the state acting like a mendicant confessing its own unwillingness to provide for its professors,"[41] no alternative plan was proposed. Only in 1958, forty-nine years later, did the University finally enroll in the Teachers Insurance and Annuity Association, the successor to the Carnegie system.

Andrews's resignation was met with grief but little surprise. His health had never been robust. The regents immediately named him chancellor emeritus. He found that his health did not improve after a trip around the world, and in 1912 he moved to Florida, where he died in 1917 in some degree of poverty. He had continued to write and study to the end of his life.

Benjamin Andrews influenced the University of Nebraska permanently. The organization of the administration, the development of the agricultural college, the nature of the curriculum, the quality of the faculty, the life of the mind, all were shaped by him. One member of his faculty, who had reason to be unhappy with him, wrote: "Here he displayed that remarkable skill in exposition and virility in discussion, that wonderful blending of high ideals, horse sense, humor, and racy anecdote, which had earlier established his eminence as a teacher."[42] He defined the mission of the University as a place of free and open inquiry, responsible to the needs of society and, beyond that, to truth itself. Courage and integrity were his primary characteristics. Some persons think him the greatest chancellor the University of Nebraska has ever had and one of the noblest men who have passed this way.

5. The Beginning of a Long Retreat: 1909–1919

{❧ *Samuel Avery*

In November 1908 Benjamin Andrews notified the regents of his imminent retirement, and in December they appointed Samuel Avery, head professor of chemistry, to be acting chancellor. The editor of the *Daily Nebraskan* said, 10 December 1908, that the selection was pleasing, "as would have been the election of any of three or four other Nebraska professors prominently mentioned [for the position]. But for a man to permanently occupy the chair of chancellor it is hoped by many students that the regents will go beyond the borders of this institution and pick for the head of the greatest university west of the Missouri river a man from the east, highly qualified as an educator and full of a progressive spirit." According to figures released by the U.S. Bureau of Education, in 1909 Nebraska stood fifth in enrollment among public universities, and its fees were lower than those at any other public university except California. It stood eighth in total income, but thirteenth in relative faculty salaries. "Kansas, Missouri and Iowa, schools that Nebraska has been in a position for several years to look down upon, now threaten its prestige," the editor of the *Daily Nebraskan* observed.

As in the previous decade, the board set out to find a distinguished scholar to serve as the new chancellor. In April 1891 the regents had approached Theodore Roosevelt, then with the Civil Service Commission in New York; in 1895 they invited Woodrow Wilson to become chancellor; and in 1900 they selected Benjamin Andrews, who was already a national figure. But in 1909 they shortly gave up the national search and put in an obscure local man, Samuel Avery. This was one of the most fateful decisions in the history of the University, for with it the University in effect withdrew from the national scene. "The choice fell on me," Avery wrote to the governor of Montana on 21 July 1915, "though I was practically unknown outside of my scientific work."[1] According to one brilliant, acerbic observer, John A. Rice, "No one, not even the regents, could ever explain how it had happened, and at the inaugural dinner the chairman of the board apologized, in the presence of the honored guest, assuring faculty, alumni, and friends that they had made a careful search but had been unable to find a man they wanted, and so had appointed the new chancellor whom he was now delighted to introduce. No one could explain, except Sam Avery, and he never did; but he knew. It had, in fact, been quite simple. He had merely been and kept on being a candidate. Whenever the regents met, whatever might happen to other names, his was always there, until at last he had worn them down to acquiescence."[2] Regent Charles S. Allen, who was president of the board when Avery was chosen, reflected a rather surprising defensive tone in his valedictory of 1914: "At the beginning of our administration [1904] the University of Nebraska compared more favorably with other ranking state universities in student attendance, buildings and equipment than it now does. Gauged by the standard of bigness, Nebraska as a competitor of Illinois, Minnesota and Missouri, has steadily lost ground in the past decade. Nor is it possible to regain the former relative position. . . . The prize of bigness is beyond our reach." Allen did not speak of quality.[3]

From his speeches and letters, one concludes that Avery was shrewd, unsentimental, and devoted to his University. But he was not an intellectual, however great his native intelligence, and he was certainly not prepared to be a leader in scholarship. Rice, a Rhodes scholar on the faculty, was fascinated by him. "Sam Avery had a nose like the neck of a whiskey bottle. . . . I remember his nose because he used it," he wrote later. "Sam Avery, when he was at ease, was as frank as a dog, with the difference that he freely used the fingers of his right hand to bring the smells to him. . . . [H]e slipped his hand inside his coat and to his armpit and came out with a real refresher. 'We-e-ell,' he would say, sniffing hungrily, 'what do you suppose [that man] was up to?' "[4]

Born in 1865, Avery was brought to Nebraska as a child and educated first at Doane College and then at the University before taking his German Ph.D. in chemistry. Warmly friendly, he was "a person one could feel at ease with at once," Mabel Lee, his director of women's physical education, recalled.[5] Others in genteel and clubby Lincoln thought him something of a peasant. John D. Hicks, the historian, said, "He was a diamond in the rough who looked more like a farmer, uncomfortable in store clothes, than like the head of a great university."[6] Avery was a politician, on and off campus, and took no unnecessary risks, on principle. As he saw it, "the chancellor as chief adviser to the Regents becomes to a very considerable extent not a directing but rather a correlating officer."[7] Avery was a survivor and he viewed the chancellorship as custodial, not visionary. He remained in office from 1909 until 1927.

For a few years, perhaps a decade, the University of Nebraska retained its eminence. In the spring of 1909 Abraham Flexner had found the University's College of Medicine "all in all the best [medical] school in the West." In 1910 Charles Bessey was elected president of the American Association for the Advancement of Science. Charles W. Wallace brought worldwide fame to the University through his discovery of important facts about Shakespeare while on extended, supported leave in London. In 1915 Lawrence Bruner was named by a special governor's committee as "the greatest living Nebraskan" because he had earned international fame as an entomologist; William Jennings Bryan was pointedly passed over. In 1917 George E. Howard was elected president of the American Sociological Society and honorary vice-president of the Institut de Sociologie in France; and also in 1917 Hartley Burr Alexander was elected president of the Western Philosophical Association. Two years later he was head of the American Philosophical Association. A number of other faculty persons were making their professional marks in this decade: Louise Pound in folklore and philology, Hutton Webster in anthropology, Guernsey Jones in English history, and Prosser Hall Frye in comparative criticism. From 1913 until 1918 the University supported the *Mid-West Quarterly*, a literary journal of general interest which was at the critical frontiers of its time. Avery inherited this faculty and all this ferment. The times called for a fresh assessment of possibilities, by the regents and certainly by the chancellor. It was not made.

❧ The College of Medicine

When Abraham Flexner visited the University of Nebraska in 1909 to prepare his celebrated report on medical education, he found the separation of undergraduate preparation in Lincoln and professional training in Omaha a "perplexing problem."[8] This division had been an achievement of the Omaha community. In 1909 when the legislature provided $20,000 to purchase land for an Omaha campus, interested Omaha citizens had promised to supply $50,000 for a classroom building and hospital. This promise was not kept, and in 1911 the legislature was asked for $100,000 for a laboratory-hospital. The appropriations bill passed only after strenuous, extended lobbying by Dr. Arthur C. Stokes of Omaha. Medical folklore has it that the bill was killed nine times before it was finally approved and signed, over the strong objections of partisans of Lincoln, Omaha partisans of the Creighton Medical College, and physicians of what are now esoteric medical methodologies.[9] Ultimately the state supreme court was called on to affirm the right of the Board of Regents to establish a branch of the University away from Lincoln.

The College of Medicine was blessed with three vigorous deans in its first half century of life. Henry Ward, professor of zoology and a distinguished research scholar, raised the academic standards of medical education between 1892 and 1909; but when the college was established in Omaha, he was not made its dean. Robert H. Wolcott, who had a medical degree but was a professor of zoology, became acting dean and remained so for three years. In 1913 with the appointment of Dr. Willson O. Bridges as dean, the direction of the college passed from Lincoln and professors of basic science to Omaha physicians. Thereafter the Omaha college acted with considerable independence of the regents and University administration. Avery rarely attempted to challenge its autonomy.

The second great medical dean, Irving S. Cutter, took his M.D. degree only in 1910, but within three years he was director of laboratories in Omaha, and in five he was dean of the college. An experienced hand at school politics, perhaps because he had formerly been an administrator in secondary schools and then an agent for Ginn and Company, a major publisher of textbooks, he was a man of decision. One did not cross him with impunity. Shrewd and extremely ambitious, he directed the College of Medicine for ten years until called in 1925 to be dean of the Northwestern University Medical School. A powerful lobbyist with successive legislatures and governors, he moved equipment from Lincoln to Omaha, built a medical library, reorganized the curriculum, and added basic science faculty to his staff. He also made full use of volunteer, unsalaried physicians for clinical teaching, paying them with the prestige of University titles. He persuaded Omaha hospitals to allow clinical training in their wards. In 1915 he was able to get an appropriation of $150,000 with which to build a teaching hospital. In 1917 he got $180,000 for a laboratory building and he established a school of nursing, a necessary adjunct to a teaching hospital. He appointed the formidable Charlotte Burgess, Ph.D., R.N., as director. During World War I she directed a Red Cross unit in Russia; and like Dean Cutter, she knew her own mind. The School of Nursing grew to more than one hundred students, who were trained on the apprenticeship model, with a minimum of basic scientific education. Conkling Hall, the dormitory–administration building for the nurses, was constructed in 1923 at a cost of $70,000 and named after an earlier benefactor of the College of Medicine.

In the Twenties, though the rest of the University suffered from low budgets, in part because the state was already in an agricultural depression, Cutter persuaded the legislature to provide another $200,000 for an extension on the teaching hospital, one which cost an additional $100,000 before it was completed in 1927. Enrollment rose from 84 students in 1913 to 146 in 1916 and then to an astonishing 322 by 1928. Resources were stretched to the breaking point but intellectual standards continued to rise, and the College of Medicine "could be trying years for students if they had not yet become mature adults or were not intellectually fitted for medicine," the official historians report.[10]

If the College of Medicine did not always match the achievements of several other midwestern schools of medicine in Cutter's time, it did not fall far behind; and he left it in 1925 at least competitive. Though Dr. C.W.M. Poynter, professor of anatomy since 1910, was the logical, ambitious successor to Dean Cutter, he did not get the post. Instead it went to Dr. J. Jay Keegan, a neurosurgeon, a fine man but without the vision or the determination of his predecessor. After three stormy years he withdrew in 1929 and was replaced by Dr. Poynter, the third great dean of the College of Medicine. Poynter remained in office until 1946. That the college survived as well as it did during the depression and World War II is in large part due to him. These three deans showed what could be accomplished by men of vision even in unfavorable times.

❧ Relocating the Campus

The first great crisis of the Avery years concerned the location of the University campus. When the University was established in 1869, only four square blocks had been allotted to it, and by 1910 it had outgrown that confined area. In the Nineties, Willard Kimball had built his proprietary University School of Music across R Street at Eleventh. The massive Temple was also off campus, at the corner of R and Twelfth. A privately-owned and -operated women's dormitory, Hays Hall, was at the corner of Q and Twelfth. On campus the buildings were inadequate and mostly decrepit. University Hall and Nebraska Hall, the oldest structures, were unsalvageable and even unsafe. Old Chemistry Hall was somewhat sturdier, but it too was falling down. The library, soundly constructed because of Chancellor Canfield's careful supervision, was much too small. Brace Laboratory was sound, but the museum and mechanic arts buildings were awkward, aborted structures, planned as wings for a larger complex that never got built. Only Richards Hall, housing mechanical engineering, seemed up to standard, perhaps because it was designed, without compensation, by Dean Charles R. Richards and supervised by his protégé, C. E. Chowins, University building superintendent. The limited sporting fields to the north, acquired by eminent domain after 1905, were underdeveloped and much too small.

As early as 1898 Charles Bessey had proposed that the University be moved to the University farm, on Holdrege Street east of Thirty-third. The growing student body – in 1910 it had grown to 4,000 – made more space necessary, and everybody assumed that enrollment would continue to rise. "[A]lmost immediately after my appointment," Chancellor Avery wrote later, "one of the Regents precipitated a civil war over the location of the University, whether it should be developed in the heart of the city or the academic part moved to the State Farm campus three miles out."[11] Avery remembered that "little was heard about removal till just before the legislative session of 1911," when "the Lancaster county delegation, though favorable to retaining the city campus, voted for a mill tax levy for removal on the grounds that such a tax seemed to be the only hope of securing adequate buildings for the University."[12] A legislative joint committee, formed to study the removal question, unanimously endorsed consolidation at the farm, but the Board of Regents split over the issue, and so did the two houses of the legislature. The student body resolutely and rather uncharacteristically tried to remain neutral, the editor of the *Daily Nebraskan* declaring on 24 January 1911: "The best interests of the school demand that the student body as a whole and individually keep out of discussions of the question at issue." Chancellor Emeritus Andrews wrote the board urging the retention of the city campus both because of the enormous expense of moving, as he saw it, and the serious inconvenience of removal to self-supporting students. The removal bill passed the senate, failed in the house; and though the 1911 legislature provided money for a law building and a plant industry building, it adjourned without deciding where the campus was to be. The issue was at deadlock.

Without taking a firm stand one way or another, Avery suggested to the 1913 legislature that the issue be submitted to a statewide referendum, and his suggestion was endorsed by both houses. The same legislature created a special University building fund, financed by a property tax of three-quarters of a mill, to run for six years. As the 1914 *Cornhusker* observed: "Nebraskans are assured, therefore, of a wonderful growth of the State University in the near future," whatever its location.[13] Those in favor of relocating at the farm argued that the cost of acquiring city lots adjacent to the old campus would be prohibitive, perhaps as much as $470,000. They saw the cost of maintaining the two campuses as greater than that of maintaining a single campus. They thought that agricultural and general education could best support one another with a minimum of duplication at the farm, and they said that the country location would remove students from the worldly temptations of saloons, gaming houses, and frivolous entertainment. On the other hand, proponents of retaining the city campus argued that removal would take students away from the cultural advantages of city life where they could participate in social and church activities, and the greater number of general students might well engulf the agriculture students. Since about half the male students were working their way through college and received something like a combined total of $100,000 a year in wages, they would be seriously disadvantaged on the farm by being far from their jobs. As for costs, opponents of the removal estimated that building up the farm would come to $1.5 million more than retaining the two campuses. All this was guesswork.

In the controversy that preceded the public referendum of 1914, Lincoln property and business interests lobbied for the retention of the city campus. Though Governor Morehead, Chancellor Avery, and the Board of Regents finally favored removal, at least at this stage of deliberation, a large group of the city fathers banded together to work against it. The people of the state turned out to be much less agitated than their officials and some Lincoln citizens. They voted nearly two to one to retain the historic city campus. Avery's "civil war" ended abruptly in 1914. He wrote the next year, "Through all the bitterness of the strife I think I have in a measure retained the confidence of the people of the state, have endeavored to act as a peacemaker and in the course of a year will have been in office longer than any of my predecessors."[14]

Extending the Campus to Fourteenth Street

A program of building was swiftly undertaken. In 1911 a law building had been authorized and situated at the corner of Tenth and R streets. A particularly handsome structure, it was planned by Berlinghof and Davis of Lincoln, the first of a number of buildings that this firm, later Davis and Wilson, was to design for the University. Ellery Davis was the brilliant young son of Dean Ellery Davis of the College of Arts and Sciences. Finished in 1913, it was stylistically unlike the other buildings on the campus. Surveying the campus in 1914, Charles Hodgdon, senior partner of the celebrated Boston and Chicago firm of Shepley, Rutan and Coolidge, now officially the University's architects, proposed a new city campus. It was to be in collegiate Georgian style: red brick with limestone trim, classical columns and pilasters, and paned windows, all arranged logically around central malls. Other state university campuses, that of the University of Minnesota, for one, were similar. They harked back to Jefferson's scheme for the University of Virginia, which had a central mall, columns, walkways, and brick. Perhaps accidentally, the orderly red brick of the public university reflected Jefferson's eighteenth-century rationalism, but nobody at the time spoke of this connection. It contrasted with the Gothic decorations of the University of Chicago and Northwestern University, which alluded to the Gothic splendors of Oxford and Cambridge. On the ag campus the Plant Industry Building, in pleasant buff brick, was constructed on a mall in 1912. The earthy buff brick of that campus seemed appropriate to the agricultural studies there.

The special building levy approved in 1913 brought the University in the next four years just under $900,000, of which $300,000 was budgeted to extend the city campus from Twelfth to Fourteenth Street, from R to U Street, and to add areas north on Tenth Street.[15] Ultimately more than $2 million was provided for building on the two campuses

in the next decade. The existing, mostly frame buildings on the campus extension tract from Twelfth to Fourteenth Street were gradually removed, but along R Street a number of large houses were put to institutional use. The palatial residence built by Frank Sheldon on the corner of Fourteenth and R was immediately claimed for a women's building by Amanda Heppner, the dean of women. It would provide "the comforts of a club house to all women of the University." She wrote, "The richly carved woodwork, the imposing court, grand staircase and balconies, the massive panelled walls, old fashioned fireplaces and mosaic floors convey an atmosphere of elegance and beauty."[16] In 1920 University alumnae proposed that it be named Ellen Smith Hall, a bit ironically perhaps, because Smith had always lived in a very modest frame house north of the campus.

A large brick house just west of Ellen Smith Hall was designated the chancellor's residence, and five other houses on this street were fitted out as women's dorms (Hays Hall, the proprietary women's dorm at Twelfth and Q streets, had become a general hotel in 1912). Heppner's plan to turn these houses into self-governing communities with a common dining room and Ellen Smith Hall as a common lounge was not successful, but she was attempting to provide accommodations for women who did not live in sorority houses. By 1915 fraternities and sororities rented or owned houses about town and set the tone of undergraduate life. Their existence was by no means uncontroversial. Egalitarians asserted that these closed, mutually supportive groups were undemocratic, and as late as 1909 a bill was introduced in the legislature to ban them from the University as they were banned from high schools.

Social Life before the Great War

The plans for Ellen Smith Hall were doubly important because The Temple had become something of a disappointment. When built, it was intended to be the center of the students' social life, but in its early years it had no café or place for informal gatherings aside from rooms occupied by the YMCA and the YWCA. Smoking was forbidden, as it was in all University buildings. The two literary societies, Palladian and Union, had headquarters in The Temple as a consequence of their raising money for its construction; and upon occasion dances were held in a second-floor "pavilion." The basement, planned as an assembly room, was soon taken over for Teachers College High School; and rooms throughout the building were periodically made available to groups from town, for a fee. In 1911 the *Cornhusker* printed "An Address to John D.":

*How hollow sound the echoes down the empty Temple
    halls;*
*How swiftly dust hath gathered on the unused floors and
    walls;*
Save only in the cellar where the Temple High kids play,
And in the lonely parlors of Y. and M. C. A.[17]

The YMCA did what it could to liven up The Temple. It opened a basement lunchroom in March 1912. The YMCA, seeing itself as a service organization, ran a job bureau for those working their way through college and kept a register of boardinghouses for those not living at home or in organized houses.

For all her good intentions, Dean Heppner was not popular. The students saw her as a wet blanket. Formerly an assistant professor of German with a B.A. in 1894 and an M.A. in 1896, she had chaperoned groups of students on summertime tours of Europe. Now as dean of women she acted as University chaperone. She surveyed the enthusiasm for ballroom dancing, especially new styles like the tango, with a baleful eye. In 1913 a committee on student organizations attempted to limit the kind of dances that could be permitted at University parties. The *Daily Nebraskan* on 8 January 1914 reported, "It is probable that the Tango, Hesitation, One-step, Castle Walk and other forms of the dance will become popular at once," but some prescriptions were laid down: "The old-fashioned but graceful waltz position, together with the modified position assumed in the Boston—the girl's right forearm resting on the man's left fore-arm will be the correct position to assume, no matter what the dance. . . . The extreme in any styles of dance will be a violation of the freedom which is extended under the new ruling." One doubts that these rules were closely observed.

Various rather unattractive restaurants situated on the edge of the campus became student hangouts. The students had dancing parties, sponsored by fraternities and sororities, in hotels and halls, and smaller gatherings in their residential houses. A number of times during the year all-University balls were held on campus. If the young men drank hard liquor or even beer, they were subject to considerable opprobrium; temperance groups, headed by the chancellor himself, were vigorous. By and large before 1917, the community was officially abstemious. Nice girls not only did not drink; they did not go out with young men who did, they said.

The literary societies, though continuing, were less commanding than they had been, and their Friday and Saturday night debates and "examinations" had competition for attendance. They became increasingly anachronistic. Lincoln was still a major stop for theatrical companies, so every week students could attend one or another play or operetta. Sunday was a solemn day and everybody went to church. If the students provided their own entertainment through their dances and mixers, the faculty too entertained one another. From early days men of town and gown gathered in dinner discussion clubs where one member read a paper which others criticized. Some of these groups—The Round Table, Crucible, The Club—were very prestigious, the members chosen with care to ensure professional balance. In one of them Roscoe Pound, challenged by E. A. Ross, was introduced to the sociology of the law; and in another James LeRossignol defended his view of business education before the criticisms of Hartley Burr Alexander. Faculty persons who left Lincoln remembered these clubs as vital. Some of them exist to this day, generations after their founding.

Women had similar clubs. Flavia Canfield, Chancellor Canfield's wife, helped found the Lincoln Women's Club, which was devoted to good works and cultural enlightenment; and other groups of women met to read serious papers on cultural topics. With restricted memberships, they held themselves to high social and intellectual standards. The women did not ordinarily meet at dinner hour, as the men did. They had homes to care for and families to feed. The men's clubs met for meals provided by the wives or at

26. Chancellor E. Benjamin Andrews
(1844–1917) is usually pictured in
profile. He lost his left eye in the siege
of Petersburg (1864). For him, it was
said, "intellectual vigor and moral integrity were the indispensable begin-
nings of all worthy education." (*Cornhusker 1909*, UNL Archives)

27. Carrie Belle Raymond (1857–
1927) was director of the University
chorus from 1894 until her death. In
1917 the local press said, "We have
here in Lincoln a musical genius."
(UNL Photo Lab)

28. The agricultural campus in the early 1900s, when the roads were still unpaved. The two buildings on the left were built before the University acquired the Moses Culver place in 1874. The brick dairy building on the extreme right was constructed in 1896, and in 1899 the experiment station building under the water tower on the left was put up. (UNL Photo Lab)

29. In this famous photograph Ina Gittings, "head of the women's gymnasium," is shown in field sports with Ruth Bryan, William Jennings Bryan's colorful daughter. The view is north of T Street between Eleventh and Twelfth. Behind them are engineering and service buildings which, though hardly more than sheds, remained in use for some fifty years. (UNL Archives)

30. The Temple was constructed as a student activities building in 1906 with $66,666 from John D. Rockefeller and local matching funds of $33,333. Chancellor Andrews, a friend of Rockefeller's, pledged $1,000 from his own salary of $6,000 and became its largest University benefactor. (UNL Archives)

31. The city campus, looking north from the top of The Temple at Twelfth and R streets, about 1908. Administration Hall, center left in this photograph, was designed in 1905 by Thomas R. Kimball of Omaha. Limestone pillars and trim were originally called for, but the cost was so high that they were replaced with terra cotta. This splendid building was razed in the 1950s to make room for the Sheldon Memorial Art Gallery and Sculpture Garden. (UNL Photo Lab)

32. The first women's dormitory, Hays Hall, was built in 1906 off campus at the corner of Twelfth and Q streets where the Lied Center now stands and was operated as a private venture. It contained a cafeteria and parlors; a chaperon was in residence. (Nebraska State Historical Society)

33. This picture of a breakfast picnic off campus appeared in the *Cornhusker 1908*. Students wear formal dress; leisure clothing was some years in the future. Most students at this time had no more than two changes of clothes. Women wore gloves and hats to class, men neckties and suitcoats. (UNL Archives)

The Lincoln Medical College

121 South 14th Street, Lincoln, Nebraska

W. S. Latta,
M. D., Dean

*Member of the
National Confeder-
ation of Eclectic
Medical Colleges*

Progressive

Thorough

Up-To-Date

Well Equipped

All State Board requirements fully complied with. Graded Course—Four terms of six months each. Either sex admitted upon equal terms. Entire class witness all operations in amphitheatre. Juniors and seniors serve as assistants.

34, 35. Before the Flexner Report (1910), even the best medical schools advertised for students. This advertisement appeared in the *Sombrero* of 1902. The dental college was only "associated" with the University before 1918. (UNL Archives)

36. According to journalists, by 1900 football "had become a topic of year-round conversation in country stores and barber shops and in city clubs as well as on the campus." Modern Cornhusker football dates from the Stiehm Roller era, so named for E. O. Stiehm, the coach from 1911 until 1914. A continuing rival was Minnesota, the Golden Gophers. (*Cornhusker 1914*, UNL Archives)

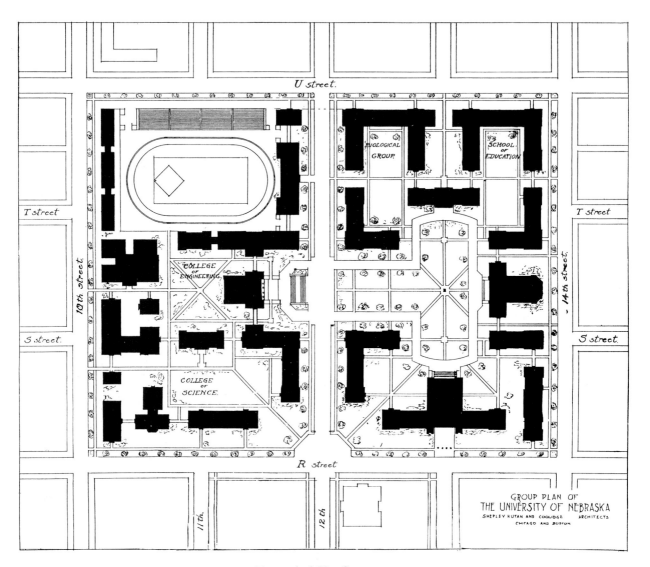

Expanded City Campus

37, 38. By 1913 the city campus and its buildings were too small for the growing student body, and Professor Bessey and others proposed that the University be moved to the farm beyond Thirty-third and Holdrege streets. After the statewide referendum of 1914 determined that the city campus should remain, however, it was expanded from Twelfth to Fourteenth Street and north to U Street. (*Cornhusker 1914*, UNL Archives)

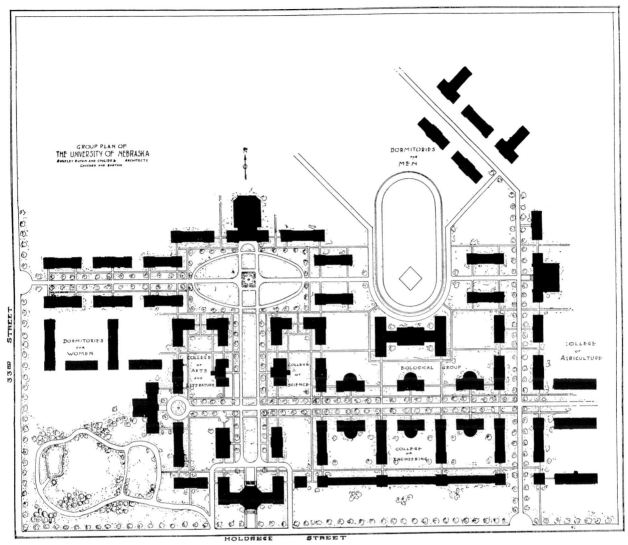

Consolidated on First Farm Site

39, 40. Agriculture faculty held Farmers' Institutes around the state after 1874. The 1913 *Cornhusker* contained these views of a professor and his farmer-students; hundreds of sessions were held on trains each year. (UNL Archives)

41. The campus of the College of Agriculture, viewed from the north, in 1917. On the quadrangle is the Plant Industries Building (1912) with the Home Economics Building (1909), right, and Agricultural Hall (1904), far right, opposite. The experiment station (1899), just opposite Ag Hall, is obscured in this picture. At the extreme left are the brick livestock judging pavilion (1915) and the dairy building, later Filley Hall (1917). The center brick building is Farm Engineering. The frame house, in the middle distance, was initially a dormitory (1874) but was used in 1917 as a lab. (UNL Archives)

42. George E. Howard (1849–1923) championed causes like racial equality, women's rights, separation of church and state, and free speech. This photograph was taken in 1917 when he was elected president of the American Sociological Society. (UNL Photo Lab)

43. Under pressure from the Nebraska Council of Defense in 1917 and 1918, the regents constituted themselves a board to receive testimony against professors and others charged with being "negative, halting, or hesitating" in their support of the war. In June 1918 hearings were held in the new law building, with five of the six regents in regular attendance. Capacity crowds appeared every day. (Nebraska State Historical Society)

44. The fence surrounding the linden tree in front of the old library carried a plaque with this inscription: "Dem grossen Dichter und Denker Friedrich Johann Schiller gewidmet am 9. Mai. 1905 Planted by Prof. Laurence Fossler." Fossler is shown here with his tree "dedicated to the great poet and thinker" Schiller. In 1938 a citizen of Omaha wrote to the University librarian: "One morning during the [1917–18] war anyone who passed by was surprised to find in place of the small iron tablet a placard containing some ribald statement or two and winding up with the statement that the tablet was interned for the period of the war. At the top of the tree was a small fluttering American flag. The information gradually leaked out that some of the law students were responsible for the situation . . . ." He suggested that "one or two of the principal characters" would be delighted to restore the tablet, but it was in fact not "restored"; it was replaced. The Sheldon Sculpture Garden surrounds the tree and fence now. Brace Laboratory is in the background. (UNL Archives)

45. This photograph of Chancellor Samuel Avery (1865–1936) was taken in his Administration Hall office for the 1917 *Cornhusker*. (UNL Archives)

46. Fred Morrow Fling (1860–1934), professor of European history, was, Mari Sandoz said, "the 'henniest,' fussiest man imaginable . . . but his approach to historical fact was impeccable." He is pictured here about 1928 with his personal library, which was given to the University by his widow, each volume carrying a gift plate with their names and a drawing of the Jacobin cap. (Nebraska State Historical Society)

hotels and restaurants. The men smoked but they did not drink at these gatherings; the women of course did neither. In all of them, town and gown met in a tone of moral responsibility, and many kept records of membership, papers, and discussion. Lincoln was not a dull city for either the students or the faculty in those days. Everybody seems to have had a passion for self-improvement.

❧ Football before the War

From its first appearance at the University in the Nineties, football was enormously popular throughout the state; and high schools, particularly Lincoln High, shortly became farms where promising players were given prep courses. With little faculty or administrative control over recruitment, coaching, and performance, scandals involving both ethics and brutality were by no means infrequent; coaches were even known to put themselves into the lineup, under false names, when losses seemed otherwise unavoidable. Professor R. D. Scott, after 1916 a faculty representative on athletic boards and a steady supporter of athletic programs, said later that "the type of intercollegiate athletics that existed between the years 1890 and 1906 [both in Nebraska and elsewhere in the region] . . . could bring nothing but discredit to any reputable institution."[18] Scott was himself a rather curious professor of English. Having spent several years as an actor-manager of theatrical stock companies, he had only drifted into teaching English, first at Lincoln High and then at the University. In both places he had assisted in coaching. As chairman of the University athletic board and its representative to the Missouri Valley Conference, he, along with the board, was a buffer for the chancellor. Avery, ever careful politically and never much interested in intercollegiate athletics, told Scott that Scott could take a lot of heat off him by serving in certain situations as the goat.

As a result of criticism and of confusion in intercollegiate scheduling, in 1906 the universities of Iowa, Missouri, Kansas, and Nebraska, plus Iowa State, Drake University, and Washington University in St. Louis, organized themselves into the Missouri Valley Conference. This conference arranged a calendar of games. They decreed that members of teams should be full-time, bona fide students carrying standard academic loads, and that they could not be paid. Players were limited to three years of competition and were expected to "observe gentlemanly conduct at all times." Enforcement of rules was left to administrative officers on individual campuses; but, meeting regularly, the conference was a "hard-bitten organization, impersonal, fearless and just."[19] For the most part the member institutions cooperated, Scott said, if for no other reason than for fear of expulsion and subsequent loss of scheduling. At Nebraska the supervising authority was an athletic board which had three academic members: the aging Grove E. Barber of the classics department, who did not know a quarterback from a javelin, one coach said; Dr. R. E. Clapp, longtime head of men's physical education; and R. H. Wolcott of the Department of Zoology. Robert D. Scott replaced Barber in 1916 and shortly became the board's chairman. The director of athletics, who was its financial officer, and an alumnus were also on the board. This group, appointed by the chancellor, stood between him and public controversy, and operated more or less responsibly from 1907 until after World War I.

Between 1906 and 1917 Nebraska dominated the Missouri Valley Conference. Under Coach W. G. "King" Cole from 1907 to 1910, Nebraska won twenty-five games, tied three, and lost only eight. When E. O. "Jumbo" Stiehm coached from 1911 until 1916 it had thirty-five wins, three ties, and only two losses. Naturally, these teams were regarded as "steam rollers," Coach Stiehm's name being pronounced *steam*. Cornhusker football for the next twenty-five years was fundamentally formed by Stiehm Roller policies.

Athletic receipts in 1915 were $35,000, and in October 1915 8,000 spectators, until then the largest crowd in Nebraska football history, paid $11,768 to see Nebraska defeat Notre Dame 20–19. When Stiehm was offered $4,500 by Indiana University in 1916, supporters including Lincoln businessmen urged the University to make a counteroffer of $4,250 to retain him. Faculty members protested vigorously, saying that no coach should be paid more than any professor; and after extended argument, the local offer was withdrawn. "Jumbo" Stiehm left. In those days the faculty, jealous of their academic reputations, considered their institution damaged by being known as a football college.[20] The athletic board, with the tacit agreement of Chancellor Avery, hired Coach E. J. "Doc" Steward. He was both competent and handsome, as handsome, it was said, "as a musical comedy juvenile though slightly over age for such a role."[21] He had two successful seasons before the football program was destroyed by wartime exigencies.

During this whole period, 1906–17, Nebraska's intercollegiate record in football earned admiration from competitors, who regarded the teams as "clean and lucky." On the whole the athletes were committed native sons who had support from home or worked their way through college with legitimate jobs. This was an amateur's game, however hard it was played. The coaches were colorful, the teams victorious, and the heroes homegrown. Vic Halligan, the first Cornhusker All-American, came from North Platte, and Guy Chamberlin, often said to be the greatest football player of them all, came from Blue Springs. People talked of replacing the wooden bleachers with concrete on the east-west field at Eleventh and T streets.

❧ The University and the Great War: 1914–1917

If the first major crisis of the Avery years was over the location of the campus, the second was over the European war. The war was immediately perceived as cataclysmic, "the disgrace of our civilization," Avery told the students. In a University convocation he asserted that "good will" was "a great local and state and universal asset," and that the "doctrine of hatred for Germany taught in French schools" and the willingness of German youth "to die for imperialism" were equally foreign to the American spirit. His views were reported fully in the *Daily Nebraskan*, 23 September 1914. President Wilson's policy of neutrality was promptly embraced in Nebraska, not least because so many of its people were first- and second-generation German immigrants. German culture and the German language were not rejected on campus or off it. The University German Verein — a social club in which students

practiced speaking German — continued to flourish after 1914, and the German dramatic club continued to present annual plays in German, directed by Amanda Heppner, not yet the dean of women. As late as January 1917 a German play and banquet for the legislators were presented and well attended in The Temple. Frank Haller, president of the Board of Regents, was known to be sympathetic to the German cause; and Chancellor Avery, like a number of the professors, had a German Ph.D.

Not all the academic community was prepared for neutrality. Fred Morrow Fling, head professor of European history, rejected President Wilson's policy out of hand and in a University convocation on 29 September 1914 proclaimed to a large audience, "Germany is on the wrong side of the issue." The German government, he asserted, was a selfish power, "carrying out the imperialistic policies of the Middle Ages." His speech was immediately protested. John G. Maher, a colorful Lincoln businessman who signed himself "Colonel," nobody knew on what authority, wrote to the public press on 5 October asserting that Fling not only had violated the neutrality proclamation but had strongly urged the students to do likewise; and following a meeting on 18 October 1914 the German-American Alliance of Lincoln wrote to the Board of Regents protesting Fling's address. "The University of Nebraska, as all other universities in the country, is greatly indebted to German models and to German ideals," the board replied, in a letter no doubt written by Avery in his peacemaking role. "The Regents believe that German academic freedom should be permitted to flourish in America and that American citizens of German descent will join them in being the last to wish to curtail it, even though at times it may be exercised in a way contrary to their personal wishes and out of harmony with the convictions of friends of the University whose good-will the Regents are most anxious to retain."[22]

But Fling continued his inflammatory addresses. He was in fact one of the best platform performers in the University. Born in Maine in 1860 and educated at Bowdoin College and the University of Leipzig (Ph.D. 1890), he came to Nebraska in 1892 on the invitation of Chancellor Canfield. While at Leipzig, perhaps caught up in the centennial celebrations of the French Revolution, he became fascinated with Honoré Mirabeau and devoted his scholarly life to a biography of him. In 1908 he brought out *The Youth of Mirabeau*, the first of four projected volumes. In the following years he produced a number of handbooks and texts dealing with the "source method" of historical study, and he worked zealously to introduce this "Nebraska method" into high schools and colleges as well as into graduate schools. His friend and colleague W. G. Langworthy Taylor, professor of economics and a considerable scholar himself, said that "Fling threw himself with almost fanatical zeal into the battle for historical truth."[23] A loner, Fling claimed that he never attended a play or a concert without carrying a book to read during intermission, and others noticed that he brought a book when he had lunch at the cafeteria in The Temple. Everyone spoke of his immaculate dress, which seemed part of his inclination to precision, completeness, and detail and made him look like a banker. Apparently without self-doubts and something of a poseur, he seemed always engaged in awesome problems.[24]

Though a splendid lecturer, Fling was a controversial teacher. The 1912 *Cornhusker* provided, rather unusually, a judgment of him: "All of his students admire Dr. Fling's ability, and would unite in his praise if it were not that his sometimes harsh and sarcastic manner antagonizes them. Old students of his classes would be pleased at nothing more than to see him mollify his sternness and show to the young people about him more of that softer side, which they feel sure he has only been concealing."[25] It may be of some significance that his multivolume biography remained in manuscript at his death, that his monumental history of civilization was never finished, and that his proposed account of the 1919 Versailles Peace Conference, which he attended as a research historian, never appeared.

Through the war years Fling continued to defend the Allied cause, and in 1917, before the official declaration of war by Congress, he asserted, as reported in the *Daily Nebraskan* on 27 March: "I'm no fire-eater, but there are some things worse than war. The young man who gives his life for some great heroic thing, to humanity, to help the realization of some of the great spiritual things, has lived a long life though he dies at 21." Fling was fifty-seven at the time. A committee of faculty members expressed their support for President Wilson's "strong foreign policy" – Wilson had long since moved from his 1914 neutrality – in a letter published 30 March 1917. The very next day a second group telegraphed Washington, with quixotic courage, urging "all honorable means of preventing American aggressive participation in the present European conflict." The campus newspaper printed both letters. Emotions ran high.

❧ *The Anti-German Witch Hunt of 1917–1918*

After the United States entered the war 6 April 1917, the antiwar group asserted their complete support of the president and the nation. Refusing to let well enough alone, Clark E. Persinger, professor of American history since 1913, claimed in the public press that a majority of the faculty continued to oppose the war; and he protested that the University was being used for war propaganda. From his previous conduct on campus, one concludes that Persinger was one kind of absolute idealist. Spoiling for a fight, he was willing, even eager, to be a martyr; he was

A daring pilot in extremity;
Pleased with the danger, when the waves went high,
He sought the storms; but, for a calm unfit,
Would steer too nigh the sands, to boast his wit.[26]

Persinger was out of step: patriotism was all the fashion. On 18 April Governor Keith Neville signed a bill establishing a Nebraska Council of Defense which was to monitor actions and speeches of persons suspected of disloyalty. On 24 April the University held a great parade down O Street and a convocation at the city auditorium, and by 3 May more than 500 students had withdrawn from classes to enlist in the armed forces. Unquestioning loyalty to government policy was required.

The University staff were looked at suspiciously, celebrated as they were for free opinion openly expressed. Not only Persinger but Professor G.W.A. Luckey, graduate dean in the Teachers College, came under suspicion. On 31 May, in a commencement address delivered at Howells,

Nebraska, Luckey was quoted in the press as saying: "I do not want to fight and die in the trenches of a foreign land in a war that is not of my making and not my war." The newspapers picked up the phrase "not my war" as an "un-American utterance" and demanded his dismissal from the University, and the Council of Defense asked the Board of Regents to deal with what they perceived as widespread disloyalty on campus. Chancellor Avery in his usual conciliatory tone asserted that whatever doubts any staff person might once have had were dispelled with the declaration of war. Regent Haller challenged the Council of Defense, but his challenge only increased the anti-German hysteria. By December he was forced to resign from the Board of Regents.

The Council of Defense continued its accusations and through the winter of 1917–18 and the following spring concerned itself with allegations of disloyalty. By May 1918 some dozen staff members, including professors of longest service, were under query. Inflammatory rumors were everywhere. Minnie Throop England, who had been made an assistant professor of economics and commerce in 1916 after writing a series of brilliant papers on international trade, appointed herself spokesman for the "patriotic" group, and in letters to the editors kept the controversial pot boiling. Always something of an enthusiast, she may not have been aware of how her conduct stirred up dissension. She supported Fling. Robert M. Joyce, chairman of the Council of Defense, and former regent George Coupland, vice-chairman, both claimed to have very definite statements from Fling as to disloyalty and expressions of it on the campus, but they seemed to have no documentary evidence.[27]

Skeptical of the validity of vague charges, the Board of Regents finally agreed, reluctantly, to schedule public hearings in the law college; and though the Council of Defense reaffirmed its original accusations, it refused to assume responsibility for prosecution. It provided the regents with what information it had against the twelve University staff members named as disloyal. The inquisition, in a quasi-legal court proceeding, took place for ten days in June and was harrowing for all concerned.

When Harry Wolfe, the remarkable teacher of psychology, died in July, many persons thought his death had been hastened by accusations made against him and his colleagues.

On 11 June the board retired to the chancellor's office to deliberate. Avery and Fling were both in Washington, Avery as a major in chemical warfare, a post he had earnestly sought, and Fling as a research historian. Avery, returning only briefly for the hearings, had done little all year to quiet the war hysteria and took a minimal part in the pseudo-trial. Judge William G. Hastings, dean of the College of Law, was left as acting chancellor. Fling did not appear in Lincoln at all, without explanation. On 18 June the regents brought out their report. They concluded that "not a student was found who had received from any teacher in any classroom or private conversation an impression of any such disloyalty" as had been charged. Of all the persons named, all were exonerated from charges of "behaving in a negative, halting, or hesitating manner in support of the government." Two professors, the board thought, had been "indiscreet" in their public utterances and had thus involved the University in public criticism. Since they had destroyed their usefulness to the institution, Persinger and Luckey were directed to tender their resignations immediately. Professor Hopt of the College of Agriculture deserved special treatment as a conscientious objector, but his resignation was also called for.[28] The careful decision was an embarrassment to both the Council of Defense and the crusading journalists who had stirred up the whole controversy.

The board came to another, interesting conclusion. They wrote that the investigation revealed dissension among members of the University staff which had resulted in the spreading of distrust: "The Board cannot hold blameless persons who have contributed to this state of affairs." They thereupon asked that F. M. Fling and Minnie T. England terminate their relationship with the University "unless they can adequately explain the circumstances before the Board." Fling in Washington was speechless with astonishment; he apparently did not understand that words are also deeds. The board reconsidered their decision when pressed by the Omaha Chamber of Commerce, and Fling did in fact return to the University in 1922, against the judgment of two of the regents. Chancellor Avery, who had tried rather successfully to remain above the controversy, wrote of Fling later, in confidence, that "while Professor Fling minutely studies evidence relating to the French Revolution, he speaks of his colleagues and associates often as the result of very erroneous impressions without applying to them the principles of evidence that he teaches in his classes."[29] England returned to classes but she did not fully recover from the excitement of the patriotic controversy. On 1 October 1919, she had to withdraw from teaching because of ill health. In the previous summer she had been divorced. She apparently had some kind of nervous breakdown. Avery saw to it that she received her salary until the end of the semester, but she soon moved to Norfolk, where there was a state mental hospital. She died there in 1941.

The Star Chamber procedures had disturbed many thoughtful people off and on the campus, but the national hysteria silenced them at the time. Persinger got a job in New Mexico with the straightforward help of Dean Hastings. Luckey, remaining in Lincoln, was vigorously defended by his colleagues and former students and eventually got a job in government. Though he appealed to the newly formed American Association of University Professors, asserting that his rights had been breached, no investigation of his case was made. Avery, who had always found Luckey willful, did nothing to help him. He found Fling difficult, too, but so did everybody else. He apparently felt sorry for Minnie England. The Council of Defense disappeared when the war ended, and everybody associated with the investigation wished to forget the whole matter.

❧ SATC

When the war came in 1917, the University had offered its facilities to the government for wartime service. In January 1917 the military department of the University became a unit of the Reserve Officers Training Corps (ROTC), through which graduating cadets could get commissions; but when young men here and everywhere enlisted in such numbers as to suggest that colleges would be depleted of students and the postwar nation deprived of trained persons, the ROTC program was converted into the Student Army Training Corps. The SATC was instituted at Nebraska in the fall of 1917, with some students studying University-level courses, others subcollegiate subjects. All lived under military discipline though they did not have uniforms for some months, the army not being able to supply them promptly. They were barracked in the new, unfinished Social Sciences Hall (now the College of Business Administration) and the armory across Twelfth Street, Grant Memorial Hall. Their mess hall was built east of The Temple. Two wooden buildings were constructed on the ag campus for additional barracks. Women – they were referred to as girls – were offered Red Cross training and instruction in nursing. The YM and YWCA prepared persons for nonmilitary support service. From October 1917 until November 1918 the campus was rather like a military installation, with soldiers and close-order drill setting the tone.

Then suddenly the war was over and the SATC was quickly demobilized. Supposed to start on 1 December 1918, the discharges were in fact not yet completed by December 18; but by the second semester the military units on campus were gone. Not all the cadets were glad to see the war end. The campus newspaper reported 8 November 1918 that many complained that it was back to the farm for them, and some even considered joining the Czecho-Slovak revolt or the enemies of the Bolsheviki in order to get action. Some students in the Office Training Corps were sharply disappointed not to get commissions. But by the beginning of the second semester, January 1919, only a few men remained in the military department, now on a peacetime basis. Wartime excitement was over.

6. A University on the Defensive: 1920–1927

ᴤ The Changed University

Chancellor Avery's third major crisis concerned the very nature of the University, but that crisis was continuing. When Willa Cather wrote, "The world broke in two in 1922 or thereabouts," she might have been referring to the general disillusion of the Twenties, to Prohibition and its consequences, to Communist witch hunts, and to the gaudy extravagances of Gatsby's generation.[1] But she could have been referring to her alma mater. In 1920 the Board of Regents published a pamphlet entitled *The University – Program of Development 1920 and After* which spelled out the requirements of a growing institution: an expanded campus, new buildings, financial security. It said nothing of goals or missions, nor did it define the nature of the University, which it simply stated was "of the people, by the people and for the people."

Unhappily, by the time the booklet was distributed, Nebraska had come upon hard times. Farm prices fell sharply after the war, and the agricultural economy was troubled. In 1921 Governor McKelvie asked for a substantial reduction in spending; in 1922 Charles W. Bryan won the governorship by campaigning against state expenditures, recommending that the state stand pat and take no risks. In 1923 the University's budget came under scrutiny by the legislature, which cut it even more than either the incumbent or the newly elected governor had proposed. In 1924 the University was forced to defend itself by asserting that the ratio of students to teachers was eighteen to one in Nebraska, compared with thirteen to one in twenty-three other state universities, and that the average cost per student in Nebraska was $159.32, compared with $281.44 at twenty-five other state universities.[2] Total enrollment rose from 4,500 in 1915 to 7,000 in 1920 to nearly 12,000 in 1927, but state allowances did not rise proportionately. On campus, competition for limited funds was keen, a competition which reduced a sense of community already battered by the internecine anti-German strife. Salary inequities were perceived to be general, faculty turnover was great, and institutional pride was challenged.

The egalitarian nature of higher education was also challenged. In 1923 for the first time students began to pay tuition in addition to minor fees. Though the cost was only one dollar per credit hour for most courses – two dollars for science and special subjects, three to five dollars for professional colleges – the die was cast: the ideal of free higher education supported for the public good was lost. Neighboring public universities, even land-grant colleges, had higher tuition than Nebraska. "Most of the large institutions of the east have a schedule of fees that amount to $6.00 to $10.00 per credit hour," Avery wrote in 1923; "the matter of fees, dues and tuition for Nebraska students is left entirely in the hands of the regents."[3] He raised no question of principle. Five years later, apparently perceiving that tuition disadvantaged some persons for whom a land-grant institution exists, the regents established one hundred tuition scholarships for undergraduates, but by 1928 more than 11,000 students were enrolled, so the scholarships were more symbolic than substantial. In spite of all this, John Hicks, the distinguished American historian who came to the University in 1923, could write later, "The University of Nebraska certainly was not Oxford, and it had many faults, but it carried the brightest torch for learning to be found anywhere between the Missouri River and the Pacific Coast."[4]

With the retirement of founding stalwarts the staff was changing. When Charles Bessey suddenly died in 1916 at age seventy, he left a gap that was impossible to fill; and though his protégé, R. J. Pool, was a man of intelligence and character, he did not have Bessey's authority. Periodically faculty and others talked of bringing in a scholar of national stature to strengthen the study of plant sciences, but nobody was hired. Notable work was continued by such persons as John E. Weaver in ecology, but no one had Bessey's eminence. The other great intellectual leader of the University in the first half century of its existence was George E. Howard. When he returned to Nebraska from Stanford, he brought fame to it through his massive three-volume history of matrimonial institutions (1904); it remains to this day a study to be reckoned with. In 1918 he went into partial retirement and spent half his year in California. Through him Hutton Webster had come to the campus in 1909. His books on primitive societies attracted international attention. An energetic and attractive man, he gathered some of the best graduate students about him, but he left teaching in 1929. He eventually made a fortune publishing textbooks and preparing classroom materials like maps.

Lucius A. Sherman, who had been head of the Department of English since the Eighties and dean of the Graduate School since Edgren's departure for the Nobel Institute in 1901, was seventy-three in 1920 and reluctant to relinquish authority. Where Edgren had aggressively encouraged graduate study, Sherman was permissive. He saw the University as offering master's and a few doctor's degrees, if anybody wanted them, but he did not promote the graduate program. In spite of faculty restlessness, Avery allowed Sherman to stay on as dean until he was seventy-nine; he did not finally retire from the chair of English until he was eighty-two, a rather pathetic old man clinging to outmoded ways. In spite of his pseudoscientific method of criticism, Sherman was in fact sensitive to the arts. One of his students remembered for many years how the old man, in reading *King Lear* to a class, became so overcome by the drama that he lost control of his emotions. Seeing him sitting there quietly weeping over Cordelia's reconciliation with her aged father —

Lear: *. . . your sisters*
    Have (as I remember) done me wrong.
    You have some cause, they have not.
Cordelia: *No cause, no cause. (VI.vii.74)* —

the students quietly closed their notebooks and left him in his tears.

Other stalwarts on the campus were also withdrawing. Through the years Laurence Fossler, professor of German, had been spokesman for worthy causes. A serious scholar and splendid teacher, a protégé of the great Edgren, he saw his relationship to students rather as that of pater familias. Wartime anti-German sentiments and gathering age restricted his authority after 1920. Clara Conklin, another student of Edgren's, head of romance languages since 1901, chaired the Department of Modern Languages when German was absorbed into it, but she was perceived as old-fashioned by 1920. In the Twenties the University community contained a number of prominent women, several among the strongest members of the staff: Hattie Plum Williams in sociology, Louise Pound in philology, H. Alice Howell in drama, Carrie Belle Raymond in music, Laura B. Pfeiffer in history, Margaret Fedde in home economics, and Mabel Lee in physical education. In 1926 M. M. Fogg, who had turned the whole state into a debating conference, suddenly died and was replaced by H. Adelbert White. Under him debating quickly disappeared. Perhaps it had run its course, but its discontinuance was a loss to the University and the intellectual life of the state. Journalism, which Fogg had promoted from a department into a school, was allowed to languish under Gayle Walker, a young assistant professor, a good teacher but with few academic qualifications. Avery was highly selective in the departments he supported.

Some physical sciences fared better than the biological sciences. The physics department, having no research leaders, saw itself almost exclusively as a service unit; but the chemistry department, Avery's home department, became a leader in research. Benton Dales, who was made acting head of chemistry when Avery became chancellor in 1909, was the grandson of the first chancellor and son of J. Stuart Dales, the longtime secretary of the Board of Regents. When he got an offer from industry, Avery allowed him to leave, which he did, bitterly. Avery appointed F. W. Upson to the chair. After taking his Ph.D. at the University of Chicago in 1910, by then a much more distinguished degree than a German Ph.D., Upson in 1918 became head of the combined departments of chemistry and agricultural chemistry. For the next generation he developed a strong cadre of excellent scientists, encouraging close cooperation between departments on the two campuses, a cooperation not always matched in the plant science departments, where competition was sometimes openly hostile.[5]

Upson had local commitments. He was married to a granddaughter of the second chancellor, Edmund Fairfield, and his sister-in-law, Kate Field, served in the registrar's office all her life. In 1929 he became dean of the Graduate School. Like Howard, Bessey, the Pounds, Fossler, and several others, he combined local loyalties with professional responsibility. Unfortunately, he retired in 1939 because of failing health, and both he and his wife died in 1942, only in their fifties. For twenty years he had tried to advance the academic standards of the University.

ᏜᏗ Hartley Burr Alexander

The intellectual center of the campus from 1910 until 1925 was Hartley Burr Alexander, who, like Bessey and Howard, combined profound scholarship with piety; that is, reverent devotion to their native soil, even like Aeneas. He was one of the most remarkable persons the University had ever produced, proficient in half a dozen disparate fields of inquiry. He and Chancellor Avery were a sharp contrast and perhaps did not understand one another. Where Avery was pragmatic, a nuts-and-bolts administrator, an instinctive politician, Alexander was a visionary. The son of a Methodist minister, he never lost his evangelical fervor. His moods of despondency, marked from undergraduate days, were the result of the failure of the world to live up to his high hopes, his friends said. At the University as an undergraduate he had studied with H. K. Wolfe, and whereas Wolfe was essentially an empiricist and Alexander an idealist, Wolfe provided him an intellectual center. From Nebraska he went to the University of

Pennsylvania on a fellowship and then to Columbia to take his Ph.D. in 1901 in metaphysics. He returned to the University in 1908, invited by Chancellor Andrews independently of the Department of Philosophy, upon the recommendation of Alvin Johnson, Alexander's undergraduate friend, another native son who returned, if only briefly.

Alexander was a poet in a fashion now outgrown, an essayist, and a philosopher; he was also an anthropologist, first of the North American Indians, later of Latin American Indians as well. In 1925 he lectured at the Sorbonne, in French, on Indian art and mythology. His most original undertaking was his invention of a new profession. In 1922 the architect Bertram Goodhue commissioned him to supervise the decorative patterns and symbolism of the new Nebraska capitol; Goodhue and Alexander agreed that a building should be read, like a book. Working with sculptors, mosaicists, painters, and other artists, he prepared the iconography and inscriptional scheme for the building. Their integration was so brilliant that Alexander was subsequently asked to program the iconography of Rockefeller Center in New York, the Century of Progress Exposition in Chicago, the public library in Los Angeles, and professional buildings around the country. For this work he was made an honorary member of the American Institute of Architects.

Alexander had large ambitions. Working with musicians, actors, and dancers, between 1915 and 1920 he wrote a series of public pageants celebrating the history and ideals of his native prairie. They were presented to large crowds in Lincoln and Omaha. He was eager through them to develop a sense of regional culture, what he called the soul of the country. In 1918 and 1919 he published *Letters to Teachers*, a series of writings as relevant to the issues of public education in later generations as they were to his own.[6] He saw teaching as less a science than an art, less a technique than a rhetoric for bringing students into participation in culture. On his home campus he founded societies to support the ideals of scholarship, leadership, and character. A generalist in a world increasingly specialized, he spoke for liberal education, for the education of free persons. Extremely sensitive, he never recovered from his daughter's death in childhood of typhoid fever.

❧ Teachers College and Professionalism

Within the University the conflict between the College of Arts and Sciences, home of generalists, and the emerging professional colleges was sharp. During the Twenties, Arts and Sciences saw a steady decline in enrollment. In 1920 more than half the students attending the University were in that college, but by the end of the decade hardly more than a fourth were generalists. Students increasingly sought accreditation in career-oriented programs. They and their parents believed that college training should prepare young people for good jobs and offer "contacts." A leading historian of American colleges from 1915 to 1940 observes: "After World War I, institutions of higher learning were no longer content to educate; they now set out to train, accredit, and impart social status to their students."[7] The conservatives on the faculty saw the University becoming what they called a trade school, whereas they wanted it to be a place of learning preparing students for life, not just for jobs. They thought students who achieved mathematical literacy and rational competence through study of the classics could apply themselves in any profession. Willa Cather wrote in 1923, "The men who control [the University's] destiny, the regents and the lawmakers, wish their sons and daughters to study machines, mercantile processes, 'the principles of business'; everything that has to do with the game of getting on in the world – and nothing else. The classics, the humanities, are having their dark hour. They are in eclipse. Studies that develop taste and enrich personality are not encouraged." Cather continued with a bit more optimism than was usual for her: "One may venture to hope that the children, or the grandchildren . . . will go back to the old sources of culture and wisdom – not as a duty, but with burning desire."[8]

The establishment of the College of Business Administration and the Teachers College illustrates the intellectual conflicts of the time. When J. E. LeRossignol, professor of economics, organized the School of Commerce within the College of Arts and Sciences in 1913, he candidly acknowledged that it provided vocational training designed "to give the students a more direct preparation for business life," but he wanted it to be combined with "a

good all-round education" and he proposed no significant shift from Arts and Sciences degree requirements. He asked that instruction in his school be primarily concerned with the *why* rather than the *how* of business, confident that there could be no sound practice not based on sound theory.[9] In 1919 the school became the College of Business Administration, enrollment having grown from 40 to more than 400; and by 1926 the college was divided into three departments: economics, business organization, and business research. By then its enrollment was about 1,000.

Dean LeRossignol was himself a cultivated gentleman. Educated in Canada and Germany – he was not a French Canadian in spite of his French name – he was first interested in philosophy and psychology and only came to economics late. He was a prolific writer of textbooks and specialized studies and was an early student of Communism. On the side he wrote stories about Quebec, where he often vacationed. Aristocratic in bearing, with a clipped mustache and round, shell-rimmed glasses, he was always treated with extreme deference in Lincoln; elsewhere he was elected to presidencies of national organizations. He remained dean until age seventy-five, in 1941, alert, witty, social, and impressive. Though the "Biz Ad" college was sometimes treated with a certain disdain by professors of English and history, it did not meet the hostility that came to Teachers College. This tolerance was due in part to the dean's dignity, but more to the fact that its influence was directed at business, not at the total educational system.

The establishment of an independent college of education was extremely controversial. Though the Teachers College had been established in 1909, its degrees were granted through the College of Arts and Sciences. Ambitious Teachers College personnel and public school administrators resented what they regarded as a restriction on their professional integrity and continually agitated for total autonomy. They thought of themselves as professional and, as such, answerable to no other group. This separatist movement reflected the mentality of the Columbia University Teachers College.

The reluctance of the College of Arts and Sciences to encourage or even allow autonomy was seen by schoolmen, as they called themselves, to be less a matter of principle than a power play. The College of Arts and Sciences wanted to control budget and courses, they said, for personal advantage. The traditionalists saw the expansion of teacher training as empire building, asserting that pedagogy did not require administrative proliferation. In 1909 the Department of Education consisted of four professors. By 1917 the collegiate school had eight departments, some with only one or two teachers; an independent Department of Educational Psychology duplicating a preexisting Department of Philosophy and Psychology; and its own graduate school. By 1920 subject-matter professors were progressively deprived of methods courses. Schoolmen both on and off the campus demanded that they alone, independently of subject-matter professors, should determine standards for teacher certification. R. W. Moritz, superintendent of schools at Seward, Nebraska, was prominent in this agitation. Subject-matter teachers, led by Philo M. Buck Jr., who had been named dean of the College of Arts and Sciences upon the death of Ellery Davis in 1918, resisted. The issue — what is the relationship of content to delivery, of subject matter to presentation? — was not negligible, and its resolution shaped public education for generations to come.

By 1920 tempers were high and perhaps Buck and his associates were sometimes less than courteous, but they in turn thought themselves insulted in public forums by the educationists. They resented the way the educationists, as they sometimes referred to them, had made a political issue of what the generalists defined as a fundamental academic matter. In the spring of 1921, under the leadership of Regent Harry Landis of Seward, the Teachers College obtained autonomy. Without guidance from the chancellor, the Board of Regents declared on 29 March that the Teachers College was professional in the same way as the colleges of agriculture, engineering, business administration, and pharmacy, and made its faculty alone responsible for teachers' degrees.[10] The subject-matter professors felt betrayed, their authority over academic matters arbitrarily usurped by laymen, the Board of Regents. Philo Buck was relieved of his deanship and put in the Department of Comparative Literature, but within a year he accepted a post at the University of Wisconsin, where he had a distinguished career. The faculty and students were sharply divided into pro– and anti–Teachers College groups.

⁂ Alexander's Proposals

The traditionalists were hostile to the Teachers College for at least three reasons. First, subject-matter professors thought that content was at least as important as technique in teaching and ought to be defined by subject-matter specialists, not specialists in teaching methods. Second, education courses were perceived as insufficiently rigorous; they were held in general disrespect by the professors of mathematics, history, literature, and the sciences. Third, the proliferation of departments in the new college seemed to draw resources from the total University budget. To pay for these departments, Teachers College robbed Peter to pay Paul, it was said.

Hartley Alexander wrote the regents protesting the direction the University was taking. He asked that the business affairs of the University be separated from the academic affairs and that academic considerations determine budgets, and he requested that a dean of students, or provost, be appointed to ensure uniform academic standards throughout the University. The total faculty, he thought, ought to have a larger share in making appointments; he saw the intellectual life of the University sliding into mediocrity, a great share of which he blamed on inferior appointments in Teachers College.[11]

Alexander's ideas did not get a serious hearing; perhaps he was quixotic in thinking that they might. The Board of Regents and the chancellor did not seem to understand what he, his associates, and his students were driving at. Instead of an academic dean-provost, in 1921 they named Fred J. Dawson, the football coach, as dean of men, presumably to get his salary high enough to bring him to Nebraska. When he proved spectacularly unsuccessful, he was replaced by Carl C. Engberg, Avery's executive dean and jack-of-all-work. No provision was made for supervision of academic programs outside college boundaries; and in 1927 T. J. Thompson, an associate professor of chemistry, was named dean of men. Though he was an honorable man in a difficult job, he was hardly the intellectual leader that Alexander and others had hoped would find a place in the chancellor's cabinet. Thompson saw extended service on both the athletic board and curriculum committees. He tried to foster scholarship and even established an annual Honors Day Convocation in 1928. L. E. Gunderson was named financial secretary in 1924 and remained in this and allied posts for many years. He had no academic qualifications. In short, Avery had no academic advisers in his office.

Inspired by Alexander's questions, students considered the general purposes of education. In the spring of 1926 a committee of students headed by a remarkable undergraduate named Douglass Orr produced a pamphlet examining the nature of the University curriculum. They had been encouraged by Dean Herman James of the College of Arts and Sciences, Buck's successor, and had held a series of weekly meetings to gather opinions. They concluded that "students who desire to have and ought to have a liberal education wander purposeless and unaided in the college." This was reported in the *Daily Nebraskan*, 5 May 1926. Orr's pamphlet – published by the University for fifteen cents – newspaper articles, and oral presentations to faculty and students caused considerable controversy but little action. The following spring, James told the local chapter of Phi Beta Kappa that it and his college were doomed "to extinction and oblivion" because of the pressure from professional schools; and the 16 November 1927 newspaper reported that educational issues remained common subjects of discussion; that there was a general "feeling that higher education is beneficial but [students were] utterly unable to see its connection to life in the world outside the college." The editor concluded, "It is the University which is falling down." C. H. Oldfather, professor of ancient history, chaired a committee to set up an honors program which would follow the tradition of what they regarded as a historic arts college, but the University community generally failed to respond to the serious questions raised in these years. The fundamental responsibilities of a large public university were not addressed.

Alexander had been profoundly discouraged with what he saw his alma mater becoming; and in 1926, after long discussions with his colleagues and students, he worked out a plan for reorganization of instruction in the College of Arts and Sciences. Leaving this program in the hands of an elected committee, he went to teach at the University of Wisconsin for the spring semester, 1927. In his absence his reforms languished. The leader was away, Chancellor Avery was ailing and unsympathetic, and the faculty was demoralized and factional because of narrow budgets. At Wisconsin, Alexander saw what he thought was missing in Nebraska: "It is a University where *ideas* are the interest," he wrote to his friend and protégé Professor Orin Stepanek. "In the University the 'Letters and Sciences' dominates everything (there is *no* T.C! only a 'Department of Ed.') and there are 'Houses' for all the languages – English, French, Spanish, German, etc. – where nothing else is spoken and letters are the concern. [Philo] Buck tells me that as yet he has discovered no faculty 'cliques' or gossip circles."[12] He talked to Alexander Meiklejohn, academic statesman and currently professor of philosophy, who, "delightful as ever," considered the schemes that Alexander and his friends had worked out in Nebraska for Meiklejohn's soon-to-be-opened Experimental College. But at home in Nebraska the "small body of men and women (about twenty, I should say) of the [intellectually committed] faculty [were] swamped by accessions to the faculty of people of meager understanding, incapable of appreciating university ideals."[13]

Nothing came of Alexander's plans and hopes. In May 1925, Chancellor Avery had announced his forthcoming resignation – to be effective in August of 1928 – and it had seemed that at last, with the appointment of a new chief executive, changes might be possible. When in January 1927 Avery's health deteriorated and he gave up his post, Alexander hoped that a new chancellor could be brought in from outside the University and that he himself would be appointed graduate dean, empowered to make extensive changes. But the Board of Regents, long accustomed to Avery's caution, rejected his proposals for reorganization, saying: "It is the belief of the Board that it should have the counsel and know the wishes of the new Chancellor regarding these matters" before making any changes.[14] Alexander thereupon accepted an appointment at Scripps

College in California, a new women's college, where he had a chance to try out his ideas. In the spring of 1928 he resigned from the University of Nebraska. The chance for renovation was past, and Regent Harry Landis, now president of the board, was quoted in the press as saying that he was perfectly satisfied with things as they were. Landis was something of an eccentric. Regent from 1917 until 1929, he was elected state district judge in 1925. On the bench he smoked continuously and young lawyers learned that it was in their best interests to bring him boxes of cigars when they appeared in his court.

Alexander's departure caused controversy both on and off campus. It was widely recognized that he had devoted the greatest portion of his mature life to Nebraska. "I have had what to me has been a great dream of cultural life in the state of Nebraska, beautifying and enriching the state in every ideal way, with its center in the University," he wrote the president of the Board of Regents. "As the years have slipped by, I have seen the means for the realization of this wasting away season after season."[15] Perhaps he was naive in his expectations for his alma mater; perhaps he was insufficiently respectful of the politics necessary in public education. Perhaps he was a late spokesman for a frontier idealism. His departure was perceived everywhere, including by the *Omaha World-Herald,* as a vote of no confidence in the state and a killing blow to hopes for academic excellence in the next generation.

❧ *"The Culture of Aspiration"*

A "culture of aspiration" flourished in the Twenties, and Alexander was not alone in seeing that college life was becoming increasingly a search for social contacts at the expense of intellectual experience. To some degree the university had always been a channel of upward mobility, but after 1920 the pressure was increased. H. L. Mencken wrote about it. "Going to college has come to [be] a sort of social necessity," the satirist said in 1929. "It almost ranks with having a bathroom and keeping a car. . . . A learned degree, once a pearl of great price, has come to have no more value or significance that the ruby-studded insignia of the Elks."[16] At Nebraska as elsewhere, new students

sought the proper fraternity insignia and new Greek-letter societies appeared on campus. Before the war there had been a dozen fraternities on campus, but by the later Twenties there were more than thirty. The number of sororities nearly doubled also. Phi Kappa Psi built the first fraternity house in 1916, but after 1920 the campus was ringed round with private dormitories, all more splendid that anything seen here before. Earlier fraternities and sororities occupied big houses constructed as private residences, but these were perceived as no longer grand enough. Self-appointed panhellenic and interfraternity councils monitored the Greek-letter societies. They were closed groups, of course, and a strict hierarchy existed among them. A generation earlier the frontier ideal of egalitarian opportunity had challenged the hegemony of the fraternity systems, so much so that even Phi Beta Kappa was rejected by some as elitist. After 1920 the literary societies and subject-matter clubs, once an alternative to the fraternity system, became increasingly unfashionable. "Camaraderie, not book learning, was the ideal" at the state university, as it was at prestigious institutions like Princeton.[17]

The regents zoned the neighborhood around the campus to provide for these privately owned dormitories. Though they constantly discussed the need to build public residence halls for women, they ignored the living conditions of men. Of the various plans for the campus after 1920, the most elaborate was the Seymour Plan, designed by Regent George Seymour, president of the board. It specified where the fraternity and sorority houses might be constructed and laid out a pattern for all future classrooms, laboratories, and halls. Seymour was a banker, a graduate of Amherst College, who had come west to make his fortune, which he did. His hobbies were landscaping, architecture, and art; and during his six years on the board (1921–27) he developed the fullest building scheme the University had yet had. His daughter was married to Frank Latenser, a prominent Omaha architect. In the next ten years the campus grew pretty much as Seymour suggested.

Bess Streeter Aldrich in her novels gives some flavor of what undergraduate life was like in the Twenties. In *A*

White Bird Flying (1931) she describes rush week, the period before fall classes began when new students were selected by fraternities and sororities as prospective members. Laura, an entering freshman, "was herded to breakfasts and luncheons and dinners, to afternoon teas and evening parties. Some of the chapter houses were gorgeous in their furnishings. One or two were not quite finished so they stepped over lath and plaster in part of the rooms." The young freshman, who had been accompanied to rush week by her mother so she would be sure to pledge the right sorority, "could not quite understand the queer quality of the atmosphere. There was something about it she had never experienced before – something tense and important, as though everyone's welfare hung in the balance. Nerves seemed taut, manners strained. An exterior of convention seemed to cover something primitive that might at any moment break its leash and bound out. Girls she had never seen before put their arms around her. Many told her she was a darling. Some confided that, honestly, she was the keenest girl that had been in the house." Young men going through rush week had similar experiences, and Laura's young male friend was "miraculously" pledged to "the aristocratic house with the cathedral-like pillars." In the midst of all the confusion Laura's mother "happened to remember that Laura must go to the huge Coliseum to register for classes. It seemed a waste of time to Eloise [the mother] but after all, it was quite true that the studies must be given some thought also."

Very shortly Laura "received her first lesson in fraternal rivalry. Standing at the window of [her] room on third [floor], she asked guilelessly: 'Why are there so many cars all around the Gamma Zeta house?' to which [her roommate] said significantly: 'it's probably because there's a stop button there. There are *never* more cars around the Gamma house than around ours. Remember that.' "[18] Not all students engaged in these games, of course, but the pacesetters, the style makers, the campus politicians could not escape the pervasive tone set by these self-perpetuating groups, nor did they try. The University was a marriage market for girls, according to Laura's mother, and a job market for young men. Under adolescent campus gaiety, life was serious business. A University was more than

an educational institution: it had become an accrediting agency for a society yearning to be stratified.

✿ Football in the Twenties

Football was increasingly important in the Twenties. Bess Streeter Aldrich's Laura "attended ball games and sang lustily with twenty five thousand others: 'There Is No Place Like Nebraska' and, carried away by mass emotion, at the moment would have cheerfully bared her breast for a sacrificial pound of flesh if Nebraska, in the guise of Shylock, had demanded it." From early years, the fans and the regents asked for facilities worthy of their winning teams, and in 1919 the legislature passed a .75-mill building levy with the understanding that half would be used for erecting a gymnasium. In March 1920 the Board of Regents asked their architects to prepare plans for a gymnasium and stadium, the gym to cost about $500,000, the stadium half that much, but state funds were insufficient.

The stadium project had a certain urgency. Omaha fans had long wanted at least one of the Nebraska football games played in Omaha, but such off-campus games were an anathema to the Missouri Valley Conference. Kansas and Missouri did not want to play in Kansas City and Des Moines, away from their home campuses. After Nebraska played Oklahoma in Omaha in 1919, Nebraska, aspiring to greater competitions, withdrew from the conference without much regret on the part of the other members. Nebraska had long dominated the region. Two years later Nebraska returned to the conference, finding that going it alone was more difficult than anticipated.

In 1920, Vincent C. "Stub" Hascall, a popular former quarterback, returned to campus as alumni secretary. He and a distinguished committee began raising money for a stadium, but not until 1922, when Harold Holtz, another veteran, became alumni secretary, did serious solicitation get under way. In a very short time more than $300,000 was subscribed from all over the state; only Omaha was undersubscribed. Soldiers Memorial Stadium seemed ensured. No lending agency, however, was prepared to put up money with pledges alone as collateral. At this point George Holmes, then president of the First National Bank in Lincoln, offered to underwrite the debt personally. He was supported by other members of the Nebraska Athletic Building Association, which was made up of leading citizens of the city and state. The First Trust Company of Lincoln thereupon promptly issued bonds, which were retired on time because practically all the stadium pledges were paid up in full and gate receipts were steady despite the bad economic times of the Twenties. What was popularly referred to as "the O Street Gang" had rescued the University athletic program, at some personal risk.

In April 1923 ground was broken and that fall the first game was played in the new Memorial Stadium. Its inscriptions, prepared by Hartley Burr Alexander, were notable. On the southwest corner, Alexander set these words:

Not the victory but the action
Not the goal but the game
In the deed the glory

The high point of the first season was surely Nebraska's defeat of Notre Dame (14–7). The ten-year series between Nebraska and Notre Dame – 1915–25 – came to an abrupt and unexplained conclusion in 1926. Nebraska had won five of the eleven games and tied one, but after his defeat in 1925 (17–0) Knute Rockne called off further contests though the date for the 1926 game had already been set. No reason for the break was ever given.

The Nebraska athletic program was conducted with considerable integrity. R. D. Scott, the faculty representative on the governing athletic board, was famous for his insistence that football players be given no special license in or out of the classroom, and he guarded the general reputation of the football program. When L. A. Sherman finally retired as head of the English department in 1929, Scott was proposed by some of the regents as his successor, but the department rebelled. The regents thereupon made him director of freshman English by way of compensation. Diligent and inflexible, he was fond of complaining that too many students "did not know a noun from a sea lion," and he habitually referred to students, athletes and ordinary students alike, as "these monkeys."[19] He was at least as devoted to football as he was to English.

Once Memorial Stadium was underway, John K. Sel-

leck, who had been named business agent for athletics and student activities in 1922, suggested that an assembly hall suitable for indoor sporting events and student convocations be constructed. Again George Holmes and his friends undertook the necessary loans, and in May 1925 the Board of Regents approved construction of the Coliseum. The first commencement was held in it on 5 June 1926. On the agricultural campus a new gymnasium built with state funding was opened in 1927. No bonding was necessary for it.

✒ Physical Education for Women

When Mabel Lee was brought to the campus in 1924 by Chancellor Avery, she noted that "football seemed to be the tail that wagged the dog at Nebraska."[20] In fact, from early times there had been a considerable interest in physical education that extended beyond competitive sports. Chancellor Canfield had set up a department of physical education in 1891 (Grant Memorial Hall having been completed in 1888), with Robert Clark, M.D., a Phi Beta Kappa from Canfield's alma mater, Williams College, as its head. By 1898 W. W. Hastings, M.D., Clark's successor, had established a special course in physical education, making Nebraska the first state university in the nation to offer such a major. Urged by Lt. John J. Pershing, Canfield in 1894 appointed Anne Barr, a young Lincoln woman, as class leader of physical education for women; and when Dr. Hastings unexpectedly resigned in December 1900, Miss Barr, now director of the women's gymnasium, was made acting head of physical education for both men and women. She held that post until R. G. Clapp, M.D., was appointed in 1902. After 1903, when they were married, the two dominated physical education in Nebraska for the next twenty years. Clapp, a formidable athlete from Yale, at various times coached basketball, track, gymnastics, fencing, and wrestling, but not football.

The unique liaison that developed between the men's and women's departments caused considerable controversy; and when Mrs. Clapp finally resigned in 1908 – her first daughter was born the next year – Dr. Clapp in effect directed women's activities. By 1918 the women's department had deteriorated so seriously that the American Physical Education Association did not even recognize its existence. Like the men's department, the women's department had become increasingly involved in competitive sports. Once basketball was introduced in 1898, both intramural and extramural games were scheduled, with rules for women's basketball devised by Louise Pound of the Department of English. She managed the women's teams, but because it was considered improper for women to appear publicly in gymnasium costume before mixed crowds, men were excluded from "demonstrations" even when the women were breaking records. By the time Mabel Lee came to the campus, enthusiasm for outdoor as well as indoor sports had increased until Mrs. Clapp could report in the 1924 *Cornhusker* that nearly all undergraduate women took some part in them.

But games were not training, and serious students over the years asked that the administration reorganize the department and bring in someone with professional competence. Chancellor Avery found Mabel Lee. Mabel Lee was no ordinary woman, and all who met her soon understood that. After graduating from Coe College in Iowa, she had two years of professional training at the Boston Normal School of Gymnastics and at Wellesley College. By the time she came to Nebraska she had directed women's physical education at Coe College, Oregon Agricultural College, and Beloit College. Beautiful, she was aware that women in physical education were often assumed to be mannish. So when she came to Lincoln to discuss the job, she wore her "prettiest hat – the lavender braid one lined in sky blue silk and trimmed by a large pink rose which broke the austerity of [her] pearl gray tailored suit and [her] premature gray hair."[21] It was the same hat and suit she had worn the year before when addressing a mixed audience at the University of Chicago on intercollegiate athletics. Beneath the pink rose and lavender braid were an iron will and steel determination.

Accepting the post as director of physical education for women with the rank of professor and the excellent salary of $3,500, Mabel Lee demanded full autonomy. Bringing in an assistant from Beloit College, Mary Wheeler, she had within five years expanded her staff and reduced the service classes from 120 to 30 pupils per section. She modernized gym costumes and varied course offerings. In place of selecting gifted women for competitive games, she promoted sports for all women. As soon as the Coliseum was finished in 1926, all of Grant Memorial Hall became her province, to the astonishment of Dr. Clapp. On campus she was received by the women students with the greatest enthusiasm. Off campus she was a national figure and in 1931 became the first woman president of the American Physical Education Association. She worked such long hours that she did not have Saturday afternoons free for football games, she said.

She was not without her critics, the chief of whom was Louise Pound, another ambitious woman, who in due course became the first woman president of *her* professional society, the Modern Language Association. When Miss Lee was appointed to the staff, Miss Pound thought she had found an ally. (The two women were always addressed as Miss Lee and Miss Pound; that is how they wanted it). Herself a formidable athlete who from earliest years engaged in competitive sports, Miss Pound wanted to best the men at their own games and became the first woman admitted to the Nebraska Sports Hall of Fame, an honor she particularly prized. Fiercely competitive, she thought that Miss Lee's professional view of physical education took all the spirit out of it. When the Women's Athletic Association asserted, "We play for the fun of the game" rather than for winning, Miss Pound responded, in disgust, "Sissies, all sissies! Bah."[22]

Miss Pound and Miss Lee were not friends, and though both achieved professional eminence, they were not at all alike. Where Mabel Lee found Lincoln full of snobs and seekers of special privilege, Louise Pound belonged to the right clubs and founded new ones. Mabel Lee wanted to earn a place in a male-dominated world; Louise Pound was an antagonist who wanted to defeat the men. Chancellors, deans, and chairmen all found Miss Pound difficult. One of them said her endless agitation took ten years off his life, and the women whom she sponsored were not advanced because deans were afraid they would become as difficult as Louise Pound. Mabel Lee also refused to bow to arbitrary administrative authority. She demanded her rights, and got them, and her protégés did not suffer. Both women developed coteries, and Miss Lee thought that Miss Pound's friends harassed her even into her retirement. Chancellor Avery supported Mabel Lee. He did not cross Louise Pound, aware that the Pounds, who had known him since undergraduate days, had powerful friends. His resignation in 1926 did not displease Louise Pound, but his departure made Mabel Lee apprehensive. Both women flourished. They were made of stern stuff.

❧ Chancellor Avery's Resignation

On 8 May 1925, Samuel Avery resigned from the chancellorship as of 1928, but by January 1927, his health broken, he took a leave of absence and he retired that summer. He was sixty-two years old. In office since 1909, he had avoided taking firm stands on controversial issues. For all his political shrewdness he had gathered many critics on and off campus. After 1920, in a time of growing economic austerity, he could conceive of no new ways to direct or organize or shape his University. He bent with the wind, and his University bent with him. Addressing alumni and faculty groups in February 1922, he said, "I can imagine Dr. Benton speaking of the Infant University, Dr. Fairfield on the Growing University, Dr. Canfield on the Booming University, Dr. MacLean on the Great University, Dr. Andrews on the Modern University. . . . But all of these periods are passed and there seems to be nothing now to do but to talk about the University in Retrenchment."[23] Twenty years later Chancellor Gustavson gave the state a new view of what the University could be, but from 1921 until 1945 it was on the defensive. The "Golden Years" – 1891 until 1917 – were followed by a long generation of economic and academic depression.

7. Depression: 1927–1938

❧ *Dean Edgar A. Burnett*

When Samuel Avery asked for immediate leave in January 1927, the regents had an opportunity for profitable reorganization; instead they turned automatically to the senior dean, L. A. Sherman, as interim chancellor. Quickly recognizing that this eighty-year-old man was not up even to temporary responsibilities, they went next to Edgar A. Burnett, dean of the College of Agriculture and director of the agricultural experiment station. Dean Herman James might have been a better appointment. Highly educated, with a law degree from the University of Chicago and a Ph.D. in government from Columbia, and son of a university president, James had thought seriously about the kinds of educational problems confronting the University of Nebraska. He had puzzled over how academic standards could be reconciled with popular education, how the good could be kept from destroying the best. Young and ambitious, he would become president of the University of South Dakota within two years and go on to greater things. But this Board of Regents turned to Burnett, who was like what they were used to.

Burnett and Avery were of an age: both were born in 1865, both were practical men, and neither was given to speculation. Both were scientists, Avery a professor of chemistry and Burnett a professor of animal husbandry. Both had long been associated with the University of Nebraska. Burnett in twenty-five years had built the College of Agriculture from an adjunct to the city campus into a flourishing, independent unit of some 750 students, with its own staff and ten large buildings. Under his guidance a comprehensive system of experiment stations was developed across Nebraska, first at North Platte and then at Mitchell and Valentine. Off-campus activities were carried to the state through agricultural extension. He used federal funds for staffing of agricultural research and extension services. By 1929 this amounted to about half a million dollars, which, combined with state funds, made the College of Agriculture a major force in the state. Like Avery, he was shrewd, and like him, politic.

Burnett was a man of authority; one did not cross him easily. He wore octagonal glasses and countenanced no funny business. "Did he have a sense of humor?" his neighbor was asked. "I can't say that he did," the neighbor replied; "he rarely smiled." Mabel Lee said that he was "not capable of being demonstrative."[1] As dean and director, he disliked controversy, professional, scientific, and certainly social; and his college decisions were handed down, not discussed. This habit of administrative authority became so firmly established in his college that it long outlasted him. As his college became increasingly separated from the rest of the University, its tone became increasingly pragmatic. Fundamental research continued to be conducted, but with little encouragement from him and sometimes without his knowledge. He thought of himself as a man of this world.

Burnett was constantly concerned with public appearances because he did not challenge the prejudices of the agricultural interests, which he saw as his constituency. H. O. Werner, a rather outspoken horticulturalist and a man of great character, remembered that Burnett tried to limit research programs to those directly requested by farmers.[2] T. A. Kiesselbach, one of the University's most distinguished research agronomists, remembered his response to some of Kiesselbach's crop-improvement experiments. Early one morning before Kiesselbach's research conclusions were to be reported to an agricultural group,

Burnett "called Professor [Erwin] Hopt and me to his office. He told us politely and calmly, 'You are both young men. What you should do is to find out what the people want to hear, and then tell them that.' " Some years later when Kiesselbach and his research team were investigating hybrid corn breeding, investigations which made them world-famous, they covered ear shoots and tassels with paper bags. "One year the Dean advised me that farmers do not cover their corn with paper bags, and that in the future we should keep this part of our experimental work somewhere back on the farm out of sight, to avoid making a bad impression."[3]

⤷ Burnett as Chancellor

When E. A. Burnett was appointed acting chancellor in January 1927, few persons on or off campus thought he was a candidate for the post permanently. For one thing, he was already sixty-two, and for another he had shown little if any interest in education generally. From the first he surprised everyone with his determined vigor. In March he entertained some 400 legislators and their wives at a dinner in the new student activities building on the ag campus. It was a splendid affair, lighted by candles on long tables, the food produced by the horticulture departments and served by young women from home economics. Music was provided by the University glee club, and short addresses were made by University officials and regents. This entertainment was so successful that it was repeated biennially, always with more than 400 guests.

From the start Burnett spelled out the University's financial needs, first at the dinner and then in pamphlets and University bulletins. These fact-filled statements, prepared by Robert Crawford, who had been his editorial assistant when he was dean, were widely distributed. They specified both the University's cultural and agricultural contributions to the state and their costs. They answered questions concerning the social life on campus and discussed the instructional work in the classrooms. Burnett and Crawford cooperated with newspaper editors, inviting them to the campus, providing them with feature stories, giving them a who's who of the University staff.

Burnett set up a speakers' bureau for the state. He actively lobbied for the University. In earlier generations the legislators had resented lobbying by state agencies, maintaining that such efforts were self-serving, as indeed they were, but a new attitude was developing in the Twenties. Burnett seemed to understand PR, Public Relations.

During his "acting" year, the campus newspaper reported on 28 April that identifying a new chancellor was a popular indoor sport, and that it was widely recognized that there were two kinds of possibilities: the administrator who was popular with the state and the legislature, and the educational leader who inspired faculty and students. Hartley Burr Alexander's discussions of the previous years had not been forgotten. By December 1927 the regents gave up their search and turned to Burnett. Regent Harry Landis, now president of the board, had opposed his initial appointment but announced that he had become impressed by Burnett's "fair and efficient administrative ability."[4] Though George Condra, the extremely well known and ambitious director of the Conservation and Soil Survey, was suggested for the post, the regents, on a motion by Regent Earl Cline at their 3 March 1928 meeting, unanimously selected Burnett for the period 1 March 1928 through 30 June 1929 on a kind of contract. It turned out to be a permanent appointment.

Burnett's appointment was received unenthusiastically by both faculty and students. It was announced, ironically, at the same meeting at which the board accepted Alexander's resignation, and it signaled the board's caution. The *Daily Nebraskan* on 7 March 1928 quoted the *Omaha World-Herald*: "Scholarship? Leadership? Idealism? Inspiration? No. Appropriation is the magic word . . . [Alexander's departure] is a loss for which neither larger appropriations nor a victory over Army next fall can begin to compensate." Burnett wrote: "The election of a new chancellor in an educational institution always raises the question of whether or not there are to be radical changes in university policy. At the present time we do not contemplate anything which will be of that nature."[5]

As during his "acting" year, Burnett spoke often of staff and faculty needs. He noted, for example, that the teaching load in the previous decade had increased 61 percent.

"What kind of professor would you like to have teach your children?" he asked the alumni. "Great teachers are indeed the most precious asset of a university." He noted repeatedly that between 1925 and 1929 the University had lost by resignation 17 full professors, 9 associate professors, 13 assistant professors, and 85 instructors out of a total of 243 faculty members.[6] His campaign seems to have paid off. The University budget in 1929 was the best in six years, though still far below the needs of the growing institution. By 1930 Burnett had gathered a small administrative group about him consisting of Robert Crawford, his public relations adviser; T. J. Thompson, the dean of students; and L. E. Gunderson, the financial officer. None of this "kitchen cabinet" were scholars, perhaps not even intellectuals, and the deans and professors felt shut out of legitimate academic decisions. Harry Cunningham, the able and colorful founder of the Department of Architecture in 1930, wrote to H. B. Alexander, "The Chancellor is a fine gentleman and would do nobly if he had not that detestable 'Kitchen Cabinet.'" He then quoted John Hicks, James's successor as dean of the College of Arts and Sciences and a historian who made his reputation with his book *The Populist Revolt* (1931) and subsequently became a national figure. "The dear Chancellor is a good judge of cattle, and sometimes of facts (when he knows them), but he is a poor judge of jack-asses."[7]

🙐 Student Life

As expected, Burnett usually left student affairs in the hands of Dean T. J. Thompson and Dean Amanda Heppner. When Thompson was appointed, he was given strict instructions by the regents to crack down on campus drinking, for throughout the Twenties there had been much talk of disorderly conduct on campus, only some of it justified. Thompson accepted this responsibility but tried to give students the benefit of doubts. He was not really unpopular. Dean Heppner was not flexible. She ruled, for example, that all University dances should end by 11:30 so that women could be in their houses by 12:15. When the student council asked to extend the hours to 12:30, she refused to allow it. She must have thought un-

dergraduate males were predatory. The chancellor remained above student controversies and students rarely saw him. The official chancellor's residence next door to Ellen Smith Hall on R Street was turned into an infirmary. Burnett elected to live in his own house near the ag campus.

The essentially cautious temper of the Board of Regents and the administration can be judged, perhaps, from actions taken by the regents in October 1929. At this meeting they allotted $400 to provide clubrooms for "colored students" under the supervision of the pastor of the Quinn Chapel, an African Methodist Episcopal church. Four hundred dollars was not an inconsiderable sum. John Adams, the pastor, was "to provide a suitable place for social purposes for colored students on all occasions and special programs for colored students on nights of All-University parties. This action [was] intended to forestall any demand on the part of colored students to participate in general student social affairs."[8] The YMCA, the YWCA, and various church groups had discussed "Negro rights" for years, but Jim Crow persisted in Nebraska. Although Chancellor Avery had cautiously denounced the Ku Klux Klan in 1921, the University administration seemed to want to establish "separate but equal" facilities and their policy apparently got no public reaction.

On 26 March 1930 an anonymous mimeographed scandal sheet headed "With Fire and Sword" appeared on campus. Its adolescent attacks should have been amusing, but they seem to have drawn blood. The paper begins by lambasting THE ADMINISTRATION as "a paternalistic, reactionary and buckpassing body, hide-bound and viciously arbitrary in spirit, and grossly inefficient in operation." The self-styled GADFLIES continue: "It personifies petty mindedness in its magnification of the insignificant." They then take after campus organizations and persons but end by asserting their support of "the bulk of the instructional staff" and lamenting the departure of the illustrious Hartley Burr Alexander, now two years gone. On 21 April a second issue of "With Fire and Sword" appeared on campus doorsteps. Dedicated as "a token of disesteem and a promise of our future antagonism" to the administration and major campus organizations, it asks questions about the profits on the previous year's senior announcements: "graft smells unto high heaven." The authors pillory three professors famously past their prime but praise others: Norman Hill in political science, O. K. Bouwsma and William Werkmeister in philosophy, Glenn Gray and C. H. Oldfather in history, L. C. Wimberly and R. W. Frantz in English, Cliff Hamilton in chemistry — a perceptive list of able young men. Though high-spirited, the authors were serious too: "Did you ever notice the number of Buick automobiles that are owned by the University big guns? And then did you know that Purchasing Agent Seaton won a gold watch in a contest among Nebraska Buick Salesmen?"[9]

Though miffed, the administration did nothing; but when a year later, on 30 April 1931, Volume II appeared, the chancellor took action. In its adolescent fashion this issue maligned several faculty members, but, more important, it complained of the incompetence of the legislators. The legislators concerned themselves with such absurdly childish matters as student smoking instead of attending to essential matters like buildings and salaries, the GADFLIES said: "The man who would vote for [an anti-smoking] bill and threaten to refuse the University any appropriations if it is not enforced, has the soul of a rat, the brains of a congenital idiot, the character of a polecat and would sell his own mother for a vote." The authors must have been reading H. L. Mencken. They then turned their vitriol on the Reverend W. C. Fawell, the Methodist student pastor: "O Wesley, what miserable pettifogging is committed in thy name!" Fawell had led the crusade against smoking. (It may be of some interest that the Board of Regents voted two years later to allow the campus newspaper to accept tobacco advertisements.)

With self-conscious indignation, the editors of the *Daily Nebraskan* offered a reward of twenty-five dollars for the arrest and conviction of the authors of "With Fire and Sword," and two days later the chancellor himself offered another fifty dollars. The authors were, in fact, not really secret. Campus bigwigs had a pretty fair idea who they were. When asked, Dean Henry Foster of the law college observed that the authors might be prosecuted for criminal libel or sued for damages. Foster, a campus char-

acter, must have offered his judgment with tongue in cheek, to please the chancellor. Surely he must have recognized a student prank when he saw it.

But the solemn chancellor was indignant. The campus newspaper reported on Sunday, 22 March, that he had employed Charles Reid of the Pinkerton Detective Agency in Kansas City to locate the authors. Pinkerton detectives were notorious. Called alternately knights of capitalism or hired hooligans, they were an unregulated private police force which operated where feelings of betrayal, suspicion, and untrustworthiness flourished. They were rarely enlisted against student shenanigans. Alan Williams, a man somewhat older then most undergraduates and the organizer of Barbs on campus — Barbs were non-Greeks — reported to the *Daily Nebraskan* on 22 March that he was questioned by Reid and offered "impunity" if he would provide information, that is, if he would be a stool pigeon. Williams called this a gangster method of inquiry. "The Chancellor says he does not know what methods are being used and evidently does not care," Williams added. When interviewed, Dean Thompson said with standard administrative loyalty that he did not think the Pinkerton methods could be called objectionable.

The authors refused to be frightened, and early in May a "second edition" appeared. Denounced by the chancellor and his dean, practically all copies were confiscated before distribution. The GADFLIES wrote: "While such asinine tomfoolery on the part of the Administration is not at all surprising and, indeed, quite in character, yet we wonder if the game is worth the candle when a gumshoe jackass from Kansas City is entertained by the University to the tune of $700.00." Cunningham wrote to Alexander, "[The administration] have handled Student matters lately in such an inhuman manner that I have simply boiled with rage." He continued, the dean knows "less about the student mentality and cares less about the Student heart, than I do about Electrolytic Dissociation Theory."[10] The Pinkerton detective returned to Kansas City by the first of June, the authors still unknown. The chancellor's curiosity was unsatisfied and his reputation with the students and faculty was unburnished.

The Wimberly Affair

Nobody was hurt in the Pinkerton affair, but in a later episode persons did in fact suffer. Lowry C. Wimberly was one of the most celebrated teachers on campus. Coming to the University before World War I "having been bitten by the writing bug at an early age," he stayed on to take a Ph.D. and founded the *Prairie Schooner* (1927), a little magazine devoted to publishing good writing that could not otherwise get a hearing.[11] For fifteen years he was the center of whatever literary life Lincoln had, and some of the most gifted undergraduates gathered around him: Robert Lasch, a Rhodes Scholar and Pulitzer Prize winner; Edward "Tuck" Stanley, novelist and journalist with the international press and national television; Loren Eiseley, the naturalist; Dorothy Thomas, the novelist; Mari Sandoz, the popular historian; Weldon Kees, the jack-of-all-arts; and others. Rudolph Umland, his longtime friend, counted some twenty books coming from the Wimberly groups in fifteen years. Wimberly himself published stories and essays in leading journals, and his scholarly study of folklore in English and Scottish balladry (1928) attracted international attention. He was very colorful: "Lowry Wimberly trudged the streets of Lincoln in a dark overcoat and black Confederate-type slouch hat, his sallow face turned into the wind, a partly smoked cigar hanging from his thin, bloodless lips. Some saw him as a tragic, Poelike figure, not only in looks but in thought," one historian has written.[12] Certainly he was not of sanguine temper. Son and brother of Calvinist ministers, he spent his final, ailing years agonizing over the fate of his immortal soul. He died in 1959, before he was seventy.

Wimberly's *Prairie Schooner* attracted national attention, and the stories he published were reprinted regularly in the annual anthologies of best stories. As such things go, the magazine cost the University very little, only a few hundred dollars a year, but "he was forced to crawl on his knees to the chancellor's office each issue to beg for funds to pay the printer," Umland reported.[13] When Mrs. Burnett, a genteel lady who wrote verses, was offended by the straightforward realism of something she read in the *Schooner*, Burnett became even more reluctant to support

it — until the *Omaha World-Herald* condemned the administration for its threat to close down the periodical. Wimberly had no friends in academic administration. He wanted none. Perhaps he should have been more politic.

On the night of 13 February 1932, Wimberly and Norman Eliason, a young teacher in the English department, were faculty chaperons at a student dance in the Coliseum. When the dance ended at 11:30, the two entered a small room off the dance floor. Umland reported what happened: "In it were Mrs. Eliason, Alan Williams [business manager of the *Prairie Schooner*], two female companions, and a small quantity of liquor brought by Williams. 'I should have poured the liquor right down a toilet bowl,' Wimberly later lamented. Almost immediately a knock sounded on the door and, when Williams opened it, five officers of the law bounded in, one after the other, in quick succession and with the precision of animated toys. Two of the officers were agents of 'Three-Gun' Howard Wilson, deputy Federal Prohibition Administrator of Nebraska."[14]

According to C. H. Oldfather, later dean of the College of Arts and Sciences, the officers had been assured they had the approval of the administration to descend upon a University building as though it were a speakeasy. "At one fell swoop the editor of the *Schooner*, the associate editor, and the business manager were taken in custody off to jail. It was all so unbelievably sudden it seemed like something out of a Gilbert and Sullivan opera. 'I was completely flabbergasted,' Wimberly said. That night he slept, or rather fitfully dozed, on a cot in a jail for the first and only time in his life. Williams was charged with possession of the liquor, ultimately found guilty, and fined five hundred dollars."[15] Bearing no permanent ill will, Alan Williams many years later endowed a scholarship fund in Wimberly's name.

Wimberly and Eliason were summoned before the Board of Regents as though to a court, Dean Foster prosecuting and Dean John Hicks defending. After considerable discussion, the regents voted four to one to suspend Wimberly and Eliason six months, until 1 September, without pay. The unyielding regent was Fred A. Marsh of Archer, who was proud of having taught the men's Bible class at the Archer Methodist church for thirty-five years.

Hicks wrote later, "The punishment assessed was out of all proportion to the crime; but it would have been even worse had not a lawyer on the board detected from the evidence (as I did not) that the whole thing was almost, if not quite, a frame-up, or at the very least a double cross."[16]

The campus was in an uproar. A lengthy petition from students protested the action, but other students, members of Farm House, an agriculture fraternity, dissented, saying that they wanted professors "whose ideals and examples will inspire and help us." A week later, on 25 February 1932, the editor of the *Daily Nebraskan* observed that the raid had been "conducted only to satisfy the public" and that this "medieval affair" and punishment were inappropriate "for breaking a law which it is literally fashionable to break." (It is not irrelevant that prohibition was repealed, even in Nebraska, after the 1932 elections.) The faculty was indignant at the general hypocrisy of the affair, for they knew that more than one member of the Board of Regents went in for sturdy drinking, and they recognized that the arrest and punishment were a public relations sop to antiliquor Puritans. Within a couple of weeks the usually timid professors schemed to modify the harsh judgment. Thomas M. Raysor, chairman of the English department, with the endorsement of both his dean and the director of the Extension Division, proposed that part-time work be found for the two men so that the financial penalty would not extend to their families. Soon thereafter John D. Hicks, a great favorite with students, who referred to him as "the jolly dean," accepted an appointment at the University of Wisconsin without even conferring with the chancellor. Eliason left the University to have a fine career elsewhere, but Wimberly stayed on, for family reasons and for the sake of the *Schooner*, he said. In any case 1932 was no time for easy moving. In later years he sometimes regretted his decision, but his local reputation as a teacher, scholar, editor, and personage was untouched by the affair. Burnett's reputation for integrity, on the other hand, suffered.

The Faculty

Wimberly was not alone in gathering students around him. The most famous faculty character of the decade was Orin Stepanek, the one-man Department of Comparative Literature. A native of Crete, Nebraska, he was a flamboyant celebrant of his Czech heritage, generations before ethnic identification was fashionable. He was hired in 1920 to teach Slavic languages, and he quickly earned a reputation for being a polyglot, which he disclaimed. He was the kind of man around whom legends collected, and students loved to exaggerate his classroom histrionics. A fascinating lecturer in part because he was so vibrant, he dramatized the texts he asked students to consider. In a time before everybody traveled, he visited Russia and India and studied at Charles University in Prague. In Nebraska he invited students to his house — he always kept a lookout for the bright ones — and listened to them by the hour. His students never forgot him, and forty years after his death in 1955, they still talked about him.

Orin Stepanek was concerned with the eternal verities as represented in the arts and saw no discontinuities between life inside and life outside the classroom. He was equally contemptuous of the "arty-guys" — the aesthetes — and the "biz ad boys," for both were one-sided, bruising body to pleasure soul, sacrificing spirit to worldly success. He himself could write poems, cobble shoes, bake bread, and play the piano. Undiplomatic and outspoken, he had the audacity to call the capitol a phallic symbol when undergraduates had to look up the word in the dictionary. More than once his chairman and dean had to protect him from administrative wrath. For years he was grossly underpaid.

F. D. Keim, chairman of the agronomy department, was remarkable in a different way. Not a distinguished research scholar as his colleague T. A. Kiesselbach most certainly was, nor so successful a teacher as his friend T. M. Goodding, he had "an uncanny ability to size students up and encourage them." He directed their careers faultlessly. According to George W. Beadle, the Nobel laureate, "Some he sent back to the farm, some to be county agricultural agents, others to teach high school, and a few to go on to graduate school. I've known half a dozen or more of the latter and have never known one to be a misfit."[17] Several of his protégés made major contributions to science. Not at all colorful like Stepanek, he was conventional, even provincial, and refused to allow his students to smoke. He taught a celebrated Sunday school class at the Warren United Methodist Church which many of his students dutifully attended. Chairman of his department from 1932 until 1952, he developed agronomy into the premier department in the University and one of the notable agronomy departments in the world.

In the Department of History, Edgar N. Johnson attracted a circle of admirers almost in spite of himself. Concerned with the largest intellectual questions, he offered a two-year course in the history of Western civilization in which he asked students to ponder the rise of rational liberalism from ancient times through the Enlightenment down to modern "scientism," one of his words. He did not pretend to be unbiased and thought that history revealed the eternal truths of civil rights. Cultural relativism was not for him. After Harley Burr Alexander left the campus, Johnson was sometimes referred to as the intellectual conscience of the University. A very intense man, rather indifferent to his appearance, he talked to freshmen as though they were his intellectual equals and to advanced students as though they were as passionately committed to the intellectual life as he was. In devoting himself to his grand ideas, he did not always seem aware of the individual students to whom he lectured, but they did not mind. He opened doors to worlds they had not known existed, and he changed the lives of some. Edgar Johnson was a synthesizer, a writer of textbooks, and a generalist.

O. K. Bouwsma in the Department of Philosophy was no generalist. He appealed to only a few students, but for those few, he made a profound difference. Stepanek, who liked him very much, called him "a word-monger," by which he meant he analyzed the meanings of words, sentences, and paragraphs so intensely that he seemed to pour the baby out with the bath water. Johnson thought Bouwsma paid too little attention to the traditions of Western thought in his microscopic examination of words. Bouwsma was insistently Socratic. He offered courses in the dialogues of Plato, and, like Socrates, he published no philosophical disquisitions. To the total astonishment of his dean and colleagues, he was among the first American professors invited to Oxford as a Fulbright scholar after World War II and there he delivered the John Locke Lectures, this on the recommendation of brilliant students and his one published essay. Bouwsma was paradoxical, for although a peerless analyst of language, he remained an orthodox Calvinist. An enigma, he left the University at sixty-five for a second career in Texas, only to be recalled to Nebraska to receive an honorary degree ten years later. O. K. Bouwsma was a great teacher but he was essentially a practicing philosopher.

The University had a number of notable personages in the Thirties. Karl M. Arndt was a popular lecturer in business and willingly served as adviser to many student organizations. H. G. Deming was a mediocre teacher but an excellent writer, and his text in beginning chemistry became a bestseller. Indeed, his publisher said that without it his company would have gone under during the depression. He retired, rich, to Hawaii. William K. Pfeiler, a splendid teacher, wrote books about German literature. Born and raised in Germany and a German soldier in World War I, he studied local history and geography when he came to Nebraska "so the country would speak to me," he said. When he returned to Europe, he was not going home. Emanuel Wishnow, born in England but raised in Lincoln, returned to the School of Music after studying violin and conducting in New York and elsewhere, and helped set the standards of musical performance. He earned the respect of his contemporaries, and sometimes their professional envy. In the Thirties the University community was relatively small, budgets were tight, opportunities for travel were limited, and the faculty knew one another intimately.

In a national survey made in 1934, six departments of the University were judged by their national peers to be worthy of offering the Ph.D. degree: chemistry, English, education, and three plant science departments — botany, plant physiology, and plant pathology. This ranked it with the University of Kansas. In 1937 the American Council on Education did not list the University of Nebraska among its major graduate degree–granting institutions, and the editor of the *Daily Nebraskan* noted on 8 December that though Nebraska did not make this list, its football team was judged number eleven in the nation.

❧ Depression Budgets

After his first, trial year, Chancellor Burnett's relationship with the faculty was uneasy. The agricultural depression that had come to the plains after the Great War had kept University budgets low, and by 1932 the hard times were intensified by the drought. The state, usually conservative, in 1932 joined the Democratic landslide and the state legislature was turned over to new men unacquainted with public institutions. A significant number were latter-day populists, even levelers, and some were anti-intellectuals. Discontent with established governmental institutions, they extended their discontent to the University. Farmers whose incomes were small and whose future was uncertain resented the financial security of tenured professors, however small their salaries. Burnett and the Board of Regents felt themselves on the defensive, as indeed they were.

To placate public opinion, Burnett decided that salaries needed to be lower still. And so in the spring of the second year of the 1931–33 biennium, he ordered that all salaries beyond $1,000 be cut 10 percent. In the fall of 1932 he asked that his own salary be reduced by 20 percent "to improve the public relations."[18] At the same time, he reminded Nebraskans that appropriations to the University were a minor fraction of state expenditures: "If the university were not there at all most people would hardly know the difference in their tax bills."[19] Since these cuts were made in the second year of the biennium, the sum saved was not "returned to the state treasury; it was spent, most of us thought, for far less important things than teachers' salaries," Dean Hicks later wrote. "I reminded the Chancellor that President Hoover, as a means of holding the depression in check, had urged businessmen not to reduce wages or salaries, and I remember well the reply I got. 'That's one point,' the chancellor asserted firmly, 'on which Hoover was wrong.'"[20]

Burnett was clearly trying to anticipate criticism in the 1933 legislature, but he misjudged. In the new session the University was attacked as it had never been before. Bills were introduced to abolish certain divisions within the University, to discontinue the Teachers College and send all teacher programs to the normal schools, to set an arbitrary limit on the salaries of officers and professors, and to withdraw the University from the North Central Association of Colleges and Secondary Schools because accrediting agencies were thought to set standards too high for this state to maintain. "Under the cloak of economy an attempt is being made to destroy the state's most valuable institution," Ray E. Ramsay, the popular secretary of the Alumni Association, wrote in a special issue of *The Nebraska Alumnus* (23 March 1933). A specially appointed legislative committee, usurping the constitutional power of the Board of Regents, even attempted to fix the salaries in the various colleges, and the resulting inequality showed the revolutionary temper of the time. The College of Agriculture was to be cut only 7.6 percent, whereas the College of Arts and Sciences was to be cut 27.4 percent, the College of Law 26.5 percent, and Teachers College 14.3 percent.

One can perceive the populist disposition in all this: Why should the impoverished citizen be asked to support students who subsequently dominate society and receive professional incomes higher than those of the supporting citizens? Critics on the floor of the legislature called the University "aristocratic," and the editor of the campus newspaper on 11 May 1933 noted that the bitter discussion showed a general hostility to education. The editor, Phil Brownell, observed that controversial academic matters were being swept under the rug by the chancellor and his administrators to avoid antagonizing critics. "This University is not worthy of the name if it cannot act and think and teach without keeping one eye open to see how the political leaders in the state react," he wrote in the *Daily Nebraskan* three days later. The integrity of the University was at stake.

The University was fortunately not without friends. In March a thousand students marshaled by student leaders like E. N. (Jack) Thompson, president of the Innocents Society, and others had met in a mass meeting in The Temple to protest the legislative action, and they sent a strong resolution to the capitol. James E. Lawrence, editor of the *Lincoln Star*, was speaker at this meeting though he was very hoarse from stumping the state in behalf of the University. Other papers in the state, including the

Omaha World-Herald, defended the University, and eight prominent Lincoln clergymen printed a pamphlet protesting the destruction of the long-established policy of public higher education in Nebraska. Spring 1933 was marked by charges and countercharges, proposals and counterproposals. Finally in May the University was voted a budget over a million dollars less than the previous biennium's, but the legislature acknowledged the authority of the Board of Regents and the unity of the institution. The University survived intact, impoverished in an impoverished state.

Nevertheless, it remained in greatest peril. The chancellor and the regents decided that the library budget should be cut a devastating 30 percent; this action caused damage from which the library could never recover and it was vigorously protested by the faculty. Part of the University hospital in Omaha was closed, and activities of the experiment stations were cut by 25 percent. Regents tuition scholarships for undergraduates were discontinued. Building construction and maintenance were postponed and numerous positions were dropped. In addition to Burnett's 10 percent, salaries were now decreased an additional 22 percent. This reduction was promised to be restored when times improved. The faculty was embittered, for they felt the chancellor had betrayed their interests by initiating reductions on his own in the middle of the previous biennium. Although universities across the country were taking similar depreciations in 1933, University personnel in Nebraska were, in fact, harder hit because they had taken the earlier, unmandated additional cut. Moreover, during the Twenties their salaries had not kept up with regional competition. For the rest of the Thirties, the University continued to get only meager support from the legislature, the farm economy remaining weak, but it did not again meet the open hostility of 1933. The promised restoration of the 1933 reduction was not made.

Football, however, continued to get generous support. In 1929 Dana X. Bible was hired away from Texas A&M at a salary of $10,000 a year when full professors nationally earned an average of $5,000 and head coaches $6,000. In his years at Nebraska, Bible coached his teams to fifty victories and six league championships. He toured the state searching out football talent, stirring up enthusiasm, but the enthusiasm did not translate into support for the University. When he left in 1936 to go to the University of Texas for $15,000 a year (and bonuses), the chancellor's salary had just been raised to $10,200.[21] The highest-paid faculty member was paid half that. Football in Nebraska seemed to have a life of its own.

❧ Campus Buildings and Student Life

In his search for money, Chancellor Burnett turned to private sources. Observing that alumni endowments had been a source of revenue in other universities, he proposed as early as 1932 that a University of Nebraska foundation be set up to receive gifts. Over the years Ralph Mueller had established funds for student loans. Charles Morrill had left one-fifth of his estate to the University, primarily for the museum; Adam Breede had given a large collection of African trophies for exhibition in Morrill Hall; and the F. M. Hall estate had financed the Nebraska Art Association collections, which were housed at the University. Nothing much came of the chancellor's suggestion until 1936, when the foundation was incorporated by thirty prominent Nebraska business and professional men and women, but it was not aggressive and its growth was slow. In the first half-dozen years it received only $42,000.

Building needs were urgent. In 1926 old University Hall was reduced to a basement and one floor and Nebraska Hall was condemned as dangerous and its upper floors were removed. That wreck of a building continued as ROTC headquarters. Some engineering laboratories were housed in makeshift sheds on T Street, and frame houses on R Street were turned into classrooms. The Temple had become a classroom building, and the library, planned for a thousand students, now tried to serve five and six times that many. Living accommodations for students were a continuing problem. The office of the dean of women carefully monitored private rooming houses for women, ensuring that they were clean and properly equipped, however drab, but boardinghouses for men were hardly supervised. The men often found themselves in firetraps infested with cockroaches. A few pleasant cooperative houses for women were established under the protection of the University in the 1930s – Howard Hall in 1932, Wilson Hall in 1933, Rosa Bouton Hall in 1936. A number of men's cooperative houses appeared also, but without University support. As late as 1939 the rooming house district surrounding the city campus was identified by Professor E. F. Witte of the Graduate School of Social Work as "one of the worst housing areas in the city of Lincoln." His conclusions were published in the *Daily Nebraskan* on 14 February of that year. If the women were restricted by rules set down by the dean of women, they had at least decent places to live; the men, unsupervised, had the choice of living in fraternities, depression cooperatives, or boardinghouses. Lincoln residents lived at home. Apartments around town were not generally available to students in these years.

The students had a good time nonetheless. The organized houses had dances and parties regularly, and several times a year all-campus dances, often in the Coliseum, provided entertainment for everybody. The Coliseum's barnlike interior was softened on these nights by dark blue velour curtains and a tentlike ceiling purchased by students with money raised under the leadership of the Innocents Society. Relatively inexpensive movies were available in ten or fifteen theaters in town, although movie houses were closed on Sundays. Churches sponsored youth groups which had gatherings on Sundays and some weeknights. A weekend date might cost a dollar, sometimes less, and the undergraduates did not feel especially put upon in spite of the depression. The Turnpike Ballroom, a large dance hall seven miles out of town, brought big-name bands to Nebraska. An evening there cost a bit more money, but the Turnpike was often filled both Saturday and Friday nights.

The success of building Memorial Stadium and the Coliseum with bonds issued against promised income suggested that women's dorms could be built on the same plan, and in 1929 the legislature provided $100,000 toward what became Carrie Belle Raymond Hall, conceived as the first unit of a larger women's residence complex. The question of men's dormitories appears not to have been raised. Opened in 1932, the women's dorm cost $35 a month for room and full board, a not inconsiderable sum in that de-

pression year. House bills at the fraternities and sororities were a bit higher. At the co-ops students could live for $20 a month by helping with housekeeping. About half the undergraduate men and a fourth of the undergraduate women worked for their board, usually as hashers. Food was cheap but money was tight. At the cafeteria in The Temple, breakfast cost ten cents and students complained when dinners cost more than twenty-five cents. In 1938 Don L. Love, former mayor of Lincoln, provided money for an extension on the women's dorm, in memory of his wife, and two years later he gave money for Love Cooperative Dormitory, also for women, on the ag campus. These were the first of his generous bequests to the University.

Alert University administrators across the country saw opportunity for building through the use of federal funds from several agencies. In 1933 Congress authorized the PWA (Public Works Administration) to provide up to 30 percent of the cost of public buildings, the remainder to be amortized over a long period. In 1935 this maximum was upped to 45 percent, the rest provided by PWA bonds. Additional support for construction could be obtained through the Works Progress Administration. Many state universities and all but eight of the land-grant colleges undertook PWA construction, and thus campuses across the country were expanded and modernized. Such construction supported local economies, of course.[22] In Omaha the Municipal University, under the leadership of President Rowland Haynes, built a whole new campus on West Dodge Street with PWA funds. The University of Nebraska College of Medicine, under the leadership of Dean C.W.M. Poynter, added several buildings to its campus, including the South Laboratory, with various kinds of federal support. If the state could not provide for the University and its students, clearly the New Deal offered an alternative.

But the Board of Regents officially refused to participate. They announced in September 1933: "It is ordered that this board does not make an official request to the Federal Public Works Committee for Nebraska to erect a student union building on the University grounds in Lincoln."[23] They did, in fact, apply unsuccessfully for an outright federal grant of some $400,000 for an armory to

47. The Board of Regents, 1920. The man with the skullcap is Dean J. Stuart Dales, secretary of the board from 1875 until 1932. Opposite him is Chancellor Avery (far right) and Judge H. D. Landis, grandfather of Senator David Landis. (UNL Archives)

48. When campus enrollment nearly doubled between 1918 and 1925, rising from 3,200 to 6,100 students, facilities were badly strained, as this cartoon from the 1924 *Cornhusker* illustrates. (UNL Archives)

49. Noontime traffic at Twelfth and R streets, 1925. Chemistry Hall, renamed Pharmacy Hall when a new chemistry building was constructed in 1916 at Twelfth and T streets, is to the left; the new Social Sciences Hall, just visible, is to the right. The tall building in the center, behind Grant Memorial Hall, was the first wing of a planned classroom building. It housed the museum until Morrill Hall was constructed in 1927. The view is to the north from the steps of The Temple. (UNL Archives)

50. By the mid-1920s the library was particularly crowded, for it had been too small even for prewar enrollment. This interior shot shows the main reading room on the first floor. (UNL Photo Lab)

51. In 1925 the cupola and the top three floors of old University Hall were removed in the interests of safety. The basement and the first floor, covered with a leaky flat roof, continued to be used for classrooms and extracurricular offices until they too were razed in 1948. (UNL Photo Lab)

52. Plans for an expanded campus were made under the leadership of the president of the Board of Regents, George N. Seymour. His scheme was generally accepted for twenty-five years, and a model of the campus was placed in the basement of the state museum in Morrill Hall. (*Cornhusker 1926*, UNL Archives)

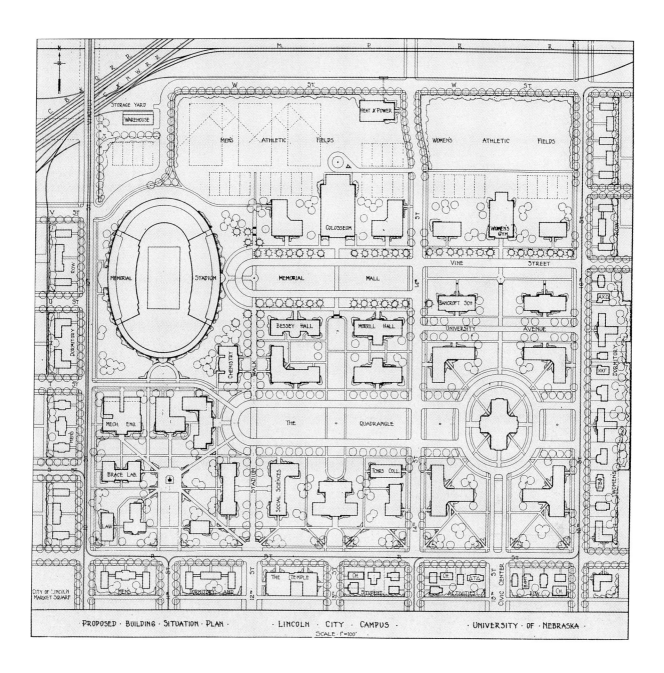

PROPOSED · BUILDING · SITUATION · PLAN ·   · LINCOLN · CITY · CAMPUS ·   · UNIVERSITY · OF · NEBRASKA ·

SCALE 1"=100'

53. When the campus was expanded from Twelfth to Fourteenth Street, the area was cleared of residences and boardinghouses. Teachers College is to the left in this view. The area being cleared is now Donaldson Garden. (UNL Archives)

54. During the campus expansion a row of large houses on R Street was acquired. The largest, a brick mansion, the Ricketts house, on the corner of Fourteenth and R, became Ellen Smith Hall, the center for women's activities. Women's groups protested vigorously when it was razed in 1958 to clear the approach to the new administration building. (UNL Archives)

55, 56. Mabel Lee and Louise Pound, two of the most prominent women in the University in their time, were not friends. Mabel Lee saw games as a means to health; Louise Pound saw them as a field of conquest. These photographs were taken about 1924, when Mabel Lee arrived, age thirty-eight, to become head of women's physical education. Louise Pound, age fifty-two, a tennis and golfing champion, was already a local legend. (Mabel Lee: *Memories Beyond Bloomers (1924–1954)*; Louise Pound: Nebraska State Historical Society)

57. Hartley Burr Alexander (1873–1939) had a vision of what his native community might become. The editors of the *Cornhusker 1926* dedicated their yearbook to him. (UNL Archives)

58. Aerial view of the city campus in
1927, looking toward the northeast
from the railroad station. The quadrangle north of Social Sciences Hall
(now CBA) and Teachers College,
though cleared, has not yet been
paved, and the foundations of Andrews Hall are only indicated, not dug.
Memorial Stadium and the Coliseum
are the most imposing buildings of the
decade. (UNL Archives)

59, 60. In the Twenties the social life of the campus was dominated by the Greek houses. These cartoons by Oz Black appeared in the *Cornhusker 1927*. By the end of the decade there were thirty-eight fraternities and twenty-three sororities on campus — and they had an acknowledged pecking order. (UNL Archives)

61. The quadrangle of the ag campus, 1927. The Agricultural Engineering Building is at the far, north end and the roof of the Plant Industry Building can be seen to the right. (UNL Photo Lab)

62. The Board of Regents, 1930. Chancellor E. A. Burnett, who usually wore octagonal glasses and a severe expression, is on the extreme left, front row. Earl Cline is third from left, front row, and Marion Shaw is in the middle of the back row. (UNL Archives)

63. The 1931 office of the *Daily Nebraskan*, usually called the Rag, was in the basement of old University Hall. The place was so infested with mice that they sometimes fell into wastebaskets from which they could not escape, to the amusement of the staff. The student second from left wearing a fashionable fedora at a rakish angle is E. N. Thompson, universally known as Jack. Phil Brownell, the editor, is third from the right. (UNL Archives)

64. The *Cornhusker 1931* pictured Orin Stepanek (1888–1955), professor of comparative literature. He was "one of the favorites of the Nebraska faculty, both in class and on the campus, a well known figure to everyone." (UNL Archives)

65. Though Memorial Stadium was not always filled on Saturday afternoons, football was the center of excitement while Dana X. Bible was coach (1929–36). In 1934 a rally was held in front of the old Lincoln Hotel on a Friday night. (UNL Photo Lab)

66. Jack Fischer, "Big Man on Campus," as student council president and then as editor of the *Daily Nebraskan* undertook to get a student union constructed, even without support from the University administration and regents — and succeeded. He appears here in September 1935 with Frances Lincoln, whom he later married. Notice the press in his trousers and his fashionable fabric belt. Frances Lincoln's jodhpurs and boots were similarly fashionable. (Courtesy of Mrs. Frances Fischer)

67. The Student Union, now the Nebraska Union, when it was opened in 1938. The PWA sign identifies the source of some of the funds used to construct it. Additions to the north were made in 1959 and 1970, and the total building underwent extensive, controversial remodeling in 1985. (UNL Archives)

68, 69. The interior of the Student Union was elegant and comfortable. The woodwork was walnut, the draperies satin, and the upholstery velvet and leather. Some of the furniture is in use to this day. (*Cornhusker 1939*, UNL Archives)

70. Theodore A. Kiesselbach (1884–1964) was a research scientist. A student of Charles Bessey's, he was said to be "one of the last of the total agronomists." He knew more about corn than any other person in the world. (UNL Photo Lab)

71. Lowry C. Wimberly (1890–1959), founding editor of the *Prairie Schooner* in 1927, is pictured here in his Andrews Hall office with Frederick L. Christensen, his longtime editorial assistant. An extremely popular teacher of writing and literature, Wimberly edited textbooks, as many others did, to supplement his meager salary. (UNL Photo Lab)

replace the crumbling Nebraska Hall, but they did not get it though the chancellor spent ten days lobbying in Washington. (Methodist ministers and other peace groups opposed the construction of an armory, as they had opposed compulsory ROTC for years.) In the fall of 1933 the University accepted money from the Civil Works Administration for stadium seating and grading and for construction of a stadium track, and in spring 1934 it allowed federal relief money to be made available to students through Dean Thompson's office, the scholarship program having been canceled the previous year. In 1935 it grudgingly accepted the offer of the Federal Emergency Relief Administration to finance street improvements on the ag campus. By 1935 straw votes on the campus indicated that President Roosevelt's programs were as popular here as they were nationally, but conservative regents resisted the New Deal. The board cut off its nose to spite its face, and the students were disadvantaged. It is not clear to this day why the University could accept federal money for agricultural services, as it had from its beginning, but could not accept money for academic programs.

Local needs were repeatedly listed, and priced, by the regents over the years, but, led by Regent Earl Cline, the regents took no action. In 1935 Regent C. Y. Thompson enumerated the needs in this order: (1) library, (2) a general classroom building, (3) a medical clinic, (4) engineering laboratories, and (5) general campus renovation;[24] and in 1936 the board proposed a ten-year building program to the state legislature. Perhaps because Governor Cochran did not endorse it, the bill failed, but by a single vote. The legislators were not told by the board and the chancellor that state money could be doubled with matching federal grants.

Jack Fischer and the Student Union

By 1935 the students felt that a student union was an urgent need, and the student council petitioned the Board of Regents to request PWA support to build one and thus to reverse their 1933 policy position. Their impressive petition had more than 2,300 signatures. This student activities building was not a new need. When Ray Ramsay became secretary of the Alumni Association in 1929, he began pressing for such a building on the city campus (one had been constructed on the ag campus in 1926). Ramsay, who had been an actor in New York City and later at the University in H. Alice Howell's drama department, had a deadpan sense of humor which made him a favorite on local lecture platforms and on the radio; and his observations about student needs got more than casual attention. After 1930 he and the students gave up much hope of a student center, but when federal money became available, their hopes revived.

The fact that the University of Nebraska finally got a student union is really the work of one student, Jack Fischer, the son of a Valentine mortician. A bespectacled young man who played both the piano and the accordion, Frank Jackson Fischer – he was always Jack – became president of the student council in the spring of 1935 and took the student union as his project. He obtained an endorsement of the idea of a union from Nebraska's congressmen and senators and, with the aid of Ray Ramsay, got the support of the Alumni Association and its president, John H. Agee, a prominent Lincoln businessman. Calling together campus leaders, he established a Committee of One Hundred, which endorsed the need for a student center and the necessity of applying for federal assistance. Since PWA money would pay only 45 percent of the $400,000 cost, the students agreed to tax themselves through fees to pay off the bonds issued for the remaining 55 percent. This combination of money in hand and bonds floated against future revenue was like what had made Memorial Stadium and the Coliseum possible twelve years earlier and the women's residence halls five years before.

Ray Ramsay, Jack Fischer, and the students had no support from the chancellor and his cabinet. Earl Cline, regent from Lincoln, and Marion Shaw, regent from David City, were irrationally hostile to accepting federal money. Still, confronted by an organized student proposal, they could not reject it out of hand; and when the students went home in June 1935, the application seemed ensured and the student union a sure thing. But the students underestimated the intransigence of the board and the administration. When they returned in September they discovered that the application had not been made, and by then nearly all PWA money had been allotted. The students, understandably, were indignant. "The committee waged a difficult campaign at the busiest time of the school year and acted in good faith thruout," Fischer wrote in the *Daily Nebraskan*, 16 September 1935. "We feel that utter disregard of our work is unjustified and that the university and student body have both suffered as a result." Fischer, who was now the editor of the *Daily Nebraskan*, reopened his campaign.

He had help. Irving Hill, the new president of the student council, was a brilliant young man from a responsible Lincoln family, and he joined Fischer to revive the issue. They learned from John Latenser Jr., the Omaha administrator of PWA funds, that very likely the new Congress would designate more money in its next session; and, always sympathetic to their cause, he encouraged them to get the University to apply for some of it. One of the undergraduates wrote to the campus newspaper on 1 October 1935, "The fellows at the house simply pass it over with 'Nobody has ever been able to get the board of regents to do anything anyway,' which is about the attitude that the board itself has. But I think it's about time someone asked the regents just who they're working for, and be able to expect at least a courteous reply."

In November, Hill and a committee of students met with members of the Board of Regents. Jack Fischer reported the outcome in his 12 November newspaper: "Today, after seeing student enthusiasm for a union building reach its greatest height on the campus, after seeing Nebraska's congressmen throw their weight behind the plan, after securing the PWA official's promise to help in every way, and then seeing the project die an unwarranted death by administrative red tape, the alumni association is decidedly put out, and with good reason." The students began collecting pledges to support the new building and by January 1936 they had more than $10,000 promised. The Alumni Association established a fund-raising committee, with George Grimes of the *Omaha World-Herald* as chairman, to provide furnishings. Chancellor Burnett did not openly support the student request for a union, apparently

thinking it impolitic to challenge the two adamant anti–New Deal members of his board. He responded to their agitation by reviving his idea of a University foundation. On 11 January 1936, the Board of Regents finally approved the application for PWA funds, and in November they voted to accept a PWA contract which paid nearly $200,000 toward the union and provided bonds for the rest. Regents Cline and Shaw voted stubbornly against accepting the contract. The front page of the *Daily Nebraskan* pictured Earl Cline, newly elected president of the board, and Jack Fischer, instigator of the drive: David had slain Goliath.

Collecting money for furnishings proved to be more difficult than Grimes, Ramsay, and Fischer at first had thought, but the faculty lounge was furnished by Professor John D. Clark of the College of Business Administration out of his own pocket. Clark, after a successful career in the petroleum industry, had taken his Ph.D. at Johns Hopkins University at the age of forty-five before coming to Lincoln. Mrs. Clark was said to be the only faculty wife with a mink coat. Later, in 1941, Clark became Dean LeRossignol's successor, and in 1946 President Truman appointed him to the initial three-member Council of Economic Advisers.

In February 1936 Regent Cline announced that he would not run for reelection. He had been a regent since 1925. Upon his retirement from the board, his law firm was named legal counsel to the University, not without some local restlessness, and Cline remained influential for the next thirty years. On legal matters he was a strict constructionist, as a subsequent administrator said, and consistently advised against innovation, even when other institutions were exploring financial and academic opportunities. In a generation of change, he stood pat. Robert Devoe, another Lincoln attorney, replaced him on the board. Less handsome than Cline and self-conscious about his appearance, Devoe wore an odd black toupee and elevator shoes. He was something of a bon vivant. But he was open to suggestions, imaginative, and flexible: an excellent regent.

The students challenged the regents in the spring of 1935 with another project, which Virginia Selleck, representing the student council, took before the board. Students had long objected to what they regarded as the exorbitant prices charged for used books, and they proposed that a University-owned bookstore buy and sell their books at a minimum markup. As with the student union project, they got little response, and over the summer their proposal was allowed to languish. Jack Fischer reported in the campus newspaper of 1 October 1935 that it had been referred to a subcommittee, but "the subcommittee apparently does not know that the book store proposal was to be considered. As a matter of fact, one regent actually did not know he was supposed to be on such a committee. A second had never heard of the book store. A third regretted that nothing had been done but promised to 'look into the matter.' " Fischer asked, "Why the sham and pretense . . . ?"

Within a month L. F. Seaton, operating superintendent of the University, canvassed college bookstores to discover the type of exchange best suited to Nebraska, and in January 1936 the regents finally agreed to establish a secondhand-book department. Unhappily, this exchange was not successful because it was not well managed. In failing to follow student recommendations, the bookstore became simply an agency of the administration, its books overpriced and limited in number. The students felt, with considerable justification, that their requests were not being considered. Though it was true that the bookstore did not have a high priority among administrative concerns, it is also true that running a college bookstore is a much more complicated matter than might appear to undergraduates.

Jack Fischer graduated from the University in January 1936 and, remaining in Lincoln, continued to interest himself in University affairs. Called "one of the greatest" by the newspaper staff upon his retirement, he was probably the most outstanding editor since Frank T. "Rag" Riley, founder of *The Nebraskan* in 1894. (It became the *Daily Nebraskan* in 1901.) All spring of 1936 Fischer kept an eagle eye on the progress of his union, monitoring the architects' plans, criticizing the proposed sites, objecting to what he regarded as the administration's persistent disregard for student desires. Ultimately he proposed a

student-faculty-alumni supervisory board for the union, which was established. Unhappily, Fischer, a man of enormous promise, died of a heart attack at age thirty-one. Irving Hill, after studying at Harvard, became a federal judge in California. Virginia Selleck died a few years later in childbirth. Other members of this remarkable collection of students were Frank Landis, son of the regent and father of Senator David Landis; Burton Marvin, one of Professor H. H. Marvin's gifted sons; Dwight Perkins, later president of a local insurance company; and Violet Cross, who combined beauty with considerable executive authority in campus organizations. Though they claimed they were not eager for what they called a tug of war, the students had had a wonderful time.

Earl Cline persisted in his views. Even as he was retiring, he wrote: "It has been, and is, my judgment that the Board of Regents should not increase the cost of securing an education either to students or their parents, nor assume this additional financial responsibility."[25] This "financial responsibility" came to a fee of three dollars a semester. By 1938 the regents allowed the athletic board to apply for PWA funds for a field house – a move seconded, significantly, by Regent Shaw, who previously had followed Cline's lead. In that same year they began investigating possibilities of PWA money for their listed building needs. Hearing that the new Agricultural Adjustment Act provided for the establishment of research laboratories around the country, the board, led by Regent Devoe, Cline's successor, in April offered Nebraska as a site and urged the state's congressional delegation to get one located here. But all this scurry of activity was too late, and the only substantial federal money that came to the University in these years was to the athletic department, whose supervisory board had a history of enterprise, and the College of Medicine, which had an aggressive dean.

The University's refusal to take advantage of federal funding was recognized at the time – and later – as a mistake from which the University could never recover. If the state money spent for buildings after World War II had instead been available to upgrade equipment and improve instruction, the University might have come closer to its earlier aspirations to excellence.

❧ The End of an Era

In July 1938 Chancellor Burnett, now an old man – he was seventy-three – requested from the Board of Regents a leave of absence, to be followed by retirement. His greatest accomplishment was that he had kept the University from being dismembered by populist politicians, but the faculty was dispirited, the campuses were seriously run down, and the professional schools were hanging on by force of habit. Even so, the University of Nebraska remained an inexpensive place to get a good education – if students chose professors and courses carefully.

8. Marking Time: 1938–1946

Chauncey S. Boucher

It had been clear by the fall of 1937 that Burnett was aging. Never very interested in education, rather like Sam Avery, he allowed the divisions of the University to run themselves. George Round, then director of publications in the College of Agriculture, remembered, "We paid no attention to chancellors at that particular time."[1] In the spring 1938 Burnett began missing board meetings and the regents started to look for a replacement. Through connections which Regent Devoe had made in national organizations, by May they had a list of possible candidates, none of them local, all with impressive qualifications. The regents, led by Devoe, set out to give the University a new direction. They were, unhappily, a decade late. In June they interviewed four men at the Cornhusker Hotel, without interference from the press; and they promptly decided on Chauncey S. Boucher, president of West Virginia University. In July they accepted Burnett's resignation – technically he was put on leave until January and then made chancellor emeritus – and appointed Boucher as his successor. Also in July they agreed to buy the Sidles house at Twenty-first and A streets for a chancellor's residence at a cost of $12,500. They set Boucher's salary at $12,000, and Burnett's retirement at a bit less than $5,000.

Chauncey Boucher, fifty-two years old, handsome and rather elegant, looked like a college president, and, indeed, his father had been a college president. At ease on golf courses and in clubrooms, he presided at public meetings with dignity. Unapproachable, "not a warm personality by any stretch of the imagination," he sought to inspire respect rather than affection.[2] His monographs on the antebellum South had won him a place in the guild of American historians, and at age forty in 1926 he had become dean of the College of Arts, Literature, and Science at the University of Chicago. There he claimed authorship of the so-called Chicago Plan, a revolutionary restructuring of undergraduate education which Robert Maynard Hutchins put into effect with much publicity. At the West Virginia University in 1935 he set about reorganizing the university according to this plan – with upper- and lower-division classes instead of freshman, sophomore, junior, and senior grades; general comprehensive examinations instead of course examinations; and interdisciplinary studies for all students. He tried to make over the athletic program as Hutchins had at Chicago. To govern West Virginia University, he set up a counterpart to Chicago's senate of full professors, but he retained considerable autonomy in hiring and firing.

Boucher met resistance from the West Virginia University faculty, whom he treated with some superciliousness. By 1938 his administration was investigated by the American Association of University Professors for violating its rules on tenure, and he lost the confidence of his board of governors. These troubles were not known in Nebraska, apparently not even to the regents; and when a *Newsweek* story about him appeared on 18 July 1938, Boucher issued a statement denying its accuracy, a bit deceitfully. Louise Pound remembered with some bemusement how defensive he was when she asked about West Virginia at a dinner party. Boucher was an educational innovator the likes of which Nebraska had not seen since E. Benjamin Andrews, but he did not seem to understand the distinction between a comprehensive public university and a private research university. He ignored any relationship between a state institution and the people who supported it.

❧ A New Order of Things

Nebraska, like other American universities, was forced to reconsider its nature in the Thirties. More students were coming into higher education than ever before, from families who had never before sent their children to college, but state support for public education did not keep pace with the growing numbers. Popular universities were indeed becoming universities of the people, and professors needed to ask what this new kind of student could most profitably be taught.

Professors Lane Lancaster and Harold Stoke of the Department of Political Science had confronted these questions locally in a series of essays published in the *Daily Nebraskan* in February 1934. Their observations underscored the changes that had been going on since the Great War. Where formerly students had "vaguely understood" that higher education prepared them for living and not just for making a living, students increasingly saw a university as a place for contacts. Now a respect for culture was replaced by a desire to acquire practical skills, the two professors said. Short-term job advantage was prized above the long-term value of education. The faculty must reaffirm their faith in the ability of education to "transform men's lives, to inform them with an intellectual and disinterested purpose, to sharpen their perception of nonmaterial values," they wrote on 16 February. Lancaster had come to Lincoln from Wesleyan University in Connecticut in 1930 because he saw greater academic opportunity away from the Ivy League's restricted tables of organization. Stoke, ten years his junior, was a brilliant teacher. He became graduate dean at Nebraska before moving on in 1940 to a distinguished career in academic administration.

Practical men of the working world, or men who thought of themselves as practical men, disagreed with Lancaster and Stoke. They found liberal education idealistic and said that students must adapt themselves to the real world of marketable skills. Traditional liberal education was a luxury, they said, appropriate only to the few.[3] In November 1935, Dean C. H. Oldfather wrote that, as he saw it, the most immediate task of his college was to offer a group of programs adapted to the varied backgrounds of the students who came to the University. As yet, he acknowledged, "The Arts college is only groping about the outskirts of this problem. . . . I am persuaded that we are almost uniquely conservative here at Nebraska in our educational thinking."[4] In May 1936, the College of Arts and Sciences reaffirmed its commitment to the traditional course of education, specifying that all entering students must bring credit for at least two years of high school mathematics, two years of foreign language, and two years of science, English, and history; and that once enrolled, they were to take more courses in foreign language, English, and physical and social science. If these prerequisites reduced the number of students enrolling at the University, then tax money could be used more effectively for the remaining few, some people said.

The requirements met organized resistance from high school and college administrators, led by Frank E. Henzlik, dean of the Teachers College. Requiring algebra and geometry in all high schools when only 20 percent of the pupils went to college was unrealistic, they said; students would be better served by a study of "subjects that will educate them for life." At a meeting reported in the *Daily Nebraskan* of 17 November 1936, high school and college people rejected the proposed entrance requirements. They asserted that many school districts could not afford to support teachers of math and foreign language only for the college-bound, and that to retain math, science, and languages in high school would mean the many were asked to support the few. Further, they said, the defense of math, science, and languages was self-serving: college professors were only protecting their own bailiwicks. Oldfather responded that "the avenues of opportunity must be kept open"; without preparation, nobody could move into the professions. Furthermore, math, science, and foreign languages were beneficial to all students, not just those bound for college.

With enrollment continuing to grow and with financial support decreasing, what courses of study should be given priority? Should students without defined preparation be excluded from the state university? What should be taught where, and to whom, and who should pay for it? These were the questions confronting Boucher and all of American society in 1938.

❧ Boucher's Innovations

When Boucher arrived in the summer of 1938, he was received with both fear and anticipation. Mabel Lee said to herself that he "no doubt was amazed at the lack of esprit de corps and the slow, easy-going tempo of faculty operations at Nebraska."[5] The depression had taken the spirit of adventure out of the local people, including the faculty. They were cautious because they feared any change would further impoverish them. They were shell-shocked.

The new chancellor immediately spelled out his plans. On 20 September 1938, addressing the faculty, he asserted that he was wary of dogmatism, by which he meant an automatic defense of the status quo; and though he did not intend to impose the Chicago Plan, or any plan, on the University, he asked the faculty to conduct intelligently designed experiments by way of departing from the established programs. He wanted to know firsthand the life of the campus, he said, but "not as a snooper."[6] He felt he was empowered by the Board of Regents to ask for change and to provide independent leadership. Coming from the University of Michigan, where he had studied, and the University of Chicago, where he had taught, he felt superior to all he surveyed here. The College of Agriculture and the place of the agricultural experiment station were outside his frame of reference, and he and William W. Burr, dean of the agriculture college, were shortly at odds. Eventually Burr and his staff came to ignore him.

Young and impatient, Boucher regularly came to his office at 8:00 in the morning. He immediately called around campus to see who was on the job. When not finding a chairman or dean at his desk, he would ask the secretary in surprise, "What, not in his office yet? When do you expect him?" Secretaries rose to their bosses' defense, and word of the chancellor's inquiries was soon out. Mabel Lee, head of the Department of Women's Physical Education, was not easily intimidated, and when her secretary reported his call, she promptly returned it, at 9:30. Wearing a well-tailored suit and a blouse with frilly lace at the

throat, she put on her sailor hat trimmed with a band of colorful daisies and went right over to Administration Hall. She explained to Boucher that she never got away from the campus before 6:00 or 7:00 in the evening – the recreational, nonelective nature of physical education necessarily meant that her activities continued late into the day – and that meetings brought her back to the campus many evenings. He need not call her early in the mornings, she assured him. Bearded in his den, he promised not to. They became great friends. "I had classified him as an intellectual smart aleck who needed to be stood up to," she later said.[7]

Through faculty committees Boucher sought to reconsider the structure and even the nature of the University. In November he appointed a committee on educational policy and practice, with Dean Oldfather as its chairman, and after Christmas he appointed a committee on research. In January he took a series of administrative rearrangements to the Board of Regents. He asked that a bureau of instructional research be established with J. P. Guilford, professor of psychology, as its director; and he transferred Robert P. Crawford, who had been Chancellor Burnett's public spokesman, into the Department of Journalism. In Crawford's place he set up a department of public relations with a full-time director and two assistants. When Ray Ramsay of the Alumni Association indicated that he had no interest in consolidating alumni actions with other University agencies, he was replaced by Elsworth F. DuTeau, who became a third assistant in the publicity department. Boucher told his staff that he had no desire to engage in public discussion or make personal appearances. Indeed, he and his secretary, Miss Mallory, exchanged messages through the letter slot in his office door.

❧ The Budget and the Junior Division

During the Thirties state support for the University was a continuing problem. In the 1929–30 biennium the state provided $210 for each student; this budget was referred to subsequently as the normal budget. By 1937–38 state support had dropped to $117 per student. In 1932 faculty salaries had been cut by 10 percent by administrative fiat, and in 1933 the legislature cut them another 22 percent. In 1935 the faculty received a 5 percent restitution made possible by federal money and tuition, but they thought they had been promised a full restitution as times improved.

When Chancellor Boucher arrived in 1938, he submitted a budget request to the legislature that was $145,497 less than the 1931 appropriaton; indeed, it was smaller than the budgets of the last three bienniums. He wrote to his budget officers in the University on 10 October 1938 that "a return to the *status quo ante* [i.e., the 1929–30 budget] would work grave injustices to individuals, departments, colleges, and schools,"[8] by which he meant that the restoration of the 1929–30 budget would allow him no opportunity to reorder priorities. He made no reference to the promised salary restitution, nor did he address the needs of an enlarged student enrollment.

The faculty was distressed, even outraged, at Boucher's meager request, for they and the deans were convinced that the University could not continue the course it was on. Classes were too large, buildings were falling into decay, equipment was antiquated, and teachers were overworked. When the chancellor proposed that enrollment be restricted in the interests of economy, many were sympathetic. They no less than he knew that 40 percent of entering students inefficiently dropped out by the end of the first year, incapable of sustaining college work or unable to pay even the low tuition. (Tuition averaged about forty dollars a semester before 1940.) The chancellor suggested that students be admitted only upon demonstrated competence in high school studies or upon evidence by special examination of academic merit. Those not prepared for University studies should be guided into vocational training, some of which could be introduced inexpensively into secondary schools.[9] The relatively expensive University could thus be reserved for those with demonstrated competence and determination. The historical open admission to the University should be abandoned. He proposed a fundamental change in public policy, and, given the economic circumstances, a defensible one.

A start in the direction of limiting enrollment had already been made before Boucher came to Nebraska. In December 1936, Oldfather and a faculty committee had proposed that a lower division consisting of the first year of University studies receive, examine, and advise all entering students. In this division, all University students would take general, nonprofessional courses that introduced them to the various branches of learning. From this lower division some students would be advanced to the colleges, others would be put into technological courses, and some would be awarded terminal associate degrees. Whatever else, it would cull unsuitable beginners and limit upper-division admissions. It would be an exit passage for many.

After much controversy, the idea of the Junior Division, as it came to be called, was accepted in April 1938, just as Boucher arrived, and it met with his hearty endorsement. He immediately appointed committees to set it in motion. He thought that with some strengthening, it could be a means not only of limiting University enrollment but of restructuring high school education into two tracks, one vocational, one professional. Potentially at least, this was revolutionary, and it met resistance on ideological grounds. All citizens must have their chance at improving their lot by higher education, egalitarian Nebraskans believed. Research professors objected on pragmatic grounds. Specialized courses would be underscribed if beginning students were enrolled only in general courses, they said.

Nevertheless, by action of the Faculty Senate in October 1939 the Junior Division was established to receive all freshmen and Nels A. Bengston of the Department of Geography was appointed its dean. Bengston softened the rigor which the chancellor sought. He was the last representative of the pioneer generation that had produced the Pounds, Bessey, Howard, Fossler, and Kiesselbach. Having emigrated as a child from Sweden, he spent his whole life in Nebraska, much at the University, and he made a national reputation through his excellence in both teaching and scholarship. Though chairman of geography at Nebraska for many years, he also regularly taught in the summers at Columbia University and was a consulting field geologist in Central and South America. He thought public higher education ought to be inclusive, not exclusive; and he thought beginning courses should be designed to develop intellectual curiosity, not to weed out weak students. Boucher's University of Chicago attracted students whose intellectual curiosity had already been awakened, he argued, whereas a state university like Nebraska needed to kindle sleeping imaginations. Under his direction provision was made in the Junior Division for late bloomers. Recognizing that the initial registration of entering students is an occasion of major importance in any educational program, he sought to give closer guidance than freshman (and others) had theretofore received. "[E]fficiency must be measured on the double basis of human as well as financial responsibility," he said.[10]

For several years the Junior Division operated more as a counseling center than as a culling agency or as a place of general education. The engineering college was reluctant to give up any of its specialized courses even at the freshman level, maintaining that their technical requirements absorbed all a student's hours. Many persons in the agricultural college found little merit in general humanities and social science courses, thinking them inessential to agriculturists. Teachers College and the College of Business Administration feared that Arts and Sciences instructors in the first year would seduce students from their specialized training. Various departments – chemistry, psychology, mathematics – were reluctant to modify basic courses from their preprofessional accent to a philosophical approach. The Junior Division thus did not fulfill the chancellor's hopes. If Boucher had been more persuasive, he might have brought fundamental change to education, but he remained cloistered in his office and the multiple sections of the University continued to squabble for their share of a diminishing pie. High schools were not significantly affected.

❧ *The Retirement Plan*

The academic community might have absorbed academic changes and even embraced some of them, but Boucher's new plan for retirement distressed them all. In its first fifty years the University had had few retirements and no retirement policy, and in more recent times retirement and retirement stipends had been handled on an individual

basis, sometimes with difficulty. Professors L. A. Sherman of English and E. H. Barbour of geology had both stayed on the teaching staff into their eighties and their dotage; and special provisions had had to be made for the financial welfare of the widows of Charles Bessey and Laurence Fossler. Finally in 1935 the regents decided that after 1936 the mandatory retirement age would be seventy-five, by 1941 it would go down to seventy, and by 1946 to age sixty-five. They proposed that retirement stipends, coming from the University's general budget, would consist of one-half the staff member's average salary in his or her last five years of service. Unscientific and unfunded, it was an arbitrary solution to a growing problem. Under its terms, in 1937 Professor F. A. Stuff of English received $1,682 when he retired at age seventy-two with thirty-five years of service; Professor G. O. Virtue of economics received $1,850 at age seventy-six after twenty-eight years; and Dean Amanda Heppner after some forty years received $1,974 at age sixty-six in 1939. By January 1939 twenty-four persons were on the retirement list; and though their stipends were not generous, in those days they were acceptable.

Boucher proposed a new plan in February 1939. The Board of Regents discussed it in the spring and adopted it in July. The stipends thereafter were to be figured on 1937 standard annuity tables based on total length of service and total compensation. It was all professional, but the difference between the old system and the new alarmed the staff. Stuff was now to receive not $1,682 but $796; Virtue, $866; Heppner, $564; and Ida Vose, who had worked in the engineering library, was to received $84.22, not $450. The University would expend $18,996 per year rather than $47,065 on retirement benefits. This plan was "intended to continue only during a transition period until the University may have in operation a joint contributory plan," the regents announced, and a committee of the board promised to investigate the possibilities of such a plan immediately.[11] Persons with long memories recalled that a pension plan proposed in 1909 was defeated in the legislature through the efforts of William Jennings Bryan, and that neither the legislature nor the regents since then had prepared a retirement scheme. When Bengston told new colleagues, "Chancellor Boucher has no friends," he was understood to mean that Boucher deserved no friends.[12]

✒ The School of Music

Changes in the School of Music exacerbated discontent with Boucher. Associated with the University since Canfield's administration, it was in effect the last of the proprietary schools. Its staff had taught on a fee-sharing basis, a system competitive and insecure. In 1930 the University had bought the privately owned school, expecting its fees to cover its costs; but in the depression this was not possible, and in 1936 the Board of Regents petitioned the legislature for $31,720 to support the School of Music. The University now assumed financial responsibility for a faculty limited to fourteen full-time men and women. The reorganization was not pleasant, for a number of persons were dropped from the rolls of approved teachers.

When Boucher arrived in 1938, he planned further reorganization and asked the board to establish a School of Fine Arts within the College of Arts and Sciences. It was to include the departments of speech and dramatic arts, music, and the graphic arts. In January 1939 Arthur E. Westbrook was named its director, over the head of Howard Kirkpatrick, who had been at the University for some forty years teaching voice, theory, and, after Carrie Belle Raymond died in 1927, choral singing. Westbrook came to Nebraska from Illinois Normal University in Bloomington, where he had been a successful administrator. Tall, ascetic in appearance, elegant in manner, he invited filial devotion and required unquestioning loyalty. He was something of an martinet. Essentially a teacher, though a good enough musician, he staffed the music department with his own students, some upon graduation, some after brief service teaching in high schools, some after further training away from Nebraska.

Westbrook saw it as his business to prepare teachers for Nebraska schools, not administer a conservatory; and though technically the School of Fine Arts was a part of the College of Arts and Sciences, under Westbrook it was, in effect, a part of Teachers College. Even before he arrived in Nebraska, Westbrook asked that the dean of Teachers

College be added to the school's course of study committee. When Howard Kirkpatrick suddenly requested retirement in May 1939, Boucher, on vacation, wired – ungenerously – that it would be "best to delete, expunge, erase, obliterate, suppress, efface, cancel and wipe out the name of Kirkpatrick."[13] Not all the musicians in Nebraska were pleased with the direction in which Westbrook (and Boucher) took the School of Fine Arts, and it was two generations before the wounds inflicted by the reorganization were healed.

✒ The Campus on the Eve of War

When the European war came in 1939, the students, like many in the nation, resisted acknowledging America's inevitable involvement. The campus newspaper was unusually full of discussions of current events, in part because prescient professors asserted that this country could not, and should not, remain neutral. Ignoring the future, the University administration called for only slight modifications in its programs. In the fall of 1939 flying instruction was offered through the Civil Aeronautics Authority to some forty students. The engineering college offered noncredit courses for persons in Lincoln, Omaha, and Hastings defense-related businesses, and as time went on, staff members provided technical assistance to war industries. If the students clustered around the radios a bit more than before, they remained, as undergraduates always had, bound up in their own lives.

Life on campus continued pretty much unchanged. Now that the Student Union was open – it was completed in 1938, a handsome building – the undergraduates could dance in the ballroom on weekends for a dime, later fifteen cents, and five times a year some 700 couples went to the Coliseum for all-campus parties. Formal season for those who could afford it opened with the Military Ball in December and continued until March, and organized groups had dancing parties at local hotels and ballrooms. Since the girls had to be in their houses by 12:30 – they were allowed a few 1:00 nights each semester – the local coffee shops such as the Tee Pee, that is, the Tasty Pastry at the Cornhusker Hotel, were crowded around midnight. During the day the students drank Cokes and coffee in the Union Grill or at The Drug on the corner of Fourteenth and S or in one or another of the cafés about the campus.

Campus politicking continued and in 1939–40 the Barbs defeated the Greek coalition for the first time since 1908, making a clean sweep of all campus offices. This astonishing political feat was engineered by a soft-spoken young intellectual from Geneva, Blaine Sloan, who was to become an international lawyer with the United Nations. Housing around the city campus remained substandard. The legendary T. H. Goodding on the ag campus had for ten years pressed for cooperative housing on his campus, with mixed success. The Ag College Boarding Club, started in 1930 with his help, had grown by 1939 to include some sixty members, and two or three other eating clubs developed as spin-offs. On the city campus the Cornhusker Co-op was founded in 1938 with some thirty young men; the Pioneer Co-op followed in 1940, and the Brown Palace in 1942.

In June 1943 Chancellor Boucher submitted preliminary plans to the Board of Regents for men's residence halls to be built between fraternity row on Sixteenth Street and Andrews Hall on Fourteenth Street and paid for by bonds like those that had funded the women's dorms. Delayed because of wartime shortages, the men's dorms were finally completed in December 1945 and inspired the editor of the campus newspaper to ask on 14 December why they had not been built years earlier. Although living costs were not high, money remained a serious problem for many students. In 1940 about 10 percent of the student body had support through the National Youth Administration (NYA). NYA support was reduced by about one-third in 1941. In March 1940 tuition fees were raised from $1.50 per credit hour to $2.50, the increase necessary to make up for the inadequate sum provided by the legislature. The administration asserted that tuition was still lower at Nebraska than at most colleges in the Midwest.

The city campus generally was not beautiful, except for one small area of the original plot. In 1940 Professor James L. Sellers, who saw himself as the campus gadfly, protested "the barren desert-like open spaces" of the downtown campus, so dissimilar to the ag campus which had trees and mowed green spaces. How could a University with a College of Agriculture and a Department of Horticulture justify this lack of planting? he asked; and he proposed that a committee of the Faculty Senate see to the landscaping of the city blocks. Within a few months the Lincoln Alumni Club began planning to landscape the grounds around the new library.[14] The new library was the most splendid building on the campus. When Don L. Love died in 1940, he left his estate of $800,000 to build it. Love, a banker, insurance executive, mayor, and philanthropist, had given money for dormitories in his wife's name a few years earlier, but this massive structure was the largest gift the University had yet received. W. E. Barkley, the executor of Love's estate and himself a major benefactor of the University later, said at the laying of the cornerstone on Friday afternoon, 12 December 1941, that Don Love had felt that "accumulated funds should be employed in a way to help young people secure better equipment for life." It was unwise, Love thought, "to handicap a few with wealth they had not earned."[15]

Football

University football continued to be almost an obsession both on campus and across the state in the prewar years. The players were home-state boys, and the fans seemed to take that fact into consideration. This could almost be called an era of sanity, one sportswriter has said: "The coaches were men of integrity and the fans let reality temper their expectations."[16] Though Dana X. Bible had won half a dozen Big Six championships, he did not get to take his team to the Sugar Bowl in 1935 because postseason games were assumed to interfere with academic life. The invitation was hushed up to avoid controversy. Memorial Stadium was not always full in those years, so John K. Selleck, business manager for the athletic department, started Band Day in 1933 to fill its seats. He invited all kinds of bands, not just high school groups. When Don Lentz arrived at the University in 1937 to direct University bands, he started High School Band Day. At half-time the massed bands put on a great show. He later remembered with some humor that "for many years, probably from

1941 until the end of the war, the only thing that saved the athletic department was that Band Day. The ticket sales were very low for the other games."[17]

When Bible went to Texas in 1937 he recommended Major Lawrence M. "Biff" Jones as his replacement. Hired at $10,000 in 1937, he was receiving $12,000 two years later. Though Biff Jones won only two conference titles in his five years at Nebraska (1937–42), he took his team to the Rose Bowl for New Year's Day 1941. The invitation to the Rose Bowl sent the students parading through the streets and theaters. Though the Nebraska team lost to Stanford, the Nebraska fans felt they had had a share of glory. This Rose Bowl game was the climax of homegrown Nebraska football. Within a year the military had called many players into service, and in 1942 Major Jones was himself on active duty. For the next twenty years Nebraska football was not consistently of national quality.

❧ The War

By 1941 America's participation in the war had become unavoidable. Professors Thomas M. Raysor of the English department and Glenn Gray of the history department, both Anglophiles, publicly attacked the isolationist America First groups. They studied the war, almost pedantically. In the spring of 1941 they and others circulated a petition to be sent to Washington urging assistance to England, "not necessarily short of war." Signed by 186 faculty members, including deans and administrators, it caused local controversy; and when it arrived in Washington, Senator Hugh Butler, who like many other Nebraskans was still isolationist, rejected it. On campus some students said old men were gambling with young men's lives.

The question of intervention became moot on 7 December 1941, and ten days later the chancellor called an all-University convocation in an attempt to settle disturbed students. It was said to be the largest assembly of students ever to meet for a campus address; some 4,000 crowded into the Coliseum. In his cool way, Boucher urged them to stay on course and await directions. "Carry on," he coun-

seled. The campus would not likely see Student Army Training Corps as it had in the last war, he said, because experience showed that that agency was a disappointment. He did not speculate about the University's part in the war.

As the months went by, the faculty became convinced that the chancellor was altogether too passive. Enrollment was already down in the fall of 1941, and with men called to service, it continued to drop. The teaching staff feared that many of them would soon become redundant. When the military asked what University facilities could be turned to wartime purposes, the chancellor made no proposals; he and his Committee on War Emergency did not endorse accelerated schedules – the quarter system suggested by the military – even when Congress offered to provide loans to support students in them. One student, Alan Jacobs, wrote in the *Daily Nebraskan* on 22 October 1942 that every university in the country, even Creighton University in Omaha, had gone on the quarter system to give students an opportunity to get their degrees before being called to military service. Nebraska students "should demand that red tape and narrow mindedness be forgotten," he said angrily. "The university has an obligation to the reservists."

But if the chancellor and his administration were dilatory, others were not. In September 1942 Samuel C. Waugh and Marvin Hurley, neither officially connected with the University but both on temporary service to the federal government in Washington, proposed Lincoln facilities, including the fairgrounds and the new, unoccupied Love Library, for troop use. When the University administration still remained passive, a faculty group of some 140 persons with Professor James Sellers as chairman wrote to the War Manpower Commission in December offering their competencies to the war effort. Their letter was quickly acknowledged by Frederick J. Kelly, specialist in higher education for the U.S. Office of Education. Kelly was a graduate of the University of Nebraska, class of 1902. Pressed by the faculty, Boucher asked his deans to canvass their staff for utilizable skills. Sellers and others thought such a canvass at least a year late.

Later in December the War Manpower Commission an-

nounced that the University of Nebraska was to participate in the Army Specialized Training Program (ASTP),
and the first contingent of corps cadets arrived in March
1943 to be housed in Love Library. In April a second group
was established in the new home economics building on
the ag campus. Also that month, the local students in advanced ROTC were called to active duty and stationed in
Love Library. In May, Alan Jacobs, now editor of the *Daily
Nebraskan*, observed that it had been a "helluva year because of continual uncertainties." He complained that the
University officials had not obtained the military units
that would provide it with the financial backbone "for the
duration." Himself an ROTC student and going on active
duty, he told his newspaper staff and the University community on 14 May: "Hold the fort until we get back. And
we will be back. If we, those of us who live, do not come
back ourselves, we will send you our representatives, the
generation that follows us." Active service was, in fact,
postponed for him and the other ROTC students: after basic
training they were returned to the campus in the fall of
1943 to live in Love Library barracks until places could be
found for them in officer candidate schools. Altogether
some 2,400 men were housed in the library and fed at the
Student Union mess hall. On the ag campus other groups
of transient soldier-students awaited assignment to other
posts. The campuses looked rather like a military camp.

The College of Medicine, which had barely survived
the depression by closing wards, limiting services, and restricting the number of entering students, now com-
pressed their four-year curriculum into four nine-month
academic sessions offered in three calendar years. Students, most in uniform, were assigned to the college and
supported by federal programs. Enrollment rose, and the
faculty spent extra hours in the wards and contended with
shortages of equipment and supplies. Dean Poynter's au-
tocratic management was rarely questioned, in part because he had a paternalistic concern for his students and
faculty, in part because he had a sense of humor, but
mostly because his integrity was obvious.[18]

The year 1943–44 was disturbed and disorderly. The
registrar reported that only about 4,000 students were on
the Lincoln campuses, including the servicemen, down by

one-third from peacetime enrollment. ASTP and ROTC men
came and went, studying very casually while in residence,
and by April 1944 nearly all of them were on their way to
military service elsewhere. The campus became quiet,
much to everyone's disappointment, the 1944 *Cornhusker*
reported.[19] In November 1944 the Board of Regents reported to Governor Griswold that the University had
served 13,769 military men and women, and that 151 staff
members were on military leave. Because of the military
programs on campus, the University had been able to retain a cadre. By January 1945 the regents and the chancellor could begin to plan for the postwar University.

The Postwar University and a Faculty Insurrection

The budget prepared for the 1945 legislature was the first
for the postwar University. The requests in 1941 and 1943
had been very modest because Senator Walter Raecke of
Central City and other friends of the University had
thought wartime conditions made support for University
programs difficult. The faculty acquiesced; but when a
meager budget was announced in 1945, they took alarm.
The chancellor and board were requesting no more than
they had in 1941 and 1943 although living costs had risen
by more than 30 percent and the state was prosperous as it
had not been for twenty-five years.

At the winter meeting of the local chapter of the American Association of University Professors there was an un-
planned explosion of indignation, induced by the failure of
the administration to ask for long-overdue salary adjustments. Tempers ran high, and Professor Sellers, president
of the chapter, called an unofficial meeting of the faculties
for Saturday morning, 17 February, in the Social Sciences
(now CBA) auditorium. There 98 faculty members signed a
statement calling for a blanket adjustment of salaries for
all members of the staff. An ad hoc committee took this
written request to the chancellor on 19 February. He responded that he saw no "necessity for us to have a special
meeting [of the board] at this time." A second general faculty meeting was immediately called for the next Saturday.
This time the attendance was 135 (the University Senate of
tenured professors had only about 120 voting members).

In a letter dated 24 February 1945, the unhappy faculty restated their alarm that no attempt had been made to secure salary restoration. They sent a request for a special meeting of the regents not only to the chancellor but to all the members of the board individually.[20] The chancellor was surprised at their anger.

The subsequent meeting with the board on 2 March 1945 was one of the notable occasions in the history of the University. Since Regent Marion Shaw was in Arizona because of his health, Regent Devoe was in the chair. The faculty committee, a formidable group headed by Sellers, included M. A. Basoco of mathematics, its secretary; W. L. DeBaufre, the most distinguished member of the engineering faculty; H. C. Filley, the most vocal member of the Department of Agricultural Economics; C. A. Forbes, a profound scholar of Latin and Greek; R. W. Frantz, chairman of English; C. W. Scott of the Teachers College; and C. M. Hicks, a highly respected young associate professor of business organization. They were joined by Dean Oldfather of the College of Arts and Sciences, Dean Burr of Agriculture, Dean Ferguson of Engineering, and Dean Henzlik of Teachers College.

The faculty presented a "General Statement" which raised questions concerning the whole future of the University; and by the conclusion of the meeting, the chancellor had agreed to send significant sections of this statement to the governor and every member of the unicameral. Legislative response was immediate. On 6 March Senator Ladd J. Hubka of Beatrice wrote Boucher and the board: "Gentlemen, as far as I am personally concerned, the only thing I can not understand is why the devil they didn't do it a long time ago!" He continued: "I think it is an outrage to think you can keep qualified men without being at least partially fair to them."[21]

Within the week the faculty committee was augmented by a faculty appropriations committee which included Dean of Students T. J. Thompson and Dean Robert Goss of the Graduate College. In a letter that had been prepared on 15 March with the cooperation of Regent Devoe, they gave the legislative appropriations committee a careful accounting of University budgets for the previous twenty years and a detailed account of present needs. The chancellor was absent from the city. On 23 March the two committees, with Dean Thompson in the chair, personally put their case to the appropriations committee in the statehouse. Their presentation was carefully planned, even orchestrated, with the chancellor, who had returned to Lincoln, speaking last. On 5 April the faculty committees presented a "Table of Stepped Salary Adjustment for Instructional Staff," a document unlike anything previously seen, and the legislative body discovered that the administration's budget did not square with the needs as defined by the faculty. The appropriations committee accepted the faculty recommendations.

On 13 April the regents presented their building needs to the legislature, listing fourteen buildings in order of priority. They clearly had been emboldened by the legislative response to faculty action; and by the end of the session they saw the authorization of a new armory to replace the decrepit Nebraska Hall, a classroom building to replace old University Hall, and an extension on Avery Laboratory of Chemistry. When the legislature adjourned, funds had been provided for salary adjustments as requested by the faculty committee; and John Selleck, secretary of the board, could write in May that the proposed increases would be effective on 1 June 1945.[22] At its June meeting the board increased the stipends of retired persons by 25 percent.

The faculty had a right to be pleased with themselves. Their actions had required courage, for their jobs had been on the line. They knew that their success could not have been possible if most of the deans and at least one of the regents had not supported them. But they could not stop now. At a general meeting on 15 May, the faculty voted to continue an executive committee to oversee the budget and administration. They elected Professor Clarence E. McNeill of the College of Business Administration as its chairman. No firebrand, McNeill was a quiet, little, conservative economist. That he should be nominated, and accepted, as successor to Sellers showed the depth of faculty discontent.

In all of this Boucher was odd man out. Never a person of high energy, he was worn down by the controversy. In a letter dated 18 January 1945, but not delivered until March, he informed the board that he wanted to retire as of 1 September 1946. He noted his growing frailty, his nervous exhaustion, and his loss of hearing. In 1946 he would be sixty years old. His letter was not made public for another year but his imminent departure was anticipated.[23]

In the spring 1946 a regents' committee to find a successor to Boucher was appointed with Robert Devoe as its chairman, and he immediately assured the faculty that their judgment would get high consideration. On 24 March the campus newspaper observed that the board and a strong faculty committee were beginning the search. In an open meeting with students the regents listed qualities necessary for a chancellor. Milton S. Eisenhower, president of Kansas State College at Manhattan, was repeatedly suggested, but so were Dean Oldfather; John D. Clark, dean of Business Administration; and George W. Rosenlof, the registrar. It was generally agreed that a new man should be brought into the University. The University had clearly come to a turning point.

During the long hiatus between early 1945 and September 1946 while Boucher was ailing and ineffectual, the University was operated by Dean Thompson. For years he had been not only dean of students but, in effect, provost. He had served as chairman of major committees and had planned most administrative changes, including the Junior Division. For twenty years he was faculty representative on the Big Six Athletic Council – all three of his brilliant sons were varsity athletes – from which he retired in 1947 when, he said, "I felt commercialism was coming in to an extent that I could not support as an educator."[24] Assisted by Claire Harper in his Office of Student Affairs, he always taught an elementary course in chemistry in order to keep in touch with the students and he required members of his staff to teach courses also. In later years he was rather austere in appearance, almost totally bald. From the beginning he was straightforward and, holding the most difficult post in the University for a full generation, he earned general respect. Unlike Boucher, he did not get tired. Many wished he were more a scholar, with an academic turn of mind, but he was a man of his word and everybody knew it.

9. "Turning the University Around": 1946–1953

❧ The New Chancellor

When Reuben Gustavson came to Lincoln as chancellor in 1946 from the University of Chicago, where he had briefly been vice president, he found an institution that had survived twenty-five years of depression and war. Structurally it was intact, however dispirited its staff. The faculty thought his arrival heralded a new day, and he did indeed "turn the University around," as the young men of the time said. Nineteen forty-six was a crisis year in its history; perhaps it was for universities across the country. Encouraged by federal funding, they were increasingly asked to become research centers, and unlike Chancellor Boucher, Chancellor Gustavson expected his university to play on the national stage.

It would be hard to imagine chancellors more dissimilar than Reuben Gustavson and Chauncey Boucher. Boucher was small, elegant, ironical, even sarcastic. Handsome, he was careful of his appearance. Gustavson was too large for any room, and his clothing looked as though it had been bought hastily off the rack in a bargain basement. A victim of polio at an early age, he wore a brace on one leg, though this was not generally known, and he suffered silently when standing for any length of time. The son of Swedish immigrants, he never forgot that he owed his eminence to public education. Boucher's self-confidence masked timidity, his graceful manner a want of energy. He left lobbying to his associates and told the legislators that his job was to let them know the University's needs; it was their job to see what they could do about meeting those needs. He rarely traveled in the state. Gustavson walked the main streets of Nebraska towns. He said that during his first year in office he made 400 speeches. No county fair

was beneath his attention. Like his two great predecessors, Chancellor Canfield and Chancellor Andrews, he took his University to the people. Called to the University with the full approval of a faculty committee, he saw himself as a member of the scholarly community.

❧ The Chancellor's Associates

The persons who worked most closely with Gustavson admired him in the extreme, and for the rest of their lives they talked about him. He inherited some excellent assistants. George Round had been recommended to Boucher as director of public relations by Joe W. Seacrest and other Lincoln businessmen in 1944. On the staff at the ag college from his undergraduate days, he had a detailed knowledge of Nebraska. He could call more persons by name than anybody else in the state, it was said. Like Gustavson, he was rather rumpled and downright. He orchestrated lobbying into a fine art. Taught by Gustavson that the University was a place where multiple points of view needed to be sheltered, he assumed nonetheless that they sometimes should be hidden from general scrutiny. He kept an eye out for public reactions. George and Margaret Round – they were a team – did not always agree with the chancellor's politics, but they loved him. Repeatedly Round said over the years, "Gus was a great, great man," and he meant it.

Round surrounded himself with especially able men to serve Gustavson. In time Edward Hirsch moved from the Office of Public Relations into the University Foundation, where he became its president in a time of trouble. Bruce Nicoll became administrative assistant to the chancellor before becoming director of the University of Nebraska Press, which he transformed into one of the leading university presses of the nation. Ken Keller was jack-of-all-trades for twenty years, writing speeches for some chancellors (never Gustavson), representing the University on radio and in print, smoothing difficulties silently when students and faculty misspoke or fell into contention. Less oriented toward agriculture than Round, these men tried to balance his representations of the University to the state. Gustavson trusted them all, and so did the faculty, and all of them admired the chancellor hardly less than the Rounds did.

Gustavson's major appointment in 1947 was Carl W. Borgmann as dean of faculties and, in essence, deputy chancellor. Borgmann, from the University of Colorado, had worked with Gustavson when Gustavson was graduate dean there, and upon arrival in Nebraska he was charged with helping to encourage research activities in the various colleges. He and the chancellor visited all the departments to discuss their unique problems and research goals. Borgmann was an excellent administrator and a shrewd judge of people, as Gustavson was not; and he was essentially fair-minded, asking that the staff be paid according to their achievements, not according to their market value. Like Gustavson, he was a liberal in a conservative state. He and his jolly wife, Mable, the parents of four daughters, used to say that Nebraska answered all their dreams: they even had a son here.

The faculty welcomed Gustavson because they saw that though he brought new ideas to the University, he expected to consult with them. In January 1946, at the suggestion of Regent Robert Devoe, the ad hoc advisory committee which had proposed the maverick 1945 budget was made into a permanent advisory group to consider "any matter concerning the operation or general welfare of the University."[1] The idea was embraced by Gustavson and Borgmann. Composed of some of the most responsible academic citizens, it made the faculty part of University governance, and in 1948 it became the Liaison Committee, which, with the Policy Committee, a faculty-staff group of six persons, met regularly with the chancellor and the dean to thrash out University policy. The chancellor also relied on the Research Council, a faculty group set up in 1939 to supervise graduate study, and increased its budget. The new chancellor and the faculty saw the University from a single point of view: this was a community of scholars with a single mission, the investigation and dissemination of truth.

Postwar Students

From the beginning Gustavson was popular with the students. They early on took to calling him "Dr. Gus," at least among themselves and in newspaper editorials. He treated them as adults. At his first all-University convocation in 1946, he talked to them of "Science and Religion." In 1947 when he returned from Mexico, where he had served with UNESCO at President Truman's request, he reported on his activities to them. When decorated by the Swedish government in 1948, he returned to tell them all about it. When the University celebrated Goethe's bicentennial in 1949, he addressed the community on "Goethe, Humanist and Scientist." Of course he wrote his own speeches. He was a biochemist of national reputation, his sympathies wide and his memory photographic. Young professors later recalled how he appeared casually in campus coffee shops in his suspenders, ready to talk to anybody. Students and faculty and Nebraskans all thought Gustavson had brought a new day.

In fact this was a new day. In the fall 1946 the University enrolled some 9,000 students and by spring 500 more had appeared, for a total twice the 1945 enrollment of fewer than 5,000. Of the 9,000, 6,500 were veterans supported by the GI Bill and half of these new to any campus. Only 2,400 were women. The enrollment continued to go up. Departments, not prepared for the swelling numbers of students, on short notice pressed many inexperienced townspeople into teaching. The ex-servicemen thought themselves adults, as indeed they were, and they expected to be treated as adults. Old rules forbidding drinking on and around campus struck them as ridiculous. Most of the veterans were well over twenty-one, and regulations designed for eighteen-year-olds annoyed them. For the next decade at least, long after the veterans had left, drinking on campus was much discussed and surreptitiously permitted, as it had never been before the war. In the postwar decades, drinking by undergraduates became a statewide issue in puritanical Nebraska, and the dean of men, charged with enforcing unpopular rules, was pressed on one side by adult students and on the other by conservative parents.

Times were changing, sometimes faster than Nebraskans recognized. When campus parking became congested, the veterans double-parked and demanded better service. Once when the city police appeared to enforce the parking rules, the students let the air out of the cruisers' tires. It was May 1948, and the weather was fine. The police overreacted and, thinking the crowd a mob, threw tear gas into a group gathered near Social Sciences Hall on Twelfth Street. At this the veterans did threaten to become a mob, and the dean of faculties – the chancellor was out of town – hastily sent the police away. For the rest of that spring day the students marched around town, first to the capitol and then to the city hall, and after lunch they paraded their cars up and down O Street, waving at pedestrians. The campus newspaper reported on 8 May, "Everybody had a fairly good time and the *Daily Nebraskan* was provided with plenty of copy for news." The "parking riot" got rather more unsympathetic reporting than it deserved. At worst, it was only an undergraduate romp. Old Dean Thompson, who had been dean of men since 1927, called the whole thing "an episode" and dismissed it.

In subsequent springs the undergraduates engaged in something called panty raids, which attracted a good deal of bad publicity to the University. In May 1952 after a water fight a group of male students ranged through the dorms and sorority houses collecting lingerie, which was often flaunted by the girls. Though some damage was done, the response of solemn Nebraskans was out of proportion to the incident and Chancellor Gustavson was called on to calm indignant citizens. In May 1954 male students had another panty raid which also got bad publicity. An Omaha Selective Service board asked for participants' names so they could be drafted into the Korean War, then being fought, and a number of students were suspended from the University for disturbing the peace. The next year students "rioted" while the legislature was in session, and again the University found itself under sharp criticism

by the old men in the statehouse. Panty raids were hardly unique to this campus; in the Fifties students across the country engaged in such shenanigans, as *Life* magazine loved to report. Old hands remembered how, in past springs, young male students had often paraded through town, their hormones churning, in what were then called shirttail parades.

The veterans played undergraduate politics with an earnestness new to the campus. At the end of the spring term, 1947, Mary Mielenz, faithful adviser to the student council, warned the students against cliques which excluded all but members of the Faction, a campus political party whose style was set by veterans. In the winter of 1949 Dean Thompson publicly condemned the Faction for its tactics of intimidation. He declared that the student council had become so political as to be unrepresentative; he thought campus politics ought to be democratic so everybody could have a chance to join any old-boy network. This public condemnation by Thompson was unique. Before, he had stood well above campus activities since his office required him to be both judge and prosecutor.

The immediate postwar campus was sometimes disrupted by TNE – Theta Nu Epsilon – the sub rosa drinking fraternity. In prewar years its members had been an occasional nuisance, painting its red skull and crossbones on sidewalks and walls, playing at campus politics, flexing adolescent muscles. But in 1950 ten TNE students were suspended for organized cheating, and in December seven or eight young men, identified as members of TNE, attacked a student at his front door, knocking out his teeth and breaking his glasses, for reasons that were not at all clear. The campus newspaper reported that several of the Greek-letter houses had been invaded by unidentified men also members of TNE who destroyed property and marched drunkenly through the rooms.

These activities reminded some of the Ku Klux Klan, and in January 1951 the student council urged Thompson to ferret out and discipline the members of TNE. The dean thanked the student council for its support, reminding it that he had stood alone on other occasions. When in May seven young men with red paint on their clothes were caught painting the TNE sign near Bancroft Hall, four were suspended. Thompson announced that not since 1940 had he come so near to exposing TNE for what it was and that the current episode was a great opportunity for disposing of this continuously disruptive group. His demand for a complete list of TNE members was endorsed by a front-page editorial in the campus newspaper on 10 May. Any reversal of his decision to dismiss the four, Thompson said, would be "against my better judgment." He was not pleased when the next week Gustavson overruled him and reinstated the four. TNE alumni had provided him with a complete list of active and inactive members, Gustavson announced, and he was amazed at how prominent some of the alumni members were. He was sure that with the list in his hand, TNE would become inactive. The old dean disapproved of this negotiated settlement, but in fact TNE never again became a serious threat to the civil order of the campus.

Though some 14,000 students were enrolled in 1948, by 1950 the number was down to a more or less permanent 7,000 or 8,000. The percentage of native Nebraskans at the University remained somewhat higher than the national average of natives at state universities. The University of Nebraska remained a regional institution.

❧ The Ideal of Research

The University budget changed dramatically in the postwar years. In 1947 the legislature passed a special levy of 1.1 mills for buildings, an action which allowed for ten-year planning and represented the first scheme for construction in twenty years. In 1948 Gustavson requested a 20 percent increase in the general budget, and though he got only a 4.5 percent raise, it was still the largest sum the University had ever received. In 1950 he asked for a 38 percent increase, and again though he got a million dollars less than requested, he yet received four and a half million more than in the previous biennium. Senator Terry Carpenter, the most colorful and probably the most powerful member of the legislature, said later that Gustavson "was a burglar. He always had my admiration. He knew what politics was and he used it and he went to any methods to extract the money from us. He was the only man that [the

University] ever had with that qualification."[2] The chancellor relied heavily on George Round, who was in the legislative chamber every day gaining the respect and affection of the legislators. He reported to Gustavson daily and together they planned their legislation campaigns.

More important than the budget, enrollment, and undergraduate disturbances was the new view of itself that Gustavson gave the University. At the annual Homecoming Dinner which Gustavson inaugurated on 22 October 1947, the new dean of faculties, Borgmann, defined his and the chancellor's purposes. The goal of any University, he said, was the vigorous search for new truths in science, economics, and the humanities. Conformity of thought — that is, automatic conventional and traditional responses to problems — would shatter the American dream of progress. The future lay with innovation, and change was to be embraced, not resisted. The University must become a research institution.

When W. W. Burr, for twenty years the cautious dean of the College of Agriculture, retired in 1948, W. V. Lambert was appointed to that post. Coming to the University from the U.S. Department of Agriculture, where he had been administrator of the Agricultural Research Administration, he was "without doubt one of the nation's top-flight research men," Gustavson said.[3] He was the first dean to have direct responsibility for all divisions of his college, and he encouraged fundamental as opposed to applied research; he told his faculty that "research is the last frontier of American life."[4] When Margaret Fedde, head of the Department of Home Economics, retired in 1950 after service since 1919, she was replaced by Doretta Schlaphoff, who had taken her doctorate in nutrition at Cornell University. Schlaphoff directed her energies, and the energies of her staff, into research. Thanks to federal funds, the agricultural campus had always had a strong research component, but Lambert and Schlaphoff called for more. Lambert noted that the nation had spent $166 million for research in 1930 but by 1947 the figure had risen to more than a billion dollars; he expected it to double in the next eight years. He vastly underestimated the rise, but it was into this world of research that the new chancellor was taking the University.

The career of Theodore Jorgensen, professor of physics, illustrates Gustavson's aspirations and methods. The son of a homesteading Congregational minister in South Dakota, Jorgensen arrived at the University of Nebraska in 1923 having been prepared for college by his mother's tutoring. She had a master's degree in mathematics and English. He was quickly recognized as brilliant by Professor L. C. Wimberly in English, Professor M. G. Gaba in mathematics, and Professor John Almy in physics and studied at the University from 1923 until 1930, taking two degrees. "My undergraduate physics training was solely in classical physics, and I think it was on a fairly competent level," he wrote many years later. "My graduate work was a continuation of my training in classical physics with hardly a whisper of the tremendous advances taking place in physics."[5] In 1938, after taking his Ph.D. at Harvard, where he had assistantships in important laboratories, he returned to Nebraska as an assistant professor at an annual salary of $2,500, a decent sum. But the period from 1938 until 1942 was a time of stagnation for him. "The physics department was essentially the same as when I left," he remembered. "I suppose I felt no different than thousands of teachers in small colleges who were not able to reach levels of their potential because they were overloaded with menial tasks, they had no research facilities, and [they lacked] stimulating colleagues."

Recruited in 1942 to work on atomic physics in the Manhattan Project, Jorgensen spent four years at Los Alamos. Reuben Gustavson found him there just as he was considering the chancellorship in Lincoln. "He looked me up to find what I could tell him about the University," Jorgensen recalled. "I suggested that the University should expand its physics department so it could offer work toward the doctorate in physics and that an [atomic] accelerator would help to get things underway. He told me that if he took the position offered to him, he wanted me to come back to Nebraska and he would find funds to get me started. He took the job and I returned to start the work on atomic physics."[6]

True to his word, Gustavson backed Jorgensen, and when Jorgensen asked for $5,000 to get his research started, "he countered with the suggestion that five thousand dollars might not be enough." Very shortly Professor H. H. Marvin, chair of the department, seeing Jorgensen's rapid progress, urged him to go after federal funds, whereupon the Atomic Energy Commission granted him $10,000 annually for a three-year term. (The National Science Foundation, which was to have such an impact on research in the next generations, was established only in 1950.) "The three years of the original contract was gradually extended for twenty years . . . and support has been continued to the present time, 1990, with funds from the National Science Foundation," he said. In the forty years after Gustavson got the initial money from a private donor, Nathan Gold, more than $4 million came to the University in support of this research.

"Little did I imagine when I first started to think about research in atomic physics that we would build a laboratory that would be recognized the world over," Jorgensen observed. "The thrust of the research done on our project is to increase our understanding of fundamental physical phenomena. Someone might ask what practical application there is to this understanding. We do not usually think of such things; we let our interests determine what problems we work on. Our curiosity drives us on."[7] Jorgensen's curiosity seemed insatiable. Not only was he a physicist; he was a specialist in Chinese cuisine and a musician of considerable amateur accomplishment. A devoted teacher, he occasionally taught a class of undergraduates into his eighties. At age eighty-eight he published a book on the physics of golf with the American Institute of Physics.

Gustavson agreed with Jorgensen that research must be driven by a desire to increase general understanding, but he realized that increasing research might turn universities into collections of specialists, not communities of scholars. If the researchers were primarily professional, he said, the liberal arts would be subordinated to professionalism and education in America would face a narrow future.[8] His desire to reconcile special and general education was reflected in his pleasure in the new library. When Love Library was finally available to the University community in September 1945, having been occupied by air cadets and soldiers during the war years, the students and faculty found two libraries under one roof. The research library consisted of nine studies for faculty, sixteen seminar rooms for graduates, and eighty-nine carrels in the stacks for advanced students. The undergraduate library consisted of four large reading rooms, one each for humanities, science and technology, social studies, and education, all with open shelves and each with a trained librarian. Books on open shelves could be used freely within the room or checked out. Specialized volumes were kept in closed stacks, and documents and reserved books were also separate but easily available. The library was designed for general as well as professional service, encouraging easy access and browsing. Frank Lundy, its director, thought students should be with, not away from, their books. Lundy, red-faced and singleminded, got a campus reputation for being difficult and grew increasingly uncooperative as the years passed, but his library system pleased general readers, expensive as it turned out to be.

Chancellor Gustavson and Dean Borgmann, the latter a chemical engineer with advanced study in Scandinavia and a Ph.D. from Cambridge, encouraged a broadening of the curriculum. They financed new programs in Latin American studies, Oriental studies, and other interdisciplinary areas. They did not perceive any department as essentially a service department, for they assumed that all were centers of scholarship. Distressed that the School of Fine Arts had become hardly more than an adjunct to the Teachers College, they were pleased when Professor Duard Laging, himself hired as an art educator, staffed his revitalized department with practicing artists who inspired students and delighted the community.

Racism and Student Life

Gustavson not only turned the University around academically, he forced it to confront social issues. When the women's residence halls were opened in 1932, they were tacitly restricted racially, although the subject of race was never raised. Race became an issue in 1942 when American students of Japanese extraction began arriving in Nebraska from the West Coast, released from the internment camps where they had been placed after Pearl Harbor. At their meeting on 28 March 1942, the Board of Regents, re-

sponding to wartime hysteria, voted that when "Japanese [sic] students appear for registration" University officials must "refer each student to the FBI for clearance before they can be accepted as students."[9] The board's policy was by no means universally endorsed. "We are fighting to free enslaved peoples and nations, but here at home there is racial discrimination," Paul E. Svoboda, editor of the *Daily Nebraskan,* wrote on 14 April 1942. "The ideal of equality and justice is besmeared by the discriminatory actions and words of persons and groups at home." He concluded, "This is the great American paradox." The registrar reported only twenty-five Japanese Americans at the University by September 1943, but these figures were probably fudged, for a great many more appeared around town. Dean Thompson was severely criticized by students both in and out of uniform when early in 1944 he dismissed a Nisei student from the University for dating a local girl and ordered him out of town. He was genuinely surprised to discover that his action was regarded as racist. "I have no racial prejudice whatsoever," he asserted later; falling back on a cliché of the time, he said, "You cannot legislate an attitude of tolerance upon an individual or upon a people."[10] In 1944 the regents felt called upon to take a position "concerning interracial social relations in connection with Women's Dormitory occupancy." The women's dorms on North Sixteenth Street were "for women students of the white race," but an "international house open to women students of any race or color" was to be available whenever a group of sixteen or more women "of the same race" applied for facilities. The board said, further, "Since it is advisable to avoid agitation of interracial questions whenever possible, it would seem to be inadvisable to set forth this statement of policy in print." This was out of respect for "a majority of the citizens of the state."[11] Feelings were running high as a result of the war in the Pacific.

International House was established in a former sorority house on R Street. In 1947 letters to the campus newspaper reported that segregation was found even within it, and they asserted that the house itself acted as a kind of racial ghetto.[12] In May some Japanese and Korean Americans reported that they had been refused service in a local café.[13] The editor of the *Daily Nebraskan* condemned bigotry in Peoria in a 22 April 1947 editorial but without mentioning local circumstances, and in November the student council sponsored a Big Six conference on racial discrimination in sports and voted to withdraw from the conference unless its discriminatory racial clauses were corrected. It will be remembered that President Truman banned segregation in the armed forces in 1948.

In October 1949 Gustavson persuaded the Board of Regents to issue a directive integrating the dorms. The board and the chancellor seemed unaware, and they certainly did not acknowledge, that both men's and women's rooming houses, privately-owned and -operated, had been integrated with the full knowledge of University authorities since 1943. Though the assistant dean of women, who had supervised the residences for women since 1925, was disturbed by the chancellor's actions, the integration brought no repercussions. Interestingly enough, segregation in men's residence halls, which had finally been opened in 1945, was never an issue, nor was it an issue when a great expansion of men's dorms was contracted for in 1952. Though fraternities and sororities were not integrated for many years, official nondiscriminatory policies were established by 1949.

The chancellor was concerned with the health of all his students. For many years they had complained, often bitterly, about student health facilities, and in 1945 a campus poll showed that half the students were seriously dissatisfied.[14] They found the records in the health office slovenly, the office itself disorderly — it looked as though a hurricane had passed that way — the facilities in Pharmacy Hall filthy, and the staff guilty of serious misdiagnosis. When the superannuated director finally retired in 1946, overdue renovation was immediate. By April 1947 a new student health center was planned with Dr. Samuel I. Fuenning as its director. When eleven wooden barracks from the Hastings Naval Depot were moved to the downtown campus to relieve temporarily the serious space shortages, one became the Student Health Center, complete with infirmary. In the second semester 1948 full health service was available to students for the first time in University history, and in 1953 a full-time psychiatrist was added to the staff through a grant from the Woods Charitable Fund. Dean

Walter K. Beggs of Teachers College said later, "Gus really created a fine student health program here at the University of Nebraska. He was entirely responsible for that."[15]

⟨ Anti-Communism on Campus

Halfway through his seven-year tenure as chancellor, Gustavson had brought the University into modern times. Its administration accepted new social responsibility for its students, and its faculty increasingly saw itself as a research as well as a teaching institution. As a matter of principle, Gustavson defended dissenting opinion that sometimes challenged Nebraska habits of mind. When Dean Frederick Beutel, a colorful, opinionated theorist, introduced an innovative curriculum in the reopened law college — it had been closed during the war for lack of students — he and the college garnered considerable criticism even though Beutel had assembled a brilliant faculty. The chancellor successfully defended them against Chief Judge Robert G. Simmons of the Nebraska Supreme Court and the Nebraska Bar Association.[16] He publicly supported the United Nations and encouraged students to set up model conferences on international affairs. Some Nebraskans saw the university as a "hotbed of liberalism" which harbored Communist sympathizers, especially after the campus played host to such persons as Trygve Lie, secretary-general of the United Nations; Ralph Bunche, the black who won the Nobel Peace Prize in 1950; and Wayne Morse, the maverick senator from Oregon. Gustavson came under attack from "patriotic" groups, local conservatives, some veterans' organizations, and political opportunists. "I am concerned about reports of extreme liberalism concerning the Chancellor of the University," Senator Terry Carpenter said; he himself did not believe the rumors that the chancellor was a Communist, he added, but he was puzzled over their persistence.[17] George Round recalled that visitors to the chancellor's residence on A Street were sometimes suspected of searching there for evidence of Communism.[18] These were the McCarthy years, and the tensions of the Korean War encouraged paranoia.

The issue of loyalty on campus came to a head in December 1952. On Monday night, 8 December, the chairman of the Un-American Activities Committee of the Nebraska American Legion told an Omaha post, "If you could find good Communist literature and really fight it, your membership will really increase." He thereupon announced that "a certain professor in the University uses a certain textbook" and that "students can't swallow the stuff." The next day an American Legion committee was appointed to investigate. The "certain professor" turned out to be E. N. Anderson of the history department and the book, *The State of Asia*, contained an essay by Owen and Eleanor Lattimore.[19] Lattimore was an established authority on Asian affairs, but he had been attacked by Senator McCarthy and others as "sympathetic to Communism." In a few days a group of prominent Omaha businessmen commended the action of Post No. 3 for exposing the use of the book. E. N. Anderson may have been mistaken for A. T. Anderson, another professor of history and earlier a liberal candidate for the U.S. Senate challenging the arch-conservative Kenneth Wherry.

The campus was immediately in an uproar. The editor of the *Daily Nebraskan*, Ruth Raymond, thundered in a front-page editorial on 10 December: "The only strength of their 'investigation' lies in the insinuation, smear and cries of 'pink' which are bound to reach the ears of state taxpayers and parents." She was right in assuming that "the entire University — students, faculty and administration will be entirely in support of Dr. Anderson." She concluded, "Are we free to think? Are we free to read? Are we free to have our own opinions? Are we free to examine, to analyze — and then to choose what we find to be right?" The local chapter of the American Association of University Professors immediately announced that they denied "the validity of witch-hunts and trials by press, innuendo, pressure groups, or agencies outside the properly constituted legal authorities."[20] Elmer Davis, a respected radio commentator and former head of the U.S. Office of War Information, reported on the fracas in his 26 December broadcast: "[P]lenty of people in the university and in the town, stood up on their hind legs and roared," he said, citing Ruth Raymond, the AAUP, the student council, the local chapter of Americans for Democratic Action, and various individuals including a retired colonel of military intelligence. Davis concluded with "a salute to the people of Lincoln, in the University and out, who know that the watchfulness of citizens is the salvation of the state. . . ."[21]

By early spring the American Legion had in effect backed away and adopted a program of "citizenship in education" written by a professor in the University, but the whole affair left a cloud over the University and a defensiveness within the faculty. Charles Thone, one of the original members of the investigation committee, resigned within days of its start and a few months later married the editor of the campus newspaper. For the next generation the two of them were public figures, Thone as U.S. congressman and governor, Ruth Raymond Thone as social activist. Freedom of expression and research was not restricted at the University, but the chancellor and his staff were put on the defensive. A liberal in a conservative, even reactionary, state, Gustavson frightened some timid Nebraskans.

ᛏ Football

For all his homegrown manner, Reuben Gustavson did not fully understand the temper of Nebraska. Football had been a passion here from earliest years, and though Chancellors Canfield and Andrews found it indefensibly brutal, they accepted it when they discovered its irresistible popularity. Gustavson could not reconcile himself to its postwar excesses. He disapproved of programs which distorted the students' educational experience and often left them with lifetime injuries. He could not overlook actions which he thought unethical, like undercover payments, nationwide recruiting, and manipulation of course credits. From his University of Denver days, he had been an outspoken critic of professionalized football. Indeed, he had left Denver for the University of Colorado at Boulder because of the antagonism which had grown up between him and his administration over football.

In Nebraska, football was a sacred cow. "Nebraska flinched its way through nine straight losing seasons following the Rose Bowl euphoria" of 1941, Wally Provost of the *Omaha World-Herald* later observed, and "a spirit of defeatism and uncertainty" pervaded the state. In 1946 Bernie Masterson, a former Nebraska quarterback, was hired as head football coach at $10,000 a year to return Nebraska to the glory days. But he had two unsuccessful seasons and "some fans never forgave Masterson for scheduling Notre Dame," which twice defeated Nebraska and "spoiled the rosy glow of the close prewar rivalry."[22] In February 1948 Masterson resigned with three years remaining on his contract. Joe W. Seacrest, publisher of the *Lincoln Journal*, had offered him $20,000 to withdraw, the sum to come from a local self-appointed committee headed by Clarence Swanson, football letterman of the Twenties and by 1948 a successful Lincoln merchant. Seacrest remembered the circumstances: "So we had a meeting at our home at 4:00 Saturday afternoon and we told the boys what Clarence Swanson and I had done. Everybody was for it, but they said, 'Now you must tell Gustavson and get his approval. We haven't any right to do any of these things.' So we set up a date to see Gustavson Sunday. I think that we were Earl Campbell [of Miller and Paine], Howard Wilson [of Bankers Life Insurance Company], T. B. Strain [of Continental National Bank] and myself. As we walked up the steps there at A Street, Earl Campbell said 'Joe, you are pretty close to this. Why don't you explain this thing?' Well, hell, I started talking around the mulberry bush – which you have to do – and finally Gus said 'What did you give the man?' and I said '$20,000.' He said 'That is an awful lot of money.' I said 'That is a hell of a lot of money. Maybe they will learn not to be drawing these contracts before they know what they are getting.' So he went along on that."[23]

After a year with George "Potsy" Clark filling in, Bill Glassford was hired as chief coach in 1949, and in the next five years Nebraska had three winning teams. When his contract came up for renewal in 1951, the chancellor was again bypassed and in anger wrote to "Mr. George Clark," who was now athletic director: "I am disturbed by the fact that this contract was drawn up and all ready to be presented to the board of regents without ever having been submitted to this office. I think we should have it clearly understood that no contract, except those routine contracts with respect to games, should ever be negotiated without this office knowing in detail and having approved just exactly what is to go into the contract."[24] Glassford stayed on.

Football fans accused Gustavson of attempting to "deemphasize" football, and they were right. He wanted to keep the game properly under academic control. In 1949 he, the Board of Regents, and the Board of Intercollegiate Athletics laid out the terms under which the game was to be played. By October 1951 when he addressed a University convocation on overemphasis in intercollegiate sports, all the heads of the Big Seven Conference, the successor to the Big Six Conference, had agreed to four restraints: no off-season practice, no freshmen on the teams, no postseason games, and normal academic progress for players. The next year, in the fall of 1952, John A. Hannah, president of Michigan State University and chairman of a special committee of the American Council on Education, joined ten other educators, including Gustavson, in an investigation of college athletics. They wanted "to cut college athletics down to size and to keep control on the campuses."[25] The heads of universities, at least in these first postwar years, seemed no longer to have full authority within their own institutions. Wally Provost observes, "While Nebraska was floundering, Oklahoma was setting the stage for the most oppressive reign by any school in conference history," in part by nationwide recruiting supported generously by extramural enthusiasts.[26]

Does an elaborate football program harm its sheltering university? It is hard to say. Clearly it brings no general financial advantage. There seems to be no correlation between winning teams and legislative beneficence. In the Twenties and Thirties when Nebraska football teams were winning, the legislature was not generous; indeed, the money supplied during Coach Bible's glory years was disastrously low. In the Forties and Fifties when winning was occasional at best, the budgets were larger than they had ever been before. Free football tickets may have pleased the legislators, but they did not open the public purse. Academically the student body does not appear to have been much injured. Though players got special advising and sometimes special courses, their numbers were so proportionately small that they did not distort the total. Gustavson was always concerned with what he took to be the hypocrisy surrounding the sport, but this hypocrisy, if it exists, is an open secret and perhaps no greater than other hypocrisies. In his consistent resistence to football, Gustavson was clearly out of phase with powerful elements in the state.

❧ The D.Ed. Controversy

The second major battle of Gustavson's administration – the first was over football – was academic. For some fifty years the Teachers College had worked to establish its autonomy, even hegemony. Until 1921 it had been an adjunct to the College of Arts and Sciences, on the assumption that public school teachers needed to be directed by subject-matter professors as much as by teachers of pedagogy. Indeed, until about 1920, methods had been taught in subject-matter departments by subject-matter professors. Educationists resented what they thought of as academic encroachment on their territory and, for a time (1914–18), even set up their own graduate school independent of the general graduate college.

Instead of cooperation, the method and the subject-matter people fell into confrontation, often hostile. By 1950 this confrontation had become acrimonious. The character of the deans of the two colleges principally involved illustrated their differences. C. H. Oldfather and Frank Henzlik had been appointed in the same year (1931). Oldfather looked like a dean: tall, handsome, angular, he peered through rimless glasses with an ironic glance that suggested he could not be surprised by any human foible. A classicist, he came from a family of classicist-missionaries. He was born in Tabriz, Persia. Very early in his administration he established faculty advisory committees because he did not like to make hard decisions alone. He held his faculty to a rather narrow definition of published scholarship, but, no pedant, he was a superb teacher and took controversial political stands at some personal risk. He believed that a classical education – Latin, higher mathematics, the British literary masters – was appropriate to the needs of Nebraska farm boys and girls. He was an academic.

Frank Henzlik was highly intelligent but not fundmentally an intellectual. Born in Montana, educated at Central Missouri State Teachers College, he was "the characteristic mid-westerner with the ragged edges modified by education and culture. His is the typical story of the farm boy who started from scratch, figuring that all one had to do to top the heap was to stay right in there and pitch."[27] After taking a law degree at Missouri, he returned to public school administration and with single-minded devotion worked for the rest of his life to develop what he thought of as professionalism in education. He was decisive in manner, never in doubt about his own judgments. His admiring successor as dean of Teachers College said that he "was one of the finest administrators this University has ever had. He was a fighter, he could be very, very abrasive, bull-headed. He made enemies but he also had some great friends."[28] Mabel Lee described him as "a dictator of the first water. He brooked no divergence of views from his own and loved to crack the whip over the heads of those in a position below him, especially women." Once, she remembered, "I was ordered out of a Teachers College faculty meeting by the dean following a too impassioned speech on my part in behalf of cutting back on requirements in so-called 'education courses' to make room for a requirement in history in the hopes of working in more cultural subjects for our captive students. I took his shouted order literally, 'If that's the way you feel, you are in the wrong college – get out of here!' I replied, 'That's exactly the way I feel' and immediately gathered up my briefcase, purse and coat, and as the rest of the faculty sat in stunned silence at this clash, I proceeded out of the room and down a long hallway with (as I was told later by one who saw and heard the entire episode), my heels clicking determinedly the entire length of that long walk."[29] A great advocate of something he called democratic education, "citizenship" education, Henzlik was himself an authoritarian. But he got things done. His staff thought that "he took a very small, I would say, virtually unknown operation and built it into a nationally known Teachers College."[30]

By 1950 the Teachers College staff and their allies in the state Department of Education, all under the influence of Henzlik, had succeeded in prescribing courses necessary for teachers' certification. The public schools were thus largely in the hands of educationists rather than subject-matter professors. With Henzlik in the lead, they asserted that it was the primary function of the public schools to teach democracy and democratic methods of decision making, not a specific subject or discipline. The question of what should be taught, how the curriculum should be determined, and who should teach it came to public attention when the Nebraska Association of School Administrators passed a recommendation in 1950 that all Nebraska colleges accept graduates of accredited high schools without regard to specific subjects. This recommendation was reaffirmed in a meeting on 30 November 1951, in Lincoln. No longer would college-bound students be required to take specific courses in English, mathematics, foreign languages, history, science, and government. To encourage breadth of experience and participatory democracy, all courses would count equally toward admittance to college.

Subject-matter specialists were alarmed. The traditionalists like Oldfather saw that this policy would require the University to offer subcollegiate courses in mathematics, science, English, languages, and the social sciences if students were to arrive at professional competence by the time they received their baccalaureate degrees. Colleges would thus become extended high schools, wasting student years and public funds. The traditionalists challenged the implied assertion by Teachers College educationists that the traditional course of study did not prepare students to meet life, especially life in a participatory democracy. The issue was basic: was it the function of public education to discipline the mind and to transmit a body of fact or was it to foster citizenship and celebrate democracy? Anti-Communist hysteria reflecting Senator McCarthy's accusations at the time sharpened the debate.

The College of Arts and Sciences, organized by the indomitable Professor James Sellers, responded to the president of the Nebraska Association of School Administrators in an open letter dated 10 December 1951. Signed by chairmen and the executive committee of the College of Arts and Sciences, it asserted that the proposed abolish-

ment of specific requirements for college admission was "unrealistic and perilous to sound education either for meeting life's problems or as preparation for more advanced and professional study." "It is surprising," they wrote, "that members of your association do not remember the experience of our nation during the late war. The armed services found our public school graduates deficient in English, in mathematics, in scientific studies (especially the physical sciences), and without knowledge of or deplorably weak in the foreign languages."[31] Reports of the controversy were carried in the state papers, and the *Omaha World-Herald* called it a "bitter battle." The following fall, in October 1952, Chancellor Gustavson appointed a committee consisting of high school principals, representatives of the state Department of Education, deans, and professors to consider entrance requirements for the College of Arts and Sciences, an endeavor that promised to be inconclusive.

The "bitter battle" was reflected on campus in the Graduate College. In December 1945 the Teachers College had requested that a degree of Doctor of Education (D.Ed.) be established with different requirements from those for the established Doctor of Philosophy (Ph.D.). The Teachers College felt that teaching and school administration constituted a profession like that of law, medicine, or engineering, and that advanced training in education should stress competence in this profession rather than skill in research, the hallmark of the Ph.D. The new degree would not require knowledge of foreign languages but would substitute for it "cultural familiarity with a foreign country." Speaking for his college, Henzlik asserted that such a degree was awarded in numerous universities across the country and a demand was felt for it here in Nebraska.[32] The Graduate College and its dean, Robert W. Goss, were unsympathetic. They countered with the suggestion that for the D.Ed. one-half the total graduate and undergraduate courses (exclusive of thesis) be outside departments of education. They asserted the necessity of foreign languages. In effect they denied the exclusive nature of education.

Teachers College and the Graduate College were at an impasse. Goss, a plant pathologist from the ag campus, was said by some to be inflexible, even obstinate, and no less persistent than Henzlik. Brought up in Fall River, Massachusetts, he retained his New England accent. He was urbane, married to a beautiful Nebraska woman of whom he was inordinately proud, a man of principle. The faculty used to say that with Gustavson, Borgmann, and Goss, the University was run by the father, the son, and the holy goss. Goss thought of himself and his Graduate College as the academic conscience of the University. In his dispute with Teachers College, he was the legitimate successor of Hartley Burr Alexander.

In 1952 at the behest of Henzlik a second proposal for the D.Ed. was brought to the Graduate College. This time it included eighteen hours of coursework outside the major concentration – but still in Teachers College departments – and a "proficiency in the tools of research which *might include* foreign language" (emphasis added), "tools of research" generally meaning statistics or a special research technique. Again Goss and his Graduate Council rejected the degree. The Teachers College found itself between Scylla and Charybdis. On the one hand, professional educators were requesting the professional doctorate; on the other, the Graduate Council and the Graduate College refused to approve it.[33] One can only wonder if much of this continuing, ugly confrontation might have been compromised if Henzlik had been less abrasive and Goss less intransigent. It is ironic that in the next generation the substitution of a "tool of research" for foreign language became standard across the Graduate College.

At this point Chancellor Gustavson asked that a special committee be appointed to resolve the conflict, but this ad hoc group from the Teachers College could not satisfy the Graduate Council; in November 1952 the proposed D.Ed.

was yet again rejected, this time by the total graduate faculty. In anger Henzlik then made a direct appeal to the Board of Regents, asking that the D.Ed. be awarded outside the Graduate College, and in April 1953 the regents authorized the conferring of both the Master of Education and the Doctor of Education degrees within the Teachers College, independently of the Graduate College. It was said that the angry chancellor thought the graduate faculty had betrayed him in failing to endorse a compromise, which he clearly wanted. The graduate faculty, the scholarly heart of the University, was also angry. They argued that their central intellectual responsibility, the definition and exercise of scholarship, had been arrogated.

But the degree stuck, and in May 1953 Gustavson resigned to become president of Resources for the Future, a division of the Ford Foundation. For a year he had felt that his service to the University was nearly over. When Dean Borgmann left to become president of the University of New Hampshire in 1952, Gustavson did not even seek an academic replacement but appointed Bruce Nicoll as his special assistant. He thought his authority had been circumscribed, first by extramural bodies and regents who built a sports program contrary to his principles, and now by a faculty who had refused his desire to resolve the conflict between the Teachers College and the College of Arts and Sciences.

The faculty always liked and admired Gus, even when they found him impolitic. They gave a magnificent party for him, presented him and Mrs. Gustavson a chestful of silver, and regretted the bitterness they knew he felt. Those who worked with him, faculty and staff and students, remembered his monumental integrity for the rest of their lives. They knew they had been dealing with a real man, perhaps a great one.

10. A Research University: 1953–1960

≈ John K. Selleck

When Chancellor Gustavson presented his resignation in May 1953, the Board of Regents accepted it "with great reluctance," for though members had disagreed with some of his policies, they had admired his intelligence and respected his honesty. It was, in fact, time for him to go. By 1952 he had misread his faculty, misjudged administrative appointments, and lost his poise in public. Ever since Carl Borgmann had left in 1952, the administration had become increasingly frayed, however hard Bruce Nicoll, the chancellor's assistant from the PR office, tried to knit it together. The board thought first to make the registrar, George W. Rosenlof, interim chancellor, but when word of this was leaked, within hours the faculty presented such a long petition opposing the appointment that the regents reconsidered. Rosenlof, a faithful Presbyterian layman, was a schoolman, having come into the University from public school administration, and had remained a faithful supporter of Dean Henzlik. He saw himself as a compromiser, a pourer of oil on troubled waters, but others saw him as a trimmer.

The board quickly named a faculty committee to advise them on the appointment of a new chancellor, and though they rejected faculty nominations for an interim chancellor, they settled many fears by selecting John K. Selleck, faithful business manager of the University, for the post. Selleck, through all his years at the University, had been careful never to express, perhaps never to have, opinions about academic matters. The son of a prominent Lincoln businessman, he had returned with his new wife to Lincoln, where they wanted to live, after working in Chicago as an electrical engineer and serving in World War I. He

had rejected the opportunity to enter his father's business or to go into one of the banks where he had "the intriguing prospect of starting at the top and sitting down," his friend Robert Van Pelt said. Instead, he got a job in the purchasing department at the University.[1] In 1921 he was thirty-two years old. Within a year Chancellor Avery sent him to the athletic department. "The Athletic Department is in the red," Avery wrote him. "Go over there and get it out."[2] He was successful. Working with Harold Holtz of the Alumni Association, he helped direct the campaign that built Memorial Stadium and then initiated a campaign that resulted in the building of the Coliseum. Through manipulation of ticket sales, especially for football, he paid off bonds issued for their construction. It was Selleck who inaugurated and sold "season books" for home games; and later, in the depression years, it was Selleck who with Don Lentz set up Band Day, which brought every band in the state into the football stadium. With federal funds matching athletic revenues, he saw the Schulte Field House constructed and paid for in 1942.

By 1941 the University finances were in a shambles, in part because of scandalous misadministration. One Sunday morning Chancellor Boucher telephoned Selleck, who was busily counting football gate receipts, to come to his house on A Street. "Selleck," he said in his magisterial way, "starting tomorrow morning you are Comptroller of the University of Nebraska."[3] In 1944 Selleck became corporation secretary to the Board of Regents, and when Laurence Seaton died in 1948, he was put in charge of all business operations. He was, he always said, a "finance, brick and mortar man"; and when the 1947 legislature passed a ten-year building program, Selleck oversaw it. John Selleck enjoyed the respect of town and gown alike, and he believed, properly, that his interim chancellorship neither required nor permitted bold planning. Much admired for his unflappable devotion to duty, he made one serious mistake: he ordered the destruction of Ellen Smith Hall, the women's building converted from a Victorian mansion at the corner of Fourteenth and R streets. Robert Van Pelt later told a story characterizing Selleck. One Saturday afternoon a friend found him standing alone at the crosswalk in the center of the University's city campus: "What are you doing here?" the friend asked. "This," said Mr. Selleck quietly, "is a great Nebraska institution and I am looking at it."[4] As a mark of gratitude for his long and faithful service, the Board of Regents in 1954 named the new dormitory complex on Fifteenth Street Selleck Quadrangle.

❧ Clifford M. Hardin

The regents with the cooperation of a strong faculty committee began a nationwide search for a replacement for Reuben Gustavson. The search was complicated by the aggressive reporting, complete with cameras and tape recorders, of the *Lincoln Journal*, and several excellent candidates refused to countenance what they regarded as harassment by the press. Even in Chicago, where the board moved to continue interviewing candidates, the press badgered them and their guests. Clifford Hardin, who was Regent Ben Greenberg's selection, came to the Stevens Hotel to be met in the lobby by John Selleck. "When he met Dr. Hardin, the pressure of the press was so intense that Hardin was practically absconded and in secrecy was brought to the [regents' hotel] room. When the interview terminated, he left via the fire escape and departed through the alley," Greenberg remembered.[5] Upon discovering that the interviewing rooms were bugged, the board moved to the Bismarck Hotel, where they were followed by reporters in cabs. Perhaps the newspaper people had seen too many movies.

The regents quickly settled on Clifford Hardin and asked him to visit Lincoln, which he did, unannounced. After some ten days of deliberation he rejected their offer. A few weeks later the board returned to him, even sending a delegation of regents to East Lansing, where they met Mrs. Hardin. One of them, probably Jack Elliott, said to

Hardin: "We have come to stay as long as necessary to get you to say 'yes' and Doc [Dr. Ben Greenberg, a bachelor] here hopes it is a long time because he has a girlfriend in town."[6] After further thought Hardin finally agreed to accept the appointment, assured by Regent Leroy Welsh of Omaha that the state tax base would shortly be broadened. Hardin said, "I remember some eight or ten years later when we were still discussing whether we should have a broadened tax base in Nebraska, Roy Welsh, sitting at the table musing, looked at me, grinned and said, 'Chancellor, do you remember that snow job I did on you when we were going to pass that sales and income tax in Nebraska?' "[7]

Whether by design or by accident, Clifford Hardin came to the University with the unanimous support of the Board of Regents. In allowing them to persuade him, he put them in his debt; and during his whole tenure they remained his supporters. He was much helped by his wife. Martha Hardin, a beautiful and clever woman, was seen by the board, and everybody else, as his chief aide and constant lieutenant. She acted as liaison to the board, especially Dr. Greenberg. The Hardins were a team unlike any pair the University had seen before.

Clifford Hardin was only thirty-eight years old when he became chancellor, and though he had held important administrative posts at Purdue University, where he had taken his Ph.D., and at Michigan State, he had held them only briefly. In eight years he had moved from professor and chairman of agricultural economics to director of the agricultural experiment station to dean of agriculture, earning a reputation as "a top-notcher, a world leader and a stem winder."[8] He had little of what is now called charisma, but he had presence. Wherever he sat was the head of the table. If his smile was a bit wooden and his humor a bit forced, he was always in charge. Unlike Gustavson, who was often addressed as "Gus" or "Dr. Gus," even in public, Chancellor Hardin was rarely called "Cliff" in public, even by close associates. Handsome and the father of four model children (a second son was born in Lincoln) often pictured with him and Mrs. Hardin — never Martha in public — he was not particularly verbal, certainly not eloquent. Many of his speeches were written by

Ken Keller. Though in time he learned to speak off the cuff, he did not in his public statements inspire those around him to rise to glorious achievement. In his first address to the faculty, for example, he said he hoped to make this the friendliest campus in the country, hardly an aspiration to startle the ambitious or inspire the scholarly. Shrewd more than intellectual, clever more than wise, he took advantage of local and national possibilities to the advantage of the University. As one of his deans said years later, he "taught us to think big about the future of the University."[9]

When Hardin came to Nebraska in the summer of 1954, he turned first to George Round, director of public relations. Round took the new chancellor to visit nearly every town and village, and as a result Hardin was seen as a spokesman for statewide interests, second only to the governor. Coming as he did from rural Indiana, educated in a land-grant college, administrator of an agricultural experiment station, he knew how to approach Nebraskans. Everywhere he was told there was too much drinking on campus — post–World War II laxity had not disappeared — so the Hardins thereafter never accepted a drink in public. Through Regent J. Leroy Welsh, who was prominent in conservative financial and political circles in Omaha and whose partner in the grain business was Senator Hugh Butler, and Regent Robert Devoe of Lincoln, whose law partner was the almost legendary C. Petrus Peterson, Hardin had immediate entrance into urban power centers. During his years at Nebraska he and Mrs. Hardin found their friends more in these circles than in the academic circles that Chancellor Gustavson had found congenial. Indeed, the Hardins never seemed totally at ease with academic types, and they never had the unquestioning support of the faculty. But within months, perhaps weeks, of arriving, Hardin had established himself with three basic constituencies: the leaders of agriculture, the professional and financial leaders in the cities, and, perhaps most important of all, the Board of Regents.

❧ The Kellogg Center

Hardin immediately put his constituencies in the service of the University. The month after his arrival he appointed a University committee to investigate the possibility of applying to the Kellogg Foundation for a national extension center which could bring Nebraskans to the University and the services of the University to the state for programs outside standard academic patterns. At Michigan State University Hardin had been involved in building such a conference center and had become well acquainted with the directors of the Kellogg Foundation. At first his Nebraska faculty committee was lukewarm to the idea of new building, knowing how desperately rundown the University's total physical plant had become. "There was an air of discouragement among the people," Hardin later remembered.[10] But when Thomas C. Woods of the Woods Charitable Fund promised $200,000 or $300,000 and the governors of Ak-Sar-Ben in Omaha also agreed to underwrite the project, they began to change their attitude.

After negotiation, in February 1958 the W. K. Kellogg Foundation of Battle Creek, Michigan, granted $1,856,000 toward building and running a conference center, with the understanding that local sponsors would provide $1,142,000, a considerable sum in those days. That very week Thomas Woods died and his successors withdrew their support. Shortly thereafter the Ak-Sar-Ben governors reneged in the face of political criticism by Senator Terry Carpenter. The center seemed doomed, but Byron Dunn of Lincoln's National Bank of Commerce, Clarence Swanson of the Hovland-Swanson clothing store, Joe W. Seacrest of the *Lincoln Journal*, and the chancellor agreed that they should not throw in the towel. They chartered a plane and with some thirty persons, including the governor of the state, flew to Michigan to persuade the Kellogg board that matching money could be raised. They succeeded. Joe W. Seacrest remembered the trip home: "Cliff got down on his knee in the aisle [of the plane] and said . . . 'How do we do it?' I said, 'We organize it right now.' I said to Vic Anderson, the Governor of the state of Nebraska, 'You're going to be chairman and Jack Thompson [the young president of the First Trust Company] you are going to be Vice-Chairman and George Cook [president of Bankers Life Insurance Company], you're going to handle all the insurance agencies.' We had the whole thing wrapped up."[11]

The chancellor himself went barnstorming. "All economic and social groups seemingly in the state became involved," Hardin recalled. The barnstormers promised to name rooms for cities according to the size of their contributions. Hardin said, "I remember going to Columbus — the first place that I went — and that evening they committed $25,000. The next night I was in Grand Island and they asked how much Columbus contributed. I finally told them and they said that they certainly could do better than Columbus and they did. That is the way it went."[12]

To everybody's delight and surprise, the necessary money was promptly raised and the Nebraska Center for Continuing Education was built at the corner of Thirty-third and Holdrege. Dedicated in 1961, it was commonly referred to as the Kellogg Center. The whole enterprise had a triple effect. First, it served to unite the state to the state University, demonstrating that Nebraskans had a continuing allegiance to *the University*, as they said it. Second, the success of the funding showed that money was available for worthy projects. The University of Nebraska Foundation had been slowly building up an endowment fund, but it had never tapped resources in this quantity and breadth. Third, the success of the Center for Continuing Education helped dispel any air of discouragement on campus. In 1994 the center was renamed the Clifford Hardin Nebraska Center for Continuing Education.

❧ Educational Television for Nebraska

Hardin conceived of the University as more than a place offering courses and granting degrees. Perhaps he was not fundamentally interested in that aspect of education. In the Twenties the University had owned a radio station, KFAB, but because of the University's poverty and a lack of foresight, Chancellor Avery had failed to develop this opportunity to strengthen public education. In 1953 Chancellor Gustavson, determined not to let television pass his university by, set up a committee on television. Operating out of the public relations office, it had a budget of $15,000 and George Round was its chairman. The next year, 1954, Round brought Jack McBride, who had been at Creighton University in Omaha and was now at Wayne State in Detroit, to head University of Nebraska television opera-

tions. Initially the committee planned to develop programs for use by commercial stations and thus to extend the service of the University beyond the campuses. It produced thirty-nine half-hour films called "The Great Plains Trilogy" on an improvised sound stage in the West Stadium. The films dealt with the paleontology, archaeology, and history of the plains and were broadcast nationally several times.[13]

This was not enough for Jack McBride. McBride, a fresh-faced young teacher of speech, had a shrewd political sense and an iron will under a deceptively bland manner. Few people could have foreseen that in ten years he would build a statewide television network operating seven days a week, with classroom programs by day and high-brow entertainment by night. In 1955 he hired Ron Hull, who became his second in command. Hull, too, was deceptive in manner. An enthusiast, stagestruck, himself an entertainer, he knew all the show tunes. But like McBride, he was politically astute, administratively meticulous, and, most important, committed to aesthetic and academic values far beyond popular standards. McBride and Hull were determined to bring the best entertainment and information to as wide an audience as they could persuade to accept it. They made Nebraska a leader in educational television almost immediately.

The possibilities of television in public education interested Hardin as they had Gustavson. Before Hardin came to Nebraska, John E. Fetzer of Kalamazoo, Michigan, had told him that he owned two television channels in Lincoln which he had bought from the Stuart Broadcasting Company when neither was making money. He knew that Lincoln could support only one commercial station, so he offered channel twelve to the University. At Hardin's invitation he met with the Board of Regents in Lincoln and extended his offer to include use of his commercial studio and technical equipment until permanent arrangements could be made by the University. Fearing the expense that such a gift could entail, the regents reluctantly accepted, but only upon the urging of the new young chancellor. In November 1954, weeks after Hardin arrived, KUON-TV began broadcasting, at first only two hours in the morning, from KOLN studios. In 1956 KUON built its own studios in

72. The Crib, sometimes called the Grill, was a favorite student hangout in the union for Cokes and cigarettes. The jukebox in the corner ran continuously and the murals depicted cartoon scenes of campus life: Ivy Day, sports events, theatrical productions, band practice, telephone conversations, and pep rallies. (*Cornhusker 1942*, UNL Archives)

73, 74. In the fall of 1942 the organized houses competed in a scrap drive rather than with the traditional Homecoming decorations. Sigma Alpha Epsilon had a sign over their front door that read "From the Sigs to the Pigs," the "Pigs" being the enemy. Members of the Innocents Society in their scarlet baldrics supervised the estimates of the scrap piles. (*Cornhusker 1943*, UNL Archives)

75. The bleak quadrangle between
Teachers College and Andrews Hall
became a drill field after 1942 when
military personnel were quartered in
the new Love Memorial Library. The
view here is to the east, with Social
Sciences Hall (now CBA), the new library (then a barracks), and Teachers
College to the right. The soldiers in
uniform are marching to and from
classes in formation. At the far end of
the quad is Uni Drug, a favorite hangout; Dirty Earl's, an unattractive eat-
ery; and frame boardinghouses. After
the war this area was cleared to make
room for Selleck Quadrangle, a dormitory. Enrollment at the University fell
from 6,500 in 1940 to 3,000 in 1943.
(UNL Photo Lab)

76. The wartime Board of Regents, with a rather wan Chancellor Boucher in the center rear. L. F. Seaton, operating superintendent, is to his right, John K. Selleck, comptroller, to his left. Marion Shaw, by this time supporting federal funding for the University, is seated on the extreme left. C. Y. Thompson is to his left. Robert Devoe with his Phi Beta Kappa key on his watch chain is at the extreme right. The picture was taken in the boardroom in old Administration Hall. (UNL Archives)

77. T. J. Thompson (1886–1970), dean of student affairs from 1927 until 1952, saw it as his job, he said, "to guide the behavior of high-spirited collegians." At the end of his career, he said he had tried to maintain his equilibrium while confiscating bathtub and basement stills in "the loudest part of the Roaring Twenties," supporting youth through economic and cultural depression in the Thirties, balancing academic and wartime pressures in the Forties, and disciplining a body of men tired of regimentation after the war. "It has been tough where I sit," he said. "More often than not I have sat alone." (*Cornhusker 1952*, UNL Archives)

78. Don L. Love Memorial Library, as seen in 1946 from the top of Memorial Stadium. The streets are full of cars gathered for a football game. In 1947 Burnett Hall, a classroom building, was constructed in the middle distance, facing the unlandscaped quadrangle before Love Library. (UNL Archives)

79. James L. Sellers, professor of history, saw himself as a campus gadfly. In this photograph, taken about 1948 in the editor's office at the *Lincoln Star*, he is flanked by James E. Lawrence, the editor, who was also a part-time lecturer at the University, and James C. Olson, who was to make his mark as a western historian and as the president of the University of Missouri. (Courtesy of Catherine Sellers Angle)

80. Reuben G. Gustavson (1892–1974) came to the University as chancellor in 1946. He was "the University's ambassador to the people of the State." (UNL Photo Lab)

81. In 1947 surplus army barracks were moved onto the crowded campus: 10,000 students were enrolled in 1948. The Student Health Service, including a twenty-six-bed infirmary, was set up in this two-story structure at the west end of the quad, north of Social Sciences Hall (now CBA), east of Grant Memorial Hall and the Former Museum. Four additional barracks were placed near Bancroft Hall for drawing labs and classrooms. In 1955, when enrollment had declined to about 7,000, these temporary buildings were removed. (UNL Archives)

82, 83. The College of Medicine in Omaha, 1948. University Hospital is in the center, the North Laboratory to the right, the South Laboratory opposite, at the left, with Conkling Hall, the nurses' residence, immediately behind it. Children's Memorial Hospital is behind the double-winged University Hospital. Lectures and class demonstrations were given in the medical amphitheater, where the students, almost all male, are attired in suits and ties. (*Cornhusker 1948*, UNL Archives)

84. Theodore Jorgensen (b. 1905) stands next to an atomic accelerator which he built for the Department of Physics and around which a graduate program developed after 1950. The photograph was taken about 1955. (Courtesy of Theodore Jorgensen)

85. Charles Henry Oldfather (1887–1954) served as dean of the College of Arts and Sciences from 1932 to 1952. An undergraduate once asked Professor O. K. Bouwsma what the requirements for being a dean were. "You have seen our dean, haven't you?" the professor said blandly. "First you must look like a dean." C. H. Oldfather looked like a dean. (UNL Photo Lab)

86. Frank E. Henzlik (1893–1977), dean of the Teachers College from 1931 until 1958, favored the development of professional education as an academic discipline and was "a fierce opponent" of those who disagreed. (*Cornhusker 1952*, UNL Archives)

87. James S. Blackman (1907–1984) was a devoted teacher. Serving in the office of the dean of engineering over many years, he amazed students with his memory of their names and lives. (UNL Archives)

88. Curtis M. Elliott (1911–1968) was both a distinguished scholar of economics and insurance and a remarkable teacher. The Alumni Association's annual prize to a distinguished retired faculty member is named the Doc Elliott Award in his memory. (*Cornhusker 1958*, UNL Archives)

89. George S. Round (1908–1992) was director of public relations for the University until 1973 and acted as liaison to the legislature for thirty-four years. He was generally credited with being a major influence on the University through his association with governors, legislators, and University administrators. (*Cornhusker 1957*, UNL Archives)

the basement of The Temple with $100,000 obtained from the Fund for Adult Education, a branch of the Ford Foundation. In that same year the Fetzer Foundation presented a transmitter, a transmission line, an antenna, and studio equipment to the University, and shortly, with foundation and federal money, McBride established a consortium of school systems to plan classroom programming and a statewide network to deliver it. In 1963 the Nebraska Educational Television Commission, a statewide town-gown group, assumed responsibility for the enterprise, and a statewide network was developed in 1965 with revenue from a state cigarette tax and matching federal funds.

The commission and the University worked in partnership throughout, and by 1967 the growing television operation found itself housed under eleven separate roofs on the downtown campus. In 1969 the legislature authorized the construction of a television center on the east campus, as the agricultural campus was now called, by means of a complicated system of revenue bonds in cooperation with the city. This Telecommunications Center, one of the most elaborate in the nation, cost some $3.4 million and was named for Senator Terry Carpenter, who after an initial suspicion became a champion of statewide educational television. Between 1954, when KUON-TV was activated, and 1992, $45,690,000.00 came into Nebraska for television from non-state revenue sources.[14] This enormous sum was the direct result of McBride's sagacity and determination, aided by Hull's lobbying. Hardin's role was indirect. As was his custom, he appointed able administrators, provided moral and financial support, and delegated responsibility. The original vision of educational television was Gustavson's. Its marvelous implementation was McBride's. Its success reflected on Hardin.

ꜱ The University of Nebraska Press

The University of Nebraska Press got Hardin's support quickly, for he thought a scholarly press encouraged scholarly research and added luster to a university. *Luster* was one of Hardin's buzzwords. In 1941 Chancellor Boucher had hired, unseen and uninterviewed, an assistant at Fordham University Press to become University editor. Emily

Schossberger, a polyglot refugee from nazi Austria, came west in the fall "with only a vague idea of what was expected of me." A large, handsome woman who never lost her Viennese *joi de vivre* or her taste for Viennese pastries (*mit Schlag*), she was to supervise all institutional publications – bulletins, scholarly studies, announcements, quarterlies, and the like. Almost immediately, lengthy manuscripts like E. B. Schmidt's study of the Nebraska tax system appeared on her desk, their authors asking for publication, and in November 1941 the regents chartered a press as a "non-incorporated agency of the board of regents" under the direction of a faculty-administrator committee that already existed. The press had no appropriation, so it was to get along on occasional subsidies and incidental handouts. Books began to appear almost at once but the press had a hand-to-mouth existence. Often in order to print and bind new books, it had to wait for income from books already published. Sometimes the press took advances from prospective authors, but it did not accept subsidies and of course all manuscripts had to pass peer review. The press's first book was a biography of J. Sterling Morton, Nebraska's pioneer statesman, by James C. Olson, brought out with support from the Morton family. Olson subsequently became a professor of history and graduate dean at the University and still later president of the University of Missouri.

Within five years Emily Schossberger and her staff of four were publishing a handful of books a year. To support expensive scholarly tomes, she produced service publications like the best-selling *Handbook for School Custodians* and professional volumes addressed to specific, targeted audiences. By the time Hardin arrived, the press, though small, could claim to be a reliable firm holding itself to national standards. In his first years it got occasional funds from the new chancellor which he collected here, there, and everywhere, and beginning in 1955 it began to receive an annual grant of $2,500 from the Ford Foundation for the publication of books not otherwise economically feasible. Its continuing existence was tenuous. Emily Schossberger had in effect created a press out of thin air, and she had a right to be proud of her accomplishment, even if her accounting was a bit irregular and her records rather chaotic.[15]

Then in 1957 Schossberger resigned, exhausted with detailed administration and with Frank Lundy, the strong-minded University librarian on her supervisory board. She shortly became head of the Notre Dame press, where, as at Nebraska, she produced handsome books. For a year the University of Nebraska Press was without a director; then Hardin and A. C. Breckenridge, his dean of faculties, reorganized it and appointed a new, scholarly advisory board and a permanent head. Hardin made Bruce Nicoll director, and Nicoll made Virginia Faulkner editor-in-chief. These were, as it turned out, brilliant and rather bold appointments. Nicoll had been an excellent journalist, hired by George Round in his Office of Public Relations. He loved to tell how an article he had sold to the *Reader's Digest* paid for his first house shortly after the war and yet never appeared in the magazine. He was an experienced University administrator, for Chancellor Gustavson had taken him into his front office as his executive assistant when Carl Borgmann resigned in 1952.

Nicoll had had no experience in publishing. Not himself a scholar, he was an enlightened and enterprising layman. While continuing to publish scholarly works of demonstrable merit, he inaugurated several notable series. His most important innovation was Bison Books, which were quality paperbacks. Its lists contained everything from translations of Euripides to autobiographies of Nebraska pioneers. Bison Books were sold off special racks in drugstores, motels, grocery stores, and tourist traps, as well as in bookshops. They were a great financial success. The press had published six books in 1950, with a sales income of $6,000, but in 1960 it brought out twenty-four books and had a sales income exceeding $80,000.[16] During the next generation it became one of the leading scholarly presses in the nation both in number of books produced and in quality.

Bruce Nicoll shared his remarkable achievement with Virginia Faulkner, who had returned to Lincoln after a spectacularly successful career as a freelance writer. In 1934 she had published her first novel, written at age twenty-two while she was an undergraduate at Radcliffe, and in subsequent years she had written for Hollywood, for the popular magazines like the *Saturday Evening Post*,

and for Broadway. In her second career, at the press, she was, Mari Sandoz often told everybody, "the best editor in the business, and I know for I have fought with them all." From her long experience on the national scene she had national standards. An extremely witty woman, and, in later years, patient with those slower than herself, she saw herself as a professional writer: she could write to order. She and Nicoll got on splendidly. His enterprise and her editorial acumen brought international attention to the press and the University.

✸ International Programs

Chancellor Hardin was interested in the international scene. Early in 1954 AID – the federal Agency for International Development – invited the University of Nebraska to help the Turkish government strengthen its system of higher education. The idea of the land-grant university, it was thought, might be imported to Turkey. In March 1955 the Board of Regents signed a contract with AID to provide technical assistance to the faculties of agriculture and veterinary science in Ankara University. In addition, the University of Nebraska would help establish and operate the new Ataturk University in eastern Turkey at Erzurum. The Nebraska staff was at first not enthusiastic, for the international commitment was made without consulting the personnel responsible for its work, and the staff feared that even with AID support, it would siphon energies from local needs. The Nebraska staff, headed by Professor Marvel Baker, arrived in Turkey in 1955 and for the next nine years contingents remained there on two-year assignments, most of them in remote Erzurum. By 1963 most of the assistance was phased out, and the contract was officially concluded by October 1968.[17]

In 1962 the University of Nebraska College of Agriculture was again approached by AID. When the government of Colombia asked the United States Department of Agriculture for assistance with a major program in agricultural research, teaching, and extension, "it is no exaggeration to say that Hardin, working with AID, the Kellogg Foundation, the Ford Foundation, Colombian high level public officials, and others, almost single-handedly succeeded in getting Nebraska designated as the University to conduct the program," Elvin Frolik, dean of agriculture, later said.[18] In Nebraska this South American program met with less hostility than the Turkish program, in part because Nebraska staff were more closely involved in planning it, in part because many Nebraskans visited Colombia over the years, in part because some of its staff was drawn from other mid-American universities.

By the end of 1967 the Nebraska staff in Colombia had grown to thirty. Clayton E. Yeutter, who was to have a distinguished career in the federal government in later years, became its chief of mission in 1968. He saw the mission from a Nebraskan's point of view: "The general reaction of most people [at home] is going to be, 'how are we going to gain from sending people off to Bogota, Colombia?' The answer is that it makes them better and broader people. It gives them a perspective on life and living that is altogether different from anything they can ever achieve in Nebraska."[19] In June 1970 the chief administrator of AID said, "The Nebraska-ICA [Colombian Institute of Agriculture] project is noteworthy for being something of a textbook example of how to do technical assistance."[20]

After 1973 the international programs became decreasingly important to the University. The long-term results in Colombia and Turkey remain problematical and the effect on the University community is difficult to determine, however important they may have been for the individuals involved, but they helped Hardin pull the University out of its provincialism.

❧ Chancellor Hardin's Vice Chancellors

Clifford Hardin was a shrewd judge of people. During his first year in office he retained Bruce Nicoll as his administrative associate, but in the summer of 1955 he invited Adam C. Breckenridge into the front office. "Breck," as he was known, a native Missourian with a Ph.D. from Princeton, had come to the University in 1946. During the Korean War he had served in the Office of the Chief of Naval Operations in Washington. An able administrator, he became chairman of the political science department in 1953, and in November 1955 the chancellor named him

dean of faculties. He was thirty-eight years old, one year younger than Hardin himself. Popular with the faculty because of his candor, he was always assumed to be one of their own, and he did in fact write half a dozen professional books during his career. Unlike the chancellor, he made quick decisions. Jim Denney, veteran feature writer for the *Omaha World-Herald*, told a friend: "Cliff Hardin was lucky. He had Adam Breckenridge who knew everything and George Round who knew everybody."[21]

Breck was the chancellor's sounding board, premier adviser, and constant business associate, but not necessarily his intimate friend. Hardin had no intimate friends, aside from his wife. He was fond of telling a story on Breck. Once when Hardin was in Breck's office the phone rang and the dean answered it himself. "Yes," he said into the receiver. "No. No. No. No." Leaning back, the chancellor asked, "Breck, what did you say 'yes' to?" "Oh," Breck replied, "he asked if this was the dean of faculties." A bachelor, Breck loved parties, where he was astonishingly forthright – about matters that did not matter. He said that he learned never to make promises at such affairs, but he certainly remained approachable. He never second-guessed the chancellor. The chancellor kept a close eye on all details. He wanted to see copies of the correspondence that left his office as well as all that came into it. "Breck and I had the ability to argue and argue and argue on issues and still keep each other's respect. I think we were good for each other. I know he was good for me," Hardin said later. "He made tremendous contributions. First, always he had good judgment; secondly, more than any other man I have ever worked with, he was organized and kept the office organized."[22] In time Breck was offered university presidencies, but he rejected them, preferring administrative control to public responsibility. In 1962 he was made vice chancellor for academic affairs, but this title hardly extended his authority.

Hardin's other chief assistant was Joseph Soshnik. Soshnik had taken his Ph.D. in finance at the University and had returned to his undergraduate alma mater, Creighton University in Omaha, where he became auditor and budget consultant. "In 1957 I was being considered for an assignment in financial administration at an eastern university," he remembered later, and Regent Greenberg asked if "I should consider moving to NU if I were invited to succeed John Selleck as comptroller here."[23] When Soshnik said yes, Greenberg promptly telephoned Hardin that he had a new comptroller. Hardin was alarmed and almost exasperated. "He said, 'Have you hired him?' I replied, 'No, but when you visit with him, you will.' In two days, he had an appointment with Dr. Hardin and was recommended for the position."[24]

Joe Soshnik was a spectacular success, first as comptroller and then in 1963 as vice chancellor for business and finance, and finally as vice chancellor for administration. In his dealings with the legislators and state officials he was always so well prepared that he put off his questioners. They used to say that they hesitated to ask him the time of day for fear he would tell them how to make the clock. Unlike John Selleck and other administrators, Joe and his handsome wife, Miriam, associated with the academic community, appearing at concerts, supporting the arts, engaging in spirited conversation. They were intellectuals. When Hardin became head of the merged University of Nebraska and Municipal University of Omaha in 1968, he named Joe Soshnik president of "the Lincoln campus and outstate activities." He did it without consulting the faculty or any search committee, and this arbitrary appointment remained a disadvantage to Soshnik – or, rather, he perceived it to be. The Liaison Committee, when informed of the appointment, were displeased, thinking that the chancellor had ignored their academic prerogatives, but they said they would not make a public issue because they admired Soshnik so much that they did not want to embarrass him. They were perfectly aware that they were not likely to find a better man for the newly created presidency.

The other high administrators and advisers in these decades were also selected with a shrewd eye. Men who subsequently became chancellors at Wisconsin, Minnesota, Missouri, Kansas, Arkansas, and Nebraska were all chosen by Hardin. He found four of the six outside the University of Nebraska. When Robert Goss retired as dean of the Graduate College in 1956, Hardin advised the faculty search committee to look at a young man he had

just observed, an assistant professor of classics at Princeton. The committee was not confident that such a young man would be ready for their post, but the next week the young man was made president of Princeton University. He was Robert Goheen.[25]

❦ Research at the University

Hardin knew how to use men according to their strengths. He knew, as Gustavson had known before him, that the future of the University lay in research supported by federal grants. In 1940 the federal government had provided $15 million to colleges and universities for research, but by 1953 the sum had risen to nearly $142 million.[26] By 1960 it was to be more than $462 million. Norman Cromwell, professor of chemistry, made himself spokesman for researchers on campus.

A diligent researcher and a member of the national research establishment, Cromwell had been brought to the University in 1939 by Cliff Hamilton, the shrewd chairman of chemistry. Hamilton was something of an authoritarian but his judgment was good. He also brought in Henry Baumgarten, Henry Holtzclaw, and several others who developed national reputations. From the start Cromwell was diligent. Though he had had ROTC training at the Rose Hulman Institute of Technology in Terra Haute, Indiana, as an undergraduate, during the war he remained at his laboratory bench, his work classified as essential to national defense. Since he published many papers, in the postwar expansion of science he was ready to serve on federal panels and national boards. From the first he maintained that through research the local economy could grow. He early saw that federal money would be available to those institutions ready to make use of it, and he lobbied incessantly for his discipline. The Department of Chemistry, already strong through the efforts of F. W. Upson and Cliff Hamilton, became one of the banner departments under his prodding; he was its chairman from 1964 to 1970. Cromwell put off some of his colleagues by his single-minded devotion to graduate studies and grantsmanship, but he had authority in his manner.

Hardin listened to Cromwell, for they both saw that

support for research was a long-term investment, not an expense. Frank Morrison, when he was governor, noted that federal grants were going primarily to scientists on the coasts, not in the Middle West. "Cliff Hardin had on the drawing board the development of a science complex at the University, including a new chemistry building. I was a wholehearted supporter of this movement," he said later. "When I was in Washington as chairman of the Midwest Governors' Conference, [in 1964] I had a group of midwestern governors with me in the White House. The President [Lyndon Johnson] called McNamara in. . . . Mc was secretary of defense at that time. . . . [McNamara] told me that they had to give the bulk of their grants to the University of California because the University of California was the only state university that had the expertise they were looking for." Morrison quoted McNamara: "I know what I'm talking about. When the people of the middle-western states decide that they want excellence in education, they can have excellence in education, but up to now the people of the middle-west have not demanded excellence in education."[27] What the governor saw as a "terrible indictment" was what Cromwell and Hardin worked to correct.

❧ The College Deans

In order to bring the University into the magic circle of research universities, Hardin needed deans who understood what this new age required; and the college deans he named were of a kind. Never appointed rashly and almost always after careful consultation with Breckenridge, they were not vigorously independent. Hardin would not countenance the intercollegiate squabbling so prominent in previous administrations. Nor did he want the colleges to be content with undergraduate teaching. In 1957 Roy Green retired as dean of engineering. Under Green the energies of the college had been devoted to developing professional engineers, with notable success. A study in 1955 reported that over 6.5 percent of its graduates were listed in *Who's Who in Engineering*. Only Dartmouth exceeded the University of Nebraska's achievement.[28] The chancellor turned to Merk Hobson, a thirty-six-year-old associate professor of chemical engineering who was one of the best

teachers in his college as well as a first-rate research scientist. Promoted to full professor, he was instructed to build the small graduate program of his department into a graduate program for the whole college. Hobson was extremely bright and had many hobbies; as time went on he showed himself more committed to education than to engineering. In building his academic career he had followed the advice of his superiors, and he now accepted responsibilities as directed by Hardin. Hobson was popular with the faculty, who thought that he sometimes allowed himself to be used to his own disadvantage. Something of an old shoe in manner because he was overweight and unpressed, he did not strike anybody as devious, as Hardin sometimes did, nor was he intimidating, as Soshnik sometimes seemed to be. He was the man next door. The fact was, he was something of an aristocrat; his self-deprecatory manner masked great intelligence, and his sense of humor hid a shrewd judgment of political possibilities. His devoted secretaries found him the kindest man in the University. Like Breckenridge, he was offered university presidencies and, like Breck, he turned them down. He was the first of Hardin's major *college* appointments.

In 1958 Bert L. Hooper retired. Dean of the College of Dentistry since 1939, he had put up with second-rate equipment and an inconvenient location, the third floor of Andrews Hall, which was otherwise occupied by English and language departments. The majority of his faculty practiced dentistry privately and devoted only part of their time to the University. Ralph Ireland was appointed to replace Hooper, in part because of his professional reputation across the country, in part because of his commitment to research. Handsome and gregarious, Ireland traveled in fashionable circles. In 1960 the Council on Dental Education of the American Dental Association declared the dental facilities at Nebraska entirely inadequate, whereupon the legislature voted a .25-mill levy to upgrade it. Ireland applied for matching federal money. The federal inspection team at first rejected his application, thinking state support sufficient, but when they learned that the college had not been provided its own structure but was allotted space only in the Elgin Building, a disused warehouse, they reconsidered. "You can't do this to Ralph Ireland," they said to the University, and Ireland got his clinic.[29] Built at a cost of more than $4 million on the east campus, the new building was dedicated in 1967. Dean Ireland and Chancellor Hardin had worked the old-boy network to Nebraska's advantage.

The College of Pharmacy was similarly moved toward research. When a new dean was appointed in 1961, the faculty had its own candidate, but "after much discussion" the appointment finally went to Robert D. Gibson, Hardin later remembered, " – again, I think, because we were attempting to get a little more research orientation into the program and a little more emphasis on some graduate work."[30] The College of Pharmacy had been given a new building on the city campus, not without controversy, in 1954, largely through the lobbying of old Dean Lyman, who had founded the college in 1908. The building was named for him. The quality of the faculty was quickly raised, and the first black person to serve in a tenured position at the University was on its staff, Patrick R. Wells, who received a Distinguished Teaching Award in 1969.

The Graduate College had always encouraged research, and in 1953 its dean, Robert W. Goss, was given additional responsibilities as research administrator. Federal and private support for research at the University grew from $131,446 in 1950 to $709,627 in 1956. When Goss reached mandatory retirement age in 1956, he was replaced by John C. Weaver, who was to have a distinguished career ending with the presidency of the University of Wisconsin. By the time he left Nebraska in 1961, the University was receiving more than $2 million annually in outside funding.

Research leaves now became more frequently available. In 1955 the University received a grant of $40,000 from the Woods Charitable Fund to support sabbatical leaves for professors in the humanities. With aid from the University, this fund made two or three annual leaves available for five years. The Woods Fund administrators hoped that their gift might prime the pump; and as money became available in the next few years, increasing numbers of faculty-development grants were awarded, more or less competitively. The University never developed a full sabbatical program, but these research leaves plus grants awarded by the University's Research Council for release from teaching encouraged study and rewarded scholarly endeavor.

Though the chancellor and his deans encouraged the professors to think of the University as a research center and themselves as scholars on the national scene, many resisted; but in Nebraska as across the country, research and development were bywords.

❧ Teachers College and Public Education – Again

When Hardin arrived on campus, he found controversy among the undergraduate colleges. Ever since 1908, when Teachers College was established, the local academic community, like the academic community nationally, had been sharply divided over the relationship of pedagogical method to subject matter in the preparation of public school teachers. In 1922 through powerful lobbying by educationists, the Teachers College was made autonomous and given sole authority to determine teachers' courses of study. In 1938 the Board of Regents determined that a student could get a teacher's certificate only if he or she had matriculated in the Teachers College; simultaneous enrollment in another college – dual matriculation – might be allowed, but only with approval from the Teachers College. The legal requirements for accreditation of public school teachers was under the control of the state Department of Education, a department staffed by Teachers College associates.

In the same generation, 1920–50, subject-matter professors became increasingly oriented toward peer approval based on narrowly defined research. They turned away from their earlier commitment to public education. Professional societies like the Modern Language Association dropped concerns for pedagogy and addressed themselves exclusively to scholarly matters narrowly defined. Thomas M. Raysor, who came to the University as chairman of the Department of English in 1930, was typical. A distinguished editor of Coleridge, he would endorse research only when it dealt with original examination of high literary texts. Ruth Odell's study of Helen Hunt Jackson, author of the popular novel *Ramona* (1884), was impermissible, he thought, because her writing was "subliterary." Louise Pound protested this view, arguing that Raysor and all those who were "homesick for Harvard Yard" drove prospective schoolteachers into the arms of Teachers College, where education courses, respected neither by the students nor by subject-matter specialists, replaced standard academic disciplines. Tired and cynical candidates for degrees moved to Teachers College because Gresham's Law – bad money drives out good – operated in education as well as in finance.

Dean Frank Henzlik was a belligerent defender of Teachers College interests. After his victories in teacher certification, he had insisted on establishing a Doctor of Education degree (D.Ed.), a "professional" degree, as an alternative to the Doctor of Philosophy degree (Ph.D.), a research degree. The controversy arose yet again with the public uproar over Sputnik. In October 1957 the Soviet Union launched the world's first manmade satellite, and others followed. American technological and cultural hegemony was challenged and the public responded with alarm. During National Education Week a few weeks later President Eisenhower asked the American people to "scrutinize your school curriculum and standards to see whether they meet the stern demands of the era we are entering."[31] Many persons both on and off campus felt that the educationists in charge of curriculum and teacher certification had lowered academic standards until nearly anybody could pass everything. As a result, high school graduates were insufficiently educated for the "stern demands of the era." Perhaps the general public did not want intellectual rigor in the public schools, preferring that Johnny acquire social skills more than intellectual excellence.

In Nebraska a response to Sputnik came promptly in November 1957 from eleven professors. The Eleven, as they were known, were among the most distinguished scholars on campus. Norman Cromwell of chemistry was spokesman for the group, but others were old hands like James Sellers of history and Miguel Basoco of mathematics. They were joined by young men like James C. Olson of history, Robert Chasson of physics, and James E. Miller Jr. of English, all of whom had distinguished careers else-

where in subsequent years, and established professors like William K. Pfeiler of German and Theodore P. Jorgensen of physics. "Education for survival must not be left to the outmoded offerings that now obtain," they announced in a public statement. Education was too important to be left in the exclusive control of educationists: "A first step to meeting the President's call is to place the authority of teacher certification in the subject matter departments," they said.[32]

Henzlik and unidentified Teachers College associates immediately replied in an open letter, asserting that the motive behind the statement of the Eleven was "to destroy the balanced program of teacher preparation which has been developed over many years." He was right. The Eleven were asking that the educational bureaucracy be modified if not dismantled and that intellectual rigor be introduced into the classroom. The function of public education, Henzlik and his group asserted, is "the fullest development of each individual as a free human spirit, not as a servant of the state." They said, "Freedom of choice must be preserved." The Eleven argued that choice came after, not before, learning, and that the end of education was disciplining of the mind and heart, not adjustment to the shibboleths of the time.

The longstanding issue could not be resolved easily, and the Board of Regents upon Hardin's recommendation in December 1957 ordered that a balanced faculty committee be appointed to consider changes in teacher certification. The committee could come to no resolution, however, and when they reported at the end of the spring semester, 1958, the problem remained. Nationally there was no major resolution either. Certification and thus the curriculum remained under the control of the education bureaucracy.

Hardin later observed, "It looked as though we never would be able to resolve that controversy." Then Henzlik reached retirement age, and in July 1958 Hardin replaced him with Walter Beggs, a man of an entirely different stripe. Beggs, who had come to the University in 1936 and taken his Ph.D. in 1939, was a Henzlik protégé. Hardin said later, "When Dean Henzlik came up for retirement, we interviewed a number of people that we might bring in to succeed him, hoping that in the process we would heal the breach. None of these worked out." Beggs had been suggested as a possible dean but seemed disenfranchised by his association with the intransigent Henzlik. Hardin said, "I invited [Beggs] to go out to the western part of the state with me on a long trip—just the two of us. We talked all the way out and back about the Teachers College." Because of Beggs's background, his feelings about some of the past mistakes, and his involvement in some of the actions, Hardin became convinced that "he perhaps was the one person who could swing the faculty around and do the things that would finally gain the respect of the Arts College."[33] Where Henzlik had been arrogant and abrasive, Beggs was conciliatory and modest. One could not imagine Walt Beggs browbeating students.[34] Educated at Tarkio College, a conservative Presbyterian college (now defunct) in northwestern Missouri, he was proud of his traditional studies. With him as dean, "practically all of the little flea bites of controversy seemed to disappear [because] everybody was so darned busy in getting things going and getting things moving," Beggs remembered afterward. "This was mainly due to Cliff Hardin's leadership."[35] If Beggs was himself neither a great scholar nor a great intellect, he admired scholarship and intellect. Where Henzlik inspired fear, Beggs earned affection.

Beggs quickly took the initiative to heal wounds. "Shortly after I became dean, Walt Militzer and I began to appear in public for lunch." Militzer, a professor of chemistry, had been appointed dean of the College of Arts and Sciences by Gustavson in 1952 without the endorsement of any faculty committee. "Shortly after that, Charlie Miller [appointed dean of the College of Business Administration in 1958] joined us and then Merk Hobson joined us. Then Elvin Frolik [dean of the College of Agriculture after 1960] joined us. Pretty soon these gentlemen started coming over to my conference room once a week at three in the afternoon for coffee. We would just kick things around. We not only became professional colleagues, but very shortly personal friends. If a controversy showed its head, we learned very quickly how to nip it in the bud." These deans shared certain qualities. Loyal to Hardin, they did not grab for power, and within their own bailiwicks they sought consensus. "We had a period of tranquility and positive building at the University that I don't think has ever existed before and it may never exist again," Beggs later said.[36] Authority rested in the chancellor's office, not in the colleges as in former administrations.

❧ Project English

However smoothed over, the issues remained. The central problem of general mathematical and verbal literacy needed to be addressed. Who should teach in the schools and who should be responsible for the curriculum? A major challenge to the status quo as defended by the educationist bureaucracy came in 1961 from the Department of English when Paul A. Olson, a twenty-nine-year-old assistant professor from Wahoo, Nebraska, undertook to revamp the English offerings of the public schools. What was being taught in each class had been determined in 1918 and left pretty much in place through all the years: *Ivanhoe* for freshmen, *Silas Marner* for sophomores, *Macbeth* for juniors and seniors. Prescriptive grammar had become holy writ. The world may have changed in forty years but the curriculum had not. The teachers were caught between outmoded subject matter and pressure from administrative bureaucrats to develop "citizenship" and "democratic ideals."

Paul A. Olson was unique. After a brilliant graduate career at Princeton University, he had elected to return to Nebraska, for like Aeneas, he had a filial reverence for home country. His friends sometimes accused him of possessing a Messiah complex, and he was in fact a devout Lutheran. He asserted that "excellence in education requires both human and monetary sacrifice." We must, he said, shed our self-delusions, our perpetual feeling that "we are what we are not, that our children are getting what they are not getting. I say this as a Nebraskan who attended Nebraska schools and who chose to return to Nebraska to teach Nebraska students. I speak from experience and not simply from statistics."[37]

In August 1961, with $10,000 seed money from the Woods Charitable Fund, Olson as chairman of the curriculum committee for the Nebraska Council of Teachers of English gathered a group of classroom teachers, professors of subject matter and of methods, and administrators to begin planning an articulated curriculum in language, literature, and composition. Some of the best scholars in the country concerned with the teaching of English worked with them to lay out a comprehensive program "so that Nebraska students could receive the best training possible in English, the backbone of our educational system." This "Curriculum for English" immediately attracted wide attention; in the next year the Bureau of Research of the U.S. Office of Education contributed $250,000, and the Woods fund continued an annual grant of $25,000 for three years.

In this new curriculum, called Project English, writing and grammar reinforced one another, and both were related to the interests and abilities of the students. The aim was sophisticated literacy. Teachers and philosophers and administrators worked together to produce lesson plans, reading lists, and classroom strategies. Thousands of pages of curriculum materials were sent to schools all over the country, and schools in all fifty states used them. In 1967, supported by the U.S. Office of Education and in cooperation with other universities, Olson and his associates from across the country undertook an elaborate three-year study of English and education, social studies and education, and science and education, geared to a reconsideration of the public school curricula. Four years later, with another $1.5 million from the U.S. Office of Education, they undertook a full study of undergraduate education in colleges.

But after 1970, social upheaval – the desegregation of schools, race riots, Vietnam protests – overtook them, and curricular studies merged with concern for civil rights. Always an activist, Olson got caught up in problems of minorities, and he and his associates turned their attention increasingly from pedagogy to civil justice. They asked how communities, parents, and teachers could learn to work together, decentralized from remote education bureaus and administrative offices. In some quarters these concerns, united with curricular revisions, looked like a wholesale attack on the establishment, and Olson and his friends met new resistance. In later years he thought perhaps they had cast their net too wide and thus lost their influence. The innovators failed to challenge the bureau-cratic control of teacher accreditation successfully.[38] Olson might have continued his public service but, though he was still young, his health began to give way. In his efforts to reconsider the nature and structure of public education, he had collected close to $6 million from foundations and federal sources. Public and educational inertia being great, however, he thought the long-term effects only problematical. This had been the largest and boldest examination of public school curriculum in several generations, and its failure to find continuing academic and political support disadvantaged the nation.

❧ The Mitchell Case

Supported by the. U.S. Department of Agriculture and other federal agencies, the College of Agriculture and the experiment station had been leaders in University research from their beginning. When W. V. Lambert, a research administrator, became dean in 1948, he reorganized the college and the experiment station so that all lines of authority came into his office. A firm believer in strong academic training, he encouraged basic as opposed to applied research. Everybody at that time acknowledged the eminence of some agricultural research, but Lambert thought that staff members in other colleges "looked with some disdain" upon it. He and some critics felt that for all its professional excellence, the ag campus was unsophisticated. Various administrators had attempted to direct the social lives of their staff, for example, by urging regular attendance at Sunday school, specifying activities like family picnics, and quoting platitudinous musings of Ella Wheeler Wilcox (1850–1919) in newsletters. One prominent chairman regularly recommended *Acres of Diamonds*, an 1888 Chautauqua lecture, for spiritual uplift.

When H. Clyde Filley retired in 1948, Lambert appointed C. Clyde Mitchell to be chairman of the newly named Department of Agricultural Economics. Mitchell, a student of John Kenneth Galbraith's and a liberal, was only thirty-two when he came to Nebraska with a doctorate from Harvard and administrative experience in this country and in Korea. He had not yet provided the evidence of scholarly achievement that would have admitted him to the University's graduate faculty, that elite group who directed research and graduate studies; but with his energy, youth, and intelligence, he could be expected to achieve this in short order. A colorful speaker, he was soon in demand for addresses on agricultural policy, then as always a vital topic in Nebraska. In them he did not distinguish clearly between opinion and research reports. Not at all diplomatic, he refused to qualify his defense of fixed farm price supports, basic New Deal policy, in a region where some farm groups wanted variable supports. He arrogantly called persons who disagreed with his views economic illiterates. Regent J. Leroy Welsh and conservative farm groups took public offense and objected to his speaking out.[39]

The matter became a question of free speech. Was a professor free to express opinions on matters of public policy? In expressing them, was he "indoctrinating" his students? The Board of Regents issued a ringing statement defending liberty of expression, written in haste by Bruce Nicoll and Ken Keller on the Saturday morning when it was adopted, 21 November 1953. Even so, Lambert asked Mitchell to report his schedule of speeches and to consider limiting their number. In January 1954 George Round "edited" a speech that Mitchell had prepared for public delivery. The next year, in February 1955, Lambert talked to Mitchell about appointing a new chairman for the department, and in September he nominated Mitchell for a government job. In October Mitchell reported that he had accepted a Fulbright appointment to lecture in Rome during the spring of 1956.

That should have been the end of this matter. But on 16 April 1956, Lambert announced that the University administration was seeking a replacement for Mitchell as chair of the Department of Agricultural Economics when he returned from leave in Rome. Since Mitchell had not been elected to the graduate faculty by his peers, he and his department were restricted in dealings with graduate students, Lambert said. The campus newspaper refused to accept this explanation for the change in chairmanship. Recalling the severe, earlier opposition to his views by the conservative Hall County Farm Bureau and by Regent Welsh, the editor asserted on 18 April 1956 that "special

interests outside the University" had forced what the editor called "a demotion." Nobody questioned the legal authority of Dean Lambert and, beyond him, Chancellor Hardin to replace administrative officials, but students and, increasingly, faculty members came to see this action as evidence that the University was yielding to external political pressures.

The Mitchell case disturbed the equanimity of the campus because the editor of the campus paper insisted on headlining it for weeks. Fresh-faced, tall, rather imposing in manner, Bruce Brugmann never questioned his own positions, which he liked to call "moral." He was fond of quoting James Reston of the *New York Times*, who said that the function of a newspaper is "to print the news and raise hell." While the chancellor and his staff were trying to wrest financial support from the conservative legislature and the conservative state, some members of the faculty, mostly liberals, asserted that there must be fire where Brugmann detected smoke. Dean Breckenridge and Howard Ottoson, who was acting chair of the Department of Agricultural Economics and in his long career at the University was to become a provost, both thought the controversy could have been avoided if Lambert had not tried to explain his actions publicly and before Mitchell's term of appointment was completed.

Though he was in touch with Brugmann, Mitchell, in fact, did not help the young man in what Brugmann asserted was an issue of free speech. Only at the last minute in May 1956 did Mitchell send his list of charges to the paper, and only in December did he finally mail a 136-page statement to the Faculty Senate's Committee on Academic Privilege and Tenure. By then he was in Mexico City with the Food and Agriculture Organization of the United Nations, and his statement came only by surface mail. It did not arrive until January 1957. During these months the campus remained restless with gossip and innuendo, exacerbated by the campus newspaper.

The committee began hearings on the Mitchell charges in February 1957 and delivered its report to the Faculty Senate on 4 June 1957. The report found in favor of Mitchell on four of his seven charges. The Lincoln papers commended the committee for their "judicious report." In presenting it, the committee moved that it be referred to the Liaison Committee for appropriate action. In a second report to the Senate at a special meeting on 5 November 1957, the Liaison Committee said the matter should now be considered closed and made no recommendations for further action. The Liaison Committee, charged with looking after faculty interest, came under severe criticism for its failure to recommend administrative change.

The Mitchell affair reached no neat conclusion. Though some came to feel that the case was blown out of proportion through the zeal of the young editor, at the same time they retained a lingering suspicion that the chancellor and the regents, for all their statements of principle, did not stand firm against special-interest groups, especially on the extreme right. In retrospect, one must conclude that the smoke was much greater than the fire, but the suspicions of administrative double-dealing poisoned the atmosphere.

The faculty was hard on the chancellor, perhaps harder than they should have been, standing as he did in the public eye, answerable always to a public constituency. In future years Dean Breckenridge, sticking to the letter of the law, nipped internal controversy in the bud. Hardin, watching the campus newspaper, more than once dissuaded energetic editors from editorial positions that he saw as a disservice to the institution – and a danger to themselves. In these fervently anti-Communist years, the University continued to get external criticism, but none was allowed to blossom. In 1958 a senator "accused" a young law professor of belonging to Americans for Democratic Action, a group in which Eleanor Roosevelt and Hubert Humphrey were prominent; and that year the legislature required professors to sign a loyalty oath, which was in fact meaningless and which nobody ever thought of again. In 1961 the editor of the campus newspaper was attacked by the Omaha American Legion for urging the abolition of the House Un-American Activities Committee, and in 1963 a lawyer from Fremont denounced the campus newspaper and the School of Journalism for preaching "liberal" doctrine. The director of the School of Journalism called the accusation "ridiculous" and graded the lawyer's documentation of charges with an F because it was so slovenly constructed. In May 1963, Karl Shapiro resigned rather theatrically as editor of the *Prairie Schooner*, charging that Dean Militzer had censored a story he sought to publish when a copyeditor was offended by its vulgar language. The matter was resolved quickly, largely because Bernice Slote assumed responsibility for the literary quarterly and brought it to new eminence. None of these matters was more than a temporary inconvenience. The chancellor and the regents each time reasserted their support of free expression and let the charges die of their own absurdity. By 1965 the University of Nebraska could be judged by university watchers like Arthur Adams of the American Council on Education to be "the best administered and the most comfortable" university in the nation.[40] The faculties nonetheless remained suspicious of the administration, suspecting it of tailoring University policy to public perceptions.

11. The University Expands: 1960–1968

❧ The Faculty

During the Hardin administration the University's budget rose appreciably. In 1955 the legislature gave the University a 19 percent increase over the previous biennum; in 1957, in spite of a poor harvest, it got another increase. In the 1960s Governor Morrison supported the University, and its budget continued to rise. Even so, the proportion of the University's appropriation to the total state budget remained nearly constant and student fees were regularly increased. According to the official historian of the University, the public seemed to "turn from the long-accepted tradition of the land-grant university characterized by low student fees and liberal entrance requirements" to an assumption that those who received higher education should bear a full share of its costs.[1] Enrollments increased year by year, from 8,700 in 1960 to 13,000 in 1964 to 19,000 in 1968, and some persons on and off the campus talked of restricting enrollments. Chancellor Hardin considered such a policy politically unwise, but open admission caused problems. Lee W. Chatfield, associate dean of student affairs, who was in effect the admitting officer, had a set of four letters, one of which he sent to each prospective new student. To those in the upper quartile of their high school classes he wrote enthusiastically, to those in the second quartile he wrote confidently, to those in the third quartile he wrote cautiously, and to those in the last quartile he wrote discouragingly. Far from destroying academic standards, the increasing enrollments of the Sixties allowed departments and professors to raise standards. As they sometimes said, it was a seller's market.

The Hardin years were a seller's market for professors also; the increasing number of students put teachers in demand, and if Nebraska salaries did not rise as fast or as high as the professors wished, the salary scale nonetheless improved markedly, as the annual AAUP ratings showed. At least as important, a funded retirement plan for University staff was finally established in 1961. By vote of the staff the University had come under the national Social Security system in September 1955. In 1959 Senator Otto Liebers got enabling legislation passed to provide for a vested retirement plan; but when the University proposed a funded system to the legislature in 1961, they discovered that the redoubtable Terry Carpenter was opposed. At the chancellor's residence one night, Hardin and George Round tried to bring him around, and the chancellor finally said, "Senator, is there a program that you would support?" When he said that he could accept one whose limit on the state's contribution was 9 percent, including Social Security, the Chancellor quickly agreed. Round later remembered that Terry Carpenter said, "Chancellor, the problem with you is that you don't know a damn thing about politics." "Yes," the chancellor replied with unperceived irony. "That's right, Senator, often we agree on the issues. Why don't you coach me on the politics?" With Carpenter's support, the legislation passed.[2]

This was the first such plan the University had ever had. Until then, retirement payments had come out of operating expenses and people had retired on what amounted to starvation incomes. The new plan was endorsed by the Board of Regents on 23 September 1961, and the University joined the Teachers Insurance and Annuity Association of America and College Retirement Equities Fund of New York for a compulsory, contributory, vested retirement system, the University matching the staff member's 6 percent of salary with another 6 percent. Thus the University became reasonably competitive with other educational institutions. In addition, in this period the faculty committee on retirement and insurance, which had been established in 1948 and endorsed by the Board of Regents in 1955, worked with the University administration, notably Roy Loudon Jr., in the personnel office to set up insurance plans. By the middle Sixties the staff was reasonably well protected from calamity as well as penury in old age.

Since it was a seller's market, Chancellor Hardin observed that as young faculty members developed national prominence, universities with greater resources hired them away. In order to stop this drain, he proposed establishing some super-professorships with resources made available through the University of Nebraska Foundation. At first these Regents Professorships paid $3,500 a year beyond the normal salary from state funds, but shortly the increment was raised to $5,000. The chancellor was eager that the professorships not be exploited by deans to build empires. "We used a committee of associate professors to select the first group, then we used the existing Regents professors to select those who were added to the list," he later explained.[3] The first two Regents Professors, selected in May 1960 and appointed in January 1961, were Norman Cromwell in chemistry and John H. Lonnquist in agronomy; others were appointed in the next few years. James E. Miller Jr. was named in 1961. He had come to the University as an assistant professor in 1953 but by 1957 was professor and chairman of the Department of English. In 1962 James C. Olson, the state historian and a member of the history department faculty; Royce Knapp of Teachers College; Curtis Elliott, a celebrated teacher of insurance in the College of Business Administration; Karl Shapiro, the Pulitzer Prize–winning poet; and George Young of veterinary science were also named. Though the chancellor and the board had hoped the Regents Professorships would attract a few academic stars from outside the University, more than three-fourths went to local persons, selected in a University-wide competition.

By the time Hardin left the chancellorship in 1968, thirty-two men — including six from the Medical Center — and one woman, Hazel Fox of the School of Home Economics, had been named Regents Professors. In 1967 only

three women in the University outside of home economics and women's physical education were full professors: Garnet Larson in the Graduate School of Social Work, M. Rosalind Morris in agronomy, and Bernice Slote in the Department of English. Mary Mielenz in secondary education had retired as a full professor one year earlier. This proportion was sharply different from that in previous generations. Before 1940 a number of women had been prominent across the University, but after World War II, women, when hired at all, were in junior posts or in women's departments. Those already on the staff were not encouraged.

In 1954 the University Foundation, at Hardin's suggestion, established annual Distinguished Teaching Awards which, like research grants, were awarded competitively, with a stipend of $1,000. Lane Lancaster was the first to be named. A longtime professor of political science, he was popular with both students and colleagues because of his urbanity, easy learning, and quick wit. Ironical, perhaps even cynical, he called himself an idealist and peered unblinkingly through rimless glasses. From 1955 to 1967, two teaching awards were made each year, one in humanities and social sciences, the other in science and technology. Mary Mielenz, who was long adviser to the student council and professor of secondary education, was the first woman to be named, in 1963.

In the Hardin years, the most prominent teacher on the city campus was probably James S. Blackman of engineering. He was in his day rather what T. H. Goodding (who retired in 1955) had been on the ag campus in the previous generation. Apparently without personal ambition, they had total loyalty from their students. Goodding was the first ag college professor to receive a Distinguished Teaching Award, in 1955, and Blackman was the first engineer to get one, in 1956. When University Builders, an undergraduate service club, began awarding teaching prizes in 1966, they gave Jim Blackman one of their first. His academic colleagues elected him to every post available to them, and the administration appointed him to their most responsible committees. Twice he served, reluctantly, as interim dean of his college. Like Goodding's, his goodwill was obvious.

Another spectacularly successful teacher was "Doc" Elliott in the College of Business Administration. Curt Elliott had come to the University in 1942, and though he made a national reputation as an economist specializing in insurance, he was locally famous for his rapport with students. "So many students congregated in his office that it was often called the western branch of the Student Union," his colleagues in Social Sciences Hall said.[4] He liked to laugh, and his classes, though rigorous, were wonderfully entertaining. He taught by television and lectured across the state. One wondered how he had time to be principal clarinetist in the Lincoln Symphony. Twenty years after his death in 1968 at the age of fifty-six, the Nebraska Alumni Association established a "Doc" Elliott Prize in his name to honor distinguished retired University teachers.

❧ The Sheldon Memorial Art Gallery

The chief ornament of the University campuses was the Sheldon Memorial Art Gallery, at the corner of Twelfth and R streets, on a site selected by its architects. When Frances Sheldon died in June 1950 at the age of fifty-eight, she left the bulk of her estate to construct and equip an art gallery. In the spring of 1950 she had visited the annual Nebraska Art Association show on the second floor of Morrill Hall and pronounced it a miserable place. Ever since 1888 the Nebraska Art Association had been sponsoring exhibitions, and after 1895 its collections had been exhibited on the top floor of the library (now Architecture Hall) in galleries designed for them. In 1927 they were moved to the new Morrill Hall, where two rather large but drab galleries had been provided.

The collections soon expanded into the corridors. Mr. and Mrs. Frank M. Hall, both of whom died in 1928, left their estate and private collections to the University, and the income from their bequest allowed for regular purchases, mostly of modern American painting. Guided in the Thirties and Forties by Dwight Kirsch, a native son, the collections by 1950 began to be important. The Sheldon family had been active in the Nebraska Art Association for many years, but nobody knew the depth of their interest or the size of their fortune. Miss Sheldon's initial bequest came close to a million dollars.

When Hardin arrived in 1954, he was immediately told of Frances Sheldon's generosity. "She had left this [bequest] in the hands of her brother Bromley Sheldon of Lexington, who was a lumber dealer there, to turn over to the Regents when he wanted to or on his death," Hardin recalled. "[H]e was managing the trust well and our conclusion was it was growing in value faster than building costs were advancing and that we shouldn't pressure him to turn it over." When Bromley Sheldon developed terminal cancer a few years later, "he began to work with us to transfer the assets of the trust most advantageously for building the Art Gallery. I remember . . . [his] being brought into Lincoln on a stretcher to look through some of the assets. He selected the ones that should be sold."[5] Upon his death in 1957 it was discovered that he had left half of his own estate to go with his sister's trust. The total was now over $4 million. The balance of Bromley Sheldon's estate was left to his wife, Olga, but she too was interested in art and requested that the gallery should itself be a work of art.

In 1958 Hardin appointed a joint town-gown committee to supervise the construction of the Sheldon Memorial Art Gallery. Norman Geske, director of University art galleries since 1950, drew up its program, a central responsibility. After canvassing the leading architects of the world, the committee selected Philip Johnson, who had already designed five art galleries. The committee rejected his first proposal, a rather radical construction with a roof suspended over lower units; but he overcame his unhappiness when told that once a plan was accepted, the committee would not second-guess him. His next proposal was a jewel box proclaiming that it contained precious contents. It was the Sheldons' gift to the whole state. Its outside walls and its center great hall were covered with travertine marble, its splayed arches giving a suggestion of columns. Its teak and bronze fittings, its floating stair and gilded ceiling, its elegant exhibition galleries, its tall windows admitting the clear light of the Nebraska sky combined to make it one of the finest small museums in the nation. Costing $67 a square foot, it was the most expensive building in the United States at the time. Carl Olson, whose local construction company had the contract to build it, said later, "All my crew who worked on that building realized that this was a significant building. A bit of love went into it."[6]

If, as students of architecture say, a good building requires a good patron, much credit for the excellence of the Sheldon Memorial Art Gallery is due Norman Geske. Working closely with Johnson, the paradoxical Geske understood the requirements of the local climate, both physical and cultural. Olga Sheldon watched over and bought works for the gallery. When it was opened, on 16 May 1963, she gave in her husband's memory a 1916 marble sculpture, *Princess*, by Constantin Brancusi; and when she died, thirty years after her husband, she left the bulk of her estate and her considerable private collection to the gallery. In the meantime other benefactors enriched the collections with generous gifts, and the contents of the Sheldon became worthy of their place. In 1959 the Woods Charitable Fund, which had long been a generous benefactor of the Nebraska Art Association, gave a quarter of a million dollars for the construction of the Nelle Cochran Woods Art Building, adjacent to the gallery, for art department classrooms and offices. With The Temple (1906) to the southeast, Kimball Recital Hall (1970) to the south, the Westbrook Music Building (1966) to the west, and the former library (1894), now Architecture Hall, across a sculpture garden, the old campus became the art center of the community. In 1990 the Lied Center for Performing Arts at Twelfth and R streets completed the quadrangle.

❧ Football

Hardin found an athletic program in some disarray in 1954. Nebraskans could not forget the glory days of Dana X. Bible in the Thirties and the Rose Bowl of 1941. The fiasco of the postwar teams had distressed the fans at least as much as the sportswriters, and when Bill Glassford was brought in as head coach in 1949 they expected a restoration. Chancellor Gustavson's insistence on "de-emphasis" had not gone down with them. They had not understood that he was, like college presidents across the country, trying to keep football from dominating the academic scene. Oklahoma was a leader in the professionalization of col-

legiate football. Its system of recruiting, extended practice, and bowl bargaining set the pace for the whole conference, and it challenged Big Seven rules as early as 1952 without reprimand. Bud Wilkinson, Oklahoma's coach, became a national hero – in some quarters.

Glassford was a disappointment. Though he had won more games than any other Nebraska coach in a decade, by 1954 his players were in open rebellion against his professional, rather impersonal relationship with them. Egged on by journalists, especially television reporters, the players "blasted" their coach, even threatening not to report for spring practice if he stayed on. In May the regents dissolved the old Board of Intercollegiate Athletics, which had overseen the athletic program for thirty-three years, and made the athletic director, Potsy Clark, directly responsible to the chancellor and themselves, a faculty committee becoming only advisory. Through the ruckus, the board supported Glassford – he had an airtight contract for five years with a second five-year option beyond that – and by the fall of 1954 he had come to terms with his players. The 1954 season was reasonably successful. Though Oklahoma defeated Nebraska 55 to 7 that fall, Nebraska was second in the conference. They went to the Orange Bowl, where they had a second loss.

Glassford's 1955 season was his last. After defeating Hawaii in 1954, in 1955 Nebraska lost to Hawaii in Lincoln and the next week was defeated by Ohio State in Columbus. Tempers ran high, inflamed by a critical press, and by the end of the season Glassford was under siege. His family was harassed by telephone calls at all hours, and he was abused in public. Hardin supported him but cannot have been unhappy when the coach rejected his second five-year option. Glassford left coaching and, assisted by George Cook of Bankers Life Insurance Nebraska, moved to Arizona for a successful career in insurance. Cook and his friends had been paying Glassford $3,500 a year beyond his contract while he coached at Nebraska. The fans were legitimately unhappy during these years, for Glassford's coaches had talented young men to work with. Bobby Reynolds was the most famous of them, but Glassford could not "put it together," as the fans said.

In 1956 Pete Elliott was promptly appointed head

coach. Elliott, who had been an assistant to Bud Wilkinson, looked like the all-American boy, blond and handsome, and he was a friend of sportswriters. He lasted one year before moving on to California. Bill Jennings, Pete Elliott's backfield coach, was next appointed. Very personable and an excellent recruiter, he changed dramatically when he became head coach. Don Bryant, a sportswriter who later became an assistant athletic director, said, "He kind of went into a shell and he became very defensive," perhaps because of "the pressure of the whole load on his shoulders . . . he was in total shock." Bryant, a shrewd and generous observer, concluded, "Bill and his staff could never get it put together except on rare occasions against topnotch foes. We had a lot of upsets during Bill's five years, but [we] never had any consistent winners."[7]

In 1961 Hardin made Joe Soshnik and Charlie Miller acting athletic directors. Miller, dean of the College of Business Administration, was at least as interested in football and businessmen as in academic matters. "By this time I had been here eight years and it was really kind of discouraging," Hardin later said. He arranged to meet Dana X. Bible in Kansas City for advice. After Bible told him to recruit a successful head coach and his whole staff, the chancellor telephoned Duffy Daugherty at Michigan State, an old friend. "What you ought to do is get Bob Devaney who has been with us at Michigan State and he's out in Wyoming," he told Hardin. "I said, 'Will he come?' I remember he said, 'Yes, if you will quit yacking at me and let me get off this phone so I can call him and tell him to.' "[8] Bob Devaney visited Lincoln, staying incognito at Joe Soshnik's house, and very shortly agreed to move, bringing his assistant coaches with him. Quietly Joe W. Seacrest, Clarence Swanson, and other Lincoln businessmen collected money to augment his contracted salary.[9]

Devaney became one of the great coaches of his generation. How did he operate? Don Bryant said, "The real key to Bob's success and his staff's was that they had all been successful high school coaches. They had learned how to win, but they also learned that you have to teach kids. You have to be patient. Everybody isn't an All-American who walks onto that field. If you go back through Bob's teams, you find there kids that he and his assistants brought along through work and coaching." He demanded a lot from them: "Of course he would get on those kids on that sideline something fierce. Guy Ingles always said, '[When] I would go back to catch a punt, all I would do is stand back there and pray that I wouldn't drop it so I wouldn't have to run off the field and face Coach Devaney.' " Bryant recalled that Devaney did a tremendous job with the black athletes. They had legitimate complaints. Bryant remembered how it had been in 1954 when Nebraska played Oklahoma: "They would not let our three black athletes stay in our hotel. We had to take them down to the black YMCA. At meal time they would let those kids come up, into the back door of the hotel, to eat with the squad and then go back out through the kitchen door." From 1962 on, Devaney "recognized that everybody on that squad was a man who had his own individual concerns and he treated them that way."[10]

Hardin had the football program he thought necessary to Nebraska. During his years as head coach, Devaney's teams won 101 times, lost 20 games, and tied 2. In 1970 and 1971 his teams won the national championship. "There is no doubt that [the 1971 team] was a fine college football team. Whether it was the best that ever played, well, that's for others to speculate about. But I feel that team could have played with any college team I've ever seen," Devaney said later.[11] Devaney became director of athletics in 1967 and held that post until 1993, when he retired reluctantly at seventy-seven.

In 1972 Devaney turned over his coaching responsibilities to Tom Osborne, who had served as his offensive coordinator. "Looking back, one of the better things that happened to me here was having Tom Osborne come to me in 1962 and ask if he could work as an assistant," Devaney said. Osborne was a graduate assistant in the Department of Educational Psychology at the time. "About the only thing we gave Tom for a couple of years was a chance to eat at the training table."[12] In 1964 Osborne received an extra thousand dollars for serving as assistant football coach for the season.[13] He took his Ph.D. in educational psychology in 1965. Hardin had already spotted him: "I thought he was one of the most able young men that we had on the faculty. At this time the Ford Foundation had a program which would let you pick a young man about thirty and they would provide living expenses and salary for him to go to another campus for a year to learn some of the tricks of university administration. I offered to nominate Tom for this with full assurance that he could come back and move into university administration. I thought he was the kind of man that in a few years could be a university president some place. He thought about it quite seriously. I shall never forget his reply when he came in several days later. He said, 'Dr. Hardin, I fully realize that you have accorded me a very high honor. I hope you will understand what I am trying to say to you when I tell you that coaching football is so much fun that I don't think I can give it up.' Now the background to this was that he was [then] at about a half-time basis helping Bob Devaney coach ends."[14] When Osborne became head coach, he made a record as distinguished as Devaney's.

⧉ The Campuses

During the Hardin years the University campuses underwent more physical changes than at any previous time in their history, changes dictated by deferred maintenance, increased enrollment, and growing research responsibilities. In 1945 the legislature had appropriated money for buildings. John K. Selleck, acting chancellor (1953–54), reported to the budget committee how the funds were disbursed among the colleges. Of the sum received, just under $5 million, 42 percent, had gone to the College of Agriculture; 17.5 percent had gone to the College of Engineering and Architecture. Under 10 percent had gone to the College of Medicine and about 7 percent had gone to the College of Arts and Sciences. General University projects had been allotted 15 percent. This was the first state-supported general building program since the construction of Andrews Hall in 1928.[15]

During Hardin's first years the University's building projects extended the campuses rather miscellaneously, according to pressing needs and in response to academic and political lobbying. The buildings were placed where spots could be found. Senator Richard Marvel, chairman of the budget committee of the legislature, concluding that

the University suffered from a lack of long-term planning, provided in the 1965 budget for a Bureau of Institutional Research. Harry Allen was its first director: "When I came here in 1965, the University really had not had a building program for many years," he later said.[16] In February 1966 Caudell, Rowlett and Scott, an architectural planning firm from Texas, was hired to draw a campus master plan, the first comprehensive scheme since the Seymour Plan of 1921. On their recommendation, streets were closed, walks were laid out, and building sites were specified. The administration, including Harry Allen, were more pleased with their suggestions than the faculty, and in the long run the planners' recommendations were considerably modified.

The city campus was expanded from Q Street north almost to the fairgrounds and east to Eighteenth Street. The ag campus, renamed the east campus by the regents in 1964, had given up research fields for married student housing and the Nebraska Center for Continuing Education and now became home to the College of Dentistry, the College of Law, and the Terry Carpenter Telecommunications Building. In Omaha, physicians returning after 1960 found new hospitals and laboratories extending many blocks around the old core at Forty-second and Dewey Avenue.

As student enrollments grew precipitously after 1960 the University seemed always behind in its attempt to provide living accommodations. In 1963, when the enrollment climbed above 10,000, the University rented four floors of the Capital Hotel in downtown Lincoln for male residences and hastily commissioned two tower dormitories, later called Cather and Pound Halls, on North Seventeenth Street. Alarmed at the increasing size of the student body, the Board of Regents offered the contractor a bonus for early completion of them. Demographers had warned that the "baby boomers" would be college age in the Sixties, but Hardin, fearful of overbuilding, had for once disregarded his advisers.

In 1963 two additional enormous residence halls were hastily planned. Abel Hall for men, named for University benefactor George Abel, was thirteen stories tall, and Sandoz Hall for women, next door, named for Mari

Sandoz, the writer, was half as large. They were paid for by bonds issued against student revenues. In 1964 women were admitted to Selleck Quad because the campus was so short of women's housing, and that year senior women were permitted by the office of the dean of women to live in apartments in town. As early as October 1964 students complained of the impersonal atmosphere of Pound Hall. Abel Hall was hardly finished (1965) before fires broke out in its trash chutes and its elevators were vandalized. Helen Snyder, associate dean of students, warned that high-rise dormitories would breed destructiveness, and she tried to organize them by floors to counteract their impersonality. In 1966 contracts were let for three more enormous residence halls, this time far to the north, on the other side of the railroad tracks beyond the classroom campus. One of them was ironically called Harper Hall, after Dean W. Claire Harper, director of University Services, who had advised against their construction. Another was called Schramm Hall after a bachelor geology professor, E. F. Schramm, who had left his fortune to the University and his landholdings to the state of Nebraska for parks. The third was named for Ellen Smith, the first woman on the faculty. In 1970 a ten-story faculty office building, Oldfather Hall, was completed on the city campus. The dean of the College of Arts and Sciences occupied its remote tenth floor, and the rest of the building consisted of offices too small for seminars. Oldfather Hall was a rabbit warren which defied the development of intellectual community, and the persons who occupied it were unhappy with its impersonality from the first day, just as students were unhappy with their high-rise residences. One critic suggested that the dorms were student warehouses, the students being commodities. The students were expected to come from their residential cubicles to go to classroom cubicles where they met professors out of their office cubicles for fifty-minute blocks of time; then students, staff, and faculty were to return to quiet anonymity.

Enrollments continued to rise, in 1964 to 13,000, in 1966 to 17,000, in 1968 to 19,000, and the quality of undergraduate life was radically changed. By 1966 the Associated Women Students (AWS), which had been the self-governing board for women for many years, announced

that it should not concern itself with protecting women. In the past the AWS had set and enforced rules governing women's hours and conduct; it would work now for their convenience. In September 1966 a young idealist named Steve Abbott appeared before the student council asking for a student bill of rights. "The administration stands on top of us, with their feet on our throats," the *Daily Nebraskan* quoted him as announcing fiercely on 15 September 1966. "We should make our own rules." The University no longer stood in loco parentis. Students wanted to be, and were, on their own. The next five years were to see changes of a major sort on campus.

❧ Expanding Colleges

In the Hardin administration the College of Agriculture took advantage of federal largess to strengthen its already vigorous research programs. In 1959 Carl Donaldson, business manager of the University, learned that the ordnance plant south of Mead, between Lincoln and Omaha, consisting of some 17,000 acres, would be listed as surplus the next year. Dean Elvin Frolik immediately saw an opportunity to expand his field laboratories. The Havelock farms, which had been satisfactory for many years, were increasingly surrounded by housing and had become too small for modern research. In the spring of 1960 Frolik and the chancellor persuaded the Board of Regents to ask for 8,000 acres of the land; that, they said, would not be too much for the University to support. On 12 April 1962 the grant was made, for the sum of one silver dollar, provided out of Donaldson's own pocket and polished by him.[17] In addition to the Mead land, the ag college made use of surplus property around Hastings. In 1964, after much controversy, the naval ammunition depot there was conveyed to the United States Department of Agriculture to become a meat animal research center. Named for Senator Roman Hruska, who had vigorously worked to have the land set aside for research, the center was supported by the USDA and the Agriculture Research Service, not the state of Nebraska. The regents had refused to take it on. Various departments and divisions of the college and the experiment station made extensive use of it nonetheless.

The College of Medicine, in Omaha, also expanded in the Hardin years, thanks to federal grants. In 1952 a committee on education of the American Medical Association had placed it on "confidential probation" because of its lack of research and teaching facilities and its limited professional faculty. Most of the clinical professors had nearly full-time private practices and were not deeply engaged in research. The Nebraska State Medical Association became alarmed and, joining the University administration, persuaded the legislature in 1953 to approve a ten-year .25-mill levy toward constructing a modern medical center. The college remained on AMA probation in 1954 nonetheless. In that year the trustees of the Bishop Clarkson Memorial Hospital decided to put up a new building on campus at a cost of $5 million. This, combined with private, county, and federal hospitals elsewhere in Omaha, greatly enlarged teaching and research facilities for the University. In 1955 the World Publishing Company announced it would construct a medical office building on Farnam Street adjacent to the medical campus. But even with all this, the medical college in 1962 was underdeveloped. It had the lowest bed capacity of all medical colleges under state support in the nation, and it lacked facilities to make use of available federal funds.

In 1956 Eugene C. Eppley, whose fortune derived from hotels in the region, had become interested in cancer research and in cooperation with the medical dean and the chancellor had begun considering support of a cancer research center in Omaha. After thorough investigation, the directors of the Eppley Foundation in 1960 made a grant of $2.5 million to the University for the Eugene C. Eppley Institute for Research in Cancer and Allied Diseases. The foundation money attracted $800,000 from the U.S. Public Health Service, and the College of Medicine added $350,000 from its building levy. According to plan the institute was to employ some 200 specialists and technicians with an annual expenditure of $2 million. It was expected to attract grants, and it would both aid the teaching program of the college and make research facilities available to physicians throughout the region. "Omaha will become one of the world's principal centers in the fight against cancer," the *Omaha World-Herald* said editorially on 5 May 1960.

In 1964 J. Perry Tollman resigned as dean of the Medical College. Over some internal objection, Hardin appointed Cecil Wittson in his place. Dr. Wittson had obtained federal funding for the Psychiatric Institute as its director and had built a large organization, the largest and probably most successful unit in the medical college. In what the official history of the College of Medicine refers to as "The Wittson Revolution," he turned the medical college into a major medical center.[18] The chancellor later said, "What he did at the College of Medicine can only be described as a miracle. He was able to bring the opposition in Omaha, one by one, into cooperation and solid support."[19] Regent Richard L. Herman considered Wittson "one of the greatest operators. Cecil had a great facility that real brilliant people have; and that is, when he saw he was getting into trouble, he would lead you off in several paths, or try to, and he'd have five or ten things going at you at once. I used to have to say, 'Cecil, let's get back over here.' "[20] On occasion Wittson mumbled strategically in his South Carolina accent, but Hardin said that he always knew completely what Wittson's game plan was.

One of Wittson's greatest coups was bringing Dr. Philippe Shubik and his team of researchers to Omaha from the Chicago Medical School Institute for Medical Research when it could no longer support them. This group had distinguished itself by pioneering research in chemical carcinogens and consisted of a dozen scientists, half of them physicians and half chemists. Their salaries were covered by federal grants, and their equipment, government-owned, was in effect their property. Philippe Shubik, born into an English family and educated at Oxford, was an American citizen married to a Chicago woman. An international figure with membership on boards in several European and South American countries, he had wanted for family reasons to remain in the Midwest.

Until 1968 the Eppley Institute had not lived up to its possibilities, but Shubik and his group got it off and running. The budget committee of the legislature continued to be startled by the costs of medical education, even with generous foundation support, and were sometimes put off by Wittson's fluency. Senator Richard Marvel, chairman of the budget committee, and other legislators felt that he and the University administration kept "a card under the table all the time" and thought Dr. Shubik and other University administrators were too clever by half. The University in these years was accused of political shrewdness and narrow professionalism, and Marvel became increasingly skeptical of their budget figures, even when presented by Joe Soshnik, the old reliable. George Round sometimes advised Soshnik to pretend not to know, to promise to "look it up," just to assure the legislators that he was not fudging his facts.[21] Hardin was aware that his credibility with the legislature was something of a problem, for though very effective in one-to-one relationships, he was not so persuasive in groups. Still, he and his advisers probably got as much money from the legislature over the years as anybody could have.

❧ The Merger with the Municipal University of Omaha

The most important development of Hardin's administration came in the last year of his tenure. By 1966 the Municipal University of Omaha was in serious financial difficulty. Founded as a Presbyterian college in 1900, it had become a municipal university by popular vote in 1937, but subsequently Omahans refused to fund it. In 1966 by a majority of 80 percent of the votes the people again refused a civic levy, and in desperation Kirk Naylor, president of the university, appealed to the legislature for support. The Omaha contingent of the legislature was not large enough to get it money, but Senator Terry Carpenter, always resourceful, saw an opportunity. State finances were in a sorry condition. In a referendum the previous year Nebraskans had voted out the state property tax, which had been the tax base from the state's beginning, but they had also rejected a proposed income tax. When the legislature met in 1966, it was thus confronted with the impossible: needs continued but no tax system existed to support them. The legislature had to act. Governor Norbert Tiemann proposed a combination sales-income tax, but this met mighty opposition. Government was at an impasse. Carpenter thereupon proposed that the state assume responsibility for the Municipal University of

Omaha and pass six other Omaha bills if, in return, Omaha legislators supported a new tax system. The gridlock seemed to be broken. The shape of higher education in Nebraska became part of larger political considerations: the state's basic tax strategy.[22]

How were the universities to be related, to each other and to the state? Hardin remembered that Naylor wanted the University of Omaha linked to the University of Nebraska, and Carpenter announced that if the University was unwilling to accept responsibility for it, he would introduce a bill to establish the Municipal University as an independent state university complete with its own regents. Afterwards, Gene Budig, assistant to the chancellor, recalled, "Most of us thought that he had the votes to do it [and we asked], What would that do to the total picture of higher education, to have two institutions at each other's throats every legislative season?"[23] Hardin began conversations with the Board of Regents; the governing board of the Municipal University of Omaha, headed by Robert Spire; and leading citizens. Not all his staff agreed that the universities should join, but all fervently wished that this important legislation did not have to be rushed. Budig, who studied the matter as chairman of the chancellor's steering committee, observed that other states took eighteen months or two years "to put everything [like this] in its place," but all was hurried here. If there had been time, all kinds of suspicions could have been avoided, he thought. Some people said that this linking was a power play to get legislative support from Omaha for the University of Nebraska, but Hardin always maintained that no such consideration existed in his mind. He thought it was simply more economical for the state to have the two universities under a single management than to have competing systems.

In January 1967 Hardin told his faculty that the joining of the universities was imminent but that they need not expect "an added layer of administration." He wrote, "The Board of Regents is firm in its position that there shall be only one chief executive officer reporting to it."[24] The "merging" of the institutions – the word *merge* does not appear in the legislation but constantly appears in the discussions – would not be at the collegiate or departmental level. Rather, the two institutions would have a coordinated graduate faculty and research effort, and it was assumed that the financial operations would be directed centrally.

The faculties at both institutions were apprehensive. The Lincoln faculty feared that state revenues would be drawn from their existing programs to build Omaha programs, which had been starved. They were not consulted about the merger, in part because of legislative urgency, in part because the chancellor habitually centralized authority in his office. The Omaha faculty feared that they would be taken over – that is, dictated to – by the older, larger university. In order not to alarm Omaha, Hardin agreed that Kirk Naylor should remain president of his university, and Cecil Wittson thereupon was designated president rather than dean of the Medical Center. The institution thus seemed to consist of three coordinate branches, when in fact they had incomparable missions. This yoking of the three dissimilar divisions as though they were alike would become persistently troublesome.

In December 1967 the people of Omaha resoundingly endorsed the absorption of the Municipal University of Omaha into a state system, and the union became official in July 1968. In the interim, twelve subcommittees worked on problems of unification and identified sixty-three different issues in twenty-four areas. Gene Budig later remembered, "[W]e were groping even for an agenda . . . here we were again, all thrown together with little, if any thought, under duress . . . a piece of legislation that comprehensive should have had a thoughtful setting of a year or eighteen months."[25]

In October 1968 the Board of Regents reorganized the University. Clifford Hardin was named chancellor, that is, chief administrative officer, of the total University, Joseph Soshnik vice chancellor for administration, and Merk Hobson vice chancellor of academic affairs. A graduate dean for the total University was designated but unidentified; Norman Cromwell was shortly named to the post. The three component parts of the University now had presidents: Kirk Naylor for Omaha, Cecil Wittson for the Medical Center, Joseph Soshnik for the Lincoln campuses and outstate activities. Hobson was in effect executive officer for the whole system and Soshnik was both financial officer of the total University and president of the Lincoln campuses. Obviously this organization was awkward and could only be temporary.

❧ The Hardins' Departure

And then in the fall of 1968, upon the election of Richard Nixon as president, Hardin was appointed secretary of agriculture, a post he could hardly refuse. "I can tell you this, George," he observed to Round some years later, "if someone had told me 'if you will walk across the street and shake hands with the President he'll put you in the Cabinet,' I would not have gone." His attention was urgently drawn away from University problems. "I had to get busy with backgrounding myself . . . [W]hen you take a cabinet post, there is no warming up period."[26] In January 1969 he took a leave of absence from the University and Vice Chancellor Hobson was made acting chancellor upon his recommendation. Hobson had to deal with the problems of the merger without the benefit of preliminary understandings, and some tentative commitments, made in good faith, dwindled away. Hardin, with his long-established prestige, was not in Nebraska to smooth over misunderstandings.

The Hardins left Lincoln with considerable reluctance. "My own time-table when we came to Nebraska was that we would not stay more than five years," he later said, but after five years had passed, things were going along so well that he and his wife decided to stay for ten. The ten years became twelve and then fourteen. "By the time 1968 had rolled around, we had about made the decision that if the people would put up with us, we wanted to stay for the duration." The Hardins' sudden decision to take a leave was contrary to what three days earlier they had thought possible.[27] In taking a leave rather than resigning, Hardin thought he had left the University administration in good hands. His closest associates referred to themselves as the Hardin 4-H Club – Hardin's Happy Hired Hands – for they all worked loyally together. Perhaps Hardin assumed that in a couple of years, having served his term in Washington, he could return, his retirement funds in place; but it became clear almost immediately that neither the Board of Regents nor the faculty wanted temporary leadership.

In June 1969 Chancellor Hardin resigned. Like James H. Canfield in 1895, he left the University three times larger than he had found it, but its budget was only twice as large. When the Hardins came, they found the institution only beginning to recover from the depression and the war; when they left, it was confident it could play on the national stage, participating in the research development of higher education. He left the graduate schools and professional colleges in better shape than they had been in for generations; and if less attention was paid the undergraduates than they could have used, they were perhaps no more neglected than students in universities elsewhere. Clifford Hardin had the great good fortune to be chancellor while the national tide was rising, and he took advantage of circumstances. If some of his success was due to matters beyond his control, during his watch the University flourished. All things considered, he ranks with Canfield and Andrews as one of the University of Nebraska's three great chancellors.

12. A Time of Discontinuities: 1968–1971

Woody Varner

Durward B. Varner, universally known as Woody, became the sixteenth chancellor of the University of Nebraska on 1 February 1970, the unanimous choice of both a search committee and the Board of Regents. He was fifty-three years old. After taking an undergraduate degree at Texas Agricultural and Mechanical University, where he was ROTC cadet colonel, he did graduate work in economics and public administration at the University of Chicago. After 1949, however, he was so deeply involved in administration at Michigan State University that he lost interest in his Ph.D. dissertation and did not complete it. In 1959 he was named the first chancellor of Oakland University in Rochester, Michigan, a branch of Michigan State, which by 1970 had grown from 500 to 5,000 students and achieved some prominence because of innovative programs, ungraded courses, off-campus study projects, and a three-semester calendar. Varner was a man of ideas, not afraid to experiment, impatient with the automatic acceptance of the conventional.

Woody Varner had irresistible charm. Whatever group he entered, a foursome or a mob, he dominated with wit, exuberant energy, and magnetism. He was exciting to be around. One man who worked near him for years said that he "was the kind of guy who could fire you in the afternoon and call you up in the evening to play bridge. You'd go over to his house and have a hell of a good time."[1] His wife, Paula, was as attractive as he; the two of them were a formidable team. One never felt their charm was insincere or merely political.

Varner and his immediate predecessor, Clifford Hardin, were sharply different. Hardin was cautious, arriving at decisions only after consultation with advisers

and the calculation of consequences. Varner was impetuous, eager to move to new ranges of experience. Unlike Hardin, who preferred working in one-to-one relationships with enduring teams of associates, Varner moved from one assistant to another. The relationship of the chancellors to the regents differed, too. Hardin dominated his board until they were almost his rubber stamp; when he left, one regent said, "Now that we have got another Chancellor, we're going to tell him what to do. He is not going to tell us what to do . . . ."[2] Woody Varner with all his persuasiveness was never able to bring his board into the unanimity that his predecessor enjoyed. This was in large part because he had to work with a larger, more contentious group, as we shall see.

A Social Revolution

When Varner came to Nebraska he was confronted with two great problems. The first of these was attractive to him: the joining of the University of Nebraska with the Municipal University of Omaha; indeed, this linking of an established land-grant institution with an urban university was one of the reasons he took the new job, he said. As chief administrative officer of three campuses, he was named chancellor and the campus officers of Omaha, Lincoln, and the Medical Center were designated presidents. After August 1971 the titles were reversed and Varner became president and the campus heads chancellors.

The second great issue confronting the new chancellor was largely unanticipated. Across the nation students on college and university campuses were increasingly, even violently, restless; and though the students in Nebraska were, as usual, slow to participate in national movements, by 1970 they too were disturbed. As it turned out, the decade 1964–74 was revolutionary on campuses everywhere.

In these years much of the restlessness within the University was fired by controversy over the Vietnam War. Few people noticed in 1962 how a group dubbing themselves Students for a Democratic Society (SDS) met in Port Huron, Michigan, and called on students to work for a society in which all persons would more fully control their own lives and their institutions. The President's Commission on Campus Unrest reported in 1970 that campus unrest began there. The commission had made an official blue-ribbon inquiry into those campus actions of the Sixties that upset the nation and marked it permanently. It noted that the students were disturbed both by the nation's involvement in Vietnam and by the injustice they saw in black ghettos. "Under the banner of participatory democracy, the SDS launched its early efforts to organize slum dwellers in northern cities," the report said.[3]

By 1964 student concern with unresolved issues of war and peace, civil rights, the plight of the poor, and the relation of universities to these serious matters was expressed in disorder at the University of California. In a series of celebrated lectures in 1963, Clark Kerr, president of the university, had made himself spokesman for the multiversity, which superseded the old university, he said. This multiversity served what he called the knowledge industry and took on the characteristics of the entrepreneur. "Sometimes industry will reach into a university laboratory to extract the newest ideas almost before they are born," he wrote.[4] The students thought that the multiversity had become subservient to the military-industrial complex which President Eisenhower had warned the nation against in 1961. It was no longer a free agent engaged in disinterested inquiry.

In the fall of 1964 the students at Berkeley reacted in a campus rebellion against all that Kerr represented. From this genesis "an authentic political invention – a new and complex mixture of issues, tactics, emotions, and setting – became the prototype for student protest throughout the decade," the President's Commission said. When Berkeley activists were deprived of a Hyde Park where they could protest what they saw as injustice, they responded with a spontaneous sit-in for thirty-two hours. A few weeks later in further demonstrations they began a large two-day sit-in at the university's administration building. Governor Edmund (Pat) Brown called in the police to settle what he considered lawless civil disorder. The President's Commission reported that "there were hundreds of arrests and many charges of police brutality," and the police action mobilized huge numbers of formerly passive students and faculty. "Classes and other normal activities came to a halt in an unprecedented strike against the university" and "many liberal, nonextremist students . . . supported protest demonstrations because the issues at stake pointed to genuine deficiencies in the university and in American society. Student protest thus reflected not a desire to destroy, but rather a sincere and constructive idealism."[5] In January 1965 Kerr took a "leave of absence."

By 1968 students protests had spread across the country with violence gradually escalating. The Vietnam War continued. A Columbia University revolt in the spring of 1968 "was important because it illustrated the spread of the Berkeley invention and the rising tide of student opposition to war and racial injustice," the President's Commission said.[6] One of its student leaders defined the issue: "The Columbia rebellion was set in motion by a nebulous group of outsiders who are variously known as the corporate power elite, the military-industrial complex, the Establishment. A friend of mine refers to them as the Biggies," James Kunen wrote. "We are fighting to recapture a school from business and war and rededicate it to learning and life. Right now nobody controls Columbia, but if we get it, we will never give it back. And there are five million college students in the country watching us. And a lot of them have just about had it with the Biggies."[7]

❧ Innovation at the University

Pandora's box was opened. The *Daily Nebraskan* regularly reported student uprisings across the country, the war in Vietnam was the topic of constant discussion, and students were restless. With enrollment in Lincoln promising to go over 20,000 by 1970, students were increasingly unhappy with traditional undergraduate regulations, on campus and off campus alike. By 1967 student committees working with Russell Brown, dean of student development, prepared "A Student Bill of Rights" which attempted to spell out student and administration areas of authority. Students asserted that social regulations should be in student hands, not left exclusively in the control of faculty-administration committees; and the old idea of the University in loco parentis was under explicit attack. In April 1967 in an unprecedented plebiscite, 7,000 students endorsed the Student Bill of Rights. It gave them great autonomy, and the chancellor appointed a six-person student-faculty administration committee, with Royce Knapp of Teachers College as chair, to implement its principles. The next fall, 1968, that committee recommended that a Council on Student Life, the majority of its members to be students, replace the old Senate Committee on Student Affairs; it was to have general policymaking power over all student social and out-of-classroom activities, subject only to the approval of the Board of Regents. "The day of the docile student body is over," Ken Keller wrote in the *Nebraska Alumnus* of September 1968. He reported that the chancellor had said at the 1968 Alumni Round-up that "when emotions have been running high in cities and on some campuses across the country, our own student leaders have demonstrated a commendable degree of maturity and responsibility."[8]

Residents of the dormitories continued to agitate. They wanted open residences, each resident with his or her own key. The women, seeing themselves as adults, protested their restrictive hours. If they were not enrolled as students but worked in town, they could live as they liked, they said. Why as students were they locked up, assumed to be incapable of making their own decisions? In February 1970 all residence halls implemented a no-hours policy, and by April 1970 the Associated Women Students (AWS), which had governed women's social life since 1911, voted itself out of existence.

Although the regents and the general public were reluctant to accept it, a social and sexual revolution had come to the nation and to this university. The campus paper, like periodicals elsewhere, was full of talk of "the Pill"; and the 28 March 1969 issue of the *Daily Nebraskan* had a page one discussion of birth control, announcing that society was in a "contraceptive revolution." When an interdepartmental course in homosexuality, which some saw as a revolutionary topic, was proposed in March 1970, the regents were upset. The students were not. The people of the state and the students on the campus viewed the world differently.

The University curriculum was generally under question in these years. In 1964 the College of Agriculture, whose director of instruction was Franklin Eldridge, very imaginatively inaugurated an honors program which allowed gifted students to design their own courses of study according to defined individual needs. With a cooperative student body, this program worked very well. In 1966 a group of students organized the Nebraska Free University (NFU), a collection of voluntary noncredit courses through which students could study subjects of their own selection, in methods of their own decision, for purposes of their own description. The NFU was an attack on what students saw as the irrelevance and inflexibility of standard courses. They were, they said, "dissatisfied with classroom trivia." Such subjects as "Psychedelic Drugs," "Human Reproduction," and "Radical Needs in Education" were undertaken by students and a few volunteer faculty.[9] Though only a few hundred students actively participated in these extracurricular studies, their existence was symptomatic and the NFU survived for several years.

The most elaborate innovation of the decade was the Centennial Educational Program, commonly referred to as Centennial College. In 1966 a university committee headed by Wallace C. Peterson, the George Holmes Professor of Economics and a native son, in considering how to celebrate the University's centennial in 1969, recommended to Chancellor Hardin that a group consider the feasibility of establishing an "innovative college" for undergraduates. By 1968 a faculty-student committee proposed a cluster college – that is, a "semi-autonomous school on the campus of a larger institution which shared, to a significant extent, facilities and services with the other schools."[10] Students in it were to live and study together for a major portion of their time, but they would join with the rest of the University for the remainder of their work.

They were thus to have the intimacy of a residential college, which allowed continuing association with a number of professors, and, at the same time, anonymity in a comprehensive university. With a $38,000 grant from the Woods Charitable Fund for planning, a faculty-student committee chaired by Robert E. Knoll, professor of English, prepared during the spring and summer for a fall 1969 opening. The curriculum was interdisciplinary and interdepartmental, defined by student interest and open to constant development as student concerns dictated. Two adjacent residence halls, one for men and the other for women, were refurbished to provide living, study, and classroom facilities; and four full-time and ten part-time professors agreed to participate. Living, learning, study, recreation were linked, under the loose guidance of resourceful teachers.

Knoll found a distinguished group of teachers, to be known as fellows, ready to undertake this innovative experiment, and it had the enthusiastic support of Merk Hobson, vice chancellor for academic affairs. The same day Hobson took the proposal for the experimental college to the Board of Regents, 14 October 1968, he also proposed that the University establish a Teaching Council whose major responsibility was to be "the encouragement, support, and coordination of innovation and experimentation in the teaching program" of the University generally. As the Research Council had long been an effective body in support of research, Vice Chancellor Hobson said, the Teaching Council would support teaching.[11] The Teaching Council met with considerably more approval than the proposed Centennial College, but both were finally approved. Whatever reservations the faculty may have had were not loudly stated. The academic community, normally conservative, seemed prepared for change. They needed to be.

The Centennial Educational Program admitted its first students in the fall of 1969. Of some 850 applications, some 125 freshmen and 40 upperclassmen were admitted on a more or less random basis. By spring "Centennial College [had] . . . become the most publicized member of the University (outside the Athletic Department)," David Buntain, a brilliant undergraduate, wrote in a column of

the *Daily Nebraskan* on 2 March 1970. "Reporters, professors, and even the Lions Club have devoted long hours to discovering the significance of what's happening at the Centennial College." Buntain concluded, "Shouldn't the University begin applying the lessons of the Centennial College to its general undergraduate curriculum?" As a matter of fact, within a short time a second interdisciplinary, interdepartmental program for undergraduates was set up, under the direction of John Scholz, professor of chemistry. It was not residential. With a $200,000 grant from the Ford Foundation, students in University Studies were helped to shape their academic programs to their individual needs. It encouraged tutorials and independent research. Much smaller than the Centennial Program, it had greater staying power and graduated some 200 students in the next twenty years, each with a curriculum organized to his or her prescription.[12]

Early in the Seventies a second faculty group began meeting for lunch in the basement of the Faculty Club to consider alternate ways of teaching undergraduates. It was named by Ned Hedges, later vice chancellor for academic affairs, the Tuesday Noon Chowder Society and Harpsichord Marching Band, and in due time a committee headed by the indefatigable Professor Robert Fuller of the physics department got a grant of $100,000 from the Exxon Corporation for a seminar in which teachers could consider how to adapt ideas from developmental psychology, especially from the Swiss psychologist Jean Piaget, to college teaching. By 1976 this group began teaching coordinated courses in physics, English, and the social sciences, based on inductive methods of reasoning, to some 90 students each semester. This project was called ADAPT, Accent on Developing Advanced Processes of Thought, an acronym invented by Professor Jerry Petr, a celebrated teacher of comparative economics and a fellow in the Centennial College. ADAPT continued for many years and influenced subsequent pedagogic studies across the University and in other universities throughout the nation.[13] The Seventies saw a growing commitment to pedagogy in departments that for generations had held themselves aloof from such concerns, but even in this decade "pure" scholars looked with some disdain on these programs and studies. Professors Fuller in physics, Walter Mientka in mathematics, Robert Narveson in English, David W. Brooks in chemistry, and others obtained federal and foundation grants to inaugurate innovative undergraduate and high school programs and so made their reputations, but their departments were not always sympathetic.

All these innovations with the exception of academic residence had a lasting effect on the regular curriculum of the University. The old idea of the professor as the authority figure dispensing received wisdom which was to be accepted with minor if any modifications was replaced by the idea of the teacher as guide through complex mazes of ideas, facts, and events. The students were to find their own way in the underbrush, rescued by their teachers when lost, assisted when confused, helped with maps and guidebooks prepared by earlier explorers. Ned Hedges later observed that many persons who subsequently achieved positions of public notice in the legislature and elsewhere had been Centennial students or in an allied experimental program as undergraduates.[14]

❧ The Campus Disturbances of May 1970

In 1967 a group of Nebraska students protesting against the dropping of napalm in Vietnam tried to keep recruiters for Dow Chemical from appearing on campus, and in 1968 a group led by Gene Pokorny began working for Eugene McCarthy for President. McCarthy appeared in Omaha in April; Robert Kennedy had stopped in Lincoln in March. The disruptions at Columbia University in the spring of 1968 were much talked about, and the *Daily Nebraskan* reported, 11 September 1968, that there were rumblings of discontent on campus. The University administration, the editor said, "would be advised to tread softly this year. The material for a Columbia riot is not here, but there are enough concerned, eloquent students to assure that the administration will be in trouble if it pursues unjust policies such as the careless expansion into the Malone center." The Malone area just east of the campus was seen as a working-class ghetto. Indignation at social injustice was linked with indignation at the continuing war in Vietnam. When students repeated the fashionable

phrase "Never trust anybody over thirty," they meant that old persons (over thirty!) were sending young men into battle and that the Establishment prospered at the expense of the poor. The students' very costumes were a public protest: their beards, long hair, disheveled clothing, and their preference for sitting on the floor rather than in chairs were self-conscious political gestures. One of this number, Jim Schaffer, said later, "For us blue jeans were a political statement." Student dissatisfaction with the status quo and the Vietnam War was reflected in the campus newspaper. On 9 October 1968, Jack Todd, editor of the *Daily Nebraskan*, wrote:

Once again it is time for the 5:30 war. . . . For half an hour real men fall, real jets spit napalm into burning villages, real refugees clog the roads out of this or that nameless Viet Cong stronghold.

At six o'clock the war is over. Out come the pop-top cans, the TV dinners, and Lucile Ball. . . .

It is a nightmare, necessary to those who have helped fight it, absurd to those who oppose it. To those who have arranged for us to be there through their neglect or tacit approval, however, it is only the 5:30 war.

We have always known it, but this latest bit of irony has made us even more aware: there is nothing sweet or proper about dying for one's country.

On 18 November the *Daily Nebraskan* reported, "The mood of the University of Nebraska is restive." And on 10 January 1969, Steve Abbott, a gentle idealist, was convicted of a federal felony for refusing to step forward for induction into the U.S. Army. The war was, he said, against his conscience. It was clear by spring that the student agitation familiar on campuses across the country might finally appear in Nebraska. The judicious Ken Keller wrote in the May 1969 *Nebraska Alumnus* that 1968–69 could be known as The Year of the Student, for the students gained not only considerable control over policies and procedures concerning student life, but significant representation on important faculty committees. All this was accomplished through orderly procedures. "If it is to be reported that much change has taken place *peacefully* on the student front, it must also be reported that this, too,

was the first year that the University experienced anything approaching a student demonstration with racial
overtones." In mid-May "150 or so students who lingered
for a couple of hours in the main hall of the Administration
building on a Thursday afternoon were by no means violent, destructive, or even discourteous. But the fact remains that when they first gathered to do their thing, they
had bricks in their hands. Some volunteer . . . explained
that the bricks were merely symbols of Black Power —
which somehow failed to make much sense to us senior citizens."[15] In May 1969 the Faculty Senate accepted guidelines to be observed in case of "disruptive action." Specific
steps for discussions, temporary sanctions, and possible
disciplinary actions were spelled out carefully.

In mid-October 1969 some 4,000 persons, mostly students but many faculty as well, marched in the rain to the
capitol protesting Vietnam. Also in October the University
Senate "called into existence" a committee on human
rights, with Paul A. Olson, Foundation Professor of English, as chair, to consider such matters as racial restric-
tions in housing, ethnocentricity in the curriculum, and
racism. In November the Senate discussed policy appropriate in the face of a threatened student moratorium or
strike or walkout against the Vietnam War, but it could
come to no general agreement. All fall, groups of students
met in the Student Union in "time out" bull sessions to
consider their "widespread dissatisfaction with the status
quo." President Soshnik and G. Robert Ross, vice chancellor for student affairs, met with them frequently. President and Mrs. Soshnik appeared on the campus at all
hours, making themselves available to students as no president or chancellor had done for generations, and they invited students to their home frequently. The Soshniks' aim
was "to be available – whether in the Union or in one of
the residence halls – either by invitation or on a drop-in
basis, to communicate one thing: we are here and available, [and we care]."[16]

By midwinter the new Council on Student Life, made
up of eight students and seven faculty and staff persons
with John Robinson, professor of English, in the chair, began its experiment in governance. Although it had legislative power over all aspects of student life outside the class-

room, from the start some of the students were impatient
with deliberations that faculty members thought necessary; and on 27 February 1970, a group of black students
walked out of a council meeting in a planned protest
against what they took to be its slowness in addressing
their grievances. On campus, students and some faculty
continued to be concerned with civil rights, and everybody
was obsessed with the engulfing Vietnam War.

The break came with the killing of four students by the
National Guard at Kent State University in Ohio. On 30
April 1970, President Nixon announced on national television that U.S. troops were being sent into Cambodia and
that the Indo-China war was thus being expanded. On
Saturday, 2 May, the Kent State ROTC building, a small
wooden barracks left over from World War II, was burned
by protesting students. "Compared with other American
universities of its size, Kent State had enjoyed relative
tranquility prior to May 1970, and its student population
had generally been conservative or apolitical," the President's Commission on Campus Unrest would later report.[17] On Sunday, National Guardsmen, called out by the
Ohio governor, who feared continuing violence, patrolled
the restless campus, and on Monday at about 12:30 P.M.
they opened fire on a crowd of students, killing four and
wounding nine others.

The response on the University of Nebraska campus,
as elsewhere, was immediate. From a rally north of the
union, which had been scheduled the day before by a self-
appointed Vietnam moratorium committee, a few students
marched to the local draft headquarters at Tenth and O
streets demanding the office be closed. Thirteen were ar-
rested for trespassing, though, according to the police,
damage was slight. That evening students gathered to
consider protest alternatives and the Association of Students of the University of Nebraska – the successor organization to the student council – met in emergency session
under the leadership of Steve Tiwald, its newly elected
president. At about 8:30 some fifty students, led by Alan
Siporin and against the advice of faculty persons, went
down the street to the Military and Naval Science Building
and occupied it. Shortly several hundred students joined
them in what the *Daily Nebraskan* reported as a carnival
atmosphere. A four-piece band played.

90. Clifford M. Hardin (b. 1915) came to the University in 1954, bringing his attractive young family to live in the A Street house provided by the University. Supported by a beautiful and capable wife, he quickly inspired business and community allegiance across the state. (UNL Photo Lab)

91. Adam C. Breckenridge (b. 1916) was dean of academic affairs after 1955. Cautious and decisive, he served the University in various administrative capacities for the next twenty-two years. This photograph was taken about 1960. (UNL Photo Lab)

92. Merk Hobson (1921–1977) was successively department chairman, dean of the College of Engineering, vice chancellor for research, vice chancellor for academic affairs, and acting chancellor when Clifford Hardin became the United States secretary of agriculture. When the Municipal University of Omaha became part of the University of Nebraska, Hobson became systemwide vice president for academic affairs. In this photograph, taken when he was named dean of engineering in 1957, he is posed in front of the first postwar engineering building, which stands where the original University Hall once stood. (UNL Photo Lab)

93. Chancellor Hardin met frequently with the student council. In this photograph Bruce Brugmann, president of the council, and Bev Deepe, a student journalist who became a correspondent in Vietnam, present Hardin with a pipe on his forty-first birthday. (*Cornhusker 1957*, UNL Archives)

94. According to rules established with their concurrence, women students had to be inside their living quarters by specified hours, and couples said good night at twelve-thirty or one o'clock on Friday and Saturday nights, earlier on weeknights. This picture was taken at the door of Carrie Belle Raymond Hall. Notice the relative formality of the dress: the men have trimmed hair and topcoats, most of the girls wear skirts and heels. On the right one young man has on blue jeans, but he is wearing a jacket. (*Cornhusker 1957*, UNL Archives)

95. Women's social and extracurricular lives were regulated by a campus-wide organization called AWS, Associated Women Students. Those who broke the established rules were called before a court of peers in Ellen Smith Hall to be heard by an elected board, pictured here. Men's hours were not regulated. (*Cornhusker 1953*, UNL Archives)

96, 97. In 1901 an annual senior spring day became Ivy Day. In 1903 the first thirteen members of the Innocents Society were "tapped" – tackled – during a gathering on the old city campus, and in 1905 thirteen girls were masked to become members of the Black Masque Society, which affiliated with the national Mortar Board Society in 1921. In these scenes of Ivy Day 1957, the presidents of Innocents and Mortar Board plant the ivy, and a new Mortar Board member is masqued while people watch from bleachers set up north of the old administration building. (*Cornhusker 1958*, UNL Archives)

98. While still very young, Paul A. Olson (b. 1932), with the assistance of students, teachers, and specialists from across the country, undertook a revision of the English curriculum of the public schools. This photograph shows him in a classroom in 1968. (Courtesy of Frances Reinehr)

99. Perhaps the handsomest building on the east campus was C. Y. Thompson Library, completed in 1965 and named for Regent Thompson, who served from 1935 to 1958. The nature of the east campus changed when the College of Dentistry, the College of Law, and the Barkley Memorial Center were located after 1968 on areas which had formerly been field laboratories. (UNL Archives)

100. Governor Norbert Tiemann spoke at the ceremonies marking the transfer of the Municipal University of Omaha to the University of Nebraska, 30 June 1968. They took place on the front steps of Arts and Sciences Hall, the oldest building on the Omaha campus. University of Nebraska Regents Schwartzkopf, Raun, Adkins, and Herman are seated behind the governor; Robert Spire, president of the Omaha University regents, is just to the right of the flag. (Nebraska State Historical Society)

101. When the Municipal University of Omaha became a part of the University of Nebraska in 1968, the Omaha campus underwent a considerable building program, as this page from the *Omaha World-Herald* of 5 November 1987, illustrates. (*Omaha World-Herald*)

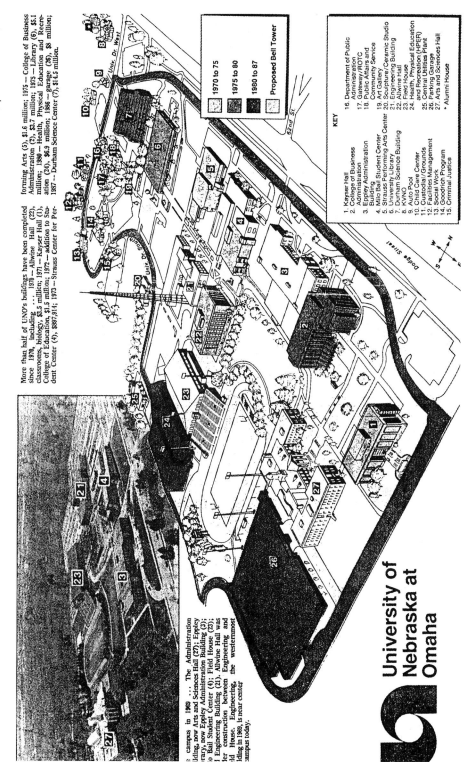

More than half of UNO's buildings have been completed since 1970, including . . . 1970 — Allwine Hall (22), classrooms, biology, $3.5 million; 1971 — Kayser Hall (1), College of Education, $1.5 million; 1972 — addition to Student Center (4), $897,914; 1973 — Strauss Center for Performing Arts (5), $1.6 million; 1975 — College of Business Administration (2), $3.7 million; 1975 — Library (6), $5.1 million; 1980 — Health, Physical Education and Recreation (24), $6.9 million; 1986 — garage (26), $8 million; 1987 — Durham Science Center (7), $14.5 million.

KEY

1. Kayser Hall
2. College of Business Administration
3. Eppley Administration
4. Milo Bail Student Center
5. Strauss Performing Arts Center
6. University Library
7. Durham Science Building
8. KVNO
9. Auto Pool
10. Child Care Center
11. Custodial/Grounds
12. Facilities Management
13. Social Work
14. Goodrich Program
15. Criminal Justice
16. Department of Public Administration
17. Gateway/ROTC
18. Public Affairs and Community Service
19. Art Gallery
20. Sculpture/Ceramic Studio
21. Engineering Building
22. Allwine Hall
23. Field House
24. Health, Physical Education and Recreation (HPER)
25. Central Utilities Plant
26. Parking Garage
27. Arts and Sciences Hall
* Alumni House

1970 to 75
1975 to 80
1980 to 87
Proposed Bell Tower

Proposed Bell Tower

Univ. Dr. West

62nd St.

Dodge Street

University of Nebraska at Omaha

campus in 1969 . . . The Administration Building, now Arts and Sciences Hall (27); Eppley Library, now Eppley Administration Building (3); Milo Bail Student Center (4); Field House (23); and Engineering Building (21). Allwine Hall was under construction between Engineering and Field House. Engineering, the westernmost building in 1969, is near center campus today.

102. This view, about 1974, looks north from the west entrance of The Temple at Twelfth and R streets. Sheldon Memorial Gallery (1963) is seen at the left, and the large white building behind it is Hamilton Hall (1971), the new chemistry building. To the right is the College of Business Administration (1920, 1970) with Oldfather Hall (1970) behind. Twelfth Street, a walkway, was closed to vehicular traffic. (UNL Photo Lab)

103. This announcement, published for the second year of what was commonly known as Centennial College, emphasizes two of its defining characteristics: students who studied together were to live together, and teacher-student relationships were exploratory rather than directive. Jerry Petr, professor of economics and one of the fellows in the program, here talks to students in their residence-classroom. (UNL Archives)

THE UNIVERSITY
OF NEBRASKA

Centennial Educational Program

An Innovation in Instruction and Experience for Undergraduates

For 1970–1971, at Lincoln

The Centennial Educational Program is for serious students who want to take a fresh approach in the individual pursuit of higher learning. It seeks to provide an alternative to standard, departmentalized education.

104. Newspapers reported that more than 2,000 students were involved in the sit-in at the Military and Naval Science Building on 4 and 5 May 1970. The sign on the north wall reads "Pull Out, Nixon." (*Omaha World-Herald*)

Finalists

105, 106, 107. The social revolution on the campus between 1960 and 1970 can be seen by comparing these photographs. The *Cornhusker 1958* presented ideal undergraduate men and women: dressed, trim, conventional. The *Cornhusker 1971* pictures undergraduates of a different sort: hirsute, extramural, self-consciously antiestablishment. (UNL Archives)

108. President Nixon came to the Nebraska campus in January 1971 to congratulate Coach Devaney and his national championship football team. They earned the title a second time the next year. Before a crowd of some 8,000 students in the Coliseum, he presented a plaque to the coach and the co-captains. Behind Devaney in this picture are Steve Tiwald and Ken Wald, campus leaders, and Chancellor Joe Soshnik. (UNL Sports Information Office)

109. Tom Osborne succeeded Devaney as football coach in 1972 and in the twenty-two following years became the winningest coach in the nation — this without the hype associated with many athletic figures. (UNL Sports Information Office)

110. D. B. (Woody) Varner became chief executive officer of the University of Nebraska in 1970. Pictured here in 1977 with his astute and ironical wife, he found himself working with a board of regents different from the board from whom he had accepted his appointment. In 1985 the regents renamed their headquarters D. B. and Paula Varner Hall. (UNL Photo Lab)

111. This caricature of the regents in the 1980s was made by David Luebke, then an undergraduate and now a professor of history at Bennington College in Vermont. It was published in *The Greek Spirit* (1979–80), a student publication, and elsewhere. In the top row, left to right, are Regents Robert E. Simmons Jr., Bud Cuca (student regent), Edward Schwartzkopf, Robert Koefoot (below), and Robert Raun; in the bottom row, Kermit Hansen, Robert Prokop, James R. Moylan, and Kermit Wagner. (UNL Archives)

112. Ronald W. Roskens (b. 1932) became chancellor of the University of Nebraska at Omaha in 1972 and president of the University of Nebraska in 1977. He served until 1990. (UNL Photo Lab)

113. Martin A. Massengale (b. 1933) was appointed vice chancellor of the Institute of Agriculture and Natural Resources in 1976 and chancellor of the Lincoln campuses in 1981. In 1990 he became president of the University. (UNL Photo Lab)

114. Graham Spanier (b. 1948) accepted the chancellorship of the Lincoln campuses in 1991. He is shown here with his wife, Sandra, and their children in the Sheldon Sculpture Garden at his inaugural ceremony on 27 April 1992. (UNL Alumni Association)

115. By 1993 the assets of the University of Nebraska Foundation surpassed $300 million and influenced the nature of University growth. In this picture are Woody Varner, former president of the foundation, and Terry L. Fairfield, his vigorous young successor. (University of Nebraska Foundation)

116. This model of the George W. Beadle Center for Genetics and Biomaterials Research was prepared in 1990 by the architects Davis Fenton Stange Darling, the successor firm to Davis and Wilson, architects for the University since the mid-1920s. The Beadle Center, located between S and Vine streets east of Nineteenth, would change the Lincoln skyline and mark a new direction for the University of Nebraska. (Davis Fenton Stange Darling)

Fearing disorder, President Soshnik; C. Peter Magrath, dean of faculties; and Vice Chancellor G. Robert Ross arrived by 10:30 to talk to the demonstrating students. They were accompanied by members of the faculty Liaison Committee. This action was according to the plan worked out the year before. Professor David Levine of psychology brought in a public address system through which students could express their indignation, and talk went on and on. Among other demands the students asked that University administration back the National Student Association strike on classes in protest of Nixon's Indochina policy. Not even the bulletin boards in the occupied building had been vandalized, and at 3:00 A.M. Soshnik said that since no rules were being broken, the students could remain there but they must not disrupt University business. Some members of the Liaison Committee stayed in the ROTC building all night. At 8:45 Tuesday morning Soshnik ordered students out, for scheduled classes were being disturbed, and privately he had begun to fear violence. He and his associates firmly resisted recommendations that they call in the police. At 10:00 when the students had not left the building, he told them that they would be suspended from the University if they remained longer. At this point Paul A. Olson and other faculty members suggested that a special Faculty Senate meeting scheduled for noon be rescheduled for 10:30 in the Student Union, whereupon the student demonstrators left the Military and Naval Science Building and marched peacefully down Fourteenth Street to attend it.

There had been no confrontation. In a special edition of the campus newspaper which appeared on the morning of 5 May, Jim Pedersen, the editor, wrote that burning buildings and breaking windows "are not effective nor positive methods of protesting the Cambodian invasion"; and Ken Wald said in his column, "The word is moderation." Steve Tiwald was equally temperate. Student leaders no less than administration and staff had acted responsibly.

The rescheduled Senate meeting, chaired by Professor Richard Gilbert of chemical engineering, was attended by several hundred faculty members. After much discussion the Senate resolved "that the sense of the faculty of the University of Nebraska is to recognize the sincerity of those faculty and students who out of conscience feel that they must protest the invasion of Cambodia by striking and recommend that their stand be respected without sanctions."[18] That afternoon, at an all-University town hall meeting in the Coliseum attended by some 7,000 students and faculty, Steve Tiwald announced: "The strike is not against the University but a strike by the University against Nixon's Indochina Policy." Students must go into the community because that's the only place change can come from, he said: "It can't happen in the Pentagon or on the campuses." We must have "a nation-wide coalition of conscience."[19] Chancellor Varner, who had not participated in the activities Monday or Tuesday, said from his office, "I fail to see a student strike solving a very difficult foreign problem." He added that the regents reported "a good deal of unhappiness in outstate Nebraska over the student demonstration."[20] Though the Vietnam War had been the occasion for disruptions, the students at Nebraska were for the most part as interested in curriculum changes and in freedom from housing restraints as in foreign policy. The war, civil rights, political injustice, and major modifications in sexual and social conventions were bound up together for them. Their parents and others in the state lived by different assumptions.

For the rest of the week students gathered with each other, faculty members, and foreign policy experts like Francis Cunningham, a retired foreign service officer living in Lincoln, for rap sessions to discuss Vietnam policy and possible student action. Though some young teachers dismissed their classes, for the most part teaching continued as usual. Even in the College of Arts and Sciences, the heart of student controversy, attendance was at 80 or 85 percent, Dean Magrath told an off-campus investigation committee that summer. Elsewhere in the nation 500 campuses and 4,000,000 students were on strike.[21]

In Lincoln, rallies were held on Saturday afternoon, 9 May, and the next day 2,500 students led by newly activated conservative groups voted to discontinue the strike. On Tuesday, 12 May, the Faculty Senate held its regularly scheduled meeting, again in the Coliseum "so that students who so desire may attend as observers," the announcement stated. At that meeting, against the strong advice of John Braeman, professor of history, the faculty reaffirmed its action of Tuesday morning. Braeman argued that the student call for a boycott and for discussion of public policy in all classrooms usurped faculty autonomy and violated academic freedom. At this contentious meeting, order was brought out of parliamentary chaos by the quick wit of young Harvey S. Perlman of the College of Law; in the next generation he was to become its dean. By the end of the afternoon, matters brought up in the previous week had been assigned to various committees. The Academic Planning Committee was to take up students' demands for a "new university" and the Calendar Committee was to consider student requests that classes be recessed for two weeks before the November elections so all could campaign full time for their candidates. Regular University procedures were honored, and Magrath observed that education had not ceased here as it had in many colleges and universities around the country.[22]

In special Senate meetings on 21 May and 2 June, the committees brought recommendations that were generally agreeable to both students and faculty. Over the summer, task forces and study groups met with faculty members, especially Paul A. Olson, David Levine, and Scott Morgan of Centennial College, and Stephen Voss of philosophy, to discuss University reform. The immediate, local crisis had passed, but its effect would resonate for the next twenty years. Many Nebraskans would feel more alienated from "their university" than they had since Chancellor Canfield's arrival in 1891, and a new board of regents unlike any other in the history of the University would frequently show a hostility toward the University. From being University cheerleaders they became University critics.

ꝰ The Rozman Case

In June 1970 the regents asked Varner to set up a seven-member lay commission to investigate the events of May. It was to discover whether laws or regents' policies had been violated, whether there were gross "improprieties," and whether there had been substantial involvement of non-University personnel. Chaired by Richard E. Spelts Jr. of Grand Island, the commission brought in a full re-

port in August. Presenting it to the board and the Legislative Council, Flavel Wright, the commission's legal counsel, said, "As I understand it, the university handled this situation (strike) beautifully – it avoided deaths, violence and damage"; and Senator C. W. Holmquist of the Legislative Council was reported in the *Daily Nebraskan* of 11 August as saying that "a fine job" had been done in May. Although the commission acknowledged the patience with which the May disturbances had been dealt, however, it suggested that a prompt use of police force would have been preferable, a view that President Soshnik, the editors of the *Daily Nebraskan*, and the Faculty Senate's Liaison Committee sharply disputed.

The commission recommended that the chancellor and the president seek out the students who had forcefully entered the ㄝlitary and Naval Science Building and take appropriate disciplinary action. More important, the commission found that "the conduct and actions of Professor Stephen L. Rozman were highly inappropriate for a teacher," and asked that a "proper faculty committee" determine "what sanctions should be applied."[23] Rozman had accompanied the students to the draft office without trying to dissuade them and had been among the initial fifty persons who occupied the ROTC building and had stayed there with them. The other faculty members at the meeting preceding the occupation of the building had apparently argued against this student action. Stephen Rozman until this time had been a rather quiet young assistant professor of political science, prominent in neither intellectual nor activist circles. Bearded and rather naive, he surprised his friends with his involvement in the May activities.

Through all of this controversy the regents and Varner were much concerned with its effects on the University's reputation across the state, for the May disturbances had received wide publicity. The chancellor, advised by the Liaison Committee, appointed an ad hoc committee – the Spelts commission's "proper faculty committee" – to investigate the propriety of Rozman's actions. It was headed by Professor Henry F. Holtzclaw Jr., a chemist of acknowledged integrity. The other members and their attorney were also highly respected. For months the

Rozman case was the subject of campus discussion by both students and faculty, and when the Holtzclaw committee brought in their report that "Dr. Rozman was not guilty of inappropriate action during the week of May 4," nobody was much surprised.[24] But the Board of Regents refused to reappoint him – he was young and untenured. Vigorous protest followed: "Charges of denial of academic freedom were made, and at least two student sit-ins, one resulting in three arrests, were held in Chancellor D. B. Varner's office," the *Lincoln Journal* reported on 16 February 1971. In the fall of 1971 the Lincoln campus got mired down in another controversy when the board refused to hire Michael Davis, a University of Michigan graduate student, because of his involvement in nonviolent protests at Ann Arbor. Davis had been recommended by the Department of Philosophy and the College of Arts and Sciences before his extracurricular activities were known. The Liaison Committee here backed the regents in their rejection; but when Davis appeared on campus under student auspices to state his case, the temper on campus was uneasy.

The Rozman case, like the Mitchell case ten years before, became a cause célèbre. In a special faculty meeting called by the Liaison Committee in February 1971, the faculty accepted a new document presented by Holtzclaw which asked for reconsideration of the University's system of governance. The Senate was displeased with the actions of the Board of Regents. Established traditions seemed to be ignored or to go unrecognized, several law professors asserted. Professor Wallace C. Peterson said that the faculty had "experienced something of a breakdown" of communication with the board and the administration.[25] So had the students. Steve Tiwald reported that the regents had refused the ASUN's invitation to discuss the Rozman case with them.

When Rozman sued in federal court for reinstatement in his University job "not only for [his] own well-being, but for the well-being of the University," Judge Warren Urbom ruled that the nonrenewal of his contract was permissible by the University, but, he went on, "I offer no view as to the wisdom of the University's action, for to do so would surpass my realm of authority." Rozman appealed,

calling the judgment "frightening," but the U.S. 8th Circuit Court of Appeals upheld Urbom's decision. That court called Rozman "an obviously well-qualified, able and talented college professor" and his dismissal "harsh punishment," but the dismissal was quite within the authority of the regents.[26] The student leaders in the May disorder subsequently had useful and in some cases distinguished careers as journalists, academics, broadcasters, and entrepreneurs. They were in no sense dropouts. But the whole nation was disturbed in these Vietnam years and paranoia was general.

ᏽ Joe Soshnik

The Rozman case and campus disorders upset Nebraskans, and Senators Holmquist, Carpenter, and others raised questions in the legislature which touched on academic freedom and civil liberty. In response Flavel Wright and George Round presented "amendments" to legislative bills which dealt with tenure without consulting the Faculty Committee on Academic Freedom and Tenure. George Round, head of public relations for more than twenty years, tended to view all University problems from his PR point of view; and Flavel Wright, a leading corporation lawyer in Lincoln, often viewed them legalistically. When they refused to show their "amendments" to faculty representatives in the hearing chambers, Professor Vernon Snow, chair of the Academic Freedom and Tenure Committee, objected angrily. Questions of tenure were at the heart of academic freedom and were therefore zealously guarded by faculties across the nation. Even Soshnik, when questioned, was forced to confess to Snow that he had not been kept informed about legislative action though he had asked to be. "As you know, under our existing organizational arrangements, legislative liaison is handled on a 'university system' basis," he wrote to Snow in February 1971.[27] Soshnik had of course dealt with the legislature for many years and had earned their highest regard.

On Saturday, 13 March 1971, President Soshnik suddenly resigned, effective midsummer, to take an assignment with Kirkpatrick, Pettis, Smith, and Polian, a

Nebraska investment banking firm based in Omaha. At fifty-one, he was leaving, he said, "a little earlier than I had assumed would be the case," but "the unanticipated availability of a most attractive 'second career' opportunity" was "extraordinary."[28] Joe and Miriam Soshnik had earned universal affection because of their character. Senator Terry Carpenter, not given to easy praise, said later that Soshnik was "one of the finest men that I have ever met"; and Val Peterson, often a sharp critic of the University, judged some years after he was governor that Soshnik was "one of the finest men that ever served the University of Nebraska." Joe W. Seacrest, publisher of the *Lincoln Journal,* thought that "he was great in everything he did." The faculty universally agreed with Professor A. T. Anderson that during the campus troubles, "Joe acted in a princely fashion."[29] When Steve Tiwald

declared, "I think the students are losing a friend with the resignation of President Joseph Soshnik," Soshnik replied that it "was one of the nicest things said."[30] People did not forget Soshnik. Peter Magrath, who became interim president when Soshnik left and was later president successively of both the University of Minnesota and the University of Missouri and still later head of the National Association of State Universities and Land-Grant Colleges, concluded some years afterward that "Joe Soshnik is one of the finest people I have ever known in my life." Magrath judged him to be a good administrator because he was a good man; "If I'm a good executive now it is because I learned from Joe Soshnik," he added. "Although maybe they won't write a full chapter on him in the next history of the University, I bet there will be more than a few pages about Joe Soshnik."[31]

13. The Governance of the University: 1971–1976

By 1971 Chancellor Varner found himself in an unenviable position. In the elections of 1970, Governor Tiemann, who had supported the University morally and financially, was replaced by J. J. Exon, who viewed the University critically and whose budget was extremely tight. "The budget recommendations have cast a long shadow over the University's operations," Varner told the faculty. "In my judgment . . . this university currently faces its most difficult budgetary situation since the depression years of the '30s."[1] Regents Ben Greenberg and Richard E. Adkins, who had been Varner's particular advocates, had lost their bids for reelection – Nebraskans were showing their displeasure with what they thought they saw happening at the University – and in January 1971 Richard Herman of Omaha, another friend, resigned to become national chairman of the Republican party. Two new regents' seats, designated when the Municipal University of Omaha joined the state system, were occupied by newcomers to University governance. Thus Varner had five inexperienced regents on a board expanded from six to eight members. One of them, James Moylan, an Omaha politician, was a registered lobbyist in the legislature with Douglas County as a principal client; the second, Robert R. Koefoot, M.D., was a physician in active controversy with the American College of Surgeons; the third, Kermit Wagner, a successful agribusinessman, was frequently absent from board meetings and often left early when he did attend; the fourth, Robert Prokop, M.D., was at best eccentric. The fifth, Kermit Hansen, was an intellectual who took to visiting classes. A sixth member, Robert Simmons Jr., came on the board three years later, replacing Jack

Elliott, who had died. He was such a maverick that he frequently voted against all the others, almost, it seemed, on principle. The two holdover members, Robert L. Raun and Edward Schwartzkopf, were not always listened to.

Somebody once asked Dean James S. Blackman, "How does a chancellor educate a new regent?" the assumption being that when regents come on the board they know less than they need to know about the operation of a comprehensive university. "Why, that's simple," Blackman had promptly replied. "You train a regent the way you train an elephant: you hitch a new one between two old ones." Varner was short of old ones. Gary Seacrest, a student writer on the *Daily Nebraskan* who in his time was to become executive editor of the *Lincoln Journal*, said, shrewdly, on 5 November 1970: "Today's election of J. J. Exon as governor [defeating Tiemann] and several new Regents clouds the University's future in addition to demonstrating the public's deep disenchantment with the University."

The new Board of Regents was like no other board in the history of the University. Traditionally, regents had seen the board as guardian of the University to which they gave general direction. In quoting Clarence Swanson, regent from 1955 to 1967, George Round described their traditional attitude: "[Swanson] always said like Jack Elliott, 'We're going to set the policy. We're not going to interfere with every little ten-cent thing that comes along. That's up to the administrator.' "[2] This new board seemed to be a collection of individuals with individual agendas. Richard E. Adkins, who had been regent for twelve years (1959–71), thought they seemed "to think they should run the University on a day to day basis instead of thinking of overall policy making."[3]

Upon taking office in January 1971, the regents immediately confronted the administration, the faculty, and the students. Questioning the budget prepared by the outgoing board, they proposed that the University ask the legislature for considerably less money than Varner and his staff thought necessary to bring the University to the top rank of the Big Eight, Varner's stated aspiration. In their attitude toward money, the board and the newly elected governor were in agreement. The holdover members, Regents Jack Elliott, Robert Raun, and Edward Schwartz-kopf, found themselves outvoiced. In September 1972, four regents, led by Kermit Hansen, rejected the chancellor's budget and presented an alternative which was $2 million lower, a budget that Elliott, Raun, and Schwartzkopf thought would hamper the implementation of Varner's "Five Year Plan," the blueprint for the future put together by faculty-administration committees and submitted to the regents in February 1972. In November 1972 the administration again came under fire when Howard R. Neville, executive vice president for administration, announced that the current budget was $1.4 million short of operating costs. Estimates of student enrollment and tuition had been far off the mark, and the source of money to cover this shortfall was not at all clear; it was even suggested that students be assessed a one-time surcharge. The students were incensed at the idea that they should have to pay for an administrative error.

It became clear that the board and the University community of students and faculty viewed the world from startlingly different perspectives. In July 1970 the board had raised questions about curricular matters which had long been held the prerogative of the teaching staff. Encouraged by Varner to consider novel interdisciplinary studies, Louis Crompton, professor of English, had organized a proseminar, that is, an advanced course for juniors, seniors, and graduate students, on homophile studies, a new subject then much discussed in intellectual communities. The course was to be team-taught by Crompton, whose book *Shaw the Dramatist* (1969) had won the Christian Gauss–Phi Beta Kappa Award, the highest academic honor a critical work can receive; James Cole, associate professor of psychology; and Dr. Louis Martin, the University psychiatrist. It was approved by the established

curricular committees and all academic authorities. But the board objected and asked that it be withdrawn.

Enormous controversy resulted, both about the subject matter and about academic procedures. Late in October, Senator Terry Carpenter, never far from political storms, held "hearings" in Omaha on a wide range of more or less related matters: sexual psychopathy, pornography, and homosexuality in prisons. C. Peter Magrath, dean of faculties, defended the proseminar, asserting that the University should be commended, not condemned, for offering such a course; "Problems," he said, "must be studied academically [if] we are to face them intelligently."[4] Carpenter "vowed to seek legislation (1) stopping the course, and (2) repealing the law which gives tenure to faculty members."[5] William O. Dobler, editorial page editor of the *Lincoln Star*, wrote, "The great misfortune of the current criticism of the homophile studies is that it does violence to man's commitment to reason,"[6] and the *Lincoln Journal* observed editorially that such a preemption of academic authority "would make the University the political football of the Legislature. It would destroy the University in short order."[7] In the spring of 1971 Carpenter's bill was called up for vote by legislators opposed to it and defeated. The controversial course was offered once and never repeated. Louis Crompton later said, "I felt I could not ask faculty to face more harassment."[8] Cole shortly began offering a course in general human sexuality in the Department of Psychology.

❧ The Regents and the Students

But the issues raised by the new sexuality were not settled. In the fall of 1971 a handbook on birth control was distributed in the residence halls. During the 1970–71 school year, the ASUN had ordered informative booklets produced by McGill University in Montreal to sell to students, but what they received was different from the sample pamphlet that they had seen. What arrived contained political statements and pictures they had not bargained for. The ASUN thought the material too controversial for them to endorse and tried to return the booklets. When this proved impossible, they turned them over to the Association for

Birth Control, a student organization; the campus YWCA sold and distributed them throughout student housing, abiding by standard regulations. The Board of Regents investigated when Paul O'Hara, executive director of the Nebraska Catholic Council, complained. Again Magrath came to the defense: "The purpose was to provide factual information on birth control to students. But it is also my view this particular booklet substantially defeats its informational purpose by the inclusion of pictures that are of questionable taste and offensive to many." He asked that political disclaimers be placed in the booklet, that policies on distribution of materials in the residence halls be reconsidered by the Council on Student Life, and that persons and groups opposed to birth control be given ample opportunity to express their views.[9]

The dust refused to settle. In October 1971 several of the regents, led by James Moylan and Robert J. Prokop, demanded that a proposed ASUN conference on human sexuality be canceled. The conference was to include discussions of homosexuality, which, they claimed, attempted to legitimize what they saw as aberrant social conduct. The regents were reminded by their legal counsel that the First Amendment of the Constitution guarantees the free exchange of controversial judgments, and the ASUN conference was thus protected. Professor Benjamin DeMott of Amherst College observed at the conference that the sexual revolution was part of the cultural revolution of the time.[10] Problems concerning the sexual revolution were not easily resolved. "The Pill" had changed the landscape, as all thoughtful people knew it would. As early as 1956, Chancellor Clifford Hardin had talked about this coming revolution, in conversations with a young faculty group dubbed the Young Turks. Together they had speculated on the form it would take. Now in 1971 it was upon them.

The relationship between the regents and the academic community was exacerbated when Regent Prokop offered a piece attacking homosexuality to the *Daily Nebraskan*. The editor, Gary Seacrest, did not publish it and Prokop thereupon printed it on 14 January 1972 in the *Douglas County Gazette*, a right-wing periodical supported by Clifton Batchelder and his politically active wife, Anne.

The essay was almost entirely copied from a well-known volume by Edmund Bergler, M.D., *Homosexuality: Disease or Way of Life?* (New York: Hill and Wang, 1957). The *Daily Nebraskan* noted this plagiarism on 10 February and the campus community was scandalized. Responses varied from anger to indignation to laughter. The ASUN unanimously passed a resolution on 16 February asking the Board of Regents to condemn plagiarism anywhere in the University, and in March a proposal of censure was offered in the Faculty Senate. It was tabled, but in April the senate asked the board to address the question of plagiarism, noting that their earlier letter had gone unanswered. In the midst of the controversy a young undergraduate, Douglas Beckwith, wrote to the campus paper on 24 February:

Dear Editor:
How much prose
Would a prokop cop
If a prokop
Could cop prose?

The confrontation between the regents and the students continued. When the ASUN planned a "World in Revolution Conference on Justice in America" in January 1972, Regents Moylan, Prokop, and Koefoot sought to control the content of the discussion, demanding guarantees that the program would "be balanced in terms of speakers and subject matter."[11] Regent Schwartzkopf, trying to resolve conflicts, listened to student complaints carefully, but Clifton Batchelder, who was running for a seat on the board, charged that some of the speakers, whom he did not name, were "known revolutionaries."[12] The conference was held as scheduled, but because of student administrative ineptness it was not a success.

During this time student fees became an issue. In addition to tuition, students paid for campus activities, publications, extracurricular lectures, concerts, and public events through assessed fees, some of which they had at one time or another voted on themselves. Both legislators and regents questioned the way this fee money was spent, asserting that it frequently brought speakers to the campus who were not congruent with conservative community opinion. Ken Bader, vice chancellor for student affairs, defended the allocation of the fees through student committees, explaining that intellectual controversy was a necessary part of any academic community. The question remained: What were the limits of student autonomy? In the midst of this continuing controversy, Senator Richard Marvel, a much respected member of the legislature and himself a professor of political science at Nebraska Wesleyan University, proposed in January 1974 that the Board of Regents be expanded to include three nonvoting student members, one from each of the campuses; and at his urging the legislature voted to submit a constitutional amendment to the people. In November the amendment passed by a very close vote decided ultimately by absentee ballots, and in the following year, 1975, the presidents of the campus student bodies were seated as nonvoting regents. Their presence on the board did not, however, resolve the dissension.

Requests for a loosening of housing regulations were a continuing source of friction between the students and the board, especially Regents Moylan, Prokop, Koefoot, and Schwartzkopf. The students felt rebuffed, even when they approached the board through the authorized Council on Student Life. They persisted in seeking an end to the University's historical role in loco parentis. In a poll held in February 1972, a large majority, 85 percent, voted to open the residence halls for coed visitation (in 1970 restrictive hours for women's dormitories had been abolished). They argued that they had received adult political status when the voting age was lowered. Now they asked for adult responsibility in the social portions of their lives. As legal adults, they thought they ought to be able to have liquor and guests in their living quarters – their rooms – at their own discretion. Former regent Adkins was rather sympathetic to the students but remained skeptical of some of their demands.[13] So was Regent Raun. He said that he did not see how alcohol could contribute to the educational atmosphere of the University. He observed that many people believed most eighteen-, nineteen-, and twenty-year-old students were not fully matured and ought to be controlled sometimes "with a kind of iron hand." Regent Schwartzkopf agreed.[14] Significantly, parents, when polled, voted

2,696 to 1,612 against liberalizing dorm rules. Chancellor Zumberge, who took office in 1972, said that his first year was an ordeal by fire because of the controversy about dormitory regulations. Since the University campus in Omaha had no dorms, the issue was moot there.

The students would not settle down. When their requests continued to be disallowed by the board, they discussed the possibility of wholesale violation of rules, in effect, a strike, knowing that no law can be sustained when a majority resist its implementation. In October 1973 the campus newspaper devoted its weekly magazine to what they called student rights and "the University as Mom and Dad." The next month the Residence Hall Association and the ASUN brought legal suit against the board and the University, claiming that the students' civil rights were being violated. In January 1974 the social privileges of Harper, Schramm, and Smith halls were suspended by the administration under pressure from the regents because of wholesale violations of regulations. Finally, in April 1974, new housing rules, developed through the Council on Student Life and endorsed by Zumberge, were presented to the board and reluctantly adopted; and these rules were liberalized in June 1975, again reluctantly. When student representatives appeared before the board in February 1976, they were treated with marked discourtesy. Regent Robert Simmons of Scottsbluff was reported as saying: "Students are children and we ought to treat them like children."[15] Clearly, what the students of the Sixties had identified as the generation gap was not closed in the Seventies. Ken Bader, the able vice chancellor for student affairs, worked constantly with the students, and Chancellor Zumberge met monthly with a round table of some ten students of his own selection to discuss campus problems. The administration was caught between student restlessness and regental and perhaps parental resistance to change. It was a time of discontinuity.

The Faculty and Administrative Authority

When the Municipal University of Omaha joined the state university system in 1968, lines of administrative authority as spelled out in the Rules and By-Laws of the Board of

Regents were strained. This strain was dramatically clear in the campus disruptions of 1970 when some faculty members spoke and acted contrary to the political views of the board. Ever since its founding in 1915 by John Dewey and A. O. Lovejoy, the American Association of University Professors had labored to spell out the responsibilities of scholars and teachers. The AAUP was roughly the equivalent of the American Medical Association and the American Bar Association in defining and representing professional responsibilities. It asserted that tenure was necessary so that a professor could follow an argument wherever it might lead, without danger of reprisals. If teachers or scholars were restrained by special-interest groups or limited by religious, political, or commercial dogmas from asking questions, they could not serve the wide interests of humankind: the search for the truth. Permanent tenure was therefore necessary to ensure intellectual freedom, and it served the total society. By the spring of 1971 these assumptions were under attack.

In April 1971 Regents Moylan and Prokop questioned the established policy of permanent faculty tenure, and in response Varner suggested that some new contractual system might be substituted for it. He and some regents thought too great a proportion of tenured faculty on a staff did not allow for diversity of opinion and also protected extremists. The Senate Committee on Academic Freedom and Tenure at once asked to meet with Varner; and the Liaison Committee appointed a special committee on tenure, headed by Harvey Perlman of the College of Law, to investigate acceptable alternate tenure systems. The Perlman committee immediately called on Varner, but he conferred with them only in the fall of 1971. He told them he preferred a contract system because it appeared that present procedures for dismissal were cumbersome. The board was divided on the matter. The Omaha faculty raised questions but took no formal action.

It had already become clear that the Rules and By-Laws under which the University operated needed reexamination. In March 1971 Wallace C. Peterson, George Holmes Professor of Economics, had proposed to the Faculty Senate in Lincoln that a University constitutional convention be called to reconsider the University's governance documents. In April the senate formally asked the board to set up a committee representing all campuses and public interests to draft a document for governance. In May the regents agreed to establish a blue-ribbon committee. This committee, with representatives from Omaha, Lincoln, and across the state, began meeting immediately, with Peterson in the chair. When he filed shortly thereafter as a candidate for the U.S. Senate, he was replaced by Richard Gilbert, professor of chemical engineering. Optimistically they hoped to have a report for the board by fall 1971. During the summer and all the next year the committee wrote and rewrote the Rules and By-Laws of the Board of Regents with advice from all quarters. Only in September 1972, a year later than originally proposed, was a draft completed.

This was an important document though considerably less comprehensive than Peterson had envisaged in calling for a constitutional convention. The faculty was apprehensive that the Board of Regents, five of whom were new to University responsibilities, and the public at large did not understand the centrality of the issues concerning academic governance and tenure that it regulated. They therefore asked that their draft be scrutinized, and modified as necessary, by every organized group on campus. They sought the widest possible agreement. Only when it had been unanimously endorsed was it taken to the board in the late fall 1972. The faculty feared that without unanimity, the regents might dangerously modify it. In January 1973 the board approved the revised Rules and By-Laws, contingent upon review by the state attorney general. This revised document preserved First Amendment rights and guaranteed academic freedom.

Though the revised Rules and By-Laws were officially adopted in January 1973, academic freedom remained insecure. In March 1973 Regent Moylan, writing in the *Douglas County Gazette*, accused the University of hushing up sexually related incidents on the Lincoln campus. He suggested that city police be called in to investigate. Vice Chancellor Ken Bader promptly denied the allegation, observing that hushing up any such incident would be to nobody's benefit. The editors of the campus newspaper, Michael (O. J.) Nelson and Tom Lansworthy, defended their old antagonist, the administration. "Moylan's statements are an unfounded, irresponsible and unjust attack on the UNL Administration," they said on 19 March 1973. The Senate Faculty Committee on Human Rights proposed that the senate officially and explicitly prohibit undercover surveillance in order to protect the constitutional rights of the administration, students, and faculty. Fearing polemical investigations, Vice Chancellor Bader and Dr. Samuel Fuenning, director of the University Health Center in Lincoln, promptly drew up careful guidelines for protecting the privacy of Health Center records.

Attacks on academic freedom and tenure continued. In a special board meeting on 7 June 1973, Regent Moylan moved that all abortion procedures in the Medical Center be prohibited. Legal counsel to the University thereupon reminded him that such an action would invite an expensive civil rights lawsuit that would be difficult to defend. In October the board discussed the abortion rights of physicians attached to the Medical Center. Medical administration and faculty took careful notice. In March 1974, Ronald Roskens, the new chancellor at the University of Nebraska in Omaha, yet again raised the issue of tenure, and in April 1975 the regents asked Chancellor Zumberge in Lincoln to bring in a plan for tenure quotas. When a special faculty meeting was called in Lincoln in response to the regents' action, more than 300 persons voted unanimously to reject a quota system. "Do they want an adversarial relationship?" the president of the Lincoln chapter of the AAUP asked.[16]

A confrontation with faculty was avoided when Steven Sample, the newly arrived vice president for academic affairs, asked for a delay so he could set up a committee to study the matter. In October 1975 he and his committee were able to report that, compared with similar universities, the University of Nebraska did not, in fact, have an alarming percentage of tenured faculty. They recommended that tenure be granted only after six full years of probation, that notification of nonappointment be given a year in advance of contract termination, and that the enforcement of any tenure policy be at departmental level. This report was in substantial accord with national AAUP recommendations and was approved by the board at their November meeting.

But the fat was in the fire. As early as 1971 a chapter of the American Federation of Teachers had been organized in Lincoln, and by February 1972 the union had a hundred dues-paying members, its president, Paul A. Olson, reported.[17] This number was far short of the minimum required for unionizing. In February 1975 the Lincoln chapter of the AAUP polled the faculty to discover if they would accept the AAUP as their sole bargaining agent for working conditions and salaries. Controversy ran high. The Board of Regents was displeased, and Varner published a piece critical of faculty unions which he claimed was nonpartisan. Professor Everett Peterson, a respected agricultural economist, supported by a faculty committee of fifteen, argued publicly and widely the disadvantages of unionizing. On February 18 collective bargaining for the Lincoln campuses was defeated by a narrow margin. It passed in the College of Law and lost in the College of Dentistry by a single vote.

In Omaha the controversy was even sharper. The Omaha senate and the Omaha administration were in frequent and sometimes acrimonious confrontation. By 1972 one-third of the faculty there belonged to the American Federation of Teachers, which agitated vigorously for collective bargaining. In the fall of 1979 the local chapter of the AAUP won by plebiscite the right to unionize the campus and represent the interests of the Omaha faculty to the board. The first contract was negotiated in 1981 and gave them a retroactive wage increase, with interest, for the previous year. Through the whole decade the relationship of the Board of Regents with the faculties on all the campuses was at best uneven, and frequently hostile.

Administrators in the Seventies

During much of the Seventies the administration of the University was unsettled, in part because the deans, vice chancellors, and chancellors changed so frequently. Joseph Soshnik was succeeded in September 1971 by C. Peter Magrath, who became interim chancellor of the Lincoln campuses. Magrath served brilliantly until February 1972, when James Zumberge was appointed chancellor. Magrath remained only a few months longer as vice chancellor for academic affairs before moving on to Bing-hampton, New York, as president of the state university campus there. G. Robert Ross, vice chancellor for student affairs, left his post in 1972 to head the University of Arkansas at Little Rock. Thereupon a kind of triumvirate of student affairs deans officiated for many months until Ken Bader could arrive from Ohio State. Bader stayed in Nebraska until 1976. In 1972 Virginia Trotter succeeded Magrath as vice chancellor for academic affairs, but in two years she resigned to go to Washington as assistant secretary for education in the Department of Health, Education and Welfare, taking John J. Stephens III, Zumberge's assistant, with her. At this point Adam Breckenridge was prevailed upon to return to that office – from the library, where he had been acting director for a year. George Round retired on 1 July 1973 after forty years of service in public relations; and in the summer of 1974 Merk Hobson, after twenty-four years, resigned as executive vice president for academic affairs to go home to Wisconsin. Also in the summer of 1974, Zumberge suddenly resigned to go to Southern Methodist University and Breckenridge became acting chancellor. In November 1976, *The Nebraska Alumnus* observed that two additional administrators and three more deans had left their posts in the previous six months. The only continuing administrator was Breckenridge. His knowledge was so wide, his commitment so established, and his integrity so complete that even the most intransigent of the regents crossed him cautiously. Some close observers thought that he alone kept the institution from total collapse on more than one occasion in these years.

The colleges were as unstable as the front office. Dean E. F. Frolik, who was nearing retirement, resigned as dean of agriculture in October 1973, but Duane Acker, his successor, did not arrive until 1974; Howard Ottoson in the meantime served as acting dean. Acker remained one year, whereupon Ottoson returned to the post for one more year, until Martin Massengale came from Arizona, in 1976. In engineering, Dean John Davis resigned in 1971, in part over frustrations with the Omaha merger, and James S. Blackman was pressed very reluctantly back into service yet once more until George P. Hanna Jr. became

the permanent, unpopular dean. The College of Arts and Sciences had four deans in six years: Robert L. Hough, a much loved teacher of English, was persuaded to serve until Magrath could arrive in 1968, but Magrath remained dean only one year, then was moved to the front office as dean of academic affairs. Hough thereupon unwillingly returned for another single year. In 1970 Melvin George arrived to stay for two years before joining the central administration. Max Larsen was acting dean from 1972 until 1975, when George returned for a few months before moving on to the University of Missouri. In those years one hardly knew who would answer the phone in Oldfather Hall.

The University of Nebraska in Omaha was hardly more stable. In August 1971, Chancellor Kirk Naylor was suddenly dismissed by the Board of Regents, meeting in Scottsbluff, upon the recommendation of President Varner. Gene Budig, later chancellor of the University of Kansas but at this time part of the Nebraska administration, recalled that Naylor lobbied almost exclusively for Omaha. "Kirk Naylor was under great pressure in Omaha to show overnight that the Omaha campus was just as good as Lincoln," he said.[18] The campus newspaper reported the sudden firing was an attempt to ease tensions between the Omaha and Lincoln campuses and quoted Varner as saying: "The reasons for this attitude of divisiveness are obviously complex and undoubtedly largely the result of a lack of clear understanding before and at the time of the merger. . . . Naylor's removal will present an opportunity to try to achieve a fresh beginning."[19] John V. Blackwell, acting dean of the College of Arts and Sciences in Omaha and formerly chair of art, was named acting chancellor. Vic Blackwell, as he was called, had a tumultuous year in office complicated by racial strife on and off campus. Ronald Roskens, vice president for administration at Kent State University, was appointed chancellor in April 1972.

Other divisions of the University were also unstable. At the Medical Center the brilliant chancellor, Cecil L. Wittson, was scheduled to retire in 1972 when he had reached mandatory age, but he left a few months early, making necessary a temporary appointment from February until summer. Dr. Robert D. Sparks, his replacement, stayed in Omaha four years. Professor Norman Cromwell became executive graduate dean of the University in 1970 for three years and was often at odds with the Board of Regents. In 1975 Carl Leopold became vice president for research, but he stayed only a year. Howard Neville was appointed vice chancellor (later vice president) for business and finance in 1970, but he moved on in 1973. The University seemed in administrative turmoil, which was the result of national uneasiness, confusing administrative relationships within the newly merged universities, and unclear definitions of responsibilities. Some of the more disaffected "youngsters" in the administration in those days occasionally got together for CRAP meetings – Counter Revolutionaries for Academic Progress – the "youngsters" being assistant vice chancellors and those just under the top ranks. They tried to figure out what really ought to be done to fix the general disorder in the place, but they usually ended in despair. One of them later said that "the organizational chart was simply impossible, and tracing specific actions through it on a chart on the wall soon looked like a bowl of spaghetti." The leading question was always "Who is the boss?" and this question could not be answered.[20]

❧ The Merger

The continuing issue of the decade was the relationship of the University in Lincoln to the University in Omaha. The word *merger* did not appear in the original legislation but the term quickly became the rubric under which necessary adjustments were conducted. *Merger* was, in fact, a misleading term, for this was really a linking of institutions which had quite different missions. Varner himself said that "the merger was never really planned to go through. It just happened and it was a political accident. And some expectations had been allowed to grow that really couldn't be fulfilled . . . ."[21] In 1970 Willis A. Strauss, a public-spirited Omaha businessman and president of the Northern Natural Gas Company, had headed a town-gown committee charged with defining the nature of what they called the urban university. He and his blue-ribbon com-

mission spelled out the relationship of the city university to the whole community, a community that included all ages, kinds, and conditions of persons. On the Omaha campus nearly half the student body of about 10,000 were part-time students, and there were no campus residences. Less concerned with the nature of its administration than with its general purposes, the Strauss Commission distinguished the Omaha university from the comprehensive research university in Lincoln, to the apparent advantage, and disadvantage, of neither.[22]

When the universities were linked, one of the first problems to be solved was how the colleges of engineering on the two campuses should be related. Since Omaha was the industrial center of the state, Omaha industrialists, including Strauss, wanted a strong engineering program there. Hobson later said that a group of consultants looking at state resources "concluded that [in] a state of a million five hundred thousand people, perhaps one engineering college was all we might need for many years to come,"[23] and certainly as much as it could pay for. Vice President Hobson worked out a compromise. Though there was to be no major duplication on the two campuses, junior-division, pre-engineering courses could be offered in both places. One full program in civil engineering, the most fully developed division at the Omaha university, could remain; and courses in elementary technology could be continued too. (This technology was later phased out, under pressure from local technological institutes.) Engineering on both campuses was to be under the direction of a single dean in Lincoln, and graduate degrees were to be offered jointly, under the authority of a central graduate office. Dean John Davis "didn't quite subscribe to the final decision"[24] and shortly resigned. The arrangement, in spite of some expensive duplication in civil engineering, worked out reasonably well for some years, but the whole question was raised again in 1993.

The total Engineering College might have been moved to Omaha in 1970 if a new $4 million laboratory-research building, funded by state and federal money, had not been under construction in Lincoln at the time. In the fall of 1972 the College of Pharmacy was moved to the Medical Center in Omaha, where it got a new building at a cost of some

$3 million, and the School of Social Work was also moved to Omaha, on the odd assumption presumably that social work is more an urban than a rural necessity. In 1973, home economics programs on the two campuses were merged under the direction of the dean on the Lincoln east campus. The fact that all this went as well as it did was due to Merk Hobson's patience.

When the legislature accepted the Omaha university as a state responsibility, the nature of its administration was not defined. Some members of the Board of Regents who were new to university experience proposed a corporate organization with strong hierarchical authority. Regent Kermit Hansen endorsed this view, but historical experience elsewhere shows that the management of institutions of higher learning does not lend itself to such easy formulation. A university is a unique institution with unique administrative problems. As Ned Hedges, vice chancellor for academic affairs, was fond of saying, a university is not a packing plant.

In 1970, upon the recommendation of Chancellor Varner and with funding from the University Foundation, the board hired the professional management consulting firm of Cresap, McCormick and Paget of Chicago to recommend an organization for the merged universities. The consulting firm and a citizens' committee headed by Thomas Nurnberger of Omaha offered suggestions for relieving what Ken Keller identified as "the confusion, the fears, and the suspicions" that they found on the campuses, especially at UNO, as the University in Omaha was now called.[25] They proposed the reversal of titles of presiding officers: campus CEOs would become chancellors; the system head would become president. These changes, Varner explained, were motivated by resentment at UNO that the central, systemwide administrator remained in Lincoln and was by his title identified with that campus, which had always had a chancellor. By making the head of each campus a chancellor, the Board of Regents hoped to indicate campus equality.[26]

Cresap, McCormick and Paget also recommended that a separate building be constructed off existing campuses to house the central administration and that this central office be separately budgeted. They thought that computer networks should be centralized; that graduate education, which had earlier been centralized, should be returned to the various campuses; and that internal budgetary procedures should be consolidated. Some of these suggestions were immediately adopted. In September 1971 campus presidents became chancellors and Varner became president, although the change of names did not settle the discontent. A building to house the central administration in seclusion from students and faculty was promptly constructed in Lincoln, on Holdrege Street, with money advanced from the University Foundation. At first called Regents Hall, it was renamed in 1985 for D. B. and Paula Varner. In 1974 Varner said, "The system office was bootlegged. It never was authorized by the merger action. . . . we're legitimatized now."[27] Other managerial recommendations were passed over. Norman Cromwell continued to monitor graduate education from Holdrege Street.

Cresap, McCormick and Paget was asked to reassess the administrative operations in 1975, for they were not smooth. All the campuses were displeased with the way the budget was shared, and all thought the central administration took too much money for itself. In 1973 Professor Carroll McKibbin, chair of political science in Lincoln, wrote for the AAUP Bulletin, "What has developed is considerable competition between the two cities over the limited financial resources available to the university system, which has resulted in such items as capital construction priorities being rebalanced between the Omaha and Lincoln campuses."[28] On both Omaha and Lincoln campuses the central administration on Holdrege Street was thought to be too expensive and too powerful.

❧ Problems of Equity

In Omaha, the most populous part of the state, UNO flourished. In the first ten years of its association with the state system, it grew from 10,000 students to 15,000. More than $21 million of state money was spent on buildings on the West Dodge campus. A million-dollar extension on the Student Union was financed from student fees, and a performing arts center was built with a gift of $1.6 million from Janet and Willis Strauss. The number of University buildings doubled in the fifteen years after 1970 as the campus grew from fifty-two to more than eight-eight acres, through condemnation, to the distress of the adjacent neighborhood. "In twenty years we went from a campus with some isolated buildings to one that is striking, cohesive, coherent," Chancellor Del Weber told the *Omaha World-Herald* on 5 November 1987. Weber added that UNO had carefully programmed its growth to develop the campus as a whole and to improve its academic quality.

By 1975 the fears and suspicions at UNO had moved to Lincoln. The Lincoln campuses feared that an inflated centralized administration worked to their disadvantage and that Omaha got a disproportionate share of the budget. Don Walton in the *Lincoln Star* of 12 February 1976 quoted Senator Douglas Bereuter of Ithaca as saying that "the quality of education on the Lincoln campus [had] been 'deteriorating' while NU [had] concentrated efforts on improving quality on the other campuses." In the preceding five or ten years, Bereuter said, NU had been "forced to prop up a medical school which was in danger of losing its accreditation" even as it "took over a very deficient municipal university in Omaha and brought it to a point of academic respectability." In addition to the West Dodge campus, UNO asked and got the legislature to fund a downtown center on lower Douglas Street at a cost of $8 million; private sources contributed an additional $5 million.

In December 1975 Varner came to the Faculty Senate in Lincoln to defend the central organization. He asserted that Nebraska had "one of the more highly decentralized systems of those studied," with only 24 professionals on the central staff, compared with the 224 at Missouri; this Missouri number included the statewide extension service, but he did not report that, if he knew it. Moreover, he said, in the previous four years 78 percent of the budget had gone to the Lincoln campuses and the Medical Center, compared with 22 percent to UNO and the systems office.[29]

Criticism of the central administration continued, however, and in both June and July of 1976 Senator John Cavanaugh of Omaha came to the Board of Regents asserting that central administration was costing too much

money.[30] In October 1976, after a summer-long committee investigation, Henry Baumgarten, Foundation Professor of Chemistry and a research chemist of considerable distinction, loudly and rather discourteously disputed Varner's conclusions about proportionate costs. Baumgarten was president of the UNL Faculty Senate. He challenged the basis on which the President's Equity Policy Committee – the group designated to ensure just treatment of all campuses – had reached its figures. He asserted that the Lincoln and Omaha campuses had both been compared to institutions which were clearly inappropriate, institutions which had different goals, responsibilities, and constituencies from theirs. The result was a distinct disadvantage to the Lincoln campuses. It was obvious, he said, "that the *ad hoc* committee was engaged in a political, not an academic, process" and that its real purpose was to "legitimize the gift of a large sum of the taxpayers' money to UNO."[31] Baumgarten's conclusions were endorsed by the Senate Executive Committee. The Board of Regents and the president seemed to them determined "to move the University to Omaha brick by brick," as was commonly said then.

The issue of campus equity was complicated by the fact that Governor Exon from the beginning of his administration had constructed hold-the-line budgets, and though the legislature sometimes voted the University more money than he recommended, the system often found itself with insufficient money for any campus. Varner noted in 1974, "While this decline [of some 18 percent] in purchasing power was occurring for members of the faculty of the University of Nebraska, the per capita purchasing power for the state as a whole was increasing by more than 20 percent"[32] In subsequent years the budget was somewhat improved but issues of equity remained.

The relationship of the College of Agriculture, the agricultural experiment station, and agricultural extension to the rest of the University, always a subject of controversy, came to a head at this time. After the Omaha and Lincoln universities were merged, President Varner and Chancellor Zumberge proposed that agricultural extension and general extension be consolidated, and they put general research funds and agriculture research funds into a single budget. This joining of divisions which for generations had been separated alarmed the state's agriculturists, led by Clare Porter, manager of NC+ Hybrids, a production and marketing corporation. When he and other agribusinessmen examined "Toward Excellence," Varner's five-year plan for the University, they feared the new specified needs of UNO would take money from agriculture. In June 1972 Porter and other spokesmen from agricultural organizations met with Zumberge and Varner to protest. Although they recognized that tremendous urban problems existed, tremendous agricultural problems existed as well, they said. They were concerned that agriculture should have more direct access to the president as well as the Board of Regents than it currently did, and they proposed a radical reorganization. They asked that the agricultural college have a chancellor and become a fourth division of the University. (Ninety years earlier, in the 1880s, agricultural interests had tried to separate the agricultural college completely from the University and had nearly succeeded.)

John Klinker, president of the Farm Bureau; Dick Goodding, its legislative representative; and others – all the farm groups in the state worked together – prepared a bill to make the agricultural college an independent entity corresponding to UNL, UNO, and the Medical Center. Chancellor Zumberge, Vice President Hobson, and President Varner were cool to the idea, and they pointed out that half the courses agricultural undergraduates took were in colleges outside agriculture and that education in agriculture should certainly be more than trade school training. They observed that the additional costs of independent administration would be great. They thought, further, that the independence of one more group within the University system would injure the unifying core of the University.

After much discussion the agricultural groups and the administration reached the Zumberge Compromise. They amended the legislative bill to ask for a vice chancellor for a semi-independent Institute of Agriculture and National Resources (IANR) which was to include Conservation and Survey, the Water Resources Research Institute, and some research divisions of particular agricultural concern as well as the College of Agriculture. The new vice chancellor would be supported by a dean in the College of Agriculture who would be in charge of college instruction, a director of the experiment station, and a director of agricultural extension. He would have direct access to the president and the Board of Regents on all matters dealing with agriculture, thus bypassing the vice chancellor for academic affairs and very often the campus chancellor as well. Hobson objected, for he thought that agricultural education was not sharply different from education in the other colleges. He later said: "I do not believe that one college had a special, elite position with respect to the other colleges."[33] Varner doubted that the new structure "made a whole lot of difference" though it had "the advantage of giving agriculture more visibility."[34] In April 1973 the legislature established the semi-autonomy of the IANR. It is worth noting that in the ten years after its founding, $24 million was spent for IANR buildings, including a $9 million veterinary science complex, and $4.5 million was spent on a new east campus union, this last paid for with bonds issued against student fees. Agricultural enrollment in this decade rose only from 1,400 to 1,500 students before going into a decline.

❧ "Toward Excellence"

From the beginning of his administration, President Varner had tried to plan ahead. Impatient with details, he thought in the largest terms, unafraid of distant goals. In this he was quite unlike Governor Exon, who seemed to give close attention only to immediate fiscal economies. In February 1972 Varner and a planning seminar made up of administrators and faculty prepared a document, "Toward Excellence: The Development of the University of Nebraska, 1972–1977," which laid out schemes for the best use of limited funds. Revised by the UNL Academic Planning Committee in the spring of 1972, it was submitted to faculty and staff for modifications in the fall before being presented to the Board of Regents in January 1973. This weighty document identified areas for support, sought areas that could survive with lesser support, and thus proposed an overall pattern of development. It called for reallocation of funds. Faculty and administrators alike had come to feel that across-the-board cuts reduced the whole institution to mediocrity, but the task of identifying areas for de-emphasis in order that others might be strengthened was so disagreeable as to cause considerable angst. Whose ox was to be gored?

The 1974 legislature required an updated version of the five-year plan, "Toward Excellence," as part of the University's 1975–76 budget request, so after more planning and more hearings a new five-year plan was submitted to the governor and the legislature. The Academic Planning Committee of the Lincoln campuses recommended agriculture and natural resources, life sciences, the musical arts, law, and the library for emphasis, but the appropriations bill provided some $440,000 for a somewhat different list of departments: animal science, chemistry, crop physiology, journalism, life sciences, and nontraditional education. The legislature seemed willing to give at least token support to the University's research activities on the Lincoln campuses.

In 1976 the legislature, responding to the prodding of Senator Douglas Bereuter, appropriated $850,000 explicitly for the improvement of undergraduate education on the Lincoln campuses. The money was to be used to replace graduate teaching assistants with full-time professionals, to lower class sizes, and to reward outstanding teachers with honoraria. The year 1976 was to be the first in a four-year program to upgrade the quality of instruction, and the regents were "instructed" to submit proposals for continuing sums with an account of previous accomplishments. Senator Bereuter had arrived at this plan after conferring with Professor Franklin Eldridge, past president of the University senate, and Interim Chancellor Breckenridge.

The bill was clearly an attempt by the legislature, and more expressly by its appropriations committee, to manage the interior operation of the University. Happy as the University was to receive the extra funds, the board felt that its constitutional authority was being usurped (previously the legislature had attempted to direct the expenditure of funds received from grants, tuition, and service fees), and so in July 1975, at the urging of Regent Robert

Koefoot, it asked its legal counsel to "seek a determination through declaratory judgment whether the board, if it submits to these infringements on its power, is meeting the responsibility and obligation that the Constitution of the State of Nebraska has placed in the Board of Regents."[35] The Nebraska Supreme Court decided that the authority of the legislature was indeed limited and that, in effect, the University could not be micromanaged from the statehouse. When Governor Exon called a special session of the legislature in the fall of 1976 to consider fiscal matters, the tension between the University and the state government was great; and the Bereuter amendment and what became identified as Bereuter funds reflected this confrontation. Some members of the University administration, among them Ned Hedges, who served in the office of academic affairs in various capacities from 1972 to 1981, doubted that this special funding was really effective.[36] The quality of undergraduate education depended on more than short-term stopgap measures, welcome as any help might be. The University needed consistent, long-term support with which to plan, and its administrators needed flexibility.

❧ Football and Other Cultural Matters

However disenchanted the public may have become with some aspects of the University in the Seventies, it continued to support Big Red football. When Woody Varner arrived in Nebraska in 1970, the University was already in the athletic big time; and when Bob Devaney's football team defeated Louisiana State University in the Orange Bowl on 1 January 1971 it became number one in the nation. President Nixon came in person to the University Coliseum to congratulate Devaney and his team. According to the campus newspaper 15 January 1971, this "special convocation resembled a football rally." Nebraskans' enthusiasm for football reached a new peak, and when in 1972, for the second year in a row, the Nebraska team again became first in the nation, Devaney was a folk hero. At his urging the legislature provided more than $21 million for a sports arena on the fairgrounds. It was opened in March 1976 and was named the Bob Devaney Sports Center.

Regent Schwartzkopf, himself a former football letterman, denied that there was too much emphasis on intercollegiate athletics, a subject of perennial discussion, but he said, "We do not have the statewide support in the same dimensions in the academic community as we do for our Big Red football team." George Round, adviser to five chancellors and an irrepressible football enthusiast, agreed: "That is one thing that has bothered me for many, many years, the inability to transfer allegiance and support to the real purpose of the University."[37] Chancellor Zumberge observed: "When the legislators pay more attention to football tickets than they do to faculty salaries, you wonder where their priorities are."[38]

In January 1973 Devaney retired as coach and became University athletic director. He had, as sportswriters like to proclaim, a permanent place in sports annals. Tom Osborne, an assistant, was named head coach in his place. As they said at the time, Devaney's was a hard act to follow. Steve Strasser, an undergraduate, compared them in a prizewinning essay: "There are at least superficial differences between the two men: Devaney the round-faced Irishman in baggy pants will be replaced along the sidelines this year by a tall, square-jawed Osborne in creased, double-knit slacks. Devaney has a little leprechaun in his eyes. Osborne has a little John Calvin in his. Before audiences, Devaney is loose on grammar and long on his patented brand of dry wit. Osborne has to force a little humor into his speech and offers to 'interact' with the audience after the talk."[39] Fortunately for football, Nebraska, and Osborne himself, the new coach turned out to be as successful as the old coach had been.

Varner was not content to let football be the only unifying experience for the state. On coming to the University, he noted that it had no program for bringing major musicians to the campus. In the summer of 1972, on his own authority, he signed up four distinguished musicians for concerts in Kimball Recital Hall. To his delight but not surprise, the series immediately sold out. In November he brought the St. Paul Chamber Orchestra to be in residence on campus – that is, both to play in concert and to meet informally with students and others. In the next year, 1973, the Performance Arts Series sold out so quickly that the

Cultural Affairs Committee, without additional money, brought the St. Louis Symphony to Lincoln for three extra, sold-out concerts. In March 1974 the campus newspaper noted that the performing arts were enjoying a phenomenal boom at the University.

Varner was eager that the arts reach people across the state. "I have been very much pleased and impressed with the responsiveness of the citizens and the leaders of the state [to my suggestions]," he said. "I have found, in the arts in particular, there is recognition that this is an important part of the good life that we talk about in Nebraska." He sought continuing support for the arts, observing that "perhaps the most important single development of the arts in this state has been the restructuring of the State Arts Council,"[40] which sponsored cultural events like concerts and art exhibits, encouraged local artistic activities, and put practicing artists and writers into the schools. Varner drew other states of the region into his projects. He took the lead in organizing a Mid-America Arts Alliance to serve Missouri, Iowa, Nebraska, and Kansas in supporting top-flight performing arts groups. If Omaha, Des Moines, Wichita, Topeka, Lincoln, and other cities were too small by themselves to support them, local groups in cooperation and with federal, state, and foundation funds could be developed. The Mid-America Arts Alliance became both a booking agency and a developer of talent. Most people agreed that it helped change the cultural face of the whole region.

Outreach: SUN and UMA

President Varner had come to Nebraska in part because he saw that the multicampus, multimission university was on the cutting edge of higher education. In many places the single-campus, residential university was being superseded by enormous public institutions which had many campuses and diversified missions. The Association of State Universities and Land-Grant Colleges reported in January 1965 that fifty-nine state and land-grant institutions in forty states and Puerto Rico were operating more than 260 permanent establishments offering degree-credit courses and programs; but in 1970 national studies showed that contemporary institutions did not provide for large segments of society needing and wanting postsecondary education. Perhaps because of his administrative experience in the extension division of Michigan State University, Varner was interested in the outreach nature of public education. So when the defunct Hiram Scott College at Scottsbluff was offered to the state in 1973 as a far western extension of the University, he recommended its acceptance. He suggested that the Hiram Scott facilities could be used for agricultural research, programs in rural health, and continuing education. The University thus got a branch in the west, but a branch which was not degree-granting or in competition with what already existed.

Varner's concern for academic outreach showed itself in what came to be called the State University of Nebraska (SUN). When he considered the splendid educational television facilities in Nebraska and the statewide network, he turned to Jack McBride, its developer and general manager. One day early in his administration, in February 1971, he got in touch with McBride. "I got a call from [Varner's] secretary asking if I could get on a private plane that afternoon and fly to Omaha and pick up [George Round] and President Varner and fly out to Holdrege," where Varner was to speak at a dinner. "And his question to me was, 'Why don't we use the television network to develop college courses for credit?' " McBride was taken aback but certainly game. "His instructions to me were, 'Now I have told you what I have in mind. Come in and eat dinner. Don't listen to my speech. Think so we can talk about it on the [flight] home.' "[41]

Very shortly, with money from the federal government and from foundations, Varner and McBride set up SUN, the State University of Nebraska. McBride was its executive director. This university without walls was to send its courses through television to students wherever they might be. Its first two pilot courses, one in psychology and the other in accounting, were ready in the fall of 1974. "Each course will include fifteen half-hour television lessons broadcast over the State's ETV network, newspaper lessons established in the 'Omaha World-Herald' and a mailed learning kit containing additional instructional materials," an announcement read. Learning centers where students could receive information and advice were located initially in Scottsbluff, Kearney, Lincoln, and Omaha. Eventually twenty-five such centers around the state were planned.[42]

Nebraska was not going it alone. In the summer of 1974 Varner and the presidents of four other universities in the region agreed to form the University of Mid-America, which would design and produce curricula for SUN-inspired programs in Kansas, Missouri, and Iowa. SUN became UMA, the University of Mid-America. This project cost the state of Nebraska very little, a total of $229,000. "I don't think that it is realistic to expect the state to pick up the full tab," Varner said. "I think all that the state could be expected to do is to help on the delivery side."[43] The ETV network already existed.

This innovative project attracted national attention, and the initial response in 1974 was gratifying. It was expected that 200 persons would register for each of the first two courses, but some 400 enrolled in accounting and nearly 300 in psychology. Only about half that number remained in the spring of 1975. But before the open university could be given a fair trial, federal policies changed sharply and federal funding was withdrawn. Foundations could not carry it alone. The whole project suddenly collapsed. In January 1976 SUN-UMA, with a deficit of $62,000, was transferred to the UNL Division of Continuing Studies, and in June 1979 the Division of Continuing Studies announced that it would discontinue SUN-UMA altogether and close the learning centers. The division would continue to offer courses by television, however. National and regional interest in an open university remained, but the great schemes for SUN and UMA had to be dropped.

❧ From President of the University to President of the Foundation

By 1975 the University administration was clearly in for a change. In 1974 George Cook of the Bankers Life Insurance Company, knowing Zumberge's time in Nebraska was up, recommended him to his friend Ed Cox, chairman of the trustees of Southern Methodist University. Cox tracked Zumberge to his summer place in Wyoming and hired him as president of SMU in a week. In late August 1975, Zumberge, who had been in Lincoln since 1972, announced his imminent departure. According to him, authority had moved increasingly away from the chancellors: it had "shifted now to a stronger central administration. Even the change in the name from systems to central administration reflects that," Zumberge said as he left.[44] By October he was in Texas.

Zumberge was an efficient if inflexible administrator. Adam C. Breckenridge, whose experience was unmatched, said repeatedly that Zumberge was the best administrator with whom he ever worked. But his relationship with his faculty was uneven, perhaps because he showed that he felt superior to most of them. A very bad judge of subordinates, he surrounded himself with assistants of limited ability; at least four of his major appointments had to be replaced promptly after he left. He looked like the movie representation of the college president. One cannot be surprised that he ended his career in Los Angeles. "A dignified, gray-haired man of patrician bearing, Zumberge seemed almost a stereotype of a university president when he arrived on the USC campus in 1980," the *Los Angeles Times* said of him on his death 16 April 1992. As president of the University of Southern California he had raised more than $640 million dollars for that university. Zumberge was succeeded in Nebraska by Roy Young, a modest man from Oregon State University.

By 1975 and 1976 the University's relations with the legislature and the governor, often adversarial, had become stormy. In November 1975, in a special session, the legislature asked for a 3 percent reduction in the current, ongoing budget, a fiscal difficulty of some magnitude. Governor Exon told the legislature not "to let the University off the hook"; and when Varner and other University officials appeared before the appropriations committee, they were met with some sarcasm. When the governor presented his budget, he and his fiscal officers used data about cash balances which University officials thought inaccurate. "I don't know the origin of his figures," Varner told Don Pieper of the *Lincoln Journal* on 29 January 1976. "I wouldn't argue that such figures could be found,

but the conclusions he reaches are simply wrong. It is a bad use of data." Exon reacted angrily.

But Varner was unrepentant. In February he returned to the legislature, asking for an $8 million dollar supplement to the budget he had already presented. The new budget would bring the University to the upper reaches of the Big Eight Conference, where in 1973 Exon had said he wanted it to be. Both Senator Marvel, chairman of the appropriations committee, and the governor were displeased. "Every time he comes here he has some radical change in the formula and we never know about it in advance," Marvel was quoted in the *Lincoln Journal* of 10 February 1976 as saying. Varner told the regents that he was laying his job on the line, and in March he recommended that the board accept the budget developed by Marvel's appropriations committee as the best they could get. In May, to balance losses, the board voted to raise tuition by some 11 percent, the first increase since 1970.

During the spring Varner concluded that it was in everybody's best interest to make a change, and in a prepared statement presented to the Board of Regents on 26 June 1976 he said, "During the past few weeks I have given a good deal of thought to the dynamics of universities in general and the University of Nebraska in particular," and, he concluded, "the University will be served if a new President moves into this leadership position."[45] To allow the board time to find his successor, Varner would stay on until January 1977. He had been chief executive officer since 1970. Later he observed that from 1971 until 1976 the state's annual general fund support for the University went from $41 million to $94 million, and that during this same period capital construction totaled nearly $100 million. "The frustrations were acute during the first two years. Following that, we've had sympathetic support," Varner told the *Omaha World-Herald* on 27 June 1976 rather generously. Later he said to George Round, "I didn't enjoy the role as chancellor and president of the University of Nebraska as much as some other roles .... I'm more atuned to working directly with people."[46]

When Flavel Wright, president of the board of directors of the University of Nebraska Foundation; George Cook, immediate past president; and Willis Strauss of Omaha heard that Varner was resigning, they immediately suggested that he join the foundation. He agreed because of his and his wife, Paula's, pleasure in the Nebraska, Lincoln, and the University. This was a brilliant appointment, for with his flair for dealing with individuals, Varner was a wonderful fundraiser. He immediately took charge of a $25 million three-year drive for basic endowment. Ed Hirsch, who had been with the foundation since 1963, said, "Before it was over — about eight months before it was over — we had already hit the twenty-five million dollars. So we announced in the newspaper that we were going for thirty-five million dollars. . . . Well, by the time we shut everything off, we had received around fifty-two million dollars."[47] In 1985 the foundation's assets had risen to more than $100 million dollars, by 1990 they had doubled again, and by winter 1993 they surpassed $300 million. Even before Varner resigned from the foundation in 1986, it had become one of the largest among all state university foundations.

Woody Varner was chancellor and president during a particularly stormy decade. He rode out the storms. When others were discouraged, he retained his high spirits, and he undertook new projects even when old ones failed. Extremely popular both on campus and off, he asked the University and the state to think in more than provincial terms. He was committed to furthering agricultural interests from his first day in Nebraska, but he never forgot that the needs of any society are greater than simple economic prosperity. If some of his major projects like SUN-UMA did not pan out, others like M-AAA did. The total University and the University Foundation were stronger when he left than when he came. Nebraskans' lives were richer because Paula and Woody Varner had been here, and Nebraskans remain permanently in the Varners' debt.

14. "Political Reality": 1977–1989

❧ Ronald Roskens

At the December 1976 meeting of the Board of Regents, Kermit Hansen moved that Ronald Roskens, chancellor of the University of Nebraska at Omaha, be designated interim president of the University of Nebraska. Diplomatically he "noted that a number of people, including some faculty and deans of the Lincoln and Medical Center campuses, had expressed the feeling that Chancellor Roskens would be an excellent choice and that he is an individual with whom they could work."[1] Hansen had been a supporter of Roskens from Roskens's first appearance in Nebraska as chancellor of UNO in 1972. Then chairman of the board of the U.S. National Bank in Omaha, he had introduced Roskens to the powers of the city. They quickly accepted him into their circle. Roskens was affable and spoke easily, indeed loved to make speeches; and he was supported by a graceful wife who charmed everybody. The Omaha citizenry, eager for the University in Omaha to be "built to a position of stature and quality that was consistent with the University as a whole,"[2] were prepared to support the energetic young man who was not yet forty. Roskens saw that his first responsibility was to represent the excellence of his institution to the city, and shortly the University in Omaha was no longer regarded as West Dodge High School. The change, in part due to state support, was automatically and properly credited to Chancellor Roskens; at the meeting of the regents in November 1976 Hansen noted that "Chancellor Roskens has just recently been elected President of the Association of Urban Universities, a group of one hundred seventy-six universities from around the nation."[3]

When the presidency of the University became vacant in 1976, Roskens along with the other two chancellors was named to the search committee charged with finding a new chief executive officer. By December all the nominated candidates were eliminated for one reason and another, and the board turned to Roskens. "We wish to emphasize that Dr. Roskens is not to act as a caretaker President," they announced.[4] Few people were surprised when the following spring they named him to the post permanently.

Woody Varner and his successor were sharply dissimilar. Where Varner was something of an enthusiast, having, it was said, more ideas per week than most people have in a lifetime, Ron Roskens was what his associates called a survivor. Varner was confident that he could manage most situations, and he could. He commanded every room he entered. Roskens also had presence, but of a different kind. Tall and bald, frequently with a large cigar in his mouth, he seemed at home in boardrooms. When Varner went to the governor and the legislature, he took, sometimes undiplomatically, a budget that reflected what he saw as the needs of his University. Roskens, on the other hand, conferring with Senator Jerome Warner, chair of the appropriations committee, tried not to "embarrass" the committee with large demands. Where Varner pressed at the limits of possibility, Roskens saw himself as a "political realist." When, for example, in 1978 Governor Exon and the legislature returned a disappointing budget, Roskens's vice president for government affairs, William Swanson, said rather plaintively, "We thought we had a reasonable request when we went in," but, he continued, "we recognize the constraints they [the legislators] are working under,"[5] and Roskens declared himself reasonably pleased by the budget. Neither Chancellor Roy Young, who came to Lincoln in 1976, nor Chancellor Del Weber, who succeeded Roskens in Omaha in 1977, could dissuade the system administration from trimming their requests to what it took to be "political reality." They sometimes asked, "What about stewardship? Are we doing our jobs if we only *begin* with what politicians have already decided?"[6]

❧ The Students and the Board of Regents

The confrontations between the central administration and the campuses continued in Roskens's administration. It was most dramatic in Lincoln. The students invited Jane Fonda, a notorious critic of the Vietnam War and a political activist, to the Lincoln campus in October 1977, paying for her visit with money collected from mandatory fees and allotted through established committees. The regents and some conservative Nebraskans objected, claiming that liberal speakers were favored at the University. They ignored the fact that William Buckley, a leading conservative editor, had recently been there. In January 1978 Regents Kermit Wagner and Robert Koefoot announced that they disapproved of using mandatory student fees for speakers because students should not be asked to pay for what many did not endorse, and in April, while asserting that freedom of expression was an "indispensable tenet of the academic community," the Board of Regents established some "guidelines" for speakers. This policy met with considerable resistance in Omaha as well as in Lincoln and students protested on both campuses.[7] The *Daily Nebraskan* reported on 23 April 1981 that Regent Robert Simmons had responded to a campus referendum on student fees by saying, "I don't think the Regents pay much attention to what the students vote on."

The students disagreed with the regents on another matter as well. Thanks to the continuing success of football, the demand for seating exceeded the capacity of Memorial Stadium, and several of the regents thought the stadium might be expanded by 6,000 seats at a cost of $6 million, to be paid for by ticket sales. The students, seeing themselves as underwriting the bonds, objected to such an expenditure when academic programs were underfunded. The exchange was sometimes acrimonious.

The board itself was disunited. The editors of the campus newspaper reported on 3 November 1976 that between January 1971 and September 1976, Regent Wagner had missed thirteen meetings and departed early from another seven, more than all the other regents combined. Regent Simmons frequently voted against the rest of the board and in September 1978 announced that he was discontent with the administration's slow and incomplete response to his requests for information. He proposed that the regents set up their own clerical staff and asked the legislature to fund it (they refused). When the University requested a 15 percent raise in 1980, he appeared before the appropriations committee to say that Governor Thone's original proposal of 8.57 percent was sufficient. The board seemed a collection of individuals, not a unified governing board.

In April 1979 Regent Prokop, the persistent maverick, claimed that University officials were attempting to "cover up" facts about the Eppley Cancer Center, veterinary testing costs, faculty consultantships, fees to an Omaha law firm, and the University Foundation. Regents Koefoot and Schwartzkopf vigorously denied Prokop's accusations, but four senators in the legislature asked for an investigation. At this meeting of the regents Kermit Hansen was reported in the *Daily Nebraskan* of April 23 as saying in exasperation to Prokop, "I'm embarrassed to sit on the same board with you," and observed that Prokop alone had never been elected to its chair. Nobody could remember such open hostility within the Board of Regents.

❧ The Roskens Administration

In these years the faculty was increasingly restless. In March 1977 Regent Simmons reported that he had received a petition signed by 331 faculty members recommending that any necessary budget cuts be made in central administration. By 1978 the College of Engineering complained publicly that it was seriously underfunded. Their spokesmen observed that their enrollment had risen more than 30 percent while their budget had hardly kept ahead of inflation. Over the years the faculty of the College of Engineering had been the most cooperative, least contentious of college faculties, but by the winter of 1978–79 a number of them were in open rebellion against their dean and felt stymied when they took their case beyond him. They and others were indignant that the 1979 budget called for an increase in staff for the College of Agriculture when Engineering, Business Administration, Architecture, and other colleges needed teachers to meet growing enrollments. In an interoffice memo of 18 June 1979, Vice Chancellor Ned Hedges wrote: "A recent visitor to our campus, after touring our instructional and research laboratories in engineering and observing our equipment, remarked: 'You people don't teach engineering – you teach the history of engineering.' "[8]

By 1979 the faculty saw the University in "the worst financial crisis of its recent history." According to their calculations, money available for operation of the University in Lincoln had declined by 22 percent over the previous ten years even as student enrollment increased by 5 percent and research activity supported by outside grants had increased by more than 100 percent.[9] In real terms faculty salaries had decreased by some 12 percent. Many legislators were displeased when they discovered in May that a chiller for the east campus had been ordered before money for it had been voted. According to George Round in conversation with Roskens, the legislature did not trust the University because the University was perceived as disorganized and its administration not entirely candid. Round observed, "I guess after having done legislative work at the University for twenty-five years myself, I was surprised that that mood developed."[10]

If the legislature did not trust the administration, neither did the faculty. In November 1979, 162 members of the College of Arts and Sciences in Lincoln petitioned the Board of Regents to dissolve the central administration. In a general college meeting, a self-appointed committee observed that between 1970 and 1979 the Lincoln campus budget had grown 125 percent while the Omaha campus budget had increased 225 percent, the Medical Center budget 314 percent, and the central administration budget 835 percent. On November 30 the Faculty Senate, considering a related motion, unanimously asked the board to "critically examine" the central administration. A similar petition was drawn up in Teachers College.[11] Privately,

administrators on all campuses thought the systems office redundant. The Lincoln faculty began to consider unionizing. In October 1979 the Omaha campus, with 95 percent of the faculty participating, voted 216 to 176 to accept the local chapter of the AAUP as their bargaining agent. The Lincoln campus, having rejected unionizing in 1976, now reopened discussions, but the issue was dropped by fall 1980, in part because the faculty wanted to see how bargaining worked for Omaha.

In the summer of 1980 Chancellor Roy Young resigned to become head of the Boyce Thompson Institute for Plant Research in Ithaca, New York. Hired by Varner in 1976, he served from 1977 until 1980 under Roskens. A tall, bald man, he had a rather diffident manner and a soft voice. Young strove to be evenhanded in his judgments. After deliberation, he had allowed the College of Dentistry to be assigned administratively to the Medical Center in Omaha, thinking this to be to their financial advantage though it might at first seem to diminish his own turf. Charged, when he was appointed, with encouraging research and garnering outside funding, he had succeeded admirably. In 1980 a record $30 million in grants, contracts, and gifts was awarded to the University, some $8 million more than in the previous year and $11 million more than the year before that. About half these funds went to support research. By his third year in office he found that external grants were up by more than 100 percent and rising. Early in his administration a system of Faculty Development Fellowships was set up, which, like sabbaticals, allowed qualified professors to go on leave for a semester or a year at half pay. These were awarded competitively across the University. The plans for them had long been in the works.

Young was also concerned with the quality of undergraduate education. In 1978 he affiliated the University with the National Merit Scholarship Corporation in an effort to provide opportunities for a larger number of Merit Scholars to attend this University. The basic Merit Scholarship was $500, but he saw this sum as only a start: "We thought it would be nice to get a few academic scholarships equal to the full ride in football," he commented unironically.[12] "Roy Young was not a squeaky wheel," the

Lincoln Star said on 18 July 1980 when he resigned. "He has simply been a dedicated, competent and eminently decent human being. That this might not have been enough is no poor reflection upon him, but rather a measure of the misplaced values and priorities that have infected so many people and so much of our political system at this time." In August the regents named Robert Rutford as interim chancellor. Young had brought Rutford to Lincoln to be vice chancellor for research and graduate studies; and as director of the Ross Ice Shelf Project, a geological undertaking set up here by Chancellor Zumberge, he could be assumed to know how the University administration operated.

ᕤ Chancellor Martin Massengale

The regents promptly appointed a town-gown search committee to find Young's successor. The first half-dozen names it submitted to Roskens and the regents in February 1981 did not seem satisfactory, and in March four more were added. When none of these were acceptable, in late March the board turned to Martin Massengale, vice chancellor of the Institute for Agriculture and Natural Resources. He had not been on the search committee lists and had not received the president's endorsement, but Roskens had no stronger candidate and thus had to accept him. Nebraska farm leaders were confident that Massengale could unify the downtown campus and the agricultural interests.

Martin Massengale, brought up in rural Kentucky, had taken his first degree in 1952 at age eighteen at Western Kentucky State Teachers College (now University). There he found that he enjoyed research and so moved on to the University of Wisconsin, where at age twenty-four he took his Ph.D. in agronomy. He was a practical man, his interests lying in crop management. After two years in the military, he went to the University of Arizona at Tucson, where by 1976 he had become a dean of agriculture and director of the agricultural experiment station. In 1978 he came to Nebraska. He defended agricultural interests tenaciously. Like Dean Frolik before him, he encouraged research related to local problems.

Massengale's appointment took the academic commu-

nity by surprise, and it was received with a degree of apprehension. Bud Cuca, the student regent from the Lincoln campuses said, carefully, "Dr. Massengale is well-qualified and a good administrator. I hope he has a good perception of what a broad liberal arts education is. The differences between it and agriculture are considerable."[13] In May, Massengale told George Round, "I don't see any reason why someone with an agricultural background can't become broad-scoped."[14] The new chancellor was a man of goodwill. What concerned many on all campuses was the difference between administrative procedures customary within universities and those practiced in agricultural experiment stations. In many experiment stations, departments had "heads," not "chairs," and administrators seemed to have an autonomy that department officers in other colleges did not seek. The staff were sometimes regarded as research specialists rather than as professors, and many members of the station staff who held appointments with the USDA taught very few courses if any at all. Locally the vice chancellor of the IANR was advised on matters of tenure and promotion by an anonymous committee, and some persons both within the college and outside it thought the system did not square with general University rules and even smacked of Star Chamber procedures.[15]

Martin Massengale liked to keep decisions, even minor ones, in his own hands. He did not have a philosophical turn of mind. "Let's get down to nuts and bolts," he was fond of saying. "You don't work *with* Martin Massengale," one of his vice chancellors said more than once, "you work *for* him." Roskens said his first administrative direction to Massengale had been: "Don't be a workaholic." The new chancellor acknowledged that he often worked from seven A.M. until midnight.[16]

ᕤ The Massengale Administration

Massengale, who was installed on Sunday afternoon, 21 September 1981, was surrounded by interim vice chancellors. Howard Ottoson, who had acted as vice chancellor of IANR before Massengale came in 1976, returned as vice chancellor until Roy Arnold was named in February 1982.

When Ned Hedges resigned his post as vice chancellor for academic affairs to return to teaching, John Strong, recently dean of the College of Law, was pressed into service, but he went on leave from August 1982 until January 1983. R. Neale Copple, dean of the newly created College of Journalism, filled in for him. John W. Goebel, chairman of the Department of Accounting, became interim vice chancellor for business and finance. He was made permanent some months later. The new chancellor liked to see how nominees operated before establishing them. In January 1982 he replaced Max Larsen in the College of Arts and Sciences with Gerry Meisels, the excellent chair of the Department of Chemistry, as interim dean. Meisels stayed on an interim basis beyond August 1982 until a second search committee appointed by Massengale put him on their list of acceptable candidates. In February 1982 Robert Egbert resigned after eleven years as dean of Teachers College, but James O'Hanlon was not named to replace him until August 1983. Stanley Liberty, dean of engineering only since 1981, and Gary Schwendiman, dean of business administration since 1977, were vigorous young men who found support for their colleges within the business community, sometimes with, sometimes without the help of the University of Nebraska Foundation and the front office. The lines of authority seemed tenuous across the University.

Massengale shaped his administration slowly. Only in 1983 did he bring John Yost into his office as "associate to the Chancellor." Yost, who had graduate degrees in theology as well as Renaissance history, became his closest adviser and all-around pinch hitter. When John Strong resigned his vice chancellorship in 1983 after serving only briefly, Yost filled in until Robert Furgason, a chemical engineer from Idaho, could take office in 1984; and when Henry Holtzclaw returned to the Department of Chemistry in 1985, Yost became vice chancellor for research and dean of graduate studies.

More articulate than Massengale in his first years, Yost often helped him with major addresses and initiated several of his major programs. Yost was, in fact, the perfect associate, for he seemed to have a gift for anonymity. At least two troublesome deans were relieved of their posts while Yost was acting vice chancellor for academic affairs, but nobody seemed to notice. Under his impetus a University-wide honors program was set up in 1985 without faculty complaint that money was siphoned from needy areas to pay for it. Studies of curriculum were now undertaken. A task force on undergraduate education, chaired by Yost when he was in the College of Arts and Sciences, was expanded in 1985 into a chancellor's commission on general, liberal education, with Dean Meisels as its chair. After hundreds of hours of hearings and discussions by faculty and students from all the campuses, this twelve-member commission issued an elaborate "Program for the Advancement of General Education" in April 1987. But shortly thereafter both Meisels and Yost left the campus and the report languished, the chancellor's attentions being drawn elsewhere.

In February 1984 Woody Varner, then president of the University of Nebraska Foundation, announced that the University had received $10 million, the largest single donation in its history, for a center for performing arts. For several years he had been talking to Christina Hixson of the Lied Trust Foundation. Ernst F. Lied, a 1927 graduate of the University, had invested in Las Vegas, Nevada, real estate, and after his death in 1980 his large foundation was administered by Hixson. The center was to have an auditorium suitable for operas and symphonies, a modular theater, spaces for dance and chorus, and generous lobbies and offices. The Lied gift was contingent upon a matching $10 million, which Varner and the foundation proceeded to raise; $7 million came from state funds and $3 million more from private donations. Varner and the foundation collected an additional $5 million for maintenance, and in 1990 the Lied Trust Foundation provided $3 million more for programming. The center opened in 1990. Massengale accepted the ultimate administrative responsibility for the Lied Center.

During these years Massengale paid attention to the landscaping of the Lincoln campuses. Because the east campus had more green space than the city campus, it had always been more attractive, but even it had not been consistently maintained over the years. When in 1968 the firm of Caudill, Rowlett and Scott of Houston, Texas, was hired by the Board of Regents to provide a comprehensive plan for buildings and grounds, they suggested replacing at least eight buildings on the city campus. They wanted to extend the campus deep into surrounding residential areas. Their recommendations for the east campus were more modest. Not much came of their plans except the closing of North Fourteenth Street to vehicles, but beautification became possible when Ron Wright and Ray Coffey, University business managers, separated the budget for grounds from the budget for buildings in 1970. For the first time, long-range plans for campus planting were possible. Wilbur (Bud) Dasenbrock, a native son who understood native flora and fauna, became director of landscape services, and Kim Todd, extremely competent and very resourceful, was hired as landscape architect, both in 1978. Together they made a remarkable team. They were supported morally, and financially when necessary, by Chancellor Massengale, an agronomist. Never before in their history had the campuses had such care or looked so splendid.

❧ Football and Other Sports

When Tom Osborne succeeded Bob Devaney as head football coach in 1973, Devaney became athletic director, a post he held until January 1993, when he was seventy-six, long beyond standard retirement age. Osborne maintained a record nearly as splendid as his predecessor's. By 1983 he had one hundred victories, like Devaney; and by 1993 the football team had appeared in twenty-four consecutive bowl games, the longest string of consecutive bowl appearances in the nation. Osborne became the winningest coach in the country even though his teams regularly lost in their postseason bowl games.

Nebraska football got a six-page spread in the 5 December 1983 issue of *Time*. Tom Callahan wrote that in Nebraska "only this football team gathers up an entire state of people and brings them to one emotional place." *Time* quoted Susan Rosowski, a young professor of English: there is a strange duality in Nebraskans' attitude, she said. "We all partake in this tribal ritual of football,

this coming together in the community, this need for a common identity. But we are a bit self-conscious about it, and [we are] saved, I suspect, by a sense of humor. I think one of the reasons Nebraskans feel as secure as we do is Tom Osborne. He's so civilized."[17]

Osborne was a pious, churchgoing Nebraskan, to whom laughter did not come easily. His no-funny-business character did not appeal to national sportswriters. He never misbehaved in off-hours, and nobody could imagine him a womanizer. In 1991 when it was public knowledge that his pay exceeded his chancellor's, he was quoted as saying, "There are a lot of people who perform more valuable functions than I do, who work just as hard and get paid one-fourth or one-tenth the amount of what I do. In that sense, I'm overpaid." But, he went on, "when compared to other successful college football coaches," he was "at the low end of the scale."[18]

Tom Osborne was not the only successful Nebraska coach. Francis Allen was repeatedly named coach of the year by the U.S. Gymnastics Federation. Terry Pettit, who coached volleyball, had come to Nebraska from North Carolina, where he had also taught creative writing. He was, in fact, a published poet. His teams were conference champions year after year. Women's sports in Nebraska dominated their conference for a decade. Cal Bentz, the swim coach, took his teams to successive Big Eight championships. Other sports, like basketball, had their ups and downs, but the Nebraska athletic program in these years held itself to standards of highest excellence.

For many years students had complained about the recreation facilities available to them on the Lincoln campuses. By 1981 Nebraska had the largest number of intramural activities in the Big Eight Conference but the smallest support staff and next to the smallest indoor facilities. In January 1987 Robert Furgason, vice chancellor for academic affairs, announced a plan for a recreational center that did not require tax funds. To $10 million raised by a surcharge on football tickets could be added $3 million from private donations and another $3 million from student fees. Massengale was proud of this complicated tax-free complex at Fourteenth and Vine streets.

✌ A College of Veterinary Medicine

One of the most disruptive issues of Massengale's administration involved a proposed college of veterinary medicine. From earliest days the University had been concerned
to provide veterinarians to the state, and in 1955 the legislature had agreed to pay the tuition for a certain number of
Nebraska students in certain out-of-state veterinary colleges. By 1979 nearly one hundred Nebraska students
were enrolled in veterinary medicine at Kansas State, Iowa
State, Missouri, and Minnesota. This contract exchange
program was regarded by successive chancellors and regents as economical and efficient.

But in 1972 the Old West Regional Commission, a
group set up by the Nixon administration to encourage cooperation among adjacent states, began reconsidering the
veterinary needs of the region. A commission consisting
of the governors of Wyoming, Montana, North Dakota,
South Dakota, and Nebraska hired a former dean of the
Ohio State College of Veterinary Medicine, Dr. C. R.
Cole, to study it. He proposed in 1974 that a regional college of veterinary medicine be established in Lincoln.
He assumed that the federal government would provide
half the cost of initial construction and the other half
would be shared among the regional participants. Ongoing maintenance costs would also be divided proportionately. The startup cost was estimated at $30 million to
$50 million.

Though the proposal was received with skepticism by
the veterinarians of the region, it was endorsed by the livestock industry. The Board of Regents treated it gingerly
and Chancellor Zumberge said in 1975, "I haven't got any
evidence that there is a shortage of veterinarians in Nebraska."[19] But in 1979 after much deliberation the legislature passed a law allowing the board to establish a college
of veterinary medicine when two or more states joined Nebraska and when the federal government funded at least
50 percent of its initial capital construction.

There was no public endorsement of this proposal. In
1978 a major study conducted by the Arthur D. Little
Company for the American Veterinary Medical Association predicted that by 1990 the country might have an over-
supply of veterinarians.[20] The faculty and the newspaper
editors were aware of the enormous expense of medical education. They observed that in a state where funds were always limited, a new medical college might well bleed the
University white.[21] Indeed, the costs of the Medical Center
in Omaha were already a concern. Between 1979 and 1983
state appropriations for the University as a whole increased by 33 percent, but those for the Medical Center increased by 41 percent. The University of Nebraska in
Omaha got a 34 percent increase, but, significantly, the Institute of Agriculture and Natural Resources increased its
budget by 43 percent even as its enrollment declined by 25
percent. At this time state support for University of Nebraska at Lincoln (excluding the IANR) dropped a startling
23 percent even though its enrollment was steady. Agriculture and medicine were already the most expensive
branches of the University.[22]

Increasingly the proposed college of veterinary medicine became a local aspiration. In 1981 the Reagan administration withdrew its support of the Old West Regional
Commission and by 1983 not one of the states of the Old
West Region had committed itself to supporting the college. But in the spring 1985, over vigorous objections expressed in newspapers and by faculty groups, the Board of
Regents, assuming federal support, voted to create a $15
million to $30 million regional veterinary college. When
Regent Schwartzkopf failed to be reelected to the board
that year, many persons thought it was due to his support
of the veterinary college; and Regent Don Fricke of Lincoln, his replacement, immediately joined Regent Margaret Robinson of Norfolk in opposing it. Regent Moylan
of Omaha defended the college. "You will always find selfish groups that will be thinking just about themselves," he
was quoted as saying. In an editorial Chris Welsch, the
unusually able editor of the campus paper wrote: "The
need for new veterinarians does not outweigh the need of
the university to preserve its core programs at *average*
level."[23]

Money was tight. Indeed, in April 1985 Chancellor
Charles Andrews of the Medical Center proposed that the
School of Nursing be discontinued. In June the faculty of
the Medical Center agreed to take lesser salary raises if by

so doing the College of Pharmacy and the nursing programs could be saved; and in July irate nurses and their friends rather indecorously picketed the Board of Regents with placards and public displays. Yet in June, over the objections of the venerable Senator Jerome Warner, the legislature authorized a college of veterinary medicine contingent upon federal help. The mercurial Governor Robert Kerrey, himself a graduate of the threatened College of Pharmacy, signed the bill, but in September he also said that the University must "reduce its scope."[24] In October he even suggested, perhaps ironically, that in order to preserve research and undergraduate programs, the professional colleges of law and medicine be curtailed or even eliminated. In November, Senator Rex Haberman of Imperial proposed that to support the vet college the legislature cut $5 million from the Lied Center budget.

By the end of 1985 it was clear that federal support for the veterinary college was not available. The project was doomed. Many on the faculty and in the state breathed a sigh of relief. In February 1987, Vice Chancellor Roy Arnold of the IANR told the Faculty Senate, "The Regional College of Veterinary Medicine does not exist and will not exist."[25] But while the controversy was going on, the University and the livestock industry had obtained several million dollars from Washington for research facilities both in Lincoln and at the Roman L. Hruska Meat Animal Research Center at Clay Center. In addition, in 1988 an $18 million animal science complex on the east campus was opened, paid for largely with state funds.

❧ The University and Industrial Research

The proposed college of veterinary medicine was only part of a general movement to make institutions of higher learning respond more immediately to the economic needs of society. Supported by public funds, public and private universities were everywhere being asked to be accountable. By accountable was often meant immediately profitable. In 1984 a group spearheaded by E. N. (Jack) Thompson, president of the Cooper Foundation, made a study of higher education in Nebraska. This Citizens Commission for the Study of Higher Education in Nebraska was

charged by Governor Kerrey to assess "(1) Nebraskans' future needs for higher education, and (2) the future role of higher education in the state's economy." Their report, "Toward the 21st Century," was presented to the governor in December 1984.

Of all its recommendations, those dealing with governance received the most attention in the media. The report suggested that for efficiency the four state colleges and the University be placed under a single appointed board. The commission's central focus, however, was economics. Though supporting "strong emphasis on a high quality liberal arts education," the report was much more concerned with "research which contributes to the development and diversification of Nebraska's economy in this era of technological change" than with the state's spiritual and cultural life.[26] Its great weight was "practical." The value of scholarship, of education for its own sake, of learning as a terminal value, was passed over. Perhaps the governor's charge demanded such a response. The report recommended that "the Legislature should authorize the creation of a Research and Development Corporation" for the "promotion of an awareness of the importance of research and its relationship to the state's economic development."[27] A university could make a dollars-and-cents contribution to economic growth, the commission assumed, for it could help local industry and lure outstate firms with research expertise.

In 1987 Governor Kay Orr, Kerrey's successor, followed up on this recommendation and proposed a Nebraska Research Initiative (NRI) to improve the quality of the University's research program. The need for improvement was dramatized when U.S. West, the communications corporation, decided to build its $50 million research laboratory in Colorado rather than Nebraska because, they said, the company relied heavily on a research capability not obviously present in Nebraska. Furthermore, in 1987 a report prepared by SRI International of Menlo Park, California, asserted that higher education should be a critical agent for change, but that the University had become stagnant because of financial setbacks.[28] The next year the legislature not only approved the funding of the NRI but promised to appropriate an extra $4 million to the University each year for the next five years for research.

On more than one occasion Chancellor Massengale spelled out how the University contributed to the economic well-being of Nebraska. In 1986, he observed, UNL had established both a Center for Productivity and Entrepreneurship and an International Center for Franchise Studies in the College of Business Administration. The College of Engineering formed a Technical Assistance Center to help businesses. In a Center for Engine Technology, scientists blended gasoline and ethanol made from fermented corn and agricultural wastes to produce a fuel that burned cleaner than gasoline alone. In the IANR the Food Processing Center developed new products and processes for Nebraska crops. In 1988 the Board of Regents approved a Center for International Policy and Research in Agribusiness, Economics and Law; the Nebraska Agricultural Product and Market Development Center; an Agricultural Marketing Center; and, at Mead, an Agricultural Research and Development Center. In the fall of 1988 the city of Lincoln and the University cooperated to establish a research and development park in the Highlands subdivision northwest of Lincoln. "The park will develop a kind of brokerage between the University and industries," John Yost told the newspapers.[29] None of these centers involved curricular changes or touched on fundamental education. They were planned as services to industry and as adjuncts to business.

The climax of this research innovation was the George W. Beadle Center for Genetics and Biomaterials Research. Beadle, a native Nebraskan and graduate of the University, had earned a Nobel Prize for his studies of the relationship of genes and proteins. Massengale and his associates obtained almost $22 million dollars from the federal government, with the persistent aid of the Nebraska delegation, Senators Exon and Kerrey and Representative Virginia Smith; $6.5 million more came from Governor Orr's NRI; and $2 million came from private donors, through the University of Nebraska Foundation. "Nebraska has a chance to be a big league player in the field of biotechnology, an area of great promise," the *Lincoln Star* announced editorially on 5 March 1991. In this Beadle Center scientists and engineers were to manipulate genes, redesign plants, change fat contents of animals, and transfer their discoveries into products.

After World War II the University, urged on by the availability of federal money, aspired to turn itself into a research institution pressing at the frontiers of knowledge. Now the University was taking a new direction. Again supported by federal money, it aspired to become a research agency of immediate commercial utility. It was to be a publicly supported laboratory for private enterprise. Not everybody in the University saw how novel this direction was. Perhaps researchers and administrators were so concerned with funding that they did not see the forest for the trees, but this new activity fundamentally modified the nature of higher education. The Beadle Center, like the other centers, redirected the relation of the University to society. The next generation would see just what that turned out to be.

❧ Salary Scales and Peer Institutions

The expanded service of the University could not be effective without a competent staff, but by the mid-1980s the salary scale at the University in Lincoln had become seriously out of phase with those at peer universities. Whereas the University had been at the midpoint on regional scales in the 1970s, it had now sunk to the bottom. Salaries of the unionized faculty at UNO fared somewhat better, but at a considerable cost, as it turned out. When extended discussion with the regents about salaries failed, the UNO bargaining agent, the AAUP, went to the Commission on Industrial Relations in the spring of 1983 for adjudication and received a 6.6 percent pay increase. Since the commission and the Board of Regents had no power to tax, twenty-one faculty positions and sixty-three classes were cut to raise the funds for salary increases. This cannibalism was unattractive in itself, but, even more important, the commission's decision put UNO and UNL in different peer groups. Omaha was lumped with Wichita State University and South Dakota State University, institutions of limited mission. Lincoln was grouped with the University of Missouri, the University of Minnesota, and other comprehensive land-grant universities. By legal decision, the Nebraska universities were now defined as two institutions and were to be measured by different standards with differing pay scales. The short-term advantage of the commission's decision may have been a long-term disadvantage to Omaha's aspirations.

Across the campuses, faculty concerns grew. They were exacerbated first by Regent Koefoot's suggestion in June 1985 that all salaries be frozen, and then by Governor Kerrey's support of Chancellor Andrews's proposal that the Lincoln nursing program and the College of Pharmacy be eliminated. In October 1985, in a special session of the legislature, Governor Kerrey proposed a 3 percent midterm cut in the University budget which President Roskens said would be so disastrous as to change the historical mission of the University. After debate, the legislature ordered a 2 percent cut. The faculty, alarmed, thought the University was in grave danger of being downgraded, its role and mission permanently diminished, and its place in the hierarchy of American universities lowered.

But the University was not without its friends. In August 1985 Senator David Landis proposed that the University be voted an extra $10 million to return salaries to a competitive level, and though his suggestion was rejected, his action identified a danger. In the fall of 1985 the *Daily Nebraskan* conducted a statewide opinion poll under the supervision of professionals. It showed that 56 percent of those polled opposed the 2 percent budget cut and only 21 percent supported it. Moreover, 64 percent of the people polled would consent to a tax increase if they knew the money was earmarked to improve the quality of University education; only 28 percent opposed it. "It appears that NU has the support of the state, but not its representatives," Vicki Ruhga, editor of the campus newspaper, concluded on 16 December 1985.

The situation the following spring was little better. In April 1986 Kerrey line-vetoed $3.1 million of the University budget, and though the legislature overruled his veto by thirty-seven to nine, Senator Jerome Warner observed sadly that the override merely deferred the further deterioration of the University; it did not halt it. That fall Kerrey called the legislature into special session for the fourth

time in a single year and asked for a fourth midyear cut in six years, trimming $1.6 million from what was at best a slender budget. Again pharmacy and nursing were singled out for elimination. "Nebraska's colleges and universities must narrow their scope," the governor said. "We've got too many things on the plate."[30]

In response, Roskens in January 1987 proposed five programs for consolidation, reduction, or elimination; and in February Regent Koefoot suggested dropping both pharmacy and dentistry from the University. Dentistry had never before been suggested as expendable, and Regent Payne responded, one assumes ironically, "Why not law?" In March, Regent Moylan moved that the nursing program in Lincoln be discontinued, and his motion failed only on a split vote. In April the appropriations committee of the legislature supported only a meager 2 percent increase for higher education. Tuition and fees in state colleges and universities had gone up 42 percent in five years. The University had come to a crisis. Was it to be a comprehensive research institution supporting professional colleges of national standing, or was it to be a provincial institution with minimal research aspirations and professional schools geared to local needs narrowly defined?

✍ Faculty Action on the University Budget

Senator David Landis again challenged the defeatists. Boldly he offered an amendment to the appropriations bill asking for $9.9 million for University salaries, and the newly elected Governor Kay Orr — Kerrey had declined to run for a second term — boldly proposed her Nebraska Research Initiative, a package for expanding research at the University. State revenues, happily, were rising.

For the first time since 1945 the faculty began to take dramatic, independent action on the University budget. In 1945 when Chancellor Boucher had proposed a budget that was so small as to limit the scope of the institution permanently, a group of faculty assembled by the AAUP had prepared an alternate budget, which the legislature approved. In April 1987 the AAUP again took action. Dermot Coyne, George Holmes Professor of Horticulture on the east campus and chapter president, and Susan Welch, the young Carl A. Happold Professor of Political Science and chair of her department, headed a group to study the budget. President Roskens, after talking to Governor Orr, was proposing a 3 percent raise, which Coyne, Welch, and their AAUP associates found entirely unsatisfactory.

In the summer of 1987, William J. Lewis (always known as Jim), new president of the Faculty Senate and associate professor of mathematics, seeing that the AAUP had turned off some agriculturists, engineers, and others by its earlier agitation for unionizing, organized a Friends of the Faculty Senate to represent the faculty case to the legislature. This group cooperated with the AAUP group, and in October he gave a detailed account of the salary situation to the senate. To reach parity with peer institutions within three years, he figured by simple arithmetic, a raise of 15 to 20 percent would be required in the first year, 15 percent in the second, and 13 percent in the third year. "Each year we delay progress, our problem becomes more severe and we increase the danger that the quality of UNL will suffer irreparable damage," he told the faculty.[31]

Lewis took his mathematical model to Chancellor Massengale and then to President Roskens and the Board of Regents. When he presented his figures, Hans Brisch, Roskens's executive assistant who was shortly to become executive assistant to Orr, observed, "You have announced your own salary plan." Though Lewis had regarded his model as a statement of need rather than a plan of action, he accepted Brisch's challenge. The newspaper reporters told him, "You are naive to think you can get this much," and Lewis replied, "Why not try?"[32] Lewis later observed that he was astonished at how wide the support for the University turned out to be once it was sought. In November the ASUN under its alert president, Andy Pollock of Ogallala, who was also a student regent, supported the salary increases. The ASUN voted to increase tuition when the legislature matched their money three to one. John Klosterman of the Ag 40, a coalition of agribusiness groups and ag college alumni, offered help. Within six weeks the Friends of the Faculty Senate and the AAUP collected some $7,000 with which to hire Jack Moors as their lobbyist, and they conferred with legislators individually. (The faculty of UNO had been hiring its own lobbyist since

1984.) They did not limit themselves to members of the appropriations committee but set out "to humanize" the University, they said, by sending individual faculty members to present their cases to individual legislators. Teachers talked to senators about classes and courses.

In December the regents adopted a growth plan similar to Lewis's, and in January Governor Orr proposed a salary increase which Lewis said came close to the regents' (and his) proposals. Orr acknowledged that her research initiative could not operate without able faculty committed to long-term service. In March the appropriations committee approved $9.3 million for salaries, and later in March the bill passed, astonishingly, forty to zero. Governor Orr's research initiative of $4 million also passed. It was the largest appropriation for the University in twelve years, Roskens observed, and was made possible by increased tax returns from a growing prosperity in the state. Students, especially Andy Pollock, had been helpful, and faculty and University lobbyists had worked together closely to support the efforts of Senators Landis and Warner, to whom the Faculty Senate later presented plaques of appreciation. Though no single element could claim total credit for the improved budget of 1988, the faculty had not been so active in its own behalf for forty years. By the summer of 1988 the future of the University looked more promising that it had for at least a decade.

President Roskens's Departure

From the beginning of his tenure as president of the University in 1977, Roskens's relationship with the Board of Regents had been uneasy. The board had appointed Massengale as chancellor of the Lincoln campus without Roskens's endorsement in 1981, and in 1983 they gave him six weeks' "administrative leave" to renew his "vigor and spirits for the tasks which lie ahead."[33] In 1984 he frequently said in public that unlimited tenure for any president was undesirable and suggested rather undiplomatically that seven to ten years was long enough at a major institution. At least three of his regents publicly agreed with him. Roskens's interests seemed to stray from the University and he took repeated trips abroad, most frequently to China. In 1986 the board hired Peat, Marwick, and Mitchell, an accounting firm with limited experience in academic matters, to study the efficiency of the University administration. Their report, returned in April 1986, was disappointingly unhelpful, though it cost $75,000, a sum supplied by the University Foundation.

In his dealings with the regents, Roskens could usually count on the support of four, but in the elections of 1988 the nature of the board changed. Andy Pollock, the student regent, wrote in the campus newspaper 10 November 1988, "The new board will be composed of regents who have new ideas and different opinions." They would check the independent authority of the central administration.

In 1987 the regents had renewed Roskens's contract for one year, surprisingly because until that time he had served without a contract. A year later the contract was renewed for two more years, and again with a salary increase. But things were different this fall of 1988. The pharmacy building on the medical campus was found to be dangerous because of faulty construction. Completed in 1976, it had begun to disintegrate by 1977. Independent architects reported that necessary repairs would cost more than $2 million. Apparently the building had been put up without supervision and accepted without critical examination of specifications. Embarrassed, the regents had to get a supplemental appropriation of $2.7 million from the legislature in April 1989 to repair it. Roskens himself had had no part in its construction, but this expensive error darkened the reputation of his administration. Also in the fall of 1988 Regent Nancy Hoch discovered that a computer costing nearly $4 million had been delivered to Nebraska Hall before the board, or the legislature, had agreed to pay for it. It had been ordered from IBM without competitive bidding. Regent Blank said, "We need a chance to study the options before purchasing a computer system."[34] Again Roskens had had no direct part in the matter, but he seemed out of touch with his own office.

One of the major issues of the spring of 1989 concerned the relation of the Kearney State College to the University. Because Kearney had grown precipitously over the years, its ambitious president, William Nester; its faculty; and regional supporters thought it ready to be named a university. The question confronting them, and the state that supported the college, was not only whether but how it was to be accomplished. Rather than set up a second university system that included all four of what had originally been state normal schools, Senator Jerome Warner thought Kearney should be added to the existing University system and brought under the authority of its board of regents. Kearney State College would then become the University of Nebraska at Kearney, analogous to the University of Nebraska at Omaha. Roskens and Warner discussed this repeatedly.

The Board of Regents could not decide what was best for the state or the University. Would the addition of Kearney to their responsibility strengthen or weaken the existing institutions, politically and academically? The faculty in Lincoln opposed it; the faculty in Omaha just as widely favored it. Public opinion polls showed that Nebraskans were evenly divided on the matter. In February 1989 the regents officially asked the legislature for a delay until a study could be made by professional consultants, but already a bill joining Kearney to the University had been introduced. The board was at least a year late and appeared to legislators and others as obstructionists, fearful of change. The regents felt that Roskens had not prepared them or the University for what he considered inevitable.

When the bill making Kearney a part of the University was discussed in the capitol, Nancy Hoch, president of the Board of Regents, appeared as witness and questioned the wisdom of the linking. Speaking for the board, she again requested a delay; but Roskens spoke informally of immediate unification. The University lobbyists were directed to change their position almost daily. "Who's the Boss?" the *Daily Nebraskan* asked on 18 April 1989 – the board or Roskens? On two separate occasions Hoch found herself publicly embarrassed by Roskens's failure to support her and the Board of Regents.

Finally the legislature voted to link Kearney to the University system. But the matter was not settled. Robert Spire, the state's respected attorney general, declared that such a linking was possible only through constitutional amendment and that the legislative bill was therefore unconstitutional. Soon the state supreme court, on a very tight vote, permitted the union; and Kearney State College in July 1991 became the University of Nebraska at Kearney, a branch of the University of Nebraska under the supervision of the Board of Regents.

In acting independently of their direction, Roskens had lost the confidence of his board. Meeting in July 1989, they adjourned preemptorily before reconfirming his appointment. Rumors were rampant, and when the board met in special session later that month, Roskens was dismissed with a single regent dissenting. The board declined to explain their reasons for what the newspapers quickly called his firing. The newspapers reported that they had been told by special counsel that "their criticism would subject the school to lawsuits."[35] The newspapers of the state disingenuously demanded that the "secret" causes for the dismissal be spelled out. In point of fact there was no secret. Brian Svoboda, a bright undergraduate columnist on the *Daily Nebraskan*, summarized it all on 7 September 1989 without benefit of inside knowledge:

In November 1988, Robert Allen and Rosemary Skrupa defeated Regents Robert Koefoot and James Moylan, two long-time supporters of Roskens and central administration. These elections, along with the 1986 defeat of Robert Simmons by Don Blank, decimated the solid pro-Roskens majority on the board. . . . [T]he newer regents sought to reassert the role of the board as the maker of policy.

Svoboda went on. In 1988

the board narrowly rejected a central administration plan to buy a $5 million IBM computer. . . . Regents were put off by specific instances in which Roskens was seen as making policy, rather than implementing directives of the board.

According to the Omaha World-Herald, *Blank felt that Roskens lied to him when the Nebraska Legislature voted to close the technical agriculture campus at Curtis. . . . And Regent Nancy Hoch was said to have been left twisting in the wind by Roskens while testifying before the Legislature's Appropriations Committee on the Fall of 1988 computer decision.*

Moreover, Svoboda said,

Reports surfaced that Roskens did not faithfully implement the regents' position on the merger, working behind the scenes to promote Kearney State's inclusion.

Regent Payne, who alone had voted against the dismissal and was quoted in the *Kearney Hub* of 10 August 1989, and Regent Allen, who was quoted extensively in the *Lincoln Star* of 14 December 1990, pretty well substantiated Svoboda's explanations in their public statements. No mystery existed, but the regents may have been impolitic in not specifying the causes of their action. The newspapers had stirred up a controversy.

The terms of Roskens's dismissal were generous. In order to get the near-unanimous vote, the board named Roskens president emeritus and professor of higher education with tenure until his contract expired on 30 June 1991. He retained his salary of $112,000 and fringe benefits. Former regents Moylan and Koefoot protested the "firing" in public and, a bit indecorously, sponsored a party for Roskens in the president's official residence before he vacated it in January 1990. They led a political vendetta against Hoch, whom they had opposed publicly on other occasions. In November 1989 President George Bush nominated Roskens to head the Agency for International Development, a post he took the following spring.

15. To the University's 125th Year: 1990–1994

The departure of President Roskens marked the beginning of a new chapter in the life of the University. It was clear to the board and the people of the state that the University needed what Regent Don Blank called "shifts in procedure," and the nature of University governance was questioned. Not only did the generous financial terms of the Roskens dismissal cause controversy, but the disunity of the board was disturbing. Under the influence of Regent Nancy Hoch, the board asked Martin Massengale to serve as interim president as well as chancellor of the Lincoln campuses until a nationwide search could be made. John W. Goebel, vice chancellor for business and finance, became, first, associate chancellor and, in January 1990, interim chancellor in Lincoln.

The search for a new president did not go easily. A search committee, aided by the professional headhunters Heidrick and Struggles, Inc., of Chicago, was set up in November 1989; but since the legislature was reviewing the governance of all public postsecondary education, the first meeting of the search committee was not held until May 1990. The following November the committee brought a list of four candidates, none local, to the board. The regents interviewed Massengale in addition. Astonishingly, only when the four names were presented did the committee and the board discover that one of the four came from an institution which was under censure by the American Association of University Professors for violation of tenure regulations; the consultant firm had clearly not done its homework. When the off-campus candidates found out that an insider was being seriously considered for the presidency, first one and then the other withdrew their names. The editor of the *Daily Nebraskan* spoke for many, but perhaps a bit unfairly, when she wrote on 14 November 1990, "Fifteen months and $200,000 later, one candidate for university president drops out and another's administration is discovered to have been under censure. What exactly are the Presidential Search Committee doing all this time?" On 20 November the regents offered the presidency to Massengale on a five-to-three vote, and the next week he accepted a three-year contract to begin 1 January 1991. The cost of acquiring a new president was seen by the public as high and the procedures irregular. *Omaha World-Herald* polls in 1989 and 1990 showed wide public dissatisfaction with the way the regents handled the removal of Roskens and the hiring of Massengale. Massengale held his post insecurely.

In January 1991 two new members came on the board, Charles Wilson, M.D., of Lincoln, and Nancy O'Brien of Omaha. Both had extensive experience on other boards of higher education. Though the regents continued sometimes to conduct their business as a collection of individuals rather than as a corporate body, the board began reconsidering its administrative procedures; and in hiring Graham Spanier as chancellor in 1991, they acted as a unit. "There was and still is a strain on the Board," Regent Robert Allen told the *Lincoln Journal and Star* on 5 September 1992 with undiplomatic candor; but a start toward its resolution had been made.

The responsibility of the board was complicated in 1991 by the creation of the Coordinating Commission for Higher Education. An amendment to the state constitution had created this body to oversee all institutions of public higher education in the state, but its authority remained unclear. The considerable friction that the commission caused distressed its initial sponsors and confused the public. The Board of Regents felt its constitutional authority was challenged.

The board and the University faced increasingly difficult financial problems in the Nineties. Confronted with declining state revenues available for higher education and increasing resistance to taxation, the University was forced to consider the elimination of total programs if it were not to reduce everything to a common mediocrity. But when Stan Liberty, the dean of engineering who was serving as UNL's interim vice chancellor for academic affairs, proposed in 1991 that the Department of Speech Communication and the Department of Classics be discontinued, both the academic and the wider community protested. A less controversial place for the cuts would have to be found.

These financial matters raised questions about the fundamental nature of a public university. Everybody understood that land-grant universities exist to provide opportunity for all, but where was the money to come from? In 1991 the board raised tuition by 7 percent; and though tuition at Nebraska was the highest it had ever been, it was not out of line with that at comparable institutions of the region. The regents and the administration talked boldly of raising entrance requirements, both to support intellectual standards and to escape the costly attrition of unprepared students. New prerequisites were established, to begin in 1997. Questions of equity complicated budget troubles. With the addition of Kearney to the state university system, questions of equity among the campuses were again raised: Against what peer group should each campus be measured? Who was to decide, the Board of Regents or the Coordinating Commission or each campus for itself? On all the campuses there was talk of gender equity; women were acknowledged to be frequently underpaid.

If the first problem of the decade was governance and the second financial, the third was sociological. In the spring of 1991 Interim Chancellor John Goebel appointed a special assistant for minority affairs, and when Graham Spanier arrived in September, he promptly announced, "I have zero tolerance for racial and sexual harassment and discrimination." He very shortly appointed Eric Jolly, a Native American, as his special assistant for affirmative action. Eager to correct gender imbalance, he nominated

Joan R. Leitzel to be senior vice chancellor for academic affairs in 1992, and in 1993 he named Priscilla C. Grew to be vice chancellor for research, both eminently qualified on scholarly grounds. They were not the only women in positions of high authority. The Board of Regents itself now contained four women. As recommended by Massengale, Carol A. Aschenbrener became the new chancellor of the Medical Center. Gladys Johnson was named chancellor of the University of Nebraska at Kearney in 1993 when William Nester retired; she was the first black administrator in the history of the University. Chancellor Spanier spoke frequently of spousal opportunity, that is, a policy allowing the hiring of a faculty member's husband or wife if he or she is otherwise qualified. Dual appointments presented admirable opportunities for excellence, he said. Indeed, his own wife was a practicing scholar with an appointment in English; and Leitzel's husband, an associate professor in the mathematics department, was well known in circles committed to mathematics education. Administratively, financially, and socially the University was into a new world. In 1995 Spanier resigned as chancellor to become president of The Pennsylvania State University, where he had begun his teaching career.

In January 1993 President Massengale announced that he would not ask for renewal of his three-year contract; it was clear that he did not have the support of the full board. In order to avoid the disruption of an interim appointment, he agreed to stay on until his successor could be named. In November 1993 L. Dennis Smith, executive vice chancellor of the University of California, Irvine, signed a three-year contract as the fifth president of the University of Nebraska. He had the unanimous endorsement of the Board of Regents, including its four student members. Smith, who was fifty-five years old, had been born and raised in Indiana. He had served on the Purdue University faculty from 1969 until 1987, when he went to Irvine as dean of the School of Biological Sciences. After 1990 he was executive vice chancellor at Irvine and in 1992–93 he served as its acting chancellor.

The problems confronting the new president were reasonably clear. First, he would need to establish a continuing and faithful relationship with the board, a board which in the previous twenty years had sometimes been fractious. Together they would need to work out a harmonious relationship with the new Coordinating Commission for Higher Education. Second, he would need to define the relationship of the various campuses to one another and all of them to his central authority. Third, he would need to adjust the University to the increasing demands across the state for locally delivered higher education. The historical identity of the University was challenged, not only because Kearney had joined the system, adding UNK to UNL, UNO, and UNMC, but because communities without a university, notably Grand Island, were asking that university courses and sometimes total programs be delivered to them at home. An engineering college was being demanded in Omaha; and advanced graduate work, traditionally limited to the comprehensive university in Lincoln, was sought at other places.

The traditional view of a university as a gathering of young people in a residential community where knowledge was discovered, preserved, and disseminated was undergoing change, perhaps transformation. New kinds of students in many locations asked now for what they thought a university could provide, some of it hardly above the level of instruction in trades. The new president and his board might well have to reshape higher education, providing immediately useful training without neglecting the philosophical underpinnings of higher education. The increasing demands on the University for transferable technology and the availability of private funding for directed research threatened to modify the historically independent mission of higher education. In a competitive world where intellectual skills were in both practical and ideal demand, the future shape of higher education would be wonderful to observe. Opportunities in Nebraska had not yet been exhausted.

Notes

❧ 1. Founding a Land-Grant University

1. Quoted in Robert N. Manley, *Centennial History of the University of Nebraska*, vol.1, *Frontier University, 1869–1919* (Lincoln: Univ. of Nebraska P, 1969), p.7.

2. Allan Nevins, *The State Universities and Democracy* (Urbana: Univ. of Illinois P, 1962), pp.14–15.

3. Adrienne Koch, ed., *Jefferson* (Englewood Cliffs, N.J.: Prentice-Hall, 1971), p.20.

4. Quoted in Laurence R. Veysey, *The Emergence of the American University* (Chicago: Univ. of Chicago P, 1965), p.45.

5. Quoted in Nevins, p.25n.

6. Howard W. Caldwell, *Education in Nebraska*, Contributions to American Educational History, ed. Herbert B. Adams, no. 32 (Washington DC: Government Printing Office, 1902), p.11.

7. Quoted in Caldwell, p.20.

8. Nevins, p.34; Caldwell, pp.38–39.

9. The 1869 charter of the University of Nebraska is reprinted entire in Manley, pp.309–12, but, curiously, not by Caldwell, who says it is now (1902) "in an extremely chaotic condition" because it "has been amended several times" (p.25).

10. J. Sterling Morton, succeeded by Albert Watkins and George C. Miller as editors, *Illustrated History of Nebraska*, 3 vols. (Lincoln: Jacob North and Co., 1907), 2:357n.

11. See James C. Olson, *History of Nebraska* (Lincoln: Univ. of Nebraska P, 1955), pp.153–56; A. Stuart Goldberg, "Augustus F. Harvey in Nebraska City and Lincoln, 1856–1870" (Master's thesis, University of Nebraska, 1947).

12. Augustus Harvey wrote to Caldwell of his memories of founding the University in a letter dated 31 July 1889, from St. Louis, Missouri, where he had become a successful insurance executive. The letter is reprinted in Caldwell, pp.18–21.

13. Quoted in Koch, p.84.

14. Quoted in Koch, pp.35–36. Caldwell, pp.17–18, notes the continuity from Jefferson's University of Virginia to the University of Michigan to the University of Nebraska.

15. Olson, p.152.

16. Quoted in Olson, p.153.

17. Report to the Board of Regents, 14 June 1871, Board of Regents Papers, 1/1/1, box 1, folder 2, University Archives (hereafter cited as UA).

18. Edna D. Bullock, "Buildings and Grounds," in *Semi-Centennial Anniversary Book: The University of Nebraska, 1869–1919*, comp. Louise Pound (Lincoln: Univ. of Nebraska, 1919), pp.36, 39.

19. Roscoe Pound, interview with Dr. Robert N. Manley at Harvard University, 12 July 1962, Biographical/Bibliographical Files, Roscoe Pound, UA.

20. Quoted by Louise Pound in "The Founding of the University," in *Semi-Centennial Anniversary Book*, p.18. Caldwell discusses the building of University Hall briefly, pp.21–22, and Manley gives a much fuller account, pp.16–21.

21. Alvin Johnson, *Pioneer's Progress: An Autobiography* (New York: Viking, 1952), p.76.

22. Quoted in Manley, pp.18, 19.

23. Bullock, p.37.

24. Olson, p.159.

25. Samuel Aughey, *The Ideas and the Men That Created the University of Nebraska* (address delivered before the University of Nebraska on Charter Day, 15 February 1881) (Lincoln: Journal Co., State Printers, 1881), p.14, Biographical/Bibliographical File, Samuel Aughey, UA.

26. Aughey, p.14.

27. George E. Howard, "Early Faculty and Equipment," in *Semi-Centennial Anniversary Book*, p.27.

28. O. W. Merrill to Regent[s], 4 February 1871, Board of Regents Papers, 1/1/1, box 1, folder 2, UA.

29. Albert Watkins, "The Regents," in *Semi-Centennial Anniversary Book*, p.77.

30. Howard, p.26.

31. W. H. James, *Addresses at the Inauguration of Allen R. Benton, As Chancellor of the University of Nebraska*, 6 September 1871 (Lincoln: Statesman Power Press Job Print for the University of Nebraska, 1871), pp.4–5, 12, Chancellor's Papers (Allen R. Benton), 2/1/0, UA.

32. *Announcement of the University of Nebraska, 1871–72* (Lincoln) [first report], pp.8–11.

33. Quoted in Veysey, p.33. See George M. Marsden, *The Soul of the American University: From Protestant Establishment to Established Nonbelief* (New York: Oxford Univ. P, 1994), pp.123–31, on Noah Porter.

34. Veysey, pp.42–43. See Marsden, pp.196–218, on McCosh.

35. Report to Board of Regents by Uriah Bruner and W. D. Scott, 16 December 1873, Board of Regents Papers, 1/1/1, box 1, folder 8, UA.

36. Nevins, pp.41–42.

37. L. A. Sherman, "The Making of the University," in *The Sombrero*, vol.3, Quarter-Centennial Number (Junior Class, University of Nebraska, 1895), p.21.

38. Louise Pound, p.59.

39. Bullock, p.37.

40. Family Correspondence of Allen R. Benton, 1881–1875, 2/1/1, UA.

41. Manley, p.53.

42. L. A. Sherman, "Admission and Curriculum," in *Semi-Centennial Anniversary Book*, p.21.

᠅ *2. Defining a University: 1876–1891*

1. Board of Regents Papers, 1/1/1, box 3, folder 28, UA.

2. Samuel Aughey, *The Ideas and the Men That Created the University of Nebraska* (address delivered before the University of Nebraska on Charter Day, 15 February 1881) (Lincoln: Journal Co., State Printers, 1881), pp.8–9, Biographical/Bibliographical Files, Samuel Aughey, UA.

3. Samuel Aughey, *Sketches of the Physical Geography and Geology of Nebraska* (Omaha: Daily Republican Book and Job Office, 1880), p.45.

4. Roscoe Pound, interview with Dr. Robert N. Manley at Harvard University, 12 July 1962, pp.1, 10, Biographical/Bibliographical Files, Roscoe Pound, UA.

5. Charles E. Bessey, "Professor Doctor Samuel Aughey," *The University Journal* 9, 2 (1912): 20.

6. Albert Watkins, *History of Nebraska from Earlier Explorations to the Present Time, with the Portraits, Maps, and Tables* (Lincoln: Western Publishing and Engraving Co., 1913), vol.3 [pt.1].

7. Biographical/Bibliographical Files, George Church, UA.

8. Quoted in William F. Muhs, "Harrington Emerson as Professor" (paper prepared for the Academy of Management, 40th Annual National Meeting, Detroit, Michigan, 10–13 August 1980), p.5, Biographical/Bibliographical Files, Harrington Emerson, UA. The Emerson correspondence is in the New York Public Library and his Engineering and Organizing Reports are in the Manuscripts Collection, Archives of Pennsylvania State University, University Park.

9. "Famous Firsts: High Priest of Efficiency," *Business Week*, 22 June 1963, pp.100, 104.

10. *Selected Letters of George Edward Woodberry*, with an introduction by Walter De La Mare (Boston: Houghton Mifflin Co., 1933), p.9.

11. George E. Woodberry, "The Ride," *Heart of Men* (New York: Macmillan Co., 1899), pp.282–83.

12. Lowry Charles Wimberly, "Oscar Wilde Meets Woodberry," *Prairie Schooner* 21 (1947): 113.

13. Biennial reports to the Governor, 1871–1921; Sixth biennial report of the Board of Regents of the University of Nebraska, 1 December 1882, p.4, 1/5, box 1, UA.

14. Samuel Eliot Morison, ed., *The Development of Harvard University since the Inauguration of President Eliot, 1869–1929* (Cambridge, Mass.: Harvard Univ. P, 1930), p.154n3.

15. George E. Howard, "The State University of America," *The Atlantic Monthly* 67 (1891): 338.

16. George E. Howard, *Evolution of the University* (first annual address to the Alumni Association of the University of Nebraska, 11 June 1889) (Lincoln: Alumni Association, 1890), p.34, Biographical/Bibliographical Files, George E. Howard, UA.

17. Board of Regents Papers, 1/1/1, box 4, folder 44, UA.

18. Eleanor Hinman, "Life of Ellen Smith," in *Ellen Smith, Registrar of the University of Nebraska, 1877–1902* [ed. Josephine Frisbie and Marjorie Stuff] (Lincoln: Univ. of Nebraska P [sic], 1928), p.9.

19. Paul Lombard Sayre, *The Life of Roscoe Pound* (Iowa City: College of Law Committee, State University of Iowa, 1948), p.52.

20. George E. Howard, "Early Faculty and Equipment," in *Semi-Centennial Anniversary Book: The University of*

Nebraska, 1869–1919, comp.Louise Pound (Lincoln: University, Lincoln, 1919), p.29.

21. J. W. Searson, "Sombrero, Vol. III, Dedicated to Ellen Smith," in *Ellen Smith*, p.31.

22. Board of Regents Papers, 15 June 1888, 1 / 1 / 1, box 7, folder 62, UA.

23. Grove E. Barker, "J. Irving Manatt," in *Semi-Centennial Anniversary Book*, p.123. Manatt sometimes signed himself Irving J. Manatt.

24. Raymond J. Pool, "A Brief Sketch of the Life and Work of Charles Edwin Bessey," *American Journal of Botany 2*, 10 (December 1915): 505–18. See also Richard A. Overfield, *Science with Practice: Charles E. Bessey and the Maturing of American Botany* (Ames: Iowa State Univ. P, 1993).

25. Thomas R. Walsh, "Charles E. Bessey and the Transformation of the Industrial College," *Nebraska History 52* (1971): 383–409.

26. Report of the Dean of Industrial College, 18 December 1888, Board of Regents Papers, 1 / 1 / 1, box 7, folder 65, UA.

27. Board of Regents Papers, meeting of 18 June 1888, 1 / 1 / 1, box 7, folder 62, UA.

28. Ronald C. Tobey, *Saving the Prairies: The Life Cycle of the Founding School of American Plant Ecology, 1895–1955* (Berkeley and Los Angeles: Univ. of California P, 1981), p.39.

29. Charles E. Bessey, "Science and Culture," *Science 4* (31 July 1896): 122, 123.

30. Annual Report of [Acting Chancellor] for the year 1888–89, Board of Regents Papers, 1 / 1 / 1, box 7, folder 68, UA.

31. Fred W. Wells, *The Nebraska Art Association: A History, 1888–1971* [Lincoln: Nebraska Art Association, 1972].

32. Guy E. Reed, "Athletics," in *Semi-Centennial Anniversary Book*, p.92.

33. Henry H. Wilson, "Allen Richardson Benton," in *Semi-Centennial Anniversary Book*, p.120.

3. "A Golden Era": 1891–1900

1. Willa Cather, *My Ántonia* (1918), book 3, chap.1.
2. James A. Canfield and Dorothy Canfield Fisher, "He Saw

the Golden Door," *The Nebraska Alumnus 34*, 2 (February 1938): 22.

3. W. F. Dann, "James Hulme Canfield," in *Semi-Centennial Anniversary Book: The University of Nebraska, 1869–1919*, comp.Louise Pound (Lincoln: University of Nebraska, 1919), p.127.

4. Charles E. Bessey, "Dr. Canfield's Coming to Nebraska," in "Canfield Memorial Number," *The University Journal 5*, 7 (April 1909): 114.

5. Howard W. Caldwell, *Education in Nebraska*, Contributions to American Educational History, ed. Herbert B. Adams, no. 32 (Washington DC: Government Printing Office, 1902), p.33.

6. *The Sombrero*, vol.3, Class of '93, pp.9–10.

7. La Von M. Guppa, "Chancellor James Hulme Canfield: His Impact on the University of Nebraska, 1891–1895" (Ph.D. diss., University of Nebraska, 1985), p.97. The critic was L. A. Sherman.

8. La Von Mary Guppa, "Chancellor James Hulme Canfield: His Impact on the University of Nebraska, 1891–1895" *Nebraska History 66* (1985): 392–410.

9. Quoted in Guppa, *Nebraska History*, p.405.

10. Miscellaneous Papers, Canfield Family Collection, Russell Vermontiana Collection, Martha Canfield Memorial Free Library, Inc., Arlington, Vermont, box 2, folder 16. The letter is headed by a handwritten note: "This is a characteristic letter of my Father, who felt a fatherly, personal concern about all the students in the universities of which he was in charge. – D.C.F. [Dorothy Canfield Fisher]"

11. C. H. Morrill, "Canfield the Executive," *The University Journal 5*, 7 (April 1909): 116.

12. Louise Pound, "The Late Dr. Canfield as Seen by His Students," and Samuel Avery, "The Late Dr. Canfield as Seen by His Students," *The University Journal 5*, 7 (April 1909): 115.

13. Ronald C. Tobey, *Saving the Prairies: The Life Cycle of the Founding School of American Plant Ecology, 1895–1955* (Berkeley and Los Angeles: Univ. of California P, 1981), pp.14–21.

14. Tobey, p.69.

15. L. A. Sherman, *Analytics of Literature: A Manual for the*

Objective Study of English Prose and Poetry (Boston: Ginn and Co., 1893), pp.vi, ix.

16. Emory Lindquist, *An Immigrant's Two Worlds: A Biography of [August] Hjalmar Edgren* (Rock Island, Ill.: Augustana Historical Society, 1972), p.9.

17. Lindquist, p.33.

18. H. Edgren, "Our Graduate School," in *The Sombrero*, Class of 1898, p.69.

19. Quoted in Donald Smythe, S.J., "John J. Pershing at the University of Nebraska, 1891–1895," *Nebraska History* 43 (1962): 171, 184.

20. Letter to the President of the Board of Regents, 28 August 1899, Board of Regents Papers, 1/1/1, box 14, folder 111, UA.

21. Smythe, p.194.

22. Quoted in Sharon McCashin, "The Development of a University Library: The University of Nebraska, 1891–1909" (Ph.D. diss., University of Nebraska–Lincoln, 1987), p.70.

23. Quoted in McCashin, p.71.

24. McCashin, p.150.

25. McCashin, p.163.

26. Quoted in McCashin, p.165.

27. McCashin, p.147.

28. Willa Cather, *The Professor's House* (1925), book 1, chap.13.

29. See Margaret R. Seymour, "Music in Lincoln, Nebraska, in the 19th Century: A Study of the Musical Culture of a Frontier Society" (Master's thesis, University of Nebraska, 1968); Marilyn Hammond and Raymond Haggh, "Willard Kimball, Music Educator on the Great Plains," *Great Plains Quarterly* 11 (Fall 1991): 249–61.

30. Canfield and Fisher, p.4.

31. Caldwell, *Education in Nebraska*, p.35.

32. *Lincoln Journal*, 6 June 1895, quoting from a printed letter by James H. Canfield to the members of the University Senate and to all others engaged in the work of instruction, dated 5 June 1895.

33. Robert N. Manley, *Centennial History of the University of Nebraska*, vol.1, *Frontier University, 1869–1919* (Lincoln: Univ. of Nebraska P, 1969), p.115.

34. Dann, "James Hulme Canfield," p.129.

35. Uncataloged manuscript discovered by Lynn Beideck-Porn in the University Archives.

36. *The Sombrero*, Class of 1898, p.16. This volume was dedicated to the new chancellor, George E. MacLean.

37. *Dictionary of American Biography* (New York: Charles Scribner's Sons, 1958), vol.22, supplement 2, pp.419–20.

38. Alvin Johnson, *Pioneer's Progress: An Autobiography* (New York: Viking, 1952), p.82.

39. See Ludy T. Benjamin Jr., *Harry Kirke Wolfe, Pioneer in Psychology* (Lincoln: Univ. of Nebraska P, 1991), pp.80–94. "During the 1895–96 school year, MacLean criticized Wolfe for teaching evolution" (p.83). "It is not known if this issue was raised again with Wolfe, nor if it was reported to the board of regents" (p.84).

40. Report to the Board of Regents, 27 April 1897, p.9, Board of Regents Papers, 1/1/1, box 13, folder 96, UA.

🙦 4. From College to University: 1900–1908

1. *The Sombrero*, vol.5, 1899 (Class of Nineteen Hundred), p.14; George R. Leighton, *Five Cities: The Story of Their Youth and Old Age* (New York: Harper Brothers, 1939), p.205.

2. Alexander Meiklejohn, *Freedom and the College* (New York: Century Co., 1923), p.50.

3. Reported in the *Daily Nebraskan*, 15 March 1904.

4. Quoted in James C. Hansen II, "Gallant, Stalwart Bennie: Elisha Benjamin Andrews (1844–1917): An Educator's Odyssey" (Ph.D. diss., University of Denver, 1969), pp.267–68.

5. E. L. Hinman, "E. Benjamin Andrews," in *Semi-Centennial Anniversary Book: The University of Nebraska, 1869–1919*, comp. Louise Pound (Lincoln: University of Nebraska, 1919), p.131.

6. Hinman, p.131.

7. Edward A. Ross, *Seventy Years of It: An Autobiography* (New York: D. Appleton-Century Co., 1936), p.87.

8. *Dictionary of American Biography* (New York: Charles Scribner's Sons, 1928), 1:270.

9. Board of Regents Papers, 1/1/1, box 16, folder 125, UA.

10. Hansen, p.26.

11. Quoted by Ken Hambleton, "And in the Beginning . . . ,"

Lincoln Journal-Star, Special Section, 8–9 September 1989, p.2x.

12. Anne L. Johnson, "The Student Writer at the University of Nebraska, 1871–1911" (Master's thesis, University of Nebraska, 1972), p.74.

13. *The Sombrero*, vol.8, Class of 1906 (Lincoln: University of Nebraska, 1905), p.155.

14. *The Sombrero*, vol.7, Class of '04 (Lincoln: University of Nebraska, 1903), p.165.

15. Alvin Johnson, *Pioneer's Progress: An Autobiography* (New York: Viking, 1952), p.170.

16. See *The University Journal* (Alumni Edition), January 1917, p.28, and Robert N. Manley, *Centennial History of the University of Nebraska*, vol.1, *Frontier University, 1869–1919* (Lincoln: Univ. of Nebraska P, 1969), pp.151–55.

17. Laurence R. Veysey, *The Emergence of the American University* (Chicago: Univ. of Chicago P, 1965), p.416.

18. Ross, *Seventy Years of It*, p.87.

19. Alvin Johnson, pp.166–80.

20. Hinman, p.132.

21. Carnegie Foundation for the Advancement of Teaching, *Papers Relating to the Admission of State Institutions to the System of Retiring Allowances of the Carnegie Foundation*, Bulletin no. 1 (New York, 1907), p.24.

22. Daniel C. Gilman, "The Launching of a University" (1902), reprinted in *Portraits of the American University, 1890–1910*, comp.James C. Stone and Donald P. De Nevi (San Francisco: Jossey-Bass, 1971), p.15.

23. William James, "The Ph.D. Octopus," originally published in *Harvard Monthly*, March 1903; frequently reprinted, as in William James, *Writings, 1902–1910* (New York: Library of America, 1987), pp.1111–18.

24. Thomas R. Walsh, "Charles E. Bessey and the Transformation of the Industrial College," *Nebraska History* 52 (1971): 400.

25. See Margaret W. Rossiter, "The Organization of the Agricultural Sciences," in *The Organization of Knowledge in Modern America, 1860–1920*, ed. Alexandra Oleson and John Voss (Baltimore: Johns Hopkins Univ. P, 1979), pp.240–41.

26. M. Eugene Rudd, *Science on the Great Plains: The History of Physics and Astronomy at the University of Nebraska–Lincoln*, University of Nebraska Studies, n.s. 71 (1992), p.19.

27. Rudd, p.37.

28. Roscoe Pound, "Legal Instruction at Nebraska," in *The Sombrero*, vol.8, pp.51–55.

29. David Wigdor, *Roscoe Pound, Philosopher of Law*, Contibutions to American History, no. 33 (Westport, Conn., 1974), p.147.

30. J. Jay Keegan, M.D., Dean, "History [of the Medical College]," in *The Caduceus of 1929* [yearbook of the Medical College], vol.1 (Omaha: Douglas Printing Co., 1929), p.31.

31. W. F. Milroy, M.D., "The College of Medicine," in *The Cornhusker*, vol.2 (1908), p.41.

32. Milroy, p.38.

33. Robert B. Coleman [and others], *The First Hundred Years of the University of Nebraska College of Medicine* (Omaha: University of Nebraska Medical Center, 1980), p.9.

34. Keegan, p.31.

35. Milroy, p.38.

36. Coleman et al., p.25.

37. Coleman et al., p.36.

38. Coleman et al., p.24.

39. Ludy T. Benjamin Jr., *Harry Kirke Wolfe, Pioneer in Psychology* (Lincoln: Univ. of Nebraska P, 1991).

40. "The Carnegie Foundation," *The University Journal* 5, 7 (April 1909): 121.

41. *Daily Nebraskan*, 3 February 1909.

42. Hinman, p.132.

❧ 5. The Beginning of a Long Retreat: 1909–1919

1. Samuel Avery to Governor Samuel V. Stewart, 21 July 1915, General Correspondence of Samuel Avery, 2/9/1, UA.

2. John A. Rice, *I Came Out of the 18th Century* (New York: Harper and Brothers, 1942), p.272.

3. Regent Charles S. Allen, "University Development," *The University Journal* 11, 3 (December 1914): 21.

4. Rice, pp.269–70.

5. Mabel Lee, *Memories beyond Bloomers (1924–1954)* (Washington, D.C.: American Alliance for Health, Physical Education, and Recreation, 1978), p.4.

6. John D. Hicks, *My Life with History: An Autobiography* (Lincoln: Univ. of Nebraska P, 1968), p.133.

7. S. Avery, "Passing of University Crises," *The University Journal* 10, 1 (October 1913): 1.

8. Abraham Flexner, *Medical Education in the United States and Canada: A Report to the Carnegie Foundation for the Advancement of Teaching*, Bulletin no. 4 (New York, 1910), p.261.

9. See J. Jay Keegan, M.D., Dean, "History [of the Medical College]" in *The Caduceus of 1929* [yearbook of the Medical College], vol.1 (Omaha: Douglas Printing Co., 1929), pp.33–34; Robert B. Coleman [and others], *The First Hundred Years of the University of Nebraska College of Medicine* (Omaha: University of Nebraska Medical Center, 1980), passim.

10. Coleman et al., p.38.

11. Samuel Avery to Governor Stewart, 21 July 1915.

12. Avery, "Passing of University Crises," p.3.

13. *Cornhusker 1914*, p.24.

14. Samuel Avery to Governor Stewart, 21 July 1915.

15. Avery, "Passing of University Crises," p.4.

16. Amanda Heppner, "University Women's Hall," *The University Journal* 15, 5 (January 1919): 7.

17. *Cornhusker, 1911*, p.278.

18. R. D. Scott and others, "The Athletic Board, University of Nebraska: A Detailed Review of Its Historical Background, Origin, Development, Activities and Achievements Covering Fifty Years of Intercollegiate Athletics, 1890–1940" [1963], p.39, 12/10/10, box 2, UA.

19. Scott, pp.43, 44.

20. Scott, p.37.

21. Frederick Ware, in collaboration with Gregg McBride, *Fifty Years of Football: A Condensed History of the Game at the University of Nebraska* (Omaha: *Omaha World-Herald*, 1940), p.29; see also James E. Sherwood, *Nebraska Football: The Coaches, the Players, the Experience* (Lincoln: Univ. of Nebraska P, 1987), pp.8–12.

22. The exchange was printed in the *Daily Nebraskan*, 9 November 1914.

23. G. W. Langworthy Taylor, "A Life of Historical Research," *The Nebraska Alumnus* 28, 10 (December 1932): p.4.

24. Robert E. Carlson, "Professor Fred Fling: His Career and Conflicts at Nebraska University," *Nebraska History* 62 (1981): 481–96.

25. "Dr. Fling," *Cornhusker 1912*, in Faculty Section, unpaged.

26. John Dryden, "Absalom and Achitophel: A Poem" [1681], ll.159–62.

27. Acting Chancellor W. G. Hastings to Professor Laura Pfeiffer, 11 July 1918, General Correspondence of Samuel Avery, 2/9/1, UA.

28. Board of Regents Papers, 1/1/1, box 27, folders 201, 202, UA.

29. Samuel Avery to R. L. Slagle, President of the University of South Dakota, 1 June 1925, General Correspondence of Samuel Avery, 2/9/1, UA.

❦ 6. A University on the Defensive: 1920–1927

1. James Woodress, *Willa Cather: A Literary Life* (Lincoln: University of Nebraska P, 1987), pp.334–35.

2. *What Do You Know about Your State University?*, Bulletin 23, ser. 29, University of Nebraska, October 1924.

3. Samuel Avery, "The Chancellor's Corner," *The University Journal* 19, 5 (May 1923): 117.

4. John D. Hicks, *My Life with History: An Autobiography* (Lincoln: Univ. of Nebraska P, 1968), p.131.

5. E. R. Washburn and J. H. Looker, "Fred W. Upson (1883–1942), Administrator and Carbohydrate Chemist," unpublished paper, Department of Chemistry, Biographical/Bibliographical Files, Fred W. Upson, UA.

6. Reprinted in *The Nebraska English Journal* 38, 1 (Fall 1988), "Special Issue on Hartley Burr Alexander," with an introduction by Robert S. Haller and edited by Samuel J. Umland.

7. David O. Levine, *The American College and the Culture of Aspiration, 1915–1940* (Ithaca, N.Y.: Cornell Univ. P, 1986), p.19.

8. Cather's essay was originally published in *The Nation*, September 5, 1923, pp.236–38. It was reprinted imperfectly in Virginia Faulkner, comp. and ed., *Roundup: A*

Nebraska Reader (Lincoln: Univ. of Nebraska P, 1957), pp.1–8.

9. J. E. LeRossignol, "The Works of the School of Commerce," *The University Journal* 12, 5 (May 1916): 54.

10. See Erwin H. Goldenstein, *The First 50 Years: The University of Nebraska Teachers College* (Lincoln: University of Nebraska, 1958), for an account as seen from within the college.

11. Some proposals were made to Chancellor Avery in August 1920. Correspondence with Academic Departments, 2/9/3, UA. Detailed suggestions were spelled out in correspondence with Regent William P. Warner, 10 January and 10, 11, 19, 20 April 1927. Correspondence with Academic Departments, 2/10/3, UA.

12. H. B. Alexander to Orin Stepanek, 13 February 1927, letter in the possession of the Stepanek family; reprinted with the kind permission of Mrs. Olga Stepanek.

13. H. B. Alexander to William P. Warner, 28 April 1927, Correspondence with Academic Departments, 2/10/3, UA.

14. Board of Regents Papers, 1/1/1, box 32, folder 242, UA.

15. Alexander to Warner, 28 April 1927.

16. Quoted in Levine, p.118.

17. Levine, p.122.

18. Bess Streeter Aldrich, *A White Bird Flying* (1931). The quoted passages are from chapters 5, 8, 9, and 11.

19. Conversation with Dudley Bailey, 13 March 1991.

20. Mabel Lee, *Memories beyond Bloomers (1924–1954)* (Washington DC: American Alliance for Health, Physical Education, and Recreation, 1978), p.10.

21. Mabel Lee, p.6.

22. In conversation with various persons, including me. Louise Pound died in 1958.

23. S. Avery, "The University in Retrenchment," 24 February 1922, Speeches of Samuel Avery, 2/92, UA.

7. Depression: 1927–1938

1. Mabel Lee, *Memories beyond Bloomers (1924–1954)* (Washington DC: American Alliance for Health, Physical Education, and Recreation, 1978), p.59.

2. Oral History. H. O. Werner, 4 December 1973, p.4, 8/16/5, UA.

3. Theodore A. Kiesselbach, "What's in a Life?" unpublished autobiography, pp.144, 168, 8/8/10, UA.

4. Minutes of Board of Regents, 10 December 1927, 1/1/2, vol.10, part 1, UA.

5. Quoted in the *Daily Nebraskan*, 11 March 1928.

6. Chancellor E. A. Burnett, "What Is a Professor Worth?" *The Nebraska Alumnus* 24, 10 (December 1928): 480.

7. H. F. Cunningham to H. B. Alexander, Easter Sunday, 1931, H. B. Alexander file, Archives, Ella Strong Denison Library, Scripps College, Claremont, California.

8. Board of Regents Papers, 19 October 1929, 1/1/1, box 33, folder 252, UA.

9. Student Publications, 38/1/3, UA.

10. Cunningham to Alexander, Easter Sunday, 1931.

11. Rudolph Umland, "Lowry Wimberly and Others: Recollections of a Beerdrinker," *Prairie Schooner* 51, 1 (Spring 1977): 18.

12. Gale E. Christianson, *Fox at the Wood's Edge: A Biography of Loren Eiseley* (New York: Henry Holt and Co., 1990), p.71.

13. Umland, p.19.

14. Umland, pp.21–22.

15. Umland, p.32.

16. John D. Hicks, *My Life with History: An Autobiography* (Lincoln: Univ. of Nebraska P, 1968), p.152.

17. George W. Beadle, "Recollections," *Annual Review of Biochemistry* 43 (1974): 3.

18. Minutes of the Board of Regents, 26 November 1932, 1/1/2, vol.12, part 1, p.83, UA.

19. Chancellor E. A. Burnett, "The University Meets the Depression," *The Nebraska Alumnus* 28, 8 (October 1932): 2.

20. Hicks, p.152.

21. James E. Sherwood, *Nebraska Football: The Coaches, the Players, the Experience* (Lincoln: Univ. of Nebraska P, 1987), pp.21, 32.

22. Alice M. Rivlin, *The Role of the Federal Government in Financing Higher Education* (Washington DC: Brookings Institution, 1961), pp.98–100.

23. Minutes of the Board of Regents, 20 September 1933, 1/1/2, vol.12, part 2, p.178, UA.

24. Board of Regents Papers, 15 February 1935, 1/1/1, box 35, folder 263, UA.

25. Minutes of the Board of Regents, 5 December 1936, 1/1/2, vol.13, part 2, p.206, UA.

❧ 8. Marking Time: 1938–1946

1. George Round, "University of Nebraska Administrators," undated, 8/16/5, UA.

2. Round, "University of Nebraska Administrators."

3. This position was set forth in a series of letters to the *Daily Nebraskan* by Gerald H. Agans, a graduate student in Teachers College, on 9, 10, and 11 January 1935.

4. C. H. Oldfather, "Adventure in Teaching," *The Nebraska Alumnus* 31, 9 (November 1935): 24.

5. Mabel Lee, *Memories beyond Bloomers (1924–1954)* (Washington, D.C.: American Alliance for Health, Physical Education, and Recreation, 1978), pp.252–53.

6. Chancellor Boucher's "Address to the Faculty," delivered at a general faculty dinner on the evening of 20 September, was printed in *The Nebraska Alumnus* 34, 8 (October 1938): 3, 22, 24, 26.

7. Lee, p.254.

8. Chancellor Chauncey S. Boucher to "Budget Officers," October 10, 1938, Boucher Papers, 2/11/4, box 37, folder 282, UA.

9. News release, 15 March 1939, Boucher Papers, 2/11/4, box 37, folder 282, UA.

10. Professor Bengston's views are recorded in the *Daily Nebraskan*, 5 April 1935. His description "University Junior Division" is in *The Nebraska Alumnus* 36, 4 (April 1940): 4–5.

11. Board of Regents Papers, 3 July 1939, 1/1/1, box 37, folder 289, UA; see also 24 February 1939, folder 282.

12. Reported by Professor Leslie Hewes, 20 February 1991.

13. Board of Regents Papers, 1/1/1, box 37, folder 284, UA.

14. University Senate Minutes, 3 October 1940, 4/1/1, UA. Action reported in the *Daily Nebraskan*, 27 April 1941 and 9 December 1942.

15. Office of the Chancellor, Subject Correspondence, 2/11/5, Love Memorial Library 1941–1942, UA.

16. Wally Provost, "It's Always Something," *Omaha World-Herald Magazine of the Midlands*, 3 September 1989, p.23.

17. Oral History, Don Lentz, 4 October 1975, p.5, 8/16/5, UA.

18. Robert B. Coleman [and others], "The Poynter Era: 1930–1946," *The First Hundred Years of the University of Nebraska College of Medicine* (Omaha: University of Nebraska Medical Center, 1980), pp.45–54.

19. *Cornhusker 1944*, p.289.

20. University Senate Minutes, 17 February 1945, 4/1/1; Office of the Chancellor, Subject Correspondence, C. S. Boucher, 1938–1946, 2/11/5, Salary Increase 1945, UA.

21. Office of the Chancellor, Subject Correspondence, C. S. Boucher, 1938–1946, 2/11/5, Legislative Business 1938–1945, UA.

22. Board of Regents Minutes, 5 May 1945, 1/1/2, p.22, UA.

23. Board of Regents Minutes, 23 March 1946, 1/1/2, UA. The board passed a resolution expressing gratitude for his service upon his resignation "because of ill-health."

24. Quoted in the *Lincoln Sunday Journal and Star*, 8 June 1952.

❧ 9. "Turning the University Around": 1946–1953

1. Boucher Papers, Subject Correspondence, 14 January 1948, 2/11/5, UA.

2. Oral History, Terry Carpenter, 16 October 1975, p.8, 8/16/5, UA.

3. Elvin F. Frolik and Ralston J. Graham, *The University of Nebraska–Lincoln College of Agriculture: The First Century* (Lincoln: Institute of Agriculture and Natural Resources, University of Nebraska–Lincoln, 1987), p.16.

4. Quoted in *The Nebraska Alumnus* 44, 9 (November, 1948): 9.

5. Theodore P. Jorgensen, "Autobiography," MS, 1993, chap.3, p.54, Biographical/Bibliographical Files, Theodore P. Jorgensen, UA.

6. Jorgensen, chap.5, p.67; chap.9, pp.94–95.

7. Jorgensen, chap.9, pp.100–101.

8. John P. McSweeney, "The Chancellorship of Reuben G. Gustavson at the University of Nebraska, 1946–53" (Ph.D. diss., University of Nebraska, 1971), p.167.

9. Board of Regents Minutes, 28 March 1942, 1/1/2, vol.15, section 2, UA.

10. Quoted in the *Daily Nebraskan*, 25 April 1946.

11. Board of Regents Minutes, 17 June 1944, 1/1/2, vol.16, section 3, UA.

12. *Daily Nebraskan*, 16, 23 March; 23 April 1947.

13. *Daily Nebraskan*, 18 May 1947.

14. Cited in the *Daily Nebraskan*, 9 March 1945.

15. Oral History, Walter K. Beggs, 22 January 1975, p.5, 8/16/5, UA.

16. McSweeney, p.170.

17. McSweeney, pp.120–21.

18. George Round, "University of Nebraska Administration," undated, 8/16/5, p.3, UA.

19. Quoted in the *Daily Nebraskan*, 10 December 1952.

20. Quoted in the *Daily Nebraskan*, 15 December 1952.

21. Quoted in full in the *Daily Nebraskan*, 15 January 1953.

22. Wally Provost, "It's Always Something," *Omaha World-Herald Magazine of the Midlands*, 3 September 1989, p.24.

23. Oral History, Joe W. Seacrest, 29 October 1974, p.5, 8/16/5, UA.

24. Gustavson Correspondence with Academic Departments, Intercollegiate Athletics, Mr. George Clark, 2 March 1951, 2/12/2, UA.

25. Quoted from *U.S. News and World Report* in the *Lincoln Sunday Journal and Star*, 28 November 1952.

26. Provost, p.24.

27. *Daily Nebraskan*, 11 December 1934.

28. Oral History, Beggs, p.2.

29. Mabel Lee, *Memories beyond Bloomers (1924–1954)* (Washington DC: American Alliance for Health, Physical Education, and Recreation, 1978), p.390, p.58.

30. Oral History, Beggs, p.2.

31. Quoted in the *Daily Nebraskan*, 11 December 1951.

32. Erwin H. Goldenstein, *The University of Nebraska Teachers College: The First Fifty Years* (Lincoln: University of Nebraska, 1958), p.49.

33. Goldenstein, p.50.

10. A Research University: 1953–1960

1. Robert Van Pelt, "A Tribute," Address given upon the occasion of the Kiwanis Club Medal for Distinguished Service, 17 November 1961, p.5, Biographical/Bibliographical Files, John Selleck, UA.

2. Quoted by Elwood Randol, "Selleck Thought NU Post Would Last 'A Few Weeks,'" *Lincoln Sunday Journal and Star*, 27 December 1953.

3. Van Pelt, p.11.

4. Van Pelt, p.14.

5. Oral History, Dr. B. W. Greenberg, 13 March 1974, pp.3–4, 8/16/5, UA.

6. Oral History, Clifford Hardin, 28 June 1975, p.5, 8/16/5, UA.

7. Oral History, Hardin, p.5.

8. Oral History, Greenberg, p.2.

9. Oral History, Walter K. Beggs, 22 January 1975, p.8, 8/16/5, UA.

10. Oral History, Hardin, p.24.

11. Oral History, Joe W. Seacrest, 29 October 1974, p.9, 8/16/5, UA.

12. Oral History, Hardin, p.25.

13. Oral History, Jack McBride, 7 June 1976, p.3, 8/16/5, UA.

14. Interview with Paul E. Few, Assistant General Manager, Administration and Finance, University Television, 2 September 1992.

15. Emily Schossberger, "Publishers on the Plains Provide 'Quality Fare,'" *The Nebraska Alumnus* 53, 4 (April 1957): 12–13.

16. Peggy Wilson, "UNP Reaching New Heights," *The Nebraska Alumnus* 56, 9 (November 1960): 17.

17. Elvin F. Frolik and Ralston J. Graham, *The University of Nebraska–Lincoln College of Agriculture: The First Century* (Lincoln: Institute of Agriculture and Natural Resources, University of Nebraska–Lincoln, 1987), pp.87–93.

18. Frolik and Graham, p.80.

19. Oral History, Clayton E. Yeutter, 6 January 1975, p.9, 8/16/5, UA.

20. Quoted in Frolik and Graham, p.84.

21. Quoted in Frolik and Graham, p.143n. In later years Breckenridge was fond of citing this footnote, with laughter and some pride.

22. Oral History, Hardin, p.9.

23. Oral History, Joseph Soshnik, 18 March 1974, p.1, 8/16/5, UA.

24. Oral History, Greenberg, p.9.

25. Oral History, Hardin, p.16.

26. James McCormack and Vincent A. Fulmer, "Federal Sponsorship of University Research," in *The Federal Government and Higher Education*, ed. Douglas Knight (Englewood Cliffs, N.J.: Prentice-Hall, 1960), pp.77–78.

27. Oral History, Governor Frank Morrison, 13 September 1976, pp.9–10, 8/16/5, UA.

28. Quoted in R. McLaran Sawyer, *Centennial History of the University of Nebraska*, vol.2, *The Modern University, 1920–1969* (Lincoln: Centennial, 1973), p.189.

29. Oral History, Hardin, p.15.

30. Oral History, Hardin, p.15.

31. Quoted in *The Nebraska Alumnus* 53, 10 (December 1957): 4.

32. These statements, quoted prominently in the newspapers of the state, were printed in *The Nebraska Alumnus* 53, 10 (December 1957): 4, 29, with the Teachers College Reply, pp.5, 30.

33. Oral History, Hardin, p.19.

34. See Mabel Lee, *Memories beyond Bloomers (1924–1954)* (Washington DC: American Alliance for Health, Physical Education, and Recreation, 1978), pp.245–46.

35. Oral History, Beggs, p.8.

36. Oral History, Beggs, p.8.

37. Paul A. Olson, "The University, the Community and Education," *The Nebraska Alumnus* 57, 8 (October 1961): 15.

38. Interview with Paul A. Olson, 25 November 1991.

39. See complete file of C. Clyde Mitchell Case, 1953–1957, University Senate Committees, Committee on Academic Privilege and Tenure, 4/2/1, UA.

40. Repeatedly quoted by Harry Allen, finally on 22 October 1991.

✍ 11. The University Expands: 1960–1968

1. R. McLaran Sawyer, *Centennial History of the University of Nebraska*, vol.2, *The Modern University, 1920–1969* (Lincoln: Centennial, 1973), p.221.

2. Oral History, Clifford Hardin, 28 June 1975, p.30, 8/16/5, UA.

3. Oral History, Hardin, p.33.

4. E. Z. Palmer, College of Business Administration [newsletter], November 1954.

5. Oral History, Hardin, p.34.

6. Quoted in Oral History, Hardin, p.35.

7. Oral History, Don Bryant, 25 February 1976, p.13, 8/16/5, UA.

8. Oral History, Hardin, p.29.

9. Oral History, Joe W. Seacrest, 29 October 1974, p.7, 8/16/5, UA.

10. Oral History, Bryant, pp.14–15.

11. Quoted by T. L Henrion, "Bob Devaney," *Omaha Sunday World-Herald Magazine*, 3 September 1989, p.11.

12. Henrion, p.11.

13. Minutes, Board of Regents, 9 October 1964, 1/1/1, UA.

14. Oral History, Hardin, p.29.

15. Office of the Chancellor, Senate Committee Correspondence, Building Committee, (Senate), 1951–1952, 2/12/5, UA.

16. Oral History, Harry Allen, 7 November 1984, p.11, 8/16/5, UA.

17. Elvin F. Frolik and Ralston J. Graham, *The University of Nebraska–Lincoln College of Agriculture: The First Century* (Lincoln: Institute of Agriculture and Natural Resources, University of Nebraska–Lincoln, 1987), pp.341–47.

18. Robert B. Coleman [and others], *The First Hundred Years of the University of Nebraska College of Medicine* (Omaha: University of Nebraska Medical Center, 1980), p.85.

19. Oral History, Hardin, p.22.

20. Oral History, Regent Richard Herman, 28 September 1979, p.15, 8/16/5, UA.

21. Oral History, Edward Hirsch, 16 October 1984, p.21, 8/16/5, UA.

22. Frederick C. Luebke, "Tiemann, Texas and the Centennial Legislation of 1967: Beginning Nebraska's Second Century," *Nebraska History* 71, 3 (Fall 1990): 111–16; Tommy R. Thompson, *A History of the University of Nebraska at Omaha* (Distributed by the University of Nebraska at Omaha Alumni Association, 1983), chap.6, "Merger with the University of Nebraska: A New Beginning," pp.101–37.

23. Oral History, Gene Budig, 8 July 1976, p.8, 8/16/5, UA.

24. Letter "To the Members of the Faculty," 26 January 1967, President's Office, Files Relating to Merger with the Municipal University of Omaha 1966–1974, 2/15/2, box 2, folder LB736, UA.

25. Oral History, Budig, p.10.

26. Oral History, Hardin, pp.39–40. The part played by George Cook, Chairman of the Board of Bankers Life Nebraska, is detailed in Oral History, George Cook, 21 January 1974, 8/16/5, UA.

27. Oral History, Hardin, p.30.

 12. A Time of Discontinuities: 1968–1971

1. Oral History, Harry Allen, 7 November 1984, p.15, 8/16/5, UA.

2. Oral History, Richard E. Adkins, 7 June 1974, p.5, 8/16/5, UA.

3. *The Report of the President's Commission on Campus Unrest* (Washington DC: Government Printing Office, 1970), p.22.

4. Clark Kerr, *The Uses of the University* (Cambridge, Mass.: Harvard Univ. P, 1963; 3d ed., 1982), pp.89–90.

5. *Report of the President's Commission*, pp.22–24.

6. *Report of the President's Commission*, p.35.

7. James S. Kunen, "Why We're against the Biggies," frequently reprinted, as in *Essays on the Student Movement*, ed. Patrick Gleeson (Columbus, Ohio: Charles E. Merrill Publishing Co., 1970), pp.45, 48. See "Clark Kerr" in Garry Wills, *Certain Trumpets: The Call of Leaders* (New York: Simon & Schuster, 1994), pp.80–84.

8. Ken Keller, "Campus Round-Up," *The Nebraska Alumnus* 63, 5 (September 1968): 20.

9. Reported in the *Daily Nebraskan*, 1 February 1967.

10. Robert E. Knoll and Robert D. Brown, *Experiment at Nebraska: The First Two Years of a Cluster College*, University of Nebraska Studies, n.s. 44 (1972), pp.1–2.

11. Minutes, Board of Regents, 4 October 1968, 1/1/1, UA.

12. Interview with Robert Haller, 21 September 1992.

13. Interview with Robert Narveson, 26 October 1992.

14. Interview with Ned Hedges, 16 March 1993.

15. Ken Keller, "Campus Round-Up," *The Nebraska Alumnus* 65, 3 (May 1969): 14.

16. Oral History, Joseph Soshnik, 18 March 1974, p.7, 8/16/5, UA.

17. *Report of the President's Commission*, p.234.

18. University Senate, Liaison Committee, "Strike," 1970, 4/2/13, box 2, UA.

19. Quoted in the *Daily Nebraskan*, 6 May 1970.

20. Quoted in the *Daily Nebraskan*, 5 May 1970.

21. James Miller, *"Democracy Is in the Streets": From Port Huron to the Siege of Chicago* (New York: Simon and Schuster, 1987), p.310.

22. Minutes, University Senate, 12 May 1970, 4/1/1, UA.

23. Report of the Commission of Inquiry on Disruptive Actions on the University of Nebraska Campus, Lincoln, 30 April–10 June 1970, Richard E. Spelts Jr., chair, 4/2/72, Rozman Case (1970), UA.

24. Report of the Special Faculty Fact-Finding Committee, Re. Stephen Rozman Matter, University of Nebraska, 1 February 1971, Henry Holtzclaw, chair, General Summary and Relevant Observations, pp.31–33, 4/2/72, UA. See also Stephen Witte, "UNL Student Reaction to the Cambodian Incursion and the Kent State Shootings, May 1970," *Nebraska History* 75 (fall 1994), pp.261–71.

25. Minutes, University Senate, 9 March 1971, 4/1/1, UA.

26. Reported in the *Lincoln Star*, 19 November 1971 and 17 October 1972.

27. Minutes, University Senate, 9 March 1971, Supplement to Exhibit 3, Letter by Vernon F. Snow to President Joseph Soshnik, 8 February 1971; the reply, 25 February 1971, 4/1/1, UA.

28. Oral History, Soshnik, p.14.

29. Oral History, Terry Carpenter on his relationship to the University, 16 October 1975, p.13; Oral History, Val Peterson as University Regent, 21 May 1974, p.14; Oral

History, Joe W. Seacrest, 29 October 1974, p.7; Oral History, A. T. Anderson, 6 July 1979, Post scriptum, 8/16/5, UA.

30. Quoted in [Ken Keller], "The Losing of a President," *The Nebraska Alumnus* 67, 3 (May 1971): 15.

31. Oral History, C. Peter Magrath, 5 October 1974, p.18, 8/16/5, UA.

13. The Governance of the University: 1971–1976

1. Quoted in the *Lincoln Journal*, 16 February 1971.

2. George Round in Oral History, George Cook, 11 November 1978, p.20, 8/16/5, UA.

3. Oral History, Richard E. Adkins, 7 June 1974, p.5, 8/16/5, UA.

4. Quoted in the *Lincoln Star*, 6 November 1970.

5. Quoted in an editorial, "How to Wreck a University," in the *Lincoln Evening Journal*, 10 November 1970.

6. *Lincoln Star*, 7 November 1970.

7. *Lincoln Evening Journal*, 10 November 1970.

8. Statement by Louis Crompton, 5 May 1992, SSF, Homophile Studies 1970, UA.

9. Quoted in "Round-Up," *The Nebraska Alumnus* 68, 1 (January 1972): 16.

10. *Daily Nebraskan*, 11 October 1971.

11. *Daily Nebraskan*, 7 February 1972.

12. Quoted in *Daily Nebraskan*, 8 March 1972.

13. Oral History, Adkins, p.8.

14. Oral History, Robert Raun, 15 March 1974, p.5; Oral History, Edward Schwartzkopf, 11 June 1974, p.5, 8/16/5, UA.

15. *Daily Nebraskan*, 16 February 1976.

16. Reported in the *Daily Nebraskan*, 30 April 1975.

17. Reported in the *Daily Nebraskan*, 25 February 1972.

18. Oral History, Gene Budig, 8 July 1976, p.8, 8/16/5, UA.

19. *Daily Nebraskan*, 10 August 1971.

20. Ned Hedges in conversation, 16 March 1993.

21. Oral History, D. B. Varner, 6 March 1974, p.3, 8/16/5, UA.

22. "Report of the Regents' Commission on the Urban University of the 70's," Willis Strauss, chair, Omaha, Nebraska, 30 September 1970, 43/1/3, UA.

23. Oral History, Merk Hobson, 19 February 1975, p.4, 8/16/5, UA.

24. Oral History, Hobson, p.4.

25. Ken Keller, "Round-Up," *The Nebraska Alumnus* 67, 6 (November 1971): 18.

26. Quoted in the *Daily Nebraskan*, 10 August 1971.

27. Oral History, Varner, 6 March 1974, p.3.

28. Carroll R. McKibbin, "The Politics of Public Higher Education: Nebraska," *AAUP Bulletin* 59, 3 (September 1973): 298. The article was quoted in the daily papers of the state, including the *Daily Nebraskan*, 25 October 1973. It had been written upon invitation as part of a symposium on the relationship of higher education to politics in four more or less representative public universities.

29. Minutes, University Senate, 9 December 1975, 4/1/1, UA.

30. Minutes, Board of Regents, 26 June, 17 July 1976, 1/1/1, UA.

31. Minutes, University Senate, 5 October 1976, "The Real Issues in the Equity Report," p.3, 4/1/1, UA.

32. Minutes, Board of Regents, 14 December 1974, 1/1/1, UA.

33. Oral History, Hobson, p.11.

34. Oral History, Varner, 6 March 1974, p.11.

35. Minutes, Board of Regents, 26 July 1976, 1/1/1, UA.

36. Interview with Ned Hedges, 16 May 1992.

37. Oral History, Schwartzkopf, p.7.

38. Oral History, James Zumberge, 23 September 1975, p.18, 8/16/5, UA.

39. The essay, written in the spring of 1973, won a William Randolph Hearst Scholarship National Award. It was reprinted in newspapers across the nation, including the *Daily Nebraskan*, 8 September 1973.

40. Oral History, Varner, 6 March 1974, p.7.

41. Oral History, Jack McBride, 7 June 1976, p.17, 8/16/5, UA.

42. "S-U-N courses begin"; "Mid-America U forms," *The Nebraska Alumnus* 70, 5 (September/October 1974): 16.

43. Oral History, Varner, 12 May 1976, p.6.

44. Oral History, Zumberge, p.4.

45. Minutes, Board of Regents, 26 June 1976, 1/1/1, UA.

46. Oral History, Varner, 26 August 1980, pp.6–7.

47. Oral History, Edward Hirsch, 16 October 1984, p.22, 8/16/5, UA.

14. "Political Reality": 1977–1989

1. Minutes, Board of Regents, 11 December 1976, 1/1/1, UA.

2. Oral History, Ronald Roskens, 17 July 1979, pp.10–11, 8/16/5, UA.

3. Minutes, Board of Regents, 20 November 1976, 1/1/1, UA.

4. Minutes, Board of Regents, 11 December 1976, 1/1/1, UA.

5. Quoted in the *Daily Nebraskan*, 12 April 1978.

6. Ned Hedges in private correspondence, 16 March 1993.

7. Minutes, Board of Regents, 21 April 1978, 1/1/1, UA.

8. Ned Hedges, 16 March 1993.

9. These figures were determined by faculty committees and reported in a faculty meeting of the College of Arts and Sciences, 29 November 1979, 12/2/1, box 2, UA.

10. George Round in Oral History, Roskens, p.20.

11. Minutes, College of Arts and Sciences Council Meeting, 15 November 1979, and faculty meeting, 29 November 1979, reported in the *Daily Nebraskan*, 20, 26, 30 November 1979. See account in *The Nebraska Alumnus* 76, 1 (January/February 1980): p.19.

12. Oral History, Roy Young, 22 July 1980, pp.16–17, 8/16/5, UA.

13. Quoted in the *Lincoln Journal*, 27 March 1981.

14. Oral History, Martin Massengale, 28 May 1981, p.5, 8/16/5, UA.

15. See report of discussion in Minutes, University Senate, 13 May 1980, 4/1/1, UA.

16. *Lincoln Journal*, 27 March 1981.

17. *Time*, 5 December 1983, pp.80–86.

18. *Daily Nebraskan*, 13 November 1991.

19. Oral History, James Zumberge, 23 September 1975, pp.12–13, 8/16/5, UA.

20. Arthur L. Little, Inc., *Veterinary Supply and Demand in the United States: A Report to the American Veterinary Association* (Cambridge, Mass., 1978).

21. Minutes, University Senate, 10 April 1979, Exhibit Four: "Resolution on Proposed School of Veterinary Medicine . . . be it resolved that the Faculty Senate shares the deep concerns expressed by Dean Max Larsen and other UNL deans regarding the addition of new programs at UNL at the expense of existing programs that are already critically underfunded," 4/1/1, UA.

22. "Toward the 21st Century: Report of the Citizens Commission for the Study of Higher Education in Nebraska," December 1984, James C. Olson, Director, pp.21–22, SSF, UA.

23. *Daily Nebraskan*, 15 April 1985.

24. Quoted in the *Daily Nebraskan*, 13 September 1985.

25. Minutes, University Senate, 10 February 1987, 4/1/1, box 8, UA.

26. "Toward the 21st Century," p.x.

27. "Toward the 21st Century," p.xii.

28. Widely reported in the media of the state, including the *Daily Nebraskan*, 19 November 1987.

29. *Daily Nebraskan*, 28 November 1988.

30. Quoted in the *Daily Nebraskan*, 4 December 1986.

31. Minutes, University Senate, 13 October 1987, Exhibit 5, "UNL Faculty Salaries – A Major Crisis in the Making," reported in the *Daily Nebraskan*, 14 October 1987.

32. Interview with William J. Lewis, 5 December 1990.

33. Minutes, Board of Regents, 17 December 1982, 1/1/1, UA.

34. Quoted in the *Daily Nebraskan*, 27 October 1988.

35. *Lincoln Star*, 21 August 1989.

Sources

Anyone interested in the history of the University of Nebraska has lots of materials to draw on. Much of it is conveniently assembled in the Don L. Love Memorial Library in Lincoln. The minutes and papers of the Board of Regents from earliest days are collected in the University Archives there. Perhaps not all the correspondence for the last century and a quarter has survived, but the files are full. The papers of successive chancellors are also in these archives, but thanks to defensive private secretaries, some letters are unfortunately missing. The minutes and committee reports of the University (Faculty) Senate are also in the archives, and so are the University bulletins, reports, directories, catalogs, and other official publications. I have consulted all these papers and documents.

Campus journals and newspapers are invaluable to anyone interested in the history of the University. The archives and microfilm collections contain complete files of the *Hesperian Student* (1871–85), *The Hesperian* (1885–99), the *Nebraskan* (1892–99), the *Nebraska-Hesperian* (1899–1901), and the *Daily Nebraskan* (after 1901). Since these papers provide a daily log of campus activities, one sees in them contemporary responses to persons and actions. I have quoted liberally from them in order to suggest the temper of changing times. Selections from early writings about Nebraska and the young University are conveniently reprinted in *Prairie Schooner*, "Nebraska Centennial Issue," 41, 2 (summer 1967), and "University of Nebraska Centennial Issue," 43, 1 (spring 1969), collected and edited by Bernice Slote. The Alumni Association's publications, the *University Journal*, which appeared several times a year from 1905 until 1924, and *The Nebraska Alumnus* thereafter, regularly record campus happenings, often with faculty and administrative commentary. These journals bring official documents to life, explaining what the minutes and catalogs only suggest. State newspapers, including the Lincoln and Omaha dailies, are on file in the Nebraska State Historical Society, down the street from Love Library. They record events and provide editorial response to University actions. In recent years the University's Office of Public Relations has collected media response to University affairs from across the state and filed clippings in the archives.

When George Round retired in 1973 after forty years of service in University public relations, he gathered materials for an oral history of the University. He interviewed some 300 persons who had been associated with the University and the state. These interviews were typed, approved for scholarly use by the men and women interviewed, and placed in the archives. They provide firsthand reports of events and controversies and explain both what happened and what the persons involved thought was happening. I have drawn on these oral histories generously. For readability, I have lightly edited typists' transcriptions, correcting spelling, punctuation, and sometimes sentence divisions, but I have not changed any words. Various published and unpublished autobiographies are also in the archives, for example, those of Hartley Burr Alexander, Theodore P. Jorgensen, and Theodore A. Kiesselbach. I have made use of them.

From the earliest days the University has had historians, for the pioneers thought they were creating a new world whose founding was worth recording. An account of its first decade is given by Samuel Aughey in an address delivered before the University on Charter Day, 15 February 1881, entitled *The Ideas and the Men That Created the University of Nebraska* (Lincoln: Journal Co., State Printers, 1881). It is detailed and colorful. A history by participants is contained in the 15 February 1894, issue of *The Hesperian*, edited by Willa Cather. Other accounts are in *The Sombrero*, vol.3, Quarter-Centennial Edition (class of '95, University of Nebraska).

The Sombrero was a more or less annual class book which appeared in eight volumes between 1883 and 1906. Thereafter it was replaced by the *Cornhusker*, which was published annually until 1972.

In 1901 Howard W. Caldwell wrote a chapter on the University of Nebraska for his volume *Education in Nebraska*, Contributions to American Educational History, edited by Herbert B. Adams, no. 32 (Washington DC: Government Printing Office, 1902), chap.2, pp.17–117. Louise Pound compiled a *Semi-Centennial Anniversary Book: The University of Nebraska, 1869–1919* (Lincoln: University of Nebraska, 1919). It consists of essays by firsthand observers and participants and contains sketches of all the chancellors except, perhaps significantly, George E. MacLean (1895–99). Later Louise Pound contributed a biographical sketch of MacLean to the *Dictionary of American Biography* (New York: Charles Scribner's Sons, 1958), vol.22, supplement 2, pp.419–20. Firsthand accounts of life at the University are contained in a number of memoirs, and I have cited in the notes those I used. Addresses, essays, and memoirs dealing with various departments can be found in the Biographical / Bibliographical files of the archives. Newsletters and bulletins issued by college deans provide further information.

A number of histories are now available. Bernice Slote provides a vivid account of life in Lincoln and the University in the 1890s in her essay "Writer in Nebraska" in *The Kingdom of Art: Willa Cather's First Principles and Critical Statements, 1893–1896*, edited by Bernice Slote (Lincoln: University of Nebraska Press, 1966), pp.3–29. In 1958 Erwin H. Goldenstein wrote *The University of Nebraska Teachers College: The First Fifty Years* (Lincoln: University of Nebraska, 1958). The University's first century was commemorated with the *Centennial History of the University of Nebraska*, vol.1, *Frontier University, 1869–1919*, by Robert N. Manley (Lincoln: University of Nebraska Press, 1969), and vol.2, *The Modern University, 1920–1969*, by R. McLaran Sawyer (Lincoln: Centennial Press, 1973). These centennial histories are supplemented by Elvin F. Frolik and Ralston J. Graham, *The University of Nebraska–Lincoln College of Agriculture: The First Century*, (Lincoln: Institute of Agriculture and Natural Resources, University of Nebraska–Lincoln, 1987). This volume is encyclopedic.

Histories of divisions of the University are now appearing. Robert B. Coleman's *The First Hundred Years of the University of Nebraska College of Medicine* is volume 3 of the Centennial Trilogy of the University of Nebraska College of Medicine and was published by the University of Nebraska Medical Center, Omaha, in 1980. In 1983 Tommy R. Thompson published *A History of the University of Nebraska at Omaha* (distributed by the University of Nebraska at Omaha Alumni Association). This volume concludes with the chapter "Merger with the University of Nebraska: A New Beginning," pp.101–37. It is illustrated and contains appendices.

Margaret Seymour's Master of Music thesis, "Music in Lincoln, Nebraska: The Musical Culture of a Frontier Society" (University of Nebraska, 1968), contains much about the history of the University School of Music. Seymour published an article, "The University of Nebraska School of Music, 1876–1894," in *Nebraska History* 54 (fall 1973): 399–419. The founding of the School of Music is considered by Marilyn Hammond and Raymond Haggh, "Williard Kimball, Music Educator on the Great Plains," *Great Plains Quarterly* 11 (fall 1991): 249–61. The history of the Department of Art is discussed by Fred W. Wells, *The Nebraska Art Association: A History, 1888–1971* (Lincoln: privately printed, 1971). Lonnie Pierson brings the history up to 1988 in *Sheldon Sampler: A Century of Patronage* (Lincoln: Sheldon Memorial Art Gallery, 1988). Anne L. Johnson's Master of Arts thesis, "The Student Writer at the University of Nebraska, 1871–1911" (University of Nebraska, 1972), is, in effect, a history of the early Department of English. It contains a number of appendices. Robert D. Stock, *The New Humanists in Nebraska: A Study of the Mid-West Quarterly (1913–1918)*, University of Nebraska Studies, n.s. 61 (1979), discusses the Department of English at a slightly later period. Leslie Hewes published "Geography at the University of Nebraska" in the *Great Plains–Rocky Mountain Geographical Journal* 2 (fall 1983): 10–18. The *Mid-American Review of Sociology* 13, 2 (winter 1988), edited by Michael J. Hill, is a special issue devoted to the early history of sociology at the University. Hill's *Guide to Sources and Materials on the History and Foundations of Sociology at the University of Nebraska (to 1930)* (1989) is available in the University Archives.

Robert E. Knoll and Robert D. Brown, *Experiment at Nebraska: The First Two Years of a Cluster College*, University of Nebraska Studies, n.s. 44 (1972), is an account of the founding of the Centennial Educational Program. A file on its subsequent development is in the University Archives. Ralph Marlette published a history of the Department of Civil Engineering in *Contacts* 8, 1–2 (fall/winter 1991); *Contacts* is a journal of the College of Engineering brought out four times a year. The fullest departmental history is M. Eugene Rudd, *Science on the Great Plains: The History of Physics and Astronomy at the University of Nebraska–Lincoln,* University of Nebraska Studies, n.s. 71 (1992).

The history of football in Nebraska has been considered, not without bias, in several monographs: Frederick Ware, in collaboration with Gregg McBride, *Fifty Years of Football: A Condensed History of the Game at the University of Nebraska* (Omaha: *Omaha World-Herald*, 1940); David Israel, *The Cornhuskers: Nebraska Football* (Chicago: Henry Regnery Co., 1975); James E. Sherwood, *Nebraska Football: The Coaches, the Players, the Experience* (Lincoln: University of Nebraska Press, 1987). The athletic department issues an annual *Nebraska Football Media Guide* which contains all kinds of historical statistics. The history of physical education for women at the University was written by Mabel Lee, *Seventy-five Years of Professional Preparation in Physical Education for Women at the University* (Lincoln: University Printing Office, 1973); a longer version of this monograph is in the archives of the Department of Women's Physical Education. Another version is in Mabel Lee, *Memories beyond Bloomers (1924–1954)* (Washington, D.C.: American Alliance for Health, Physical Education, and Recreation, 1978). This fascinating volume is useful for lots of purposes. Other departments have been considered in books dealing with more general subjects. I have cited them in the notes.

Acknowledgments

This book was written with the help of all my friends. My home department of English has supported me morally and financially from the inception of my work on it, and I am particularly indebted to Dudley Bailey, the late John Robinson, Frederick Link, and Stephen Hilliard, all of whom have chaired the department. I have had continuous support from and been provided information by Franz Blaha, Louis Crompton, Robert Haller, Ned Hedges, Lee Lemon, Melvin Lyon, Mordecai Marcus, James McShane, Charles Mignon, Robert Narveson, Paul A. Olson, Linda Pratt, Hilda Raz, James L. Roberts, R. D. Stock, Susan Rosowski, Leslie Whipp, and Dorothy Zimmerman. I am grateful to them all.

When I started this project, Wallace Peterson told me that I ought to write this history in terms of its people. "People are interested in people," he said repeatedly. James Rawley asked that I consider the local scene against a national and international background. Frederick L. Luebke repeatedly challenged my historiographic assumptions; Dale L. Gibbs asked for balance. The late James N. Ackerman, John Baylor, William E. (Pat) Daugherty, Ted Kooser, J. Robert Sandberg, James Stange, and F. M. Tuttle have been my Thursday noon sounding board; Ellery H. Davis, the late Robert Dobson, Lee Stover, and E. N. (Jack) Thompson have been my Tuesday sounding board. All have challenged my assumptions and tried to strengthen my frailties.

At the University library I have had constant assistance. Joseph Svoboda and Michele Fagan, archivists, have helped a lot, and so have Lois Peterson and other members of the archives staff. My chief and constant supporter has been Lynn Beideck-Porn. Nothing has seemed too much trouble for her. She seems to know where everything I have lost could be rediscovered. Kate Kane cheerfully helped me in the microfilm room. Eva M. Sartori has been available when I needed her,

which was often, and so have Kathleen Johnson and Kent Hendrickson. As I said in my first monograph nearly forty years ago, librarians are hugely responsible for this country's community of scholarship, and we are all in their debt.

In my search for pictures, I have had consistent cheerful help from Lois Brinton in the University Photography Laboratory, from Ann Billesbach and John Carter in the Nebraska State Historical Society, and from various officials in the libraries of the *Lincoln Journal and Star* and the *Omaha World-Herald*. They have all gone out of their way to help me. Robert E. Sheldon, Michael Mulnix, and others in University Public Relations have assited me on a number of occasions; and Terry L. Fairfield and his administrative assistant, Linda Daiker, of the University of Nebraska Foundation have inconvenienced themselves repeatedly for me.

Over the years I have constantly quizzed my friends. Many of them will have forgotten these conversations. They include Harry Allen, A. C. Breckenridge, Robert Carpenter, Wilbur (Bud) Dasenbrock, John W. Goebel, James V. Griesen, Frank Hallgren. Martin Massengale, J. B. Milliken, Howard W. Ottoson, Robert Pazderka, and Kim Todd from the administrative staff. I am indebted to members of college staffs: Franklin Eldridge, Donald G. Hanway, Ted Hartung, and Irvin T. Omtvedt in the College of Agriculture; Larry H. Lusk and John Peters in the College of Arts and Sciences; Gary Schwendiman in the College of Business Administration; Stanton D. Harn and Donald T. Waggener in the College of Dentistry; Ezekiel Bahar, the late James Blackman, Stanley Liberty, and Ralph Marlette in the College of Engineering; R. Neale Copple in the College of Journalism; Richard S. Harnsberger and Harvey Perlman in the College of Law; David Brooks, Robert D. Brown, Erwin Goldenstein, the late John Prasch, and R. McLaran Sawyer in Teachers College; Paul Few, Ron Hull, Marshall Jamison, and Jack McBride in

University Television; Bruce Baker II and William Pratt at the University of Nebraska at Omaha.

Other colleagues and friends have been consulted formally and informally over the years. I recall talking with John Janovy Jr. and James Rosowski in the School of Biological Sciences; Henry Baumgarten, the late Norman Cromwell, Michael L. Gross, Henry Holtzclaw, and John Scholz in chemistry; C. J. Kennedy and Jerry Petr in economics; Leslie Hewes and Dean Rugg in geography; C. Bertrand Schultz and T. M. Stout in geology; Patrice Berger, Peter Maslowski, and Benjamin Rader in history; William J. (Jim) Lewis and the late Donald Miller in mathematics; Robert M. Beadell, Raymond J. Haggh, Margaret Seymour, and Emanuel Wishnow in music; Theodore Jorgensen, M. Eugene Rudd, and Leo Sartori in physics; Donald D. Jensen in psychology; Tice Miller in theatre arts and dance; and Ruth Levinson in women's physical education. I am also indebted to Nanette Graf, Helen Kiesselbach Green, James McKee, James C. Olson, and the late Rudolph Umland for lots of help. There are many more. I hope they do not feel slighted in not being named here.

I would like to thank Linda Rossiter and her office staff. The manuscript of this book was typed and retyped by LeAnn Messing and others, including Maggie Kahler. Roma Rector has cheerfully corrected my spelling, standardized my bibliography, questioned my inconsistencies, and improved all she has touched. Large portions of this manuscript were read carefully by Ken and Maxine Keller, to whom I am especially indebted; Ned Hedges, who made significant additions; J. B. Milliken, who corrected errors; Paul A. Olson; Melvin Lyon; R. D. Stock; and Frederick Luebke, who commented critically. The total manuscript was read with great care by Senator Jerome Warner and the late Betty Warner. They made helpful comments, as did James C. Olson, who also read the manuscript in full. Kay Graber ably edited my text. My daughter Elizabeth Knoll, herself a professional book editor, has read several chapters. My other children, Sarah Knoll German and Benjamin L. Knoll, have listened, criticized, and supported me in the selection of pictures. My beloved wife, Virginia, has listened patiently, cautioned me frequently, edited manuscripts as I brought them to her, and supported me as always.

As in all my life, I have found assistance everywhere, and I am grateful. Nobody but me can be responsible for what is printed here, but this book would be much poorer indeed without all this help from everybody. My thanks to them all.